TND:

I dedicate this book to my wife and best friend

Charlene,

and to my parents

Norbert and Carole Duening

GNS:

I dedicate this book to my wife, partner, and best friend

Jennifer,

and to my parents

Rudy and Norma Stock

CONTENTS

ACKNOWLEDGMENTS

Each book has its own development lifecycle, challenges, and joys. This one is no different. Developing this book with the support of our publisher, Kendall Hunt, has been one of the joys. We want to thank William England and Sarah Flynn, whose enthusiastic support of this project was essential to its gestation and completion.

Writing a text is always a challenge. Finding the time to write the original text, edit the content, and make sure all of the exhibits have proper permission, citations are formatted correctly, and key terms are defined requires incredible attention to detail and patience. We want to thank Shawna Markiewicz for her diligent attention to the details and for managing the chapters as they were completed.

Finally, no book could be completed without the support and patience of family and friends. We want to thank our wives, Charlene Duening and Jennifer Stock, for their indulgence of our many working weekends and evenings.

As usual, despite all of this wonderful support, we accept full responsibility for any errors of omission or commission that remain in this book.

Congratulations on your decision to engage in entrepreneurship education. Your life is about to change and we are delighted to play a part in that transformation. There is no question that entrepreneurship is a fundamental component of successful economies. Studies have indicated that most job creation in the United States over the past twenty years is due primarily to new ventures—not large companies. In fact, over the past several decades new ventures have created on average over three million new jobs each year, while large companies have averaged net job destruction. That is, large companies focus on cost reduction, and this usually involves reducing the number of people required to produce a given amount of output.

Your future as an entrepreneur is entirely undetermined. And that's part of what makes it so exciting. Your decision to study entrepreneurship differentiates you from other business students in a number of ways. Consider the future careers of those who confine their studies only to one of the several disciplines in the business school. They are targeting jobs in large companies and can practically map out their entire careers before they get started.

Entrepreneurship, by contrast, is a journey to the frontiers of the economy and careers in entrepreneurship are as varied as the people who choose to become entrepreneurs. Your future may, in fact, take you into industries, venture types, and career tracks that currently don't even exist. And that's what makes entrepreneurship so exciting and varied a career path.

We wrote this book specifically to introduce people like you to a new way of thinking about entrepreneurship. Rather than taking you through the standard approaches to teaching entrepreneurship, where you might write a business plan or prepare a simulated investor presentation, we wrote this book to introduce you to the **entrepreneurial method.** An emerging line of research suggests that there is a method that underlies all entrepreneurial ventures despite their wide range of differences.

To understand what we mean by the *entrepreneurial method,* it is useful to think of it as an analogy to what is called the "scientific method." You may have been exposed to the concept of the scientific method in your science classes in high school. In fact, you may have learned and still recall some of the key components of the scientific method, such as "hypothesis testing" and "experimentation." Although you may not have become a scientist, you still recall elements of the scientific method and may even use your knowledge of it to choose between conflicting ideas that you are exposed to. Consider that there are many shows on television today purporting to involve hunting for ghosts. Someone steeped in the scientific method would have to question whether this is self-deceptive. For example, how is it that ghosts can walk through doors yet stand on the floor? How is it that they seem only to reside in cold, dark, abandoned buildings? A scientifically minded person would likely ask such questions.

A new and insightful line of research in entrepreneurship education suggests that expert entrepreneurs practice the entrepreneurial method when exploring economic opportunity via new ventures. While this line of research is relatively new, it has been able to discover and articulate some fundamental principles of the entrepreneurial method. We have built this textbook on those discoveries and have embedded them in the standard tools of entrepreneurship to provide you with an entirely new perspective on the subject.

For example, many entrepreneurship courses focus on helping students become entrepreneurs during school or immediately after. We are not under the illusion that you are prepared to become an entrepreneur right now. In fact, we recommend in this book that it may take you up to ten years of **deliberate practice** to become expert in the entrepreneurial method. The entrepreneurial method provides you with an understanding of what it will take successfully to pursue economic opportunity, but you will likely need to hone your skills in applying the entrepreneurial method for many years before you achieve higher levels of success.

This last assertion may have you wondering why you should study a course in entrepreneurship if you must go out and practice for another ten years to attain expert status. Our response is that it is important to your eventual success that you practice the *right* things. We have attempted in this book to provide you with an overview of what you need to practice. Don't be fooled by those famous entrepreneurs who were fortunate enough to achieve tremendous success with their first ventures. People like Mark Zuckerberg, who became one of the world's forty wealthiest people in his late 20s, are far and away the exception rather than the rule. Zuckerberg's great idea, the creation of Facebook, was in the right place at the right time. Most entrepreneurs are not as fortunate. Most entrepreneurs have to work a long time and against many odds to build their ventures. It is more likely than not that you will not achieve the instant success of a Zuckerberg. It is also more likely than not that you *will* succeed as an entrepreneur in your own way and at your own pace.

This textbook is based on the fundamental belief that everyone can become an entrepreneur. But, just as not all scientists become an Einstein or Curie, not all entrepreneurs become a Zuckerberg or Gates. Everyone who studies this text must accept the challenge of becoming an entrepreneur in his or her own way. Each person must match his or her unique talents, experiences, and skills to appropriate economic opportunity. How do you know what's appropriate? If you are attempting to start a venture that leverages your greatest talents, you are most likely to succeed. However, you must also be careful to leverage your talents in an industry that has a good chance to grow. For example, if you have artistic talent, you could elect to create paintings and hope that people will pay for your work. On the other hand, you may elect to ply your craft in the homes of wealthy people who want original murals or other types of wall art in their homes. From this you can see that the entrepreneurial method is based on helping you match your natural talents and skills to high-growth potential economic opportunities.

Throughout this text we have attempted to convey an accurate and realistic perspective of what it is like to become an entrepreneur. We have also attempted to make sure that the information and opinions expressed in this book are based on the best and most current research in entrepreneurship. Thus, each chapter includes a number of citations that you may want to explore for further understanding of the material we present.

It is our fervent belief that entrepreneurship is the driver of economic success in free societies. We also believe that anyone can become an entrepreneur, and that means that you can be successful as an entrepreneur. Finally, we are convinced that teaching entrepreneurship via the entrepreneurial method provides you with the best chance of creating your own entrepreneurial career in a manner best suited for you. We encourage you to retain this text as a guide and reference as you build your ventures and grow your entrepreneurial career. Entrepreneurship is best regarded as a team sport and we are delighted that you have allowed us to be part of your team.

Tom Duening

Greg Stock

December, 2012

ABOUT THE AUTHORS

Dr. Thomas Duening, is the El Pomar Chair of Business & Entrepreneurship and Director of the Center for Entrepreneurship in the College of Business at the University of Colorado, Colorado Springs. He is a 1991 graduate of the University of Minnesota with a PhD in higher education administration and an MA in philosophy of science. He began his academic career as the assistant dean for the University of Houston's College of Business Administration. There, he was also a visiting faculty member in the Marketing Department, and a co-founder of its Center for Entrepreneurship & Innovation. That unit is now considered to be one of the top entrepreneurship centers in the southern United States.

Dr. Duening launched his first venture while a graduate student. His international consulting firm served the electric utility industry with information products centered on the issue of health effects associated with electric and magnetic fields (EMF) from high voltage power lines. Duening and his partner launched the venture in 1984. He left in 1991 upon completion of his doctorate to assume the assistant dean position in Houston.

After his 9-year stint as assistant dean, Dr. Duening founded several more companies. With a partner, he co-founded U.S. Learning Systems in 1998. The firm provided e-learning content to providers around the country. U.S. Learning Systems was acquired in December 1999 by Aegis Learning. Aegis provided e-learning services to corporations around the world. Dr. Duening left Aegis in 2002 to launch the Applied Management Sciences Institute (AMSI). The organization was created to develop educational products for business students. As part of this firm, Professor Duening co-wrote three business textbooks, which now enjoy wide circulation around the world.

Dr. Duening next founded INSYTE Business Services Group and launched a project to study best practices in business process outsourcing. The result of this effort was two trade books: "Business Process Outsourcing: The Competitive Advantage" and "The Essentials of Business Process

Outsourcing". Both books were published by John Wiley & Sons in 2004 and 2005, respectively. As he was conducting the research for these books, Dr. Duening co-founded INSYTE InfoLabs India, Pvt. Ltd., a business process outsourcing firm based in Bangalore, India. The firm provides outsourcing services to a wide range of companies, enabling them to reduce their cost structure. Infolabs was acquired by ANSR Source in 2004.

In 2004, Dr. Duening accepted a position with Arizona State University's Ira A. Fulton School of Engineering as Director of its Entrepreneurial Programs Office. In that role, Dr. Duening taught courses in Technology Entrepreneurship to engineers at the graduate and undergraduate levels. He also co-authored a textbook titled "Technology Entrepreneurship: Creating, Capturing, and Protecting Value" published by Elsevier.

Dr. Gregory Stock graduated in 1995 with a Ph.D in business administration from the University of North Carolina. He also holds BSE and MS degrees in electrical engineering from Duke University. Prior to his academic career, he was a design engineer at several electronics firms, beginning with a corporate startup unit in the Semiconductor Division of General Electric and ending with a small firm that designed and marketed telecommunications integrated circuits.

Dr. Stock's academic career has included faculty appointments at the University of Hartford, Arizona State University West, Hofstra University, the China-Europe International Business School, Northern Illinois University, and the University of Colorado, Colorado Springs. He has taught courses in operations management, supply chain management, innovation management, quantitative methods, research methods, and entrepreneurship. His research focuses on innovation, technology implementation, new product development, and healthcare management, and he is the author of more than forty peer-reviewed publications.

Dr. Stock is currently Professor and Associate Dean of Faculty and Operations in the College of Business at the University of Colorado, Colorado Springs. He is also the Co-Director of the Bachelor of Innovation™ Program at UCCS. The Bachelor of Innovation™ Program is a family of degrees in which students majoring in business and engineering work together in cross-disciplinary teams on innovation projects throughout their degree program. The innovation core curriculum supplements their major courses in business or engineering with education and practical experience in innovation, entrepreneurship, and teamwork.

THE ENTREPRENEURIAL METHOD

Learning Objectives

As a result of studying this chapter, students will be able to:

- **Understand** what is meant by the term "entrepreneurial method" and how it is the foundation of this text.

- **Recognize** the similarities and differences between the scientific method and the entrepreneurial method.

- **Apply** the techniques of expert entrepreneurs in their own lives.

- **Recognize and use** effectual reasoning as it contrasts with standard causal reasoning.

- **Learn** how expert entrepreneurs select an appropriate level of venture risk and act to push creatively to increase return.

- **Assess** opportunity and the "doability" of a new venture.

- **Understand** that anyone can be an entrepreneur but that each person must learn to be an entrepreneur in his or her own unique way.

- **Apply** the five principles of the entrepreneurial method in a variety of settings and in any industry.

INTRODUCTION

It is not possible to teach something to someone else unless the teacher and student each have clear and common goals in mind. That should be obvious. For example, I can't teach you to ride a bike unless you and I both agree that you, in fact, want to learn how to ride a bike unassisted. If I brought a bike into the classroom, I could teach you how to repair it, the names of each of its parts, or how to ride it. Clearly, we'd have to be in agreement that you want to learn how to ride a bike unassisted, and I would need to have the requisite understanding of, and prior training in, bike riding to help you learn. Without that common understanding and prior preparation of the teacher, it is not clear that teaching and learning would take place. If I endeavored to teach you the names of all the parts of a bike when you really were interested in learning to ride it, there probably would not be much teaching and learning taking place.

Yet, for the past three decades entrepreneurship teachers have been attempting to teach entrepreneurship without really understanding what it is or what the proper goals of teaching should be. As a result, there are today a wide range of approaches to teaching entrepreneurship, with varying degrees of apparent effectiveness.[1] We say "apparent" because it is not even agreed what counts as "effective outcomes." If we measured the effectiveness of entrepreneurship teaching by the number of students who become successful entrepreneurs within five years of graduation, the results likely would be dismal. Many students don't become entrepreneurs until long after they have left the university, and the effect of their university experience on their success is difficult to track. Others who do start businesses right out of school are probably not much more likely to succeed than those who did not receive formal education in entrepreneurship.

With this mixed record of teaching focus and measures of "success," it is no wonder that entrepreneurship scholars continue to search for something more concrete to teach via textbooks and in the classroom. Research into what makes entrepreneurs successful has ranged over a number of factors. For example, early research assumed that successful entrepreneurs possess certain unique personality traits.[2] These traits, it was supposed, are the critical factors that lead to entrepreneurial success when they are present and to entrepreneurial failure when they aren't. And, it was thought, if certain personality traits were found to be critical to success in entrepreneurship, it would stand to reason that teaching *those* traits would be fundamental to entrepreneurship education.

Unfortunately, after many years of effort spent trying to identify unique personality traits that are essential to entrepreneurial success, none were found. In other words, there are no specific personality traits that are necessary for success in entrepreneurship. For example, a common misunderstanding about entrepreneurs is that they are notorious risk takers. In fact, many people avoid entrepreneurship because they believe that it involves taking risks they simply don't want to take. In reality, the research into entrepreneurship has revealed that the risk taking personalities among the entrepreneurial population is no more prevalent than among the population in general.[3] Of course, there are some risk takers who also are entrepreneurs, but the research is very clear that entrepreneurs in general are no more risk takers than non-entrepreneurs. And today it is far more common to talk about expert entrepreneurs as risk minimizers than excessive risk takers.

What we have learned about expert entrepreneurs is that they have become adept at minimizing their exposure to a wide range of business risks. Where non-entrepreneurs see excessive risk in pursuing an opportunity, expert entrepreneurs have learned how to eliminate or reduce that risk to tolerable levels. Expert entrepreneurs have learned how to risk no more than they can reasonably afford to lose. As you will learn later in this chapter, this is called the "Affordable loss principle." It simply means that expert entrepreneurs are aware of the limits of their own risk tolerance, and they pursue entrepreneurial opportunities only within those limits.

Of course, there are ways that entrepreneurs may be distinguished from the population of non-entrepreneurs other than by their respective personality traits. Another major line of research undertaken by entrepreneurship scholars attempted to identify unique behaviors that may be essential to success in entrepreneurship.[4] For example, it was thought that entrepreneurs might be more oriented toward leadership behaviors than non-entrepreneurs or to have a propensity to be extroverted rather than introverted.

This line of research was actively pursued for a number of years and, despite a few promising leads, it simply is not possible today to say that any specific behaviors are necessary and/or sufficient for success in entrepreneurship. For example, it is possible to find successful entrepreneurs who tend toward introversion, and it is also possible to find those who tend to be extroverts. Some entrepreneurs have classic leadership personalities, and some clearly do not.

In light of these thorough research projects to identify either the personality traits of successful entrepreneurs or their behaviors, one might think that there is little left for scholars to identify as factors in entrepreneurial success. Perhaps, one might think in light of this discussion, that entrepreneurial success is simply a matter of "luck." Fortunately, there are things that one *can* learn that will facilitate the goal of becoming an expert entrepreneur. What scholars now tend to think is that success in entrepreneurship is correlated with the relative effectiveness of applying an identifiable and repeatable *entrepreneurial method* and with specific cognitive skills or *entrepreneurial mindsets*.[5] This chapter introduces you to the entrepreneurial method, and Chapter 2 introduces entrepreneurial mindsets. These two concepts are highly intertwined in that becoming effective in the entrepreneurial method in fact requires developing particular entrepreneurial mindsets.

The notion of the entrepreneurial method has evolved out of a relatively new line of entrepreneurship research that is centered on the concept of *effectuation*. Effectuation, simply stated, places the entrepreneur and his or her behaviors, decisions, character, and social connections in the center of research into entrepreneurial success. Effectuation asks, "What do expert entrepreneurs really do to achieve their success?"[6] It would seem that this is a straightforward question—one that should have been asked long ago. Well, it was asked a long time ago. The problem was, despite the fact that many entrepreneurship scholars were looking at what expert entrepreneurs do, most were confining their investigations to a narrow field. For example, scholars with finance backgrounds looked at how expert entrepreneurs deal with the financial issues. Scholars with marketing backgrounds would examine the marketing activities of expert entrepreneurs. It is only in the last decade that entrepreneurship scholars have been focusing on the larger picture of entrepreneurial expertise. They have attempted to encapsulate all of the thoughts, experiences, and performances of the expert entrepreneur under a single theoretical framework. Of course, it could turn out that there is no such thing. It could turn out that "luck" or predestination, or favorable genes is all that separates expert entrepreneurs from non-entrepreneurs.

As it turns out, scholars have identified an expertise that successful entrepreneurs possess and use to varying degrees of effectiveness. This expertise has been encapsulated in the term *effectuation* and embodied in the principles of the *entrepreneurial method*. A working definition of effectuation is: "A logic used by expert entrepreneurs to solve problems in highly uncertain market environments."[7] Further, "entrepreneurs can learn to think and act effectually, thereby increasing their ability to create successful ventures."

According to the effectual way of thinking, nearly anyone can become a successful entrepreneur if he or she applies the entrepreneurial method effectively to business opportunities. That is not to say that timing, circumstances, and luck don't play a role in entrepreneurial success—they most certainly do. There is no way to avoid the circumstances in which one finds oneself—the current economic conditions, the availability of needed resources, and the potential for customers to afford what one is attempting to bring to the market. At the same time, extensive research into the techniques used by expert entrepreneurs has begun to reveal that there is in fact a method behind their success. This entrepreneurial method has recently become the topic of intensive research, and the fruits of that research constitute the foundation for this textbook. To understand what we mean by the *entrepreneurial method,* it is helpful to examine another well-known method that can be applied by nearly anyone to solve problems in a wide range of situations: The scientific method.

THE SCIENTIFIC METHOD

Most of you reading this textbook have probably heard of the **scientific method**. In fact, most of you probably learned a bit about what constitutes the scientific method in one or more of your science classes during your primary education years. You may have learned about the concept of a hypothesis, the importance of testing hypotheses through experimentation and observation, and the need for experimental results to be replicated in order to consider them to be established facts.

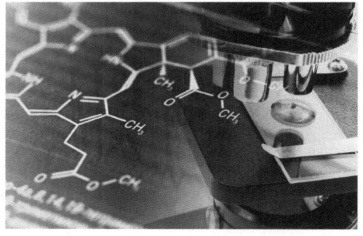

Even though most of you have learned about the scientific method, and some of you may have also applied it in laboratory settings either in high school or in college, most of you probably are not practicing scientists. In that sense, you've learned something useful about how knowledge is discovered and verified, but you don't actually expect to earn your living as a scientist. The method that you learned is useful as a tool to determine valid from invalid knowledge and beliefs. Our world is awash in a wide variety of belief systems, and the scientific method is one way for you to choose among them. People who subscribe to the scientific method and use it to judge valid beliefs from invalid ones generally are more effective in life than those who subscribe to belief systems that include, for example, ghosts, leprechauns, or fairies.

Practicing scientists have learned how to approach problems and questions through hypothesis testing, experimentation, and a complex array of statistical and mathematical techniques of analysis. All professional scientists must use the scientific method in order to be accepted among their peers, and they must be able to report how they used the scientific method to arrive at the results they obtain in their experiments. Some scientists rise to the top of their profession because they are particularly gifted at applying the scientific method to problems. Richard Feynman, for example, was a gifted scientist whom many revere for his insightful application of scientific method to uncommon and common problems alike. For example, Feynman was appointed to a commission to investigate the 1986 Challenger space shuttle explosion. In one incredibly insightful television moment, Feynman took a chunk of material from the shuttle that was suspected to have become brittle during the frosty morning launch of the Challenger and dipped it into a glass of ice water. The substance became brittle as a result of Feynman's impromptu experiment, and he ultimately was proved right. A major cause of the Challenger disaster was that the rubbery material that was supposed to form a seal between the fuel tank and the heat of the engine failed due to its becoming brittle in the low temperatures experienced on launch day.[8]

Other scientists are less adept at the application of scientific method but become successful because they have learned to use the method to achieve highly predictable and repeatable results. Most scientists are like this: They are people who have learned the scientific method, they've mastered it to a certain degree, and they spend their lives working on problems that require diligent application of the scientific method. Most of them are involved in solving novel problems, but the problems are not significant to the world and not many people are aware of them.[9] Think of the legions of scientists who toil in energy companies, pharmaceutical companies, universities, and other organizations and who never receive the public accolades of a Feynman, Einstein, or Curie.

The scientific method can be applied to the mundane problems of inventing new and beneficial drugs or to the monumental questions about the formation and ultimate fate of the universe. Not all scientists have the passion to pursue the mundane questions, and not all have the creative capability to pursue the great big questions. Yet, all professional scientists must apply the scientific method to be recognized by their peers as "doing science."

In the same way, the entrepreneurial method can be applied to mundane opportunities that arise in everyday life, or to great and culture changing types of opportunities. The small business owner who simply wants to open a corner bakery has to apply the entrepreneurial method to be successful. Similarly, but on a different scale, founders of Facebook, Groupon, and Netflix all had to apply the entrepreneurial method to create their disruptive and culture-changing technologies. Let's turn next to an examination of some of the fundamental principles of the entrepreneurial method.

THE ENTREPRENEURIAL METHOD

Although you are probably familiar with the scientific method, this is very likely the first time you've encountered the concept of the **entrepreneurial method**. The previous section was offered merely to remind you of how you were introduced to the scientific method and, hopefully, to highlight how it still influences your life, regardless of whether you are a practicing scientist.

Learning about and applying the entrepreneurial method can similarly affect your entire life. Scientists become experts after applying the scientific method again and again over a number of years. The research into how people become expert in anything indicates that it takes on average ten years to achieve expertise. And that occurs only through what is referred to as **deliberate practice**. Deliberate practice is the process of trying out a new skill or technique, observing the results, reflecting on the results, and improving your performance over time.[10]

In light of this understanding of what it takes to become an expert, it should be clear that becoming an **expert entrepreneur** requires deliberate practice in the entrepreneurial method. It should also be clear that it may take you as long as ten years of such deliberate practice to achieve expert levels of performance and success.

As we mentioned in the Introduction, the research underlying this text is centered on the concept of effectuation. **Effectuation** has engendered a new understanding of entrepreneurship from the perspective of the expert entrepreneur. Effectuation basically says that it is what entrepreneurs actually do, rather than what they are or who they are, that is important to their success. This research simply investigates what expert entrepreneurs actually do and attempts to extract lessons. The following Research Link highlights some of the key research underlying the effectuation perspective.

RESEARCH LINK

Research into the definition, role, and domain of entrepreneurship has been ongoing for several generations. Once thought to be a fairly well-defined domain of practice and inquiry, entrepreneurship is now thought to be a way of being and doing that applies in a wide range of domains. For example, it is now reasonable to talk about corporate entrepreneurship, social entrepreneurship, and others. Leaders of the effectuation movement in entrepreneurship have suggested that attempts to put entrepreneurship into a fixed domain are misguided. In fact, they argue, entrepreneurship is not a singular domain of inquiry and practice, but rather defines a *method* that can be applied in many domains and in many ways. This research has been supplemented by others who argue that there are some essential things about entrepreneurship that must be present, but its domain of possible practice and inquiry is open-ended.

Saras D. Sarasvathy and Sankaran Venkataraman, "Entrepreneurship as Method: Open Questions for an Entrepreneurial Future," *Entrepreneurship Theory & Practice*, January 2011, pp. 113–135; Ronald K. Mitchell, "Increasing Returns and the Domain of Entrepreneurship Research," *Entrepreneurship Theory & Practice*, July 2011, pp. 615–629.

Effectuation has also revised our understanding about how entrepreneurs think about the future. Teaching entrepreneurship based on traditional business thinking and reasoning would teach what is referred to as **causal reasoning**. Causal reasoning begins with a very clear goal in mind and attempts to gather and deploy the resources that are required to achieve that singular goal. The objective of the entrepreneur under causal reasoning would be to choose among various alternative means available to achieve the stated goal. For example, someone who has his or her heart set on serving an Italian dinner would gather the resources (recipes, pasta, spices, etc.) necessary to achieve that goal.

By way of contrast, effectual reasoning does not begin with a clear goal in mind. Most expert entrepreneurs will readily admit that the goals they've achieved often were unexpected at the time they launched their business. **Effectual reasoning** begins with the means, rather than the ends. That is to say, expert entrepreneurs look to the assets that they currently control and attempt to create any number of possible alternative future outcomes. On this way of thinking,

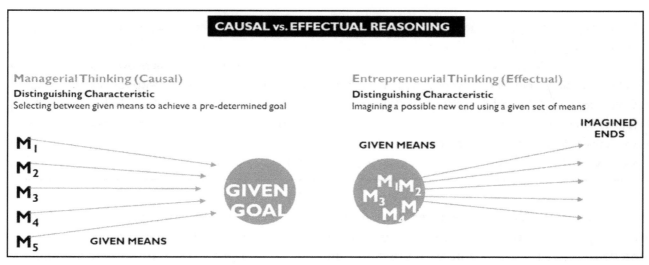

EXHIBIT 1.1

Source: Society for Effectual Action. http://effectuation.org

a variety of the alternative future outcomes could reasonably constitute a successful outcome. For example, rather than wanting to fix an Italian dinner, imagine being hungry and looking into the cupboards and refrigerator to find what you can. You then prepare a meal from those unexpected and varied foods that was not anticipated when your stomach first growled.

In graphic form, the difference between causal reasoning and effectual reasoning is presented in Exhibit 1.1.

Managerial or causal reasoning is depicted on the left side of the diagram. Note that this model assumes a well-defined given goal. The challenge confronting the entrepreneur/manager is to gather the assets needed to pursue that singular goal. All measures of success and/or effectiveness are related to whether that goal was achieved.

The right side of this diagram depicts what is referred to as effectual reasoning.[11] This is the reasoning that has been linked to expert entrepreneurs. As you can see, expert entrepreneurs begin with the means that they currently control and then they use those means to pursue economic ends. Effectual reasoning, however, does not pursue any *particular* end. The expert entrepreneur realizes that achieving economic ends is a discovery process and that the ultimate end is unknown in the present.[12] The following Mini-Case discusses how two entrepreneurs fundamentally changed their business model and found exciting new levels of success using effectual reasoning.

MINI-CASE

Fabulis Evolves to Fab and Success Follows

Jason Goldberg and Bradford Shellhammer founded Fabulis.com in January 2010. The site was a lifestyle reviews and recommendations platform targeting gay men. Goldberg and Shellhammer had garnered $1.75 million in financing, but Fabulis was not growing the way they and their investors expected. Membership had grown rapidly at first, but had topped out at around 30,000. In early 2011, the entrepreneurs began to think that they needed to change their business model. After several meetings to figure out what to do, they decided to change course. Goldberg says that he told his partner, "Let's put this all aside. If we could do anything, what would we do? We're smart, we're creative, and we want to build a big business. What are the talents of our team?" As a result of this conversation, the entrepreneurs evolved an entirely different business model and website called Fab.com, which features daily design inspirations and deals. Goldberg said, "We did $65,000 to $70,000 in sales each day from the beginning." In July 2011, the founders received $8 million in funding for Fab.com. Their ability to leverage current assets and shift goals was critical to their newfound success.

Source: Adapted from "Fab Forward," by Jason Ankeny, *Entrepreneur*, November 2011, pp. 32–38.

A good way to understand the difference between causal reasoning and effectual reasoning is from the perspective of managing risk. A common misunderstanding of entrepreneurs, as we have stated, is that they are people who are comfortable taking larger risks than non-entrepreneurs. In reality, expert entrepreneurs are good at evaluating risk, minimizing risk, and managing risk.[13] Expert entrepreneurs become aware of the level of risk they personally are willing to take to explore new venture opportunities.[14] Then, within the limits of that personal risk tolerance level, expert entrepreneurs act to maximize the returns available.

By way of contrast, a banker, for example, would start out with the expected rate of return as a very specific goal.[15] With the expected rate of return in mind, the banker works diligently to reduce the risk associated with deploying assets to gain that rate of return. In graphic form, the difference between our hypothetical banker and the expert entrepreneur looks like Exhibit 1.2.

This graphic clearly depicts the contrast between how an expert entrepreneur understands and manages risk and how a banker understands and manages risk. The entrepreneur, consistent with our previous graphic that suggests any one of several alternative futures could be considered a successful outcome, sets out to maximize returns while managing risk. As the lefthand side of

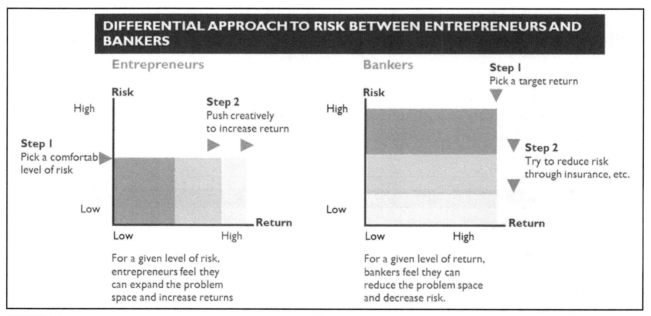

EXHIBIT 1.2

Source: Society for Effectual Action. http://effectuation.org/

the graphic indicates, the level of risk remains the same while the entrepreneur acts creatively to increase potential returns without knowing exactly what the final outcome will be.[16]

The righthand side of the diagram indicates the banker picks a target rate of return and then endeavors to reduce the risk associated with that level of return. The banker has begun with the outcome in mind—the target rate of return—and endeavors to minimize the risk exposure of the assets controlled.

In essence, then, the entrepreneur overturns the standard understanding of risk and return as taught in most corporate finance courses. That standard understanding is based on the assumption that financial returns increase with increased risk. The entrepreneur, by way of contrast, uses his or her creativity to increase the problem space that can be addressed by the assets under his or her control. This increase in the problem space increases the potential returns without increasing the associated risks. For example, a software entrepreneur might set out to create a solution to a particular problem faced by companies in the healthcare industry. To reduce the risk associated with serving a single industry, the entrepreneur may expand the problem set to include other related industries. Risk is not increased because including other industries expands the potential market for the entrepreneur's software. In addition to managing the risk, the entrepreneur has also increased potential returns. If both the original healthcare market and the new markets adopt and purchase the entrepreneur's software, the returns will be greater than they would be if the entrepreneur had pursued only the healthcare market.

Finally, the expert entrepreneur is adept at choosing which opportunities to pursue. This includes a great deal of self knowledge and understanding of the need to control a given set of resources in order to increase the chances of success. Exhibit 1.3 is a good representation of the types of questions the expert entrepreneur has learned to ask regarding potential opportunities.

The expert entrepreneur asks questions both about the market and about his or her own personal resources, talents, contacts, and other personal factors. Each of these types of questions is evaluated in terms of **feasibility** and **value**. Regarding market feasibility, the entrepreneur must determine whether the product or service he intends to build a venture around is technologically, economically, and otherwise feasible. Is it possible to bring the projected product or service to market and find a buyer? From a personal feasibility perspective the expert entrepreneur has learned to ask the exceedingly difficult question "Can *I* bring this product/service to the market?" This involves not only an analysis of one's personal skills and experience, but also an analysis of the resources the entrepreneur currently controls, the resources that the entrepreneur readily and inexpensively can obtain, and other resources the entrepreneur can attract to the venture, especially human resources.

In terms of value, the entrepreneur must ask whether adequate returns can be generated to assume the risk of the business opportunity. While the interest in returns differs between the expert entrepreneur and, for example, banker, as we have seen, the expert entrepreneur still, minimally, must be concerned that she will be able to generate enough cash to pay expenses. This minimal required rate of return is usually supplemented with a vision of higher potential returns, even if it is not yet clear exactly how those returns can or will be generated. These higher potential returns are expected to be generated through the entrepreneur's own creative exploration of market opportunities, as we noted in Exhibit 1.3.[17]

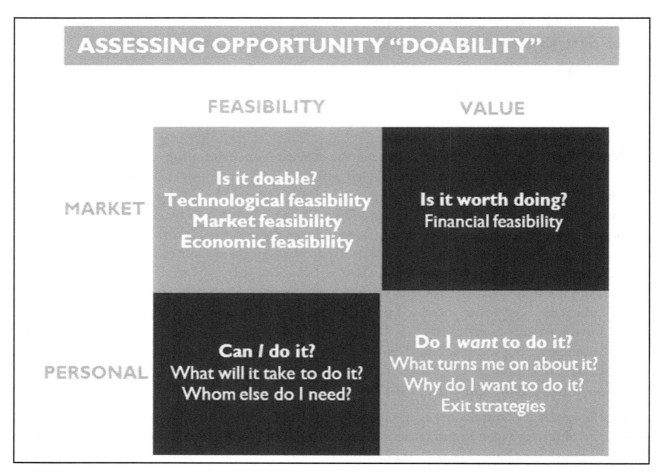

EXHIBIT 1.3

Source: Society for Effectual Action. http://effectuation.org/

If the entrepreneur decides that she has the personal and other resources that will be necessary reasonably to pursue the opportunity, the final question to ask is, "Is it personally worth it?" This question will encompass a host of considerations. Among these is whether the entrepreneur harbors sufficient interest or passion in the industry/product/service to warrant pursuing the suspected opportunity.[18] If the opportunity does not provoke the entrepreneur's interest and/or passion, there does not seem to be any reason to proceed. Launching a new venture is difficult enough even with extreme levels of passion. The expert entrepreneur knows that, at times during the life of a venture, passion will absolutely be required to keep moving forward. Other considerations that the entrepreneur should take into account regarding the value of the opportunity from a personal perspective is the effects on family and other aspects of the entrepreneur's private life. If these effects are too costly, in terms of time, money, or other sacrifices, then it doesn't make sense to pursue the opportunity.

On the other hand, if a project seems feasible from a market and personal perspective, and there is potential value in terms of monetary and personal returns, then the opportunity may be a good one for the entrepreneur to pursue.

Table 1.1 provides a summary of the scientific method and the entrepreneurial method. As you can see, there are similarities in the evolution of the general understanding of how knowledge is created and how ventures are created. Both of the respective methods began with the "unique person" perspective. Scientific knowledge was thought to be the result of a unique person, such as

Comparing the Entrepreneurial Method with the Scientific Method

Comparison	Scientific Method	Entrepreneurial Method
Similarities in historical development	Early explanations: Some special people are able to (are even born to) "read the signs" – from the True Book (of God or Nature) Real science is born when the experimental method of the craftsmen is adopted by the university-scholar and the humanistic literati Scholars begin to argue that: There is no qualitative difference between the processes of revolutionary science and journeyman science – i.e. anyone can learn to do science and do it well	Early explanations: Some people are able to (are even born to) see opportunities while others are not University-scholars (whether they are theoretical social scientists or empirical policy researchers) begin to understand what actual entrepreneurs really DO Scholars begin to argue that: Key elements of the entrepreneurial method can be the same for the extraordinarily successful entrepreneur as well as the ordinary entrepreneur – i.e., it can be taught and learned
Differences in content	Harnesses the potential of Nature Purpose: To achieve human ends Aims to discover general "laws" – the emphasis is on universality and inevitability Focus is on the objective Mechanisms involve data gathering, formal models, analytical techniques, and testing for correspond-	Unleashes the potential of human nature Purpose: To engender new ends as well as achieve old ones Aims to generate and redefine design principles – the emphasis is on locality and contingency Focus is on the inter-subjective Mechanisms involve action, interaction, reaction, transformation, and explicit co-creation

TABLE 1.1

Source: Saras D. Sarasvathy and Sankaran Venkataraman, "Entrepreneurship as Method: Open Questions for an Entrepreneurial Future," *Entrepreneurship Theory & Practice*, January 2011, pp. 113–135; Ronald K. Mitchell, "Increasing Returns and the Domain of Entrepreneurship Research," *Entrepreneurship Theory & Practice*, July 2011, pp. 615–629.

an Isaac Newton, who had some special gifts that enabled the creation of the insights. Similarly, entrepreneurship was thought at first to be dependent on unique personhood—embodied in the likes of a Henry Ford or Andrew Carnegie.

Fortunately, these perspectives have both been revised over time to shift the focus from the individual to the methods used. In the end, there's no question that some people are inherently better at implementing the scientific or entrepreneurial methods, but that's not to say that those less gifted can't be scientists and/or entrepreneurs. Knowledge creation, like venture creation, is done on a spectrum from the humdrum to the revolutionary. Anyone can participate in science and/or entrepreneurship, but not everyone can be a Newton or a Ford.

Finally, we want to highlight some simple things the entrepreneur can do to determine the fit between an entrepreneurial opportunity and one's personal circumstances. This is perhaps best represented in the fundamental question that all entrepreneurs must ask themselves:

> *Given who you are, what you know, and whom you know, what types of economic and/or social artifacts can you, would you want to, and should you create?*

THE ENTREPRENEURIAL METHOD: BASIC PRINCIPLES

The concept of effectuation has radically altered our understanding of how expert entrepreneurs actually achieve their success. Instead of focusing on personality traits or behaviors, effectuation-based research takes what expert entrepreneurs do as the starting point. That shift has led to the new understanding of how to teach entrepreneurship, embodied in what we're calling the entrepreneurial method. Of course, it might have turned out from research that every expert entrepreneur uses a completely different method to achieve success. If that were the case, this textbook would not exist nor would something called the entrepreneurial method exist. But scholars have discovered that expert entrepreneurs tend to follow a similar method, even though most have never been schooled in a method the way today's scientists are schooled in the scientific method. Nonetheless, scientists practicing prior to the "discovery" of the scientific method were using such a method, even though they were doing so less consciously than scientists of modern times.

The entrepreneurial method that has been discovered by effectuation scholars has been encapsulated in five fundamental principles. These principles have been revealed through investigation of expert entrepreneurs in a wide range of fields, from technology to restaurants, and from product oriented to service oriented. The five principles underlying the entrepreneurial method are:

1. The Bird in the Hand Principle
2. The Affordable Loss Principle
3. The Lemonade Principle.
4. The Crazy Quilt Principle.
5. The Pilot in the Plan Principle

The Bird in the Hand Principle

The Bird in the Hand Principle is related to the effectual logic that we learned about in the previous section. Effectual logic, as you'll recall, differs from causal logic in that it starts with a given set of means (resources) and deploys those means to achieve a wide range of potential goals, any one of which could be determined to be a "success." The Bird in the Hand Principle encourages aspiring entrepreneurs to take stock of those resources they currently control. These may include any from the following non-comprehensive list:

- Capital (cash and access to cash)
- Talent (personal and other stakeholders)
- Physical equipment
- Access to lucrative markets
- Specialized knowledge
- Patents or other intellectual property
- Key insights into a specific industry

The expert entrepreneur starting a venture would begin by taking stock of the resources that are currently controlled and those that can readily be acquired. He would know from experience that the ends being pursued are not clear, other than to build a venture that earns more than it spends—hopefully, a lot more. The novice who has not learned the entrepreneurial method might be more inclined to hesitate in getting started as he attempts to acquire more knowledge about the market, set a clear goal, and then analyze whether it was possible to acquire the resources necessary to achieve that goal. The expert doesn't wait. The expert starts and relies upon her experience and personal resourcefulness to get by until appropriate goals begin to emerge. The expert entrepreneur also seeks to gather additional resources as the venture grows to help accelerate that growth. Of course, this approach is limited by the expert's desire to risk only as much as she is prepared to lose, which leads us to the second principle.

The Affordable Loss Principle

The Affordable Loss Principle stipulates that expert entrepreneurs risk no more than they are willing to lose when they launch new ventures. This concept concerns more than just the financial risk that expert entrepreneurs are willing to take. You've probably learned the meaning of **opportunity cost**. Expert entrepreneurs realize that by launching a new venture—and considering the time, energy, and general sacrifice that will be required to build it up over time—they are thereby NOT doing something else that might work out better. Expert entrepreneurs have learned to minimize opportunity costs by focusing on the opportunity they've chosen and giving it their best efforts to make it successful. Novice entrepreneurs, by way of contrast, may attempt to "hedge their bets" and try to minimize risk by attempting to pursue all of their opportunities at the same time. This doesn't take into account the natural limitations that all people have, and the potential to spread oneself too thin to be successful at anything.

Affordable loss also takes into account the effects of building a new venture on the entrepreneur's family, friends, and other key relationships. The expert entrepreneur has learned to manage time and maintain a work/life balance that enables preservation of these relationships. In fact, many expert entrepreneurs will attest to the importance of supportive and accepting relationships as they struggle with the difficulties of building a growing enterprise.

Despite the expert entrepreneur's ability to assess the risk of starting a new venture and manage that risk to stay within his personal risk tolerance limits, that doesn't mean that launching a new venture is smooth sailing. Even the experts will encounter unexpected obstacles, experience setbacks, and learn tough lessons. This brings up the third principle, which we call "The Lemonade Principle."

The Lemonade Principle

The Lemonade Principle is based on the old adage that goes: "If life throws you lemons, make lemonade." In other words, make the best of the unexpected. Expert entrepreneurs have learned that predictability is reserved for only narrow domains in business and in life. Most of what happens as one is building a new venture could not have been predicted. And yet, in the face of all

© PrairieEyes, 2012. Used under license from Shutterstock, Inc.

the uncertainty, the expert entrepreneur has learned how to build successful ventures. The expert realizes that adaptability is key to building a successful new venture. Stubbornly sticking to original business models, or refusing to heed the market's desire for lower prices, better features, or something else is simply not an effective strategy. On the other hand, the expert entrepreneur has also learned that there must be reasons behind shifting business strategies, so that one is not shifting without cause. The causes of changing a venture's strategy are many, and the expert entrepreneur has learned that some are more potent evidence of the need for change than others. For example, if a single group of customers demands lower prices, the expert entrepreneur will realize that it's not possible to please everyone. On the other hand, if one's target customers consistently vote with their feet and choose the lower-priced alternative offered by competitors, it is time to shift strategy.

Adapting to changing environments, or adapting to new information that changes one's original assumptions, is vital for success in building a new venture. Of course, such shifts may require that the entrepreneur expand her range of resources to be able to exploit the newly recognized opportunities. One way to ensure that such resources will be available when needed is to constantly seek to expand the number of people who have a stake in the outcome of the venture. Expert entrepreneurs are continuously seeking to expand their social network by forming advisory boards, attending networking meetings, and other strategies. This is the basis for the fourth principle, which is called the "Crazy Quilt Principle."

The Crazy Quilt Principle

The Crazy Quilt Principle is based on the expert entrepreneur's tendency to continuously seek out people who may become valuable stakeholders of his or her venture. Many entrepreneurs learn the value of establishing knowledgeable advisory boards. Advisory boards can be as large or small as needed, but they should include people who can add value to the venture. Adding value can be achieved in a number of ways, including contributing needed investment capital, providing insights about how a particular market works, opening doors to potential customers, and many others.

In addition to advisory boards, expert entrepreneurs know they will often need to supplement the talents of their employees with consultants. Consultants who provide vital knowledge and insights as the venture grows are, in the long run, relatively inexpensive compared to hiring new employees. Consultants provide entrepreneurs with just-in-time, as-needed talent. Among the consultants that most ventures will need are industry-savvy attorneys and small business accountants. Others may hire firms to assist with site selection for operations, support in managing finances, and many, many others.

The Crazy Quilt Principle advises the novice entrepreneur to expand his or her network of associations and contacts on a continuous basis. It also advises that the entrepreneur seek out ways to ensure that key individuals become stakeholders to the venture. That is to say, they have a stake in helping the venture to become successful. This is most often done via distribution of ownership in the venture. Investors naturally receive an ownership stake in a venture by virtue of the capital they invest. But advisory boards are often also provided with small equity stakes to increase their incentive to work hard to advance the venture.

The Pilot in the Plane Principle

The Pilot in the Plane Principle is based on the concept of control. In most business classes that focus on large organizations, the primary focus is control of outcomes. We saw this in the difference between causal logic and effectual logic. Causal logic focuses on acquiring the means to attain a single, clearly defined outcome. Effectual logic, in contrast, focuses on the means that are currently under one's control and applying those means to the entrepreneurial opportunities at hand.

The unique aspect of control under effectual logic is that the future is unpredictable. It takes a bit of a leap to think in this manner. Most of your education and life instruction has urged you to be careful and to focus on goals that you can predict. Getting good grades in school, brushing your teeth after each meal, looking both ways before crossing the street are all things we do to lessen our exposure to the unpredictable. Yet, we are urging that expert entrepreneurs don't focus so much on controlling outcomes, they focus on controlling the resources at their disposal.

The desire to control events in our environment seems to be a natural human tendency. Expert entrepreneurs believe they can control their individual futures best by applying the entrepreneurial method to the resources they currently control. In other words, expert entrepreneurs do not focus on adapting to their environment; they focus on adapting their environment to them. This perspective highlights the difference between market exploitation and market creation. Expert entrepreneurs are fully aware that oftentimes market participants don't know what they want until they are presented with novel and useful products and/or services. Apple and Pixar founder Steve Jobs, for example, was notoriously critical of market research. He once remarked, "Why do we want to do market research when customers don't know what they want until we show them?"[19]

THE EXPERT ENTREPRENEUR

The background to this text is the emerging research into what expert entrepreneurs actually do to achieve their success. This line of research is only a few years old, but it has already begun to bear significant fruit. The research is primarily centered in the concept of effectuation. It is important to understand what this term means and why it is considered to be an important new contribution to understanding what expert entrepreneurs actually do.

Traditionally, entrepreneurship education has been taught in business schools. Only in the last few years has the teaching of entrepreneurship migrated to other areas within the academy, including the arts, liberal arts, engineering, and other departments. Despite this slow migration out of the business school, the foundation of teaching entrepreneurship remains deeply entrenched in business concepts, principles, and processes.

For example, standard programs in entrepreneurship, regardless of what department they might be located in, provide students with textbooks and instruction that covers generic topics, including the following:

- Opportunity identification and feasibility analysis
- Business plan development and writing
- Entrepreneurial accounting and finance

- Go-to-market strategy and market research

- Pricing, distribution, and sales strategies

- Managing and leading the entrepreneurial venture

These topics are vitally important, but they don't provide much insight into how expert entrepreneurs actually make decisions and create their success. For example, when conducting interviews with expert entrepreneurs, effectuation scholars learned that most of them don't spend too much time or money conducting standard market research. The quotes below were taken from the research:

I don't believe in market research actually, I just go sell it.

Traditional market research says you do very broad based information gathering, possibly using mailings. I wouldn't do that. I would literally target, as I said initially, key companies who I would call flagship and do a frontal lobotomy on them.

Of course, these two examples don't upend decades of teaching entrepreneurship, but they are suggestive of the kind of disconnect that has generally existed between what is taught in the entrepreneurship classroom and how expert entrepreneurs actually behave. Expert entrepreneurs are more inclined to run experiments with their sales offerings to learn what the market wants than they are to conduct standard market research. This propensity among entrepreneurs toward taking action as opposed to conducting more analysis had been suspected for some time. Effectuation scholars took their research into the field to discover what the expert entrepreneurs are actually doing and how they actually are doing it. What is unique about the effectual approach to understanding entrepreneurship is that it reveals that expert entrepreneurs believe they are *creating* markets as much as they are *exploiting* them. [20]

Market creation is a novel understanding of entrepreneurial behavior. If entrepreneurs create markets rather than exploit pre-existing markets, then standard "market research" is not merely disregarded, it would literally be useless. Creating markets is a process of discovery, adjustment, adaptation, and only then exploitation. A good example of market creation is the advent of the personal computer. Prior to Apple's creation of a computer—the Macintosh—that was easy to operate, affordable, and could fit within the average home office, not many people envisioned the ubiquitous market for personal computers that exists today. In fact, many computer industry leaders were unaware that the market for personal computers could be created and could be so comprehensive in extent. Here are some examples of what the so-called experts thought about the future of the computer industry prior to Apple's creation of the personal computer market:

I think there is a world market for maybe five computers.

Thomas Watson, chairman of IBM, 1943

Computers in the future may weigh no more than 1.5 tons.

Popular Mechanics, 1949

640K ought to be enough for anybody.

Bill Gates, Microsoft Founder, in 1981

If Steve Jobs and Steve Wozniak had conducted standard market research to determine whether they should take the risk of building and marketing the Apple Macintosh computer, we might not be enjoying the remarkable utility that computers have brought to all of our lives. Jobs and Wozniak followed their instincts, and through the genius of elegant design and provocative marketing engendered the PC revolution.

© Diego Cervo, 2012. Used under license from Shutterstock, Inc.

A LIFETIME OF ENTREPRENEURSHIP

One of the key outcomes of the research into what we are calling the entrepreneurial method is that it provides rich material for the classroom. After all, what is the use of entrepreneurship professors and entrepreneurship classes if not to help people become entrepreneurs? That is an obvious objective of not only courses in entrepreneurship but of this very textbook.

The problem is, with the research into personality types and behavioral characteristics having reached ostensible dead ends, the question of what to teach in the entrepreneurship classroom weighed heavily. If we are not teaching toward specific behavior and/or personality traits, then just what should we be teaching?

The notion that successful entrepreneurs apply a method to achieve their success answers that question. Scholarship that has examined what expert entrepreneurs actually do to become successful has revealed some fundamental methods that seem to apply regardless of the type of venture or individual entrepreneur. We will be discussing elaborating the principles and concepts of the entrepreneurial method throughout the rest of this book. Suffice it to say for now that enough research has been conducted to provide content for a textbook of this nature and that the research seems to be fruitful enough that future editions of this book will build on the material in this one.

The interesting thing about the new focus on entrepreneurial method is that it provides a strong response to the often-asked question familiar to all professors of entrepreneurship: "Who can be an entrepreneur?" Sometimes it is phrased in more of a nature versus nurture manner in the form of "Are entrepreneurs made or born?"

Under the concept of effectuation, and given our new understanding of both the entrepreneurial method and entrepreneurial mindsets, the answer to the question "Who can be an entrepreneur?" is: Anyone. Anyone can learn the methods and mindsets of successful entrepreneurs to the extent that scholars can identify them and put them into teachable lessons. The same thing happened when scholars began to shift their thinking about successful scientists. Originally, successful scientists were thought to be supremely gifted people who had some special connection to nature or the universe. Only after it was determined that science is the careful, deliberate, and transparent application of a method did it occur that anyone could be a scientist.

And today, as we have already discussed, the notion that anyone can become a scientist has literally come true. It has come to be such a deeply accepted belief in Western societies that young people routinely are taught the scientific method at a very young age. It doesn't matter that there is some dispute about the exact boundaries of the scientific method. We have enough convergence of thinking around the notion that, at minimum, for something to be called a component of scientific method it must be based on experiment, it must be open to refutation by future experiments, and it must cohere with what is considered to be appropriate practice amongst the scientific professionals.

We are at a similar place today in our understanding of entrepreneurs and entrepreneurship. Rather than regarding successful entrepreneurs as lucky geniuses who were born with all the gifts needed for their success, we now regard them as individuals who have effectively applied a common method. That method is the entrepreneurial method. And, just like we now regard it as possible to teach the scientific method, we can also teach the entrepreneurial method. Further, just as we now regard it as reasonable to believe that anyone could become a scientist, it is also now reasonable to believe that anyone can become an entrepreneur.

As we now regard it reasonable to believe that anyone can be an entrepreneur, that naturally extends to you. If you have the ability to learn the entrepreneurial method, and there is every reason to believe that you do, then you can become a successful entrepreneur. Of course, understanding the entrepreneurial method from a textbook won't guarantee that every venture you launch will be a success. In fact, recent research indicates that people who study entrepreneurship prior to leaping into the fray increase their chances of success, but only by a little bit.

Learning the entrepreneurial method doesn't guarantee that every idea that you attempt to build into a business venture will be successful. But it does ensure that you will begin a journey through your entrepreneurial career with your eyes wide open and your expectations appropriately set. This alone can hasten your ultimate success and prevent you from having to pay the heavy price that many novice entrepreneurs must pay to attend the school of hard knocks.

You should be aware that learning the entrepreneurial method empowers you to recognize and solve problems, but it doesn't necessarily prepare you to make a profit. Nor does it aspire to prepare you to make a profit. The expanding world of what is referred to as "social entrepreneurship" requires the same method and deliberate application of that method as profit-seeking entrepreneurship. Social entrepreneurs are interested in solving major global problems, but these problems don't always have a "market" that is willing and/or able to pay for the solutions. In such cases, other sources of capital must be sought in order to fuel the value-creating and value-delivering engine. Social entrepreneurs must often appeal to alternative funding sources such as governmental agencies, foundations, and others for the capital needed.

The entrepreneurial method that you will learn in this book prepares you for a life of problem recognition and problem solving. It also prepares you to be a leader among your peers and in whatever industry you should choose. Whether you become the CEO of your own entrepreneurial venture or become an employee in a large organization, you are prepared to identify and solve major problems. The entrepreneurial method, like the scientific method, is a force for change in our world. We intend to empower you with that force and ask only that you use it to create value for others in an ethical manner.

SUMMARY OF LEARNING OBJECTIVES

1. **Understand** what is meant by the term "entrepreneurial method" and how it is the foundation of this text. *The entrepreneurial method is a relatively recent and new understanding of entrepreneurship. Scholars have begun to view entrepreneurship as the application of a method, and that method can be learned and one can develop expertise in its application. To that extent, it resembles another social phenomenon known as the scientific method. Most people learn the scientific method as part of their basic education. Scholars argue that most people should also learn the entrepreneurial method as part of their basic education.*

2. **Recognize** the similarities and differences between the scientific method and the entrepreneurial method. *The scientific method is a social phenomenon that helps people develop reliable knowledge. Entrepreneurial method is a social phenomenon that helps people start and launch successful companies.*

3. **Be able to apply** the techniques of expert entrepreneurs in their own lives. *Each aspiring entrepreneur has the potential to develop expertise in the entrepreneurial method. Most of us will improve with practice, as with any form of expertise.*

4. **Recognize and use** effectual reasoning as it contrasts with standard causal reasoning. *Effectual reasoning differs from causal reasoning. Causal reasoning begins with a single, specific goal in mind and then attempts to gather the resources necessary to pursue that single goal. Effectual reasoning begins with the resources (means) at the disposal of the entrepreneur and then deploys those means toward any of a number of ends, any one of which would constitute a successful outcome.*

5. **Learn** how expert entrepreneurs select an appropriate level of venture risk and act to push creatively to increase return. *Expert entrepreneurs have learned how to assess the risks involved with a business opportunity and to determine if those risks are acceptable to them. If the risk level is acceptable, the expert entrepreneur takes action to attempt to maximize the returns available at that level of risk.*

6. **Be able to assess** opportunity and the "doability" of a new venture. *Expert entrepreneurs have learned to assess a potential opportunity from a number of salient perspectives. The key questions to ask are: Is it doable? Is it worth doing? Can I do it? and Do I want to do it? This approach combines both market and personal perspectives, as well as feasibility and value perspectives.*

7. **Understand** that anyone can be an entrepreneur but that each person must learn to be an entrepreneur in his or her own unique way. *As we discuss throughout this chapter and this entire text, entrepreneurship is a highly personal undertaking. That is, the expert entrepreneur has learned that success comes from matching one's personal talents, experiences, and background with the opportunities that one discovers in the marketplace. Naturally, the diversity of human beings in general suggests a diversity of entrepreneurial types.*

8. **Apply** the five principles of the entrepreneurial method in a variety of settings and in any industry. *The five principles of the entrepreneurial method were pointed out to be (1) The Bird in the Hand Principle, (2) The Affordable Loss Principle, (3) The Lemonade Principle, (4) The Crazy Quilt Principle. Each of these principles applies to any type of entrepreneurial venture in any industry, and (5) The Pilot in the Plane Principle: Expert entrepreneurs act according to these principles as they build their ventures over time.*

QUESTIONS FOR DISCUSSION

1. Explain the difference between *effectual logic* and *causal logic*. When do you think it is more appropriate to use causal logic in business? Effectual logic? Explain your responses.

2. What do you think the term *entrepreneurial method* means? Do you think some people will be more talented than others in the application of this method? Explain why you think the way you do.

3. How do people use the scientific method? Have you ever used the scientific method in your life? What did you apply the method to? How did that work out for you? Do you think you will be able to use the entrepreneurial method in your life?

4. Explain how expert entrepreneurs actually behave as opposed to the way in which entrepreneurship has traditionally been taught. Do you think that expert entrepreneurs know something that business professors don't know? Explain your response.

5. Compare and contrast the way an expert entrepreneur understands and manages risk versus the way a banker understands and manages risk. Give an example of how this difference would be demonstrated in the real world.

6. Do you agree with the notion that "anyone can be an entrepreneur"? Explain why you think the way you do. Do you have any examples to prove your point of view?

7. What are the steps involved in becoming an "expert entrepreneur"? Describe some of the ways you can develop your expertise in the entrepreneurial method over the next three to five years.

8. If you decide today that you want to become an entrepreneur at some future point in your life, what is your first step toward that goal? How will you ensure that you are successful in that first step? What is the next step after that?

IN-CLASS EXERCISE

The recognition of opportunity is essential to entrepreneurship. It is a skill that develops over time in most entrepreneurs, suggesting that it is a skill that can be learned and refined. The research literature describes the process of opportunity recognition as akin to the pattern recognition that is developed in individuals who are deemed experts in a field. Expert entrepreneurs are able to review and understand "deals" more rapidly than novices. Expert entrepreneurs tend to use heuristics that they've developed from their own experiences and from watching others. A good way for students to begin to develop the ability to evaluate deals includes:

*   Allow students to evaluate nascent entrepreneurial ventures and encourage them to track those ventures over time. Have them track the venture and provide periodic updates throughout the semester on the progress (or lack of progress) the venture displays.

*   Review a set of mature and defunct entrepreneurial ventures whose outcomes are not revealed to the students. Ask them to use their evaluation skills to judge which of them were successful and which failed.

KEY TERMS

Causal reasoning: Reasoning that begins with a very clear goal in mind and attempts to gather and deploy the resources that are required to achieve that singular goal.

Deliberate practice: The process of trying out a new skill or technique, observing the results, reflecting on the results, and improving your performance over time.

Effectual reasoning: Reasoning that begins with the means, rather than the ends. That is to say, expert entrepreneurs look to the assets that they currently control and attempt to create any number of possible alternative future outcomes.

Effectuation: What entrepreneurs actually do, rather than what they are or who they are, that is important to their success.

Entrepreneurial method: The putative method used by entrepreneurs of all types to create value within an industry.

Expert entrepreneur: One who has deliberately practiced the entrepreneurial method for ten years or more.

Feasibility: Regarding market feasibility, the entrepreneur must determine whether the product or service he or she intends to build a venture around is technologically, economically, and otherwise feasible.

Market creation: If entrepreneurs create markets rather than exploit pre-existing markets, then standard market research is not merely disregarded, it would literally be useless. Creating markets is a process of discovery, adjustment, adaptation, and only then exploitation.

Opportunity cost: Expert entrepreneurs realize that by launching a new venture—and considering the time, energy, and general sacrifice that will be required to build it up over time—they are thereby NOT doing something else that might work out better

Scientific method: The putative method used by scientists of all types to conduct research into questions and problems within a discipline.

Value: In terms of value, the entrepreneur must ask whether adequate returns can be generated to assume the risk of the business opportunity.

ENDNOTES

[1] There is a large number of articles in the scholarly literature that pertain to this fundamental challenge for teaching entrepreneurship. A short list of some of these includes: D.H. Streeter, R. Kher, and J.P. Jacquette, Jr., "University-wide Trends in Entrepreneurship Education and the Rankings: A Dilemma," *Journal of Entrepreneurship Education,* 14(2011): 75–92; A. Lautenschlager and H. Haase, "The Myth of Entrepreneurship Education: Seven Arguments Against Teaching Business Creation at Universities," *Journal of Entrepreneurship Education,* 14(2011): 147–161; S.C. Vetrivel, "Entrepreneurship and Education: A Missing Key in Development Theory and Practice," *Advances in Management,* 3(8) (2011): 18–22.

[2] Zhao, H., S.E. Siebert, and G.T. Lumpkin, "The Relationship of Personality to Entrepreneurial Intentions and Performance: A Meta-Analytic Review," *Journal of Management,* 36(2)(2010): 381–404.

[3] Caliendo, M., F. Fossen, and A. Kritikos, "Risk Attitudes of Nascent Entrepreneurs—New Evidence from an Experimentally Validated Survey," *Small Business Economics,* 32(2)(2009): 153–167.

[4] Brown, T.C., and D. Hanlon, "Validation of Effective Entrepreneurship Behaviors," *Academy of Management Annual Proceedings* (2010): B1–B6.

[5] Ward, T.B., "Cognition, Creativity, and Entrepreneurship," *Journal of Business Venturing,* 19(2)(2004): 173–188.

[6] Read, S., and S.D. Sarasvathy, "Knowing What to Do and Doing What You Know: Effectuation as a Form of Entrepreneurial Expertise," *Journal of Private Equity,* 9(1)(2005): 45–62.

[7] This definition of *effectuation* is derived from the Society for Effectual Action website: www.effectuation.org

[8] Feynman's simple application of the scientific method can be viewed on YouTube here: www.youtube.com/watch?v=6Rwcbsn19c0

[9] The seminal discussion of how practicing scientists engage primarily in "normal" as opposed to "revolutionary" science is Thomas Kuhn's book *The Structure of Scientific Revolutions* (Chicago: University of Chicago Press, 1970).

[10] Day, D.V., "The Difficulties of Learning from Experience and the Need for Deliberate Practice," *Industrial & Organizational Psychology,* 3(1)(2010): 41–44.

[11] Sarasvathy, S.D., "Effectual Reasoning in Entrepreneurial Decision Making: Existence and Bounds," *Academy of Management Proceedings* (2001): D1–D6.

[12] Wiltbank, R., N. Dew, S. Read, and S.D. Sarasvathy, "What to Do Next? The Case for Non-predictive Strategy," *Strategic Management Journal,* 27(10)(2006): 981–998.

[13] Macko, A., and T. Tyszka, "Entrepreneurship and Risk Taking," *Applied Psychology: An International Review,* 58(3)(2009): 469–487.

[14] Hao, Z., S.E. Siebert, and G.E. Hills, "The Mediating Role of Self-Efficacy in the Development of Entrepreneurial Intentions," *Journal of Applied Psychology,* 90(6)(2005): 1265–1272.

[15] Sarasvathy, S.D., H.A. Simon, and L. Lave, "Perceiving and Managing Business Risks: Differences Between Entrepreneurs and Bankers, *Journal of Economic Behavior & Organization,* 33(2)(1998): 207–222.

[16] Sarasvathy, S.D., "Causation and Effectuation: Toward a Theoretical Shift from Economic Inevitability to Entrepreneurial Contingency," *Academy of Management Review,* 26(2)(2001): 243–263.

[17] Read, S., N. Dew, S.D. Sarasvathy, M. Song, and R. Wiltbank, "Marketing Under Uncertainty: The Logic of an Effectual Approach," *Journal of Marketing,* 73(3)(2009): 1–18.

[18] Gabrielsson, J., and D. Politis, "Career Motives and Entrepreneurial Decision Making: Examining Preferences for Causal and Effectual Logics in the Early Stage of New Ventures," *Small Business Economics,* 36(3)(2011): 281–298.

[19] Isaacson, W., *Steve Jobs* (New York: Simon & Schuster, 2011).

[20] Dew, N., S. Read, S.D. Sarasvathy, and R. Wiltbank, "On the Entrepreneurial Genesis of New Markets: Effectual Transformations versus Causal Search and Selection," *Journal of Evolutionary Economics,* 21(2)(2009): 231–253.

ENTREPRENEURIAL MINDSETS

Learning Objectives

As a result of studying this chapter, students will be able to:

- **Identify** the five key mindsets that Harvard scholar Howard Gardner believes are essential for everyone in the 21st century.

- **Identify** the five key mindsets of the expert entrepreneur.

- **Develop** these mindsets over the course of their lives via deliberate practice.

- **Understand** how these mindsets contribute to effective application of the entrepreneurial method.

- **Apply** the techniques of deliberate practice to develop and hone your entrepreneurial expertise.

- **Realize** that there is no right time/right place to begin your efforts to refine your entrepreneurial expertise.

- **Seek out** opportunities to learn and grow throughout your life.

INTRODUCTION

As we discussed in the previous chapter, early efforts to identify the key personality traits and/or behavioral characteristics of successful entrepreneurs proved fruitless. The range of personality traits and behavioral characteristics among expert entrepreneurs is as varied as that of non-entrepreneurs. We also emphasized that despite the inability of researchers to discover key personality or behavioral characteristics of expert entrepreneurs that would provide a rationale for entrepreneurship education, the discovery of the entrepreneurial method now adequately fills that void. Learning the principles, techniques, and practices of the entrepreneurial method will undoubtedly prepare you for a lifetime of entrepreneurship.

In addition to recent discoveries about the methods used by expert entrepreneurs to achieve their success, there have also been recent discoveries about the way expert

© Alexander Sherstobitov, 2012. Used under license from Shutterstock, Inc.

entrepreneurs think. Research into the cognitive (thinking) skills of entrepreneurs has proven to be very fruitful over the past decade. **Cognitive skills** are not innate or inherited via one's DNA; they can be learned and improved over a lifetime of entrepreneurial endeavors. Of course, some people may be predisposed to learn certain cognitive skills more quickly or with greater facility than others, but that's not to say that they aren't available to everyone. You've learned a lot of things during your years in school, and some things probably came fairly easily and naturally to you and some things not so easily. That's true of all of us and provides for the great diversity of businesses, nonprofit organizations, and other innovations in our modern world.

Cognitive skills are best defined as patterns of thought in response to internal and external cues. Expert entrepreneurs have learned to respond to a variety of external cues with specific thought patterns and behavioral responses. For example, one well-established response exhibited by expert entrepreneurs has been defined as the **overconfidence bias**. The overconfidence bias means that expert entrepreneurs tend to believe they are able to solve the problems that confront them. People lacking in this bias might be inclined to shrink from the major challenges that expert entrepreneurs have learned to confront. Of course, an overconfidence bias can be counterproductive if it leads one to believe that no other people need to be consulted to solve difficult problems. Not even an expert entrepreneur can solve all the problems a venture is likely to face, and consulting with others to craft alternative responses can be helpful.

Understanding the **entrepreneurial mindsets** allows you to evaluate both the advantages and disadvantages that these mindsets create. Expert entrepreneurs tend to develop a very deep understanding of their own strengths and limitations. With that knowledge, they are not likely to misuse their overconfidence bias. An expert entrepreneur knows that solving problems oftentimes means bringing in other people to help. The expert entrepreneur is confident that the problem will be solved through his or her efforts, efforts that may include bringing the right people together to develop and implement effective solutions.

In this chapter, we introduce you to some of the expert entrepreneur mindsets that have been discovered by scholars. Many of these discoveries have revealed subtle shortcuts, thought patterns, and emotional responses that expert entrepreneurs have developed over their entrepreneurial careers. Rather than provide a catalog of each of the various subtle cognitive skills that expert entrepreneurs have been found to possess, we have aggregated these skills into five fundamental categories:

1. Opportunity recognition
2. Design thinking
3. Risk management
4. Resilience
5. Effectual reasoning

These categories of underlying skills enable you to develop techniques to practice and improve on your own cognitive skill sets. For example, opportunity recognition is part analytic and part intuitive. There are a number of analytic techniques that you can learn to evaluate opportunities, and we'll teach you those in this book. But there are also a number of intuitive factors that are easy to point out, but difficult to master. For example, a new venture may appear to have cutting-edge technology that you think will be incredibly valuable to a particular target market. What you cannot observe directly is exactly how the market will respond and whether the venture can sustain itself long enough before sales accelerate. This is something that expert entrepreneurs have learned to evaluate based on their own experiences in starting ventures.

In the next section, we introduce you to Harvard scholar Howard Gardner's analysis of the five mindsets that everyone needs to be successful in the future. Gardner believes that the five mindsets he identifies should be the focus of general education.

We have borrowed from Gardner's approach to develop five mindsets that entrepreneurs will need to be successful in the future. Research into the cognitive skills of expert entrepreneurs has discovered a large number of predispositions, biases, and thought patterns among the population of expert entrepreneurs. We've aggregated this wide range of cognitive skills exhibited by expert entrepreneurs into five categories. The five mindsets that we have identified provide you a target to work on throughout your life.

After we introduce you to the five mindsets of the expert entrepreneur you will then be introduced to the concept of deliberate practice. **Deliberate practice** is a formal process that enables you to take charge of developing your skills in the entrepreneurial method and the five minds of the entrepreneur. We begin with a brief introduction to Howard Gardner's five minds for the future.

FIVE MINDS FOR THE FUTURE

This chapter borrows from a book written by Harvard psychologist Howard Gardner. Gardner's book, *Five Minds for the Future,* purports to be, among other things, an intellectual foundation for general education.[1] Gardner has written extensively on human intelligence, creativity, and cognition. Most recently, he has published on what he believes to be the essential "minds" that are necessary for a person to be effective in the future. He says, "With these 'minds,' as I refer to them, a person will be well equipped to deal with what is expected, as well as what cannot be anticipated; without these minds, a person will be at the mercy of forces that he or she can't understand, let alone control."[2]

Education Theory and Becoming an Expert

Whether you know it or whether you are aware of it, you have been subjected to a variety of educational theories throughout your years of formal schooling. Educational theories provide teachers and school administrators with a rationale for the types of curriculum and other programs they bring into the classroom. For example, during the late 1950s and 1960s when America was caught up in the so-called Cold War most students were exposed to a curriculum called "New Math." The intent was to create a generation of math-literate scientists and engineers to help America advance technologically. It is important for you to be aware of the educational theories that drive your past, present, and future education. Being aware of the theories that underlie the classroom methods will help you take control and give you more power to become the type of person you want to be. Howard Gardner's latest work on the Five Minds of the Future is one such theory. Later, we explore the concept of *deliberate practice*. Deliberate practice is necessary for any type of expertise. It is a way for you to take control of your own learning and build your entrepreneurial expertise.

Sources: Paul Ward et al., "The Road to Excellence: Deliberate Practice and the Development of Expertise," *High Ability Studies,* 18(2)(2007): 119–153; Howard Gardner, *The Five Minds for the Future* (Cambridge, MA: Harvard University Press, 2007).

In his book Gardner develops detailed arguments for five specific "minds" that individuals will need to be effective in the future. The minds he proposes are really synthesized categories comprised of myriad cognitive sub-skills that can be defined, packaged for delivery and consumption at various levels of student maturity and readiness, and ultimately measured and assessed on an individual basis. Gardner's five minds, no doubt, can and will be debated, but they are useful targets for personal development.[3] In devising these categories as an intellectual foundation for personal development, Gardner has followed in the footsteps of renowned educational theorists such as Jean Piaget, Benjamin Bloom, Albert Bandura, and others. Gardner's five minds are discussed in the next sections.

The Disciplined Mind

This mind is based on Gardner's observation that to be an effective adult in the modern world requires mastery of at least one discipline. The disciplined mind knows how to define and solve unique types of problems. It also knows how to distinguish useful contributions to a field of knowledge from errant or fraudulent ones. The disciplined mind builds on and extends its capability, constantly seeking to expand the range of problems that can be addressed. This capacity helps a person individuate and gain independence. As Gardner put it: "Without at least one discipline under his belt, the individual is destined to march to someone else's tune."[4]

The Synthesizing Mind

This mind describes the capability to gather, organize, and digest diverse facts and ideas—both from within the disciplinary perspective and from new perspectives. In the modern world individuals are exposed to far more knowledge and information each day than they can adequately absorb and comprehend. To function in this world of information requires the ability to synthesize disparate data to develop opinions and reasoned actions. The synthesizing mind "takes information from disparate sources, understands and evaluates that information objectively, and puts it together in ways that make sense to the synthesizer and also to other persons."[5]

The Creating Mind

The creating mind is able to break new ground by combining information, ideas, and artifacts in novel ways; by asking provocative and counterintuitive questions; and by absorbing new ideas and creations into the stream of everyday life to enable new and unexpected outcomes. As the call for greater levels of innovation in our globally competitive economy grows louder, the creating mind is increasingly important. The ability to create is important not just within the creative disciplines (arts, literature) but across the spectrum of human endeavor.

The Respectful Mind

The respectful mind is critical to our ability to live together in a world that is growing increasingly interdependent. This mind prepares individuals to cope with cultural, attitudinal, and behavioral variety. Gardner stresses that the respectful mind is not without conviction or values. That would be unsupportable. Rather, the respectful mind is able to tolerate differences among humans, seeks to resolve conflicts between varying perspectives through dialog when possible, and promotes tolerance and respectfulness among others.

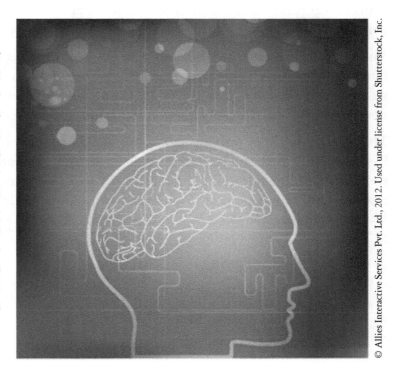

© Allies Interactive Services Pvt. Ltd., 2012. Used under license from Shutterstock, Inc.

The Ethical Mind

The ethical mind is also necessary in a world that has become increasingly secular and choice-laden. Individuals growing up in most parts of the world are less constrained by the value systems and strictures that formerly were endemic to family and religious life. As the influence of these shapers of ethical behavior wanes, individuals must develop their own ethical systems and values. Unfortunately, the "values-free" education of the United States and much of the rest of the Western world does not provide students with the tools to create their own ethical and value systems. Gardner thinks that the ethical mind is an important personal development goal and must be a high priority in this complex world.

Gardner asserts that these five minds are more than theoretical constructs. They are essential capabilities for individuals to be effective in the future. As Gardner states, "One cannot even begin to develop an educational system unless one has in mind the knowledge and skills that one values, and the kinds of individuals one hopes will emerge at the end."[6]

In the next section we extend Gardner's five minds approach to individuals who aspire to follow the entrepreneurial path to success in life. We believe that Gardner's five minds are essential to everyone, including aspiring entrepreneurs, who want to succeed in the 21st century. Those who want to succeed as entrepreneurs should develop Gardner's five minds, to be sure, but they should also focus on developing the five entrepreneurial mindsets that we discuss in the next section.

FIVE ENTREPRENEURIAL MINDSETS

As the new line of research into the differentiating cognitive skills of entrepreneurs continues to bear fruit, the question of how this research affects entrepreneurship education must be asked. For example, it seems natural to assume that *if* entrepreneurs in fact possess certain cognitive skills and *if* these skills can in fact be learned and/or improved upon, then it seems only reasonable for aspiring entrepreneurs to focus their efforts on building these skills.

The research literature on the cognitive skills of entrepreneurs is evolving rapidly, and there is much fruitful work that remains to be done in this area. Nevertheless, with nearly a decade of work already completed, it does seem reasonable for aspiring entrepreneurs to begin to focus on developing the mindsets of expert entrepreneurs.

This chapter will not provide an overview of all of the relevant and highly specific research that has been published on the cognitive skills of entrepreneurs. There have been several very useful summaries of this research published in the past few years.[7] Here, the concern is to translate the research into language that is useful to curriculum builders. I have borrowed the approach of Howard Gardner and describe the aggregated cognitive skills unique to entrepreneurs in terms of "minds."

- The Opportunity Recognizing Mind
- The Designing Mind
- The Risk Managing Mind
- The Resilient Mind
- The Effectuating Mind

Each of these five minds for the entrepreneurial future is explored in greater detail in the section that follow.

The Opportunity Recognizing Mind

Research into the cognitive skills unique to entrepreneurs has reported observation of a distinct **opportunity recognition** capability.[8] In fact, some scholars have asserted that opportunity recognition capability is a fundamental concern of entrepreneurship research.[9] Opportunity recognition has been observed to be a form of pattern recognition that develops over time among seasoned entrepreneurs.[10] Experience teaches entrepreneurs that certain patterns in consumer behavior, economic conditions, resource availability, and other factors are associated with new venture opportunities. Non-entrepreneurs who have not learned to recognize these patterns either through experience or academic study are less likely to recognize the higher-level economic opportunity the patterns represent.

Entrepreneurship scholars have been examining the opportunity recognition mind and have identified several attributes that this mindset embodies. These attributes include both analytic elements and intuitive elements. The analytic side of the equation includes developing such skills as the ability to read financial projections, analyze cost estimates, and understand the operational challenges that a new venture will face. The intuitive side of the equation includes such things as the ability to assess the credentials and experience of the top management team of a new venture. It also includes a feel for where a company is likely to fit within its industry, and whether its purported competitive advantages will be unique and sustainable enough to carve out market share. Intuitive understanding of these and other issues generally is achieved only through experience. For example, venture capitalists are better at picking winners among a set of new ventures than an entrepreneurial novice, but even the most experienced VC will be wrong more than 50 percent of the time.[11]

The Designing Mind

In the world of the entrepreneur, design plays a key role in a variety of ways. Entrepreneurs must either design a novel product and/or service to bring to a market, or they must be able to recognize such design novelty. Alternatively, they may design techniques for bringing existing products and services to underserved markets. In either case, the ability to design a solution to customer problems is vital to success in entrepreneurship.

In addition to designing the product/service offering, the design of the entrepreneurial venture itself is a singularly important act that entrepreneurs carry out with intent and over time.[12] The location of the venture, the reporting structure and job titles, the supply chain, and other elements must be designed for maximum efficiency and effectiveness. Not least, most entrepreneurs are constantly in money-raising mode and must be capable of designing a deal structure that is attractive to investors.

The concept of **design thinking** has received increasing attention beyond the realm of the entrepreneur. Design thinking is defined as "the way designers think: the mental processes they use to design objects, services, or systems."[13] This is a distinct way of thinking focused on projects. In contrast, traditional managers tend to think in terms of permanent job assignments. Herbert Simon was an early advocate of design thinking. In his acclaimed book, *The Sciences of the Artificial,* he noted: "Engineering, medicine, business, architecture and painting are concerned not with the necessary but with the contingent—not with how things are but with how they might be—in short, with design."[14] Only recently have investigators begun to use the concept of design thinking in the context of entrepreneurship.[15] It is emphasized here as one of the five minds of the entrepreneurial future because it seems to offer a richness of reference that "organizing" or "operating" lack.

The Risk Managing Mind

A common (mis)perception often expressed is that entrepreneurs are notorious risk takers. This perception has become commonplace because of the many exemplary entrepreneurs who in fact exceed the average tolerance of risk. Erroneously, the risk-taking propensity is identified as essential to their relative success. Of course, some entrepreneurs are risk takers to an extraordinary degree—but the frequency of risk taking among entrepreneurs is similar to that of the general population. What is actually the case is that entrepreneurs have become exceedingly adept **risk**

minimizers. They are able to look at situations that, of course, include elements of risk and they have learned techniques that enable them to reduce the risk to levels that are tolerable.[16] By way of contrast, someone who has not developed this risk-minimization capacity will avoid the situation and its associated risks.

Entrepreneurship scholars have in the last several years begun to examine not only how entrepreneurs recognize economic opportunity, but also how they evaluate the risks associated with that opportunity.[17] Managing risk involves internal and external components. Internally, the expert entrepreneur has learned to live with risk and to adapt to the ambiguity that it usually entails. Externally, the expert entrepreneur has learned to minimize risk through a multitude of actions. Raising capital from external investors, aggregating required resources, honing in on essential and advantage-providing knowledge, and others are techniques the expert entrepreneur routinely employs.

The Resilient Mind

Resilience is a term that has been used to refer to the ability to survive and even thrive under conditions of turbulence, change, or trauma. In general, it refers to an ability to absorb defeat and/or bad news without losing one's focus on goals and objectives.[18] This characteristic is especially useful for entrepreneurs since it is common knowledge that entrepreneurship as a lifestyle will occasion failure.[19] The ability to rebound from entrepreneurial failure and continue the entrepreneurial lifestyle is a textbook example of what is referred to as resilience. The ability to continue in the wake of entrepreneurial failure includes confronting a range of obstacles. Among these are personal and internal obstacles, including emotional state, financial condition, family matters, and others. Resiliency means being able to manage these various pressures in a manner that enables the continuance of the entrepreneurial lifestyle, regardless of whether a particular venture continues. Entrepreneurial failure also brings a number of external pressures to bear, including the entrepreneur's reputation among peers, investors, and others with potential influence. This reputation may influence the entrepreneur's future ability to launch a new venture, raise necessary funds, or acquire needed resources.

As a personality trait, resilience requires **emotional intelligence** as well as social awareness. Emotional intelligence includes the ability to recognize disappointment, frustration, and even depression as legitimate emotions associated with loss.[20] When the entrepreneur loses his or her business, it should be expected that some negative emotional state will arise. The ability to accept a negative emotion, deal with it effectively, and move on to new challenges is a major component of resilience. So is the ability to move about in the social world during periods of challenge and difficulty. Withdrawing into some neutral corner or lashing out at forces beyond one's control as responses to entrepreneurial failure can damage the entrepreneur's social reputation. Resilience certainly also includes the ability to maintain one's equilibrium in social settings, which in the case of entrepreneurial failure publicly known generally leads to *enhanced* reputation.

The Effectuating Mind

Entrepreneurship certainly calls for an action orientation on the part of its practitioners. It is not possible to claim success as an entrepreneur without understanding, at least, how to *do* two things: (1) Create or acquire something of value and (2) deliver that value to a market willing to pay prices in excess of costs. Both of these essential ingredients of entrepreneurship require intentional actions, but neither is sufficient unto itself. The inventor in the garage who creates the next iPod, but lacks the action orientation to find a way to deliver the product to a market will listen in isolation to whatever media his invention plays back. The salesperson who has a world-class contact list of willing buyers will dial the phone in vain unless he is able to lay claim to something those buyers value.

Entrepreneurship requires focused action. The effectuating mind is oriented toward closing the gap between current and future reality and toward traversing the pathway between them. Creativity may play a role in pioneering a path to be traversed, but that is not necessarily required. Many entrepreneurs are expert followers or "second movers," following the pathways blazed by pioneers. What the effectuating mind requires is a predisposition to nonpredictive control of current resources and an action orientation.

Research into the effectuating mind or action orientation of the entrepreneur is replete with cognitive heuristics and biases, and emotional predilections.[21] Effectuation is decidedly an action orientation that is fundamentally at odds with several staple beliefs about entrepreneurship education. For example, many entrepreneur educators focus on market analysis and business planning as the core of their curriculum. Yet, effectuation research indicates that expert entrepreneurs don't rely on predictive or causal knowledge and are prone to rely on an action, feedback, new action approach to venture development.[22] The Bullet Breakout box highlights both Gardner's five minds and the mindsets of the expert entrepreneur that we've identified.

BULLET BREAKOUT

Mindsets for Your Success in the Future

Howard Gardner's Five Minds for the Future:

- The Disciplined Mind: Learn how to excel in a particular discipline, such as the law, one of the sciences, or one of the many creative arts and literature fields.

- The Synthesizing Mind: Learn how to synthesize disparate facts into a coherent whole.

- The Creating Mind: Learn how to combine information, ideas, and artifacts in novel ways to create new value.

- The Respectful Mind: Learn how to tolerate diverse viewpoints and how to argue your own point of view with persuasion, civility, and skill.

- The Ethical Mind: Learn how to make ethical choices and decisions that are consistent with your own value system.

- The Opportunity Recognizing Mind: Learn how to evaluate entrepreneurial opportunities from a market perspective and a personal perspective.

- The Designing Mind: Learn how to design teams of people, incentives, and organizations to achieve successful outcomes.

- The Risk Managing Mind: Learn the techniques for managing risk and for bringing the risk of a new venture into line with your own risk tolerance.

- The Resilient Mind: Learn how to manage your own levels of stress and learn to balance your life so that you can work at peak effectiveness.

- The Effectuating Mind: Learn to become comfortable with the non-predictive control of resources that is at the heart of entrepreneurial expertise.

Now that you have explored the five minds of the expert entrepreneur and learned some of the fundamentals of the entrepreneurial method, it is useful next to consider how you can practice these things so you can begin your journey toward entrepreneurial expertise. Fortunately, the scholarly literature on expertise has identified some things that you can do. The research has identified a process known as *deliberate practice* that is necessary for developing nearly any type of expertise. We explore this process in the next section.

DELIBERATE PRACTICE

Your journey to becoming an expert entrepreneur will be filled with both disappointments and successes. The lessons that you learn along the way can either be derived by accident—you start ventures that may succeed or fail with no intention of learning lessons—or they can be lessons derived in a more deliberate manner.[23] Deliberate practice refers to experiments, exercises, and incremental steps that you can take to hone your entrepreneurial skills.

Individuals who engage in deliberate practice acquire superior knowledge structures and subsequently develop superior performance. Real expertise exhibits three characteristics: (1) It leads to performance that is consistently superior to that of the expert's peers, (2) it produces concrete results, and (3) it can be replicated and measured.[24] The principles of deliberate practice that you can use to develop your entrepreneurial expertise include:

- **Motivation:** Individuals must be motivated to undertake deliberate practice and develop expertise. Aspiring entrepreneurs should tap into whatever motivations are strongest for them, whether it is acquisition of wealth, solving a major social problem, or the sheer enjoyment of starting companies.

- **Understandability:** Rather than studying stories of successful entrepreneurs, which are mostly unique and non-repeatable, your efforts to develop entrepreneurial expertise should focus on becoming skilled in the entrepreneurial method. This principle of deliberate practice means that you can't practice what you don't understand. The entrepreneurial method has broken down the tenets of expert entrepreneurship into meaningful and understandable principles and mindsets. This means that, as an aspiring entrepreneur, you can learn to develop the arsenal of methods and mindsets that can be applied across the entrepreneurial domains and opportunities that you will encounter in your lifetime.

- **Feedback:** For deliberate practice to affect learning, there must be immediate feedback on performance. This part of the learning process is critical as you try new behaviors and modify them in the face of feedback. This process of trial and feedback is used by experts as they continuously upgrade their cognitive skills. Look for opportunities to practice new behaviors and understandings and gather immediate feedback on those performances.

- **Repetition:** Deliberate practice involves repeated performance of the same or similar tasks. The motivation required to repeatedly practice is one of the key distinctions between experts and people who merely have experience. Of course, practicing new behaviors will be awkward and uncomfortable for awhile. You will not discover new behaviors that become comfortable over time until you try them, practice them, and only then determine whether they are making things better for you and your venture.

- **Fit:** This component of deliberate practice asserts that the tasks being practiced must fit the individual and the contextual circumstances. For example, a person who aspires to be a concert pianist must not only have appropriate equipment, but must also be fortunately endowed with piano-playing talent. If either is lacking, there would be no fit between the practice and the goals. Nascent entrepreneurs must learn that success is a function of talent, expertise, environment, and other factors. Expert entrepreneurs have either consciously or unconsciously responded effectively to the fundamental question of effectuation: "Given who you are, what you know, and whom you know, what types of economic and/or social artifacts can you, would you want to, and should you create?"[25]

Of course it may be difficult to find opportunities to practice while you are striving mightily to build a company. Recognizing this, expertise scholars have developed a slightly different approach that you can use to develop your skills while you are striving to make your venture successful. This slightly different approach has been referred to as **deliberate performance**.[26] Deliberate performance differs from deliberate practice in that deliberate performance occurs on the job. Practice typically refers to undertaking simulated performance with the intention of improving performance in the real world. But it is often the case with aspiring entrepreneurs that the opportunities to practice are limited. Many are likely already to be in the real world and need to begin to create results.

Deliberate performance includes most of the same characteristics as deliberate practice. That is, feedback, repetition, being motivated, and finding a good fit are vital and necessary components of both deliberate practice and deliberate performance. Four additional elements are recommended for deliberate performance:

Estimation: Developing the ability to estimate the amount of resources that are necessary for the various stages of venture growth and development is a vital element of entrepreneurial expertise. You should observe various types of ventures and understand the relative amount of resources that are necessary for them to have a successful launch. For example, many business types such as manufacturing and medical device development are highly capital intensive.

Others, such as many of the new social media Internet business models, are far less capital intensive. In fact, a whole new type of venture capital has emerged to take advantage of the relatively low costs of launching new web-based ventures. YCombinator, TechStars, and others are examples of this new type of venture capital firm.[27] These firms invest very small amounts of capital—between $15K and $35K—and they invest in a lot of ventures to maximize their potential for at least one of them to be a big winner. YCombinator, for example, funded more than 300 startups between 2005 and 2011, approximately thirty per year.

Experimentation: Experimentation has been identified as the most important learning process that we engage in.[28] Experimentation entails trying something new, observing the results of that effort, and then deciding to adopt, reject, or continue to experiment. This type of learning is also referred to often as trial and error learning. There are three different ways in which aspiring entrepreneurs can learn via experimentation. The first way is called *exploratory experiment*. Exploratory experiment is best described as playful activity in which we try out and get a feel for behaviors, performances, and processes. Another type of experiment is referred to as *move testing*. This type of learning occurs when a person takes a particular action to produce an intended change. The move is evaluated based on how well the intended change was achieved and taking into account any other changes that resulted from the move. For example, giving a child a treat to stop it from crying may stop the crying, but it may produce more frequent crying to attain the treat reward. The final type of experimentation is termed *hypothesis testing*. This type of experimentation first conceives and then tests two or more competing hypotheses.

Extrapolation: Extrapolation refers to the way people learn from prior incidents, including examples they've heard about, to apply any lessons learned to other, similar, experiences. Usually, surprises lead to reflection, and failures lead to the most intense learning experiences. The primary goal of the extrapolation approach is not to avoid repeating mistakes, it is to improve your mental models. As such, details of prior incidents are less important than the lessons that were learned from the incident. Skilled performance, and improving performance over time, results from understanding causal relationships, not recalling the details of the event.

Explanation: This approach to learning aims at developing a narrative for the learning that has taken place and the mental models one tends to use to solve problems in the real world. Explanations are the result of reflecting on the incidents and lessons learned. They should be done naturally in the course of performing with the intention of improving future performances. Thus, an aspiring entrepreneur may reflect, for example, on the results obtained at a networking event. Was the event a good use of time? What types of opening lines did the aspiring entrepreneur use to meet new people? What type of people should be avoided in the future? What type of people should be pursued more assertively?

Another important element of deliberate practice/performance is coaching. Some scholars, in fact, assert that coaching is an *essential* element of deliberate practice. A coach is someone who is able not only to demonstrate to the learner the types of behaviors that are preferred, but who can also help reflect on and evaluate the learner's performances. For many aspiring entrepreneurs, it is simply not possible to find someone who will literally coach them as they launch one venture after another. More likely, the aspiring entrepreneur will be able to find a willing and capable mentor. A mentor can provide the same assistance in the reflection and learning process as a coach. Eventually, the aspiring entrepreneur should also learn how to coach him- or herself.

PRACTICING THE FIVE MINDS

The five minds of the entrepreneurial future are categories of a range of underlying cognitive subskills that have been identified as unique to entrepreneurs. This concluding section highlights some things you can do to practice the five mindsets of the expert entrepreneur.

The Opportunity Recognition Mind

The recognition of opportunity is essential to entrepreneurship. It is a skill that develops over time in most entrepreneurs, suggesting that it is a skill that can be learned and refined. The research literature describes the process of opportunity recognition as akin to the pattern recognition that is developed in individuals who are deemed experts in a field. Successful entrepreneurs are experts in this manner. They are able to review and understand "deals" more rapidly than novices. Successful entrepreneurs use heuristics that they've developed from their own experiences and from watching others. Things you can do to help develop this mind include:

- Evaluate nascent entrepreneurial ventures and track those ventures over time. Try to predict whether they will succeed or fail. What factors do you think are most relevant to your prediction?

- Go to entrepreneurial meetings to meet venture capitalists or listen to them via the many online video sources. Listen for the criteria VCs use to determine where and when to invest.

The Designing Mind

This mind defines the need to combine disparate ideas, people, or physical objects in novel ways that appeal to others. Entrepreneurs must design their products and services, the structure of their ventures, the structure of their equity and debt offerings, and other things. There are several things you can do to help create the designing mind:

- Design thinking is inherently interdisciplinary and combinatory. Work on projects at school or in your spare time that require multiple perspectives to achieve positive outcomes.

- Designing requires relentless prototyping. Review your business ideas with trusted others for feedback that results in evolutionary and incremental improvements in your original concepts. Be open to changing your original idea.

- The outcome of design is a narrative or story. Interview a successful entrepreneur near you and develop a compelling story to share with others.

The Risk Managing Mind

The ability to manage risk refers both to the ability emotionally to manage perceived risk and the ability to reduce actual risk through specific actions. Both of these elements of the risk management mind are amenable to curricular interventions and measurement. Some techniques that you might use to develop the risk management mind include:

- Develop your stress recognition and management skills. Learn to recognize signs of stress in yourself and develop techniques for dealing with and relieving stress that are productive and contribute to your life (i.e., don't simply resort to alcohol).

- Learn about the variety of financial resources available to entrepreneurs. Successful entrepreneurs have learned to leverage multiple financial resources, including other people's money, banks, credit cards, and others.

- Learn how to network successfully with others. Successful entrepreneurs are able to aggregate human resources to help them solve business problems that they could not solve on their own. You can become a more adept networker by going to entrepreneur gatherings, interacting with others, and following up with those who you think bring additional value to your venture and/or your life.

The Resilient Mind

This mind may be the most difficult to practice, as successful entrepreneurs develop resilience only through multiple real-world failures. The goal in practicing the resilient mind, then, would be to somehow accelerate the failure process. This is best done under conditions that produce the same type of emotions—although likely not as intense—that entrepreneurs feel when experiencing venture failure. Experiencing the actual emotion with the lessons about failing and how to avoid it in the future not only helps cement those lessons in the mind, but it is arguable that learning to cope with the emotions associated with failure is, in fact, the primary lesson. Often, nothing general can be learned from a failed venture that becomes a useful heuristic for future ventures. Nonetheless, the emotional coping skills can be applied in multiple and unrelated settings. Several techniques may be useful in helping you develop a resilient mind:

- Enter competitive situations where there is potential for you to suffer loss and/or fail. Focus on the emotions that you feel when you lose. A good resource for becoming better at handling failure is Martin Seligman's book *Learned Optimism*.[29]

- Talk with entrepreneurs who have recently failed. Listen carefully to how the entrepreneur felt in the face of failure. Ask the entrepreneur what he or she did to overcome the failure and move on to the next thing.

- With a group of trusted friends who are also interested in developing resilience, talk about a personal failure that had an emotional impact on you. You should provide sufficient detail to help conjure some level of emotion in yourself and also in the discussion partners. Discussion should focus on how to think about the failure in new ways—especially in ways that maintain emotional balance.

The Effectuating Mind

This mind is about taking action in a world of uncertain and often unpredictable outcomes. The effectuating mind has been the subject of scholarship in entrepreneurship for just shy of a decade.[30] It is based on the assumption that there is something like entrepreneurial expertise, and that this expertise can be learned via a process of deliberate practice.

- Assess your personal talents and strengths. Be realistic about what you are really good at and about your personal weaknesses. Expert entrepreneurs leverage their talents and strengths, and find ways to minimize their weaknesses.

- Put yourself in situations that currently are beyond your comfort zone. Assess your performance and resolve to continue to improve. For example, many young people have an aversion to public speaking. If that is a challenge for you, join a local Toastmasters organization and stick with it until you achieve new levels of public speaking expertise.

HOW/WHEN TO START PRACTICING

There are many opinions about when is the right time to become an entrepreneur. Some believe that entrepreneurship is only for the young. The many technology companies that have been launched by youthful entrepreneurs over the last several decades highlight this perspective. Of course, it is possible that the overweighting toward youth in the technology startups of the last two decades may be related in part to the newness of the technologies. Older entrepreneurs simply were not bred on the technologies and don't understand them as well as youth who have been using and learning the new technologies from a young age. We are now seeing a trend toward second-generation technology entrepreneurs—those who had a successful startup when they were young are now launching their second and third startups at more advanced ages.

Youth is helpful when new technologies are rapidly emerging, but even the Internet is now two decades old and more mature and savvy business models are taking over. Youth may also be helpful in that tremendous levels of energy are normally required to launch new ventures. On the other hand, greater levels of experience among older entrepreneurs may lead to greater efficiencies and less stress and strain.

In reality, there is no single time in life when it is better to launch your entrepreneurial career. In fact, the average age of the first-time entrepreneur is probably older than you think. Research has indicated that the average age of the first-time entrepreneur is 39.[31]

Another factor that often concerns aspiring entrepreneurs is the amount of capital they have at their disposal. There is common misunderstanding that launching a new venture requires large amounts of capital. In reality, the average amount of startup capital in new ventures is just $25,000.[32] Expert entrepreneurs have learned that there are many significant ways to keep costs low when launching a new venture. As a college student, you are probably only too familiar with strategies to keep expenses low. Expert entrepreneurs practice the same cost-reducing strategies when starting and operating their ventures. They have learned through experience that managing costs is paramount to long-term success. Of course, cost management means making difficult choices—such as forgoing fancy office space in favor of a larger marketing budget. If you are managing your costs well as a college student, continue those frugal ways into your entrepreneurial life and you are on the right track.

Another important lesson that expert entrepreneurs learn is that they must surround themselves with other effective people to become successful. A common mistake of aspiring entrepreneurs, by way of contrast, is to go into business with friends or family members because they are a friend or a family member. This more often than not leads to strains in the business and strains in the relationship. We are not saying that you shouldn't go into business with friends or family members, but you should be certain that you are doing so for the right reason. Anyone—including a friend or family member—that you decide to align with as a business partner must have the necessary personal capabilities and skills to help the business succeed. It is hard enough to be successful in business when everyone is aligned toward building the business and has the skills to do so without thinking about dragging along others who cannot contribute.

Finally, we will stress once again the need to find a good fit between your unique talents and the type of business that you launch. With entrepreneurship on the rise around the world, it is becoming increasingly difficult for new entrepreneurs to find and fill a niche. You are far more likely to be successful if you build your business on talents that you possess to a greater extent than the average person. If you are a talented musician, find a way to build a business around that talent. If you are a talented writer, build a business around that talent. Not all of us can be Internet zillionaires or computer gamers—two of the more rapidly growing business categories in recent years. Yet, all of us possess some unique talent that can be leveraged in myriad ways to become successful. The following mini-case highlights a Colorado entrepreneur who has a talent for designing greeting cards.

MINI-CASE

Bloomin Greeting Cards

Don Martin graduated from college and immediately went to work for a major greeting card company. He was a talented greeting card designer and developed a deep appreciation for the industry while employed with the large company. Despite his rapid advancement in the greeting card firm, Don's entrepreneurial spirit had him thinking of ways to start his own firm. However, he knew the industry was exceedingly competitive, and he would need an edge to launch his own firm and be successful. A friend of his, Tom Noyes, was dabbling in creating paper that contained seeds for flowers, trees, and other plants. Don put two and two together and realized that his friend's seed paper and his greeting card design skills could be combined to create the edge he needed to start his own venture. Don and Tom launched their venture, Bloomin, in 1995. Today, the company's products are distributed around the United States and twelve foreign countries. Don leveraged his unique talents to create a brand new niche in the greeting card industry.

Source: Adapted from "Experience Starting an Export Business," The StartUp Experience DVD Series, Businesses2Learn, Colorado Springs, CO. www.thestartupexperience.com

SUMMARY OF LEARNING OBJECTIVES

1. **Identify** the five key mindsets that Harvard scholar Howard Gardner believes are essential for everyone in the 21st century. *Howard Gardner has identified five minds that he believes are the foundation of effective general education. According to Gardner, these five minds are critical for success in the 21st century. The five minds he identifies are (1) the disciplined mind, (2) the synthesizing mind, (3) the creating mind, (4) the respectful mind, and (5) the ethical mind.*

2. **Identify** the five key mindsets of the expert entrepreneur. *Similar to Gardner's approach to identifying five minds necessary for personal success in the 21st century, this book identifies five minds that aspiring entrepreneurs will need to cultivate and develop for entrepreneurial success. These five minds are (1) the opportunity recognizing mind, (2) the design thinking mind, (3) the risk managing mind, (4) the resilient mind, and (5) the effectuating mind.*

3. **Develop** these mindsets over the course of their lives via deliberate practice. *Deliberate practice has been identified as a key technique for developing expertise in a wide range of disciplines. Applying deliberate practice to become an expert entrepreneur can take as long as ten years. Aspiring entrepreneurs can blend deliberate practice with deliberate performance (on-the-job training) to achieve their goals of becoming expert entrepreneurs.*

4. **Understand** how these mindsets contribute to effective application of the entrepreneurial method. *Aspiring entrepreneurs can develop these five mindsets via deliberate practice. Appropriate challenges can be designed by the aspiring entrepreneur either in real-world venture situations or in simulated situations that will help develop the key mindsets over time.*

5. **Apply** the techniques of deliberate practice to develop and hone your entrepreneurial expertise. *Deliberate practice requires that aspiring entrepreneurs take on challenges that will help them develop their expertise in application of the entrepreneurial method, and in developing the entrepreneurial mindsets. Deliberate practice requires that the challenges undertaken are a good fit for the aspiring entrepreneur's current level of expertise and that feedback on the performance is gathered and evaluated.*

6. **Realize** that there is no right time/right place to begin your efforts to refine your entrepreneurial expertise. *The average age of the first-time entrepreneur is 39, but entrepreneurs come in all ages. In fact, the fastest growing age for first time entrepreneurs is people over 50. If you are a young student, you should begin the deliberate practice process immediately to develop and hone your entrepreneurial expertise.*

7. **Seek out** opportunities to learn and grow throughout your life. *Whether you use deliberate practice, in simulated environments, or deliberate performance, you should be actively seeking opportunities to learn and grow in your quest to develop entrepreneurial expertise.*

QUESTIONS FOR DISCUSSION

1. Explain what is meant by the Opportunity Recognizing Mind. Provide some examples of how you might develop this mindset in the coming years as you aspire to entrepreneurial success.

2. Explain what is meant by the Designing Mind. What types of things to entrepreneurs design? Do you agree that creating a company is a design process? Explain.

3. Explain what is meant by the Risk Managing Mind. How can you develop this mindset? Give some examples of how you might develop this mindset.

4. Explain what is meant by the Resilient Mind. Do you think you have a resilient mind? Explain. What steps can you take to develop a resilient mindset?

5. Explain what is meant by the Effectuating Mind. What is the difference between this mindset and the mindset that you are learning in your other business courses?

6. Describe the key elements of deliberate practice. What are some things that you can do to use this approach to learn the entrepreneurial method?

7. When is the best time to begin practicing toward becoming an expert entrepreneur? Explain.

8. Is it a good idea to choose your friends or family members for business partners? Explain why or why not.

IN-CLASS EXERCISE

For this exercise the class should be divided into diverse groups of five. The point of this exercise is for each group to create a deliberate practice or deliberate performance activity that they and their classmates might use to develop entrepreneurial expertise. This exercise should be conducted according to the following:

1. Divide the class into diverse groups of five. You will need at least 45 minutes for this exercise.

2. Assign the groups the task of identifying a particular entrepreneurial mindset that they are interested in. Try to make sure that each of the five mindsets is covered by the groups.

3. Each group is to devise and design a deliberate practice or deliberate performance exercise that can be conducted either individually or with feedback from others.

4. The deliberate practice or deliberate performance exercises designed by the student teams must include the following:
   - The particular mindset that the exercise addresses
   - The nature of the practice or performance that must be undertaken
   - The key measures that one should look for as a result of the practice or performance
   - The strategies that one might use to improve performance over time.

5. Next, have each of the student teams present its deliberate practice or deliberate performance exercise to the class and discuss.

6. Ask each team to find time to undertake its particular practice or performance within the next week or two and to then report back to the class on its experiences.

KEY TERMS

Cognitive skills: Best defined as patterns of thought in response to internal and external cues. Expert entrepreneurs have learned to respond to a variety of external cues with specific thought patterns and behavioral responses.

Deliberate performance: Deliberate performance differs from deliberate practice in that deliberate performance occurs on the job.

Deliberate practice: A formal process that enables you to take charge of developing your skills in the entrepreneurial method and the five minds of the entrepreneur.

Design thinking: The way designer's think: the mental processes they use to design objects, services, or systems.

Emotional intelligence: Emotional intelligence includes the ability to recognize disappointment, frustration, and even depression as legitimate emotions associated with loss.

Entrepreneurial mindsets: Ways of thinking that expert entrepreneurs tend to exhibit and that are important to their success as entrepreneurs.

Opportunity recognition: A form of pattern recognition that develops over time among seasoned entrepreneurs. Experience teaches entrepreneurs that certain patterns in consumer behavior, economic conditions, resource availability, and other factors are associated with new venture opportunities.

Overconfidence bias: When expert entrepreneurs tend to believe they are able to solve all the problems that confront them.

Resilience: The ability to survive and even thrive under conditions of turbulence, change, or trauma. In general, it refers to an ability to absorb defeat and/or bad news without losing one's focus on goals and objectives

Risk minimizers: Entrepreneurs are good at managing and minimizing the risks associated with new ventures. They are able to look at situations that, of course, include elements of risk, and they have learned techniques that enable them to reduce the risk to levels that are tolerable.

ENDNOTES

[1] Gardner, H., *The Five Minds for the Future* (Cambridge, MA: Harvard Business School Press, 2007).

[2] Ibid., p. 2.

[3] Sheffield, R., "Why Discipline, Synthesis, Creativity, Respect, and Ethics Are Literally Quintessential." (Book review). *People Management,* 13(12)(2007): 53.

[4] Gardner, H., op cit., p. 3.

[5] Ibid.

[6] Gardner, H., op cit., p. 14.

[7] Baron, R.A., "Potential Benefits of the Cognitive Perspective: Expanding Entrepreneurship's Array of Conceptual Tools,"*Journal of Business Venturing,* 19(2)(2004): 169–173.

[8] Baron, R.A., and M.D. Ensley, "Opportunity Recognition as the Detection of Meaningful Patterns: Evidence from Comparison of Novice and Experience Entrepreneurs. *Management Science,* 52(9(2006)): 1331–1344.

[9] Venkataraman, S., "The Distinctive Domain of Entrepreneurship Research," In J. Katz (Ed.), *Advances in Entrepreneurship, Firm Emergence and Growth,* Vol. 3 (Greenwich, CT: JAI Press, 1997), pp. 119–138.

[10] Baron, R.A., "Opportunity Recognition as Pattern Recognition: How Entrepreneurs 'Connect the Dots' to Identify New Business Opportunities," *Academy of Management Perspectives,* 20(1)(2006): 104–119.

[11] Fiet, J.O., and P.C. Patel, "Evaluating the Wealth Creating Potential of Business Plans," *Journal of Private Equity,* 10(1)(2006): 18–32.

[12] Sarasvathy, S.D., "Making it Happen: Beyond theories of the Firm to Theories of Firm Design." *Entrepreneurship Theory & Practice,* 28(6)(2004): 519–531.

[13] Dunne, D., and R. Martin, "Design Thinking and How It Will Change Management Education: An Interview and Discussion," *Academy of Management Learning & Education,* 5(4)(2006): 512–523.

[14] Simon, H., *The Sciences of the Artificial,* 3rd ed. (Boston: MIT Press, 1969), p. 111.

[15] Jacoby, R., and D. Rodriguez, "Innovation, Growth, and Getting to Where You Want to Go," *Design Management Review,* 18(1)(2007): 10–15.

[16] Janney, J.J., and G.G. Dess, "The Risk Concept for Entrepreneurs Reconsidered: New Challenges to the Conventional Wisdom." *Journal of Business Venturing,* 21(3)(2006): 385–400.

[17] Keh, H.T., M.D. Foo, and B.C. Lim, "Opportunity Evaluation under Risky Conditions: The Cognitive Processes of Entrepreneurs," *Entrepreneurship Theory & Practice,* 27(2)(2002): 125–148.

[18] Mangurian, G.E., "Realizing What You're Made Of." *Harvard Business Review,* 85(3)(2007): 125–130.

[19] Timmons, J.A.,"Entrepreneurship and the Creation of High-Potential Ventures," in D.L. Sexton and R.W. Smilor (Eds.), *The Art and Science of Entrepreneurship* (Cambridge, MA: Ballinger, 1986), pp. 223–239.

[20] Goleman, D., *Emotional Intelligence* (New York: Bantam Books, 1995).

[21] Sarasvathy, S.D., "Causation and Effectuation: Toward a Theoretical Shift from Economic Inevitability to Entrepreneurial Contingency," *Academy of Management Review,* 26(2)(2001): 243–263.

[22] Read, S., and S.D. Sarasvathy, "Knowing What to Do and Doing What You Know: Effectuation as a Form of Entrepreneurial Expertise," *Journal of Private Equity,* 9(1)(2005, Winter): 45–62.

[23] Day, D.V., "The Difficulties of Learning from Experience and the Need for Deliberate Practice," *Industrial & Organizational Psychology,* 3(1)(2010): 41–44.

[24] Ericsson, K.A., M.J. Prietula, and E.T. Cokely, "The Making of an Expert," *Harvard Business Review,* 85(7/8)(2007): 114–128.

[25] Sarasvathy, op. cit.

[26] Fadde, P.J., and G.A. Klein, "Deliberate Performance: Accelerating Expertise in Natural Settings." *Performance Improvement,* 49(9)(2010): 5–14.

[27] See www.ycombinator.com and www.techstars.com

[28] Schank, R.C., "What Can be Taught," *eLearn Magazine,* Retrieved December 31, 2009, from http://elearnmag.org/subpage.cfm?section=opinion&article=120-1

[29] Seligman, M., *Learned Optimism,* (New York: Knopf Publishing, 1991).

[30] Sarasvathy, S.D., *How do Firms Come to Be? Towards a Theory of the Prefirm.* Doctoral dissertation thesis, Carnegie Mellon University, 1998.

[31] Shane, S., *The Illusions of Entrepreneurship: The Costly Myths That Entrepreneurs, Investors, and Policy Makers Live By* (New Haven: Yale University Press, 2007).

[32] Ibid.

CHAPTER 3

VENTURE IDEA GENERATION

Learning Objectives

As a result of studying this chapter, students will be able to:

- **Identify** the four different venture types that aspiring entrepreneurs can choose among.

- **Develop** venture ideas using a five-step approach.

- **Weigh** the potential advantages and disadvantages of launching a B2B or B2C venture.

- **Create** an opportunity register to keep track of their venture ideas and refine them over time.

- **Understand** the variety of business models and decide which of them might be right for their venture.

INTRODUCTION

The age-old question for aspiring entrepreneurs is: What business should I start? Aspiring entrepreneurs are often confounded by the challenge of developing a credible idea for a new venture. Consulting one's friends and family can be a useful start in trying to refine an idea for a venture, but that may not be the best approach. Your family and friends will likely be interested in telling you what they think you want to hear, rather than providing critical feedback on your idea. Or, perhaps the more-often-encountered reaction, they will think you are out of your mind for considering entrepreneurship in the first place.

© oliveromg, 2012. Used under license from Shutterstock, Inc.

Venture idea generation begins with an awareness of the myriad ways that entrepreneurs create new ventures. The range of possible entrepreneurial ventures is truly as broad as the human imagination. Today, we are witnessing the first private space ventures launched by some of the leading entrepreneurs of the era. New forms of retail, both online and traditional "bricks and mortar," are launching nearly every day. For example, how many new varieties of hamburger and pizza franchises can the world endure? Seemingly, there is no end to the proliferation of venture types. Fortunately, most ventures can be understood as one of only four fundamental types. We will explore these four types in detail in this chapter.

Understanding the four venture types is just the beginning of your quest to identify an idea that you can turn into a thriving venture. Once you've decided on the type of business you'd like to start, you need to generate an idea for a product or service that can be delivered via that venture type. We have developed a five step process for you to use to generate your idea. This process will help you determine a target market, develop and refine a product/service concept, review and adopt a business model, decide how to bring the product or service to market, and consider how the business will scale over time.

Expert entrepreneurs know that identifying viable ideas that can be developed into thriving ventures is an iterative process.[1] That means most ideas aren't hatched fully formed, but rather change and develop over time as new information is gathered and results of experiments are analyzed. Expert entrepreneurs know that no matter how well you think you know a market, it will nearly always behave differently than you expect. The expert entrepreneur is determined to make his idea successful, but he has also learned to be flexible and adaptable. Sticking to an original idea out of stubbornness or pride will not make a bit of difference to your market. Ultimately, the goal of every entrepreneur and entrepreneurial venture is to create value for customers. And customers have many alternative choices today if your product or service does not fit with their needs and desires.

Because idea generation is iterative, it is useful for aspiring entrepreneurs to keep what we call an opportunity register. The opportunity register is a type of a personal journal that is dedicated to helping you keep track of your evolving venture ideas, and ultimately to helping you decide on which of your ideas is the most well developed. An opportunity register can also be a means of recording intellectual property that you are creating. In this chapter we will introduce you to the concept of an opportunity register and how to keep a formal one for yourself.

Finally, in case you are getting stuck in developing ideas, we introduce you to some alternative sources of idea generation. The most likely source of idea generation is your own experience, talents, and background. Still, on occasion, aspiring entrepreneurs are not able to generate a spark of insight or innovation on their own. They need an external stimulus to get their creative juices flowing.[2] Sometimes people can be inspired by reading something different from their normal fare, or they can be inspired by listening to inspiring people, and there are other techniques that we recommend.[3]

Let's begin this chapter by exploring the four fundamental venture types that aspiring entrepreneurs can consider.

FOUR FUNDAMENTAL VENTURE TYPES

Expert entrepreneurs are among the most creative people on the planet. Imagine all the myriad ventures that have been created just in the past decade. Some of these ventures have had dramatic impacts on our economy, society, and ways of life. Facebook has tens of millions of users worldwide and people are now staying connected to extended family and friends like never before. Twitter has revolutionized the art of the pithy comment. Tesla Motors has created the first all-electric sports car. In addition to these companies, here's just a short list of companies that were founded by entrepreneurs and that have the potential to change the way we live and work in the future:[4]

- Craigslist
- YouTube
- Zynga
- Netflix
- Pandora
- WordPress
- Amazon
- Meebo
- FourSquare
- LinkedIn
- Second Life

Of course, most of these are technology- or Internet-related ventures, but there are many other non-tech new ventures that have also changed our lives. Think of how FedEx has affected package delivery. Think about how the Kindle has changed book buying and selling. Think about beverage companies that have made bottled water—bottled water!!!—nearly ubiquitous. The mini-case below describes another disruptive technology that has vastly changed the way students buy and sell college textbooks.

Chegg.com Disrupts the Textbook Industry

When Aayush Phumbhra arrived at Iowa State University in 2000 to begin his graduate studies, he was nearly broke. Needing to save money, he became an avid user of Cheggpost.com, which had been started that year by three fellow students to buy and sell textbooks and ISU merchandise.

"I realized the business had the potential to disrupt the textbook market," says Phumbhra, 33, who teamed with the Cheggpost founders and helped take the concept national under the name "Chegg" (a combination of "chicken" and "egg") in December 2007. He said, "Textbook prices have drastically outpaced the rate of inflation and are a huge pain point for college students. There was so much room to innovate and make a difference in the lives of students."

Chegg succeeded in large part by paying close attention to comments on Facebook and Twitter pages for ideas on how to improve and make customers happy. Phumbhra said, "From the very beginning, Chegg focused on customer feedback to create an experience that was far superior to anyone else in the textbook industry. As a result, we have a tremendous net promoter score, which is a tool that measures the loyalty of a company's customer relationships, and glowing reviews from our customers."

Adapted from N. Zmuda, "Chegg Expands from Textbook Rentals Into 'Social Education' Platform," *Advertising Age*, November 28, 2011; L. Girard, "Fast Growing Chegg Aims for High Marks with Students," *Entrepreneur.com*, http://www.entrepreneur.com/article/222655; accessed January 19, 2012.

Despite the many ways that entrepreneurs make millions through new ventures, in reality there are four fundamental venture types that can be created. The four types are depicted in Exhibit 3.1.

As Exhibit 3.1 indicates, you can launch a venture that creates value for business customers or for consumers. For example, Chegg's business model focuses on consumers (students). You can also create a venture that is primarily product centric or services centric. That's really about it—only four fundamental venture types. This framework provides a handy starting point in your venture

	Business	Consumer
Product	Enterprise software, heavy machinery, mainframe systems	Aspirin, personal computers, DVD players, cars, motorcycles
Service	Building maintenance, shipping, training, accounting, travel planning	Daycare, landscaping, television repair, roofing, dentist,

OFFERING (vertical axis)

CUSTOMER (horizontal axis)

EXHIBIT 3.1

idea-generation process, but it is usually not as simple in reality. Many ventures offer both products and services to their clients. For example, new ventures that specialize in enterprise software often also have a strong service component to their businesses. Software providers might need to help install the new software for their clients, and many charge a fee for such services. Many also offer maintenance plans for a fee, including access to technical support in the event that problems arise with software usage.

Many new ventures also serve both business and non-business customers.[5] For example, Dell sells computers both to business customers and retail customers. The company has separate web environments to service the different types of customer. Their corporate structure and reporting alignment likely separates these two business functions because the types of products, price points, marketing strategies, and service arrangements are vastly different for each customer type.

In general, aspiring entrepreneurs should attempt to limit their idea generation—at least initially—to only one of the quadrants from Exhibit 3.1. It is difficult enough to create value for a single type of customer without having to worry about serving two vastly different customer types. A venture launched in one quadrant can always develop products or services in the other quadrants as its capabilities and resources expand. Let's explore each of these four quadrants in more detail, beginning with business to business ventures.

Business to Business

Ventures that are launched to sell to other companies are referred to as **business to business** or "B2B" companies. There are many good reasons to consider launching a B2B venture. One good reason is that businesses usually have more money than consumers and may better be able to purchase the products and/or services that you are thinking about creating. B2B ventures come in many varieties because the needs of business are many. For example, many companies today provide cafeteria and food services to their employees. Now, it would be possible for a business to prepare and serve food to their employees, but that is not its core competence (unless it is a food service company). As a result, most businesses that provide cafeteria services to employees elect to outsource that function to another company (referred to as a third-party provider). In other words, they hire another business that specializes in food service to provide that service to their employees. One company that provides such a B2B service is Sysco. Over the past 40 years, the market for food service providers has grown to over $200B.[6]

There are many other services that businesses need to function effectively. For example, the outsourcing phenomenon accelerated rapidly over the past decade. Today, businesses outsource many of their non-core business functions, opening the door for aspiring entrepreneurs to offer those services to business clients.[7]

New B2B ventures don't have to confine their business models to providing outsource services to other companies. There is just as much need for innovative new products and services among businesses as there are among consumers. If you are thinking about ideas that will target other companies as your target market, there are three primary ways to create value:

1. Help companies make more money
2. Help companies save money
3. Help companies comply with community norms

B2B ventures have to provide value in one of these three categories, or they simply won't attract business customers. Businesses are not interested in fashion or whimsical items in the way consumers often are. Most businesses are focused on making profits, and the only way to do that is through increasing sales or decreasing costs.

Helping businesses increase sales is a popular area for new venture creation. Software designed to make the sales force more effective is a very crowded arena for venture development. Sales force automation, lead generation, and customer relationship management are just three types of enterprise software that target this space. Each of these three categories is crowded both with major incumbent firms, such as SalesForce.com, and a steady stream of new entries. Even though the space is crowded, significant new innovation over the existing products can still break through. However, any aspiring entrepreneur should be aware that most companies are slow to change their existing ways of doing business, including shifting from one software type to another. There can be many costs associated with switching that prohibit consideration of a new product or service provider.

Good cost-saving ideas for business almost always find a market among business customers. The focus for many of today's medium-sized and large companies is what is referred to as "lean." Lean is the catch-all term for constant attention to cost and cost saving tactics. The lean enterprise is generally organized around specific programs, such as Six Sigma, but there is plenty of room for innovative new approaches to cost saving.

As we previously mentioned, one of the most potent new approaches to cost saving over the past decade is business process outsourcing.[8] Businesses have learned that they can outsource their non-core functions to other companies that perform that function as their primary business activity. Entrepreneurs who saw this emerging trend were able to capture this booming business. Of course, many of the top outsourcing firms, such as InfoSys and Tata Group, are located in India. These ventures have been among the fastest growing companies in the world. For example, Infosys was founded by six Indian engineers in 1989, and the company reported 2011 revenue of over $6 billion.

Another category for B2B entrepreneurship that has emerged in recent years concerns the desire by companies to demonstrate conformity to prevailing community norms. Not all of the efforts to comply with community norms are directly related to increasing sales or decreasing costs. Most are seen primarily as preventive in nature. For example, many companies today have implemented extensive, and often expensive, sustainability programs.[9] Many such programs have little direct impact on a company's sales or costs. However, proponents of such programs argue that having a sustainability program promotes positive impressions of the company in the community and prevents possible sales losses. Many entrepreneurs have taken the initiative to develop products and services to serve this type of business demand. For example, Sustainable Minds is a venture that was formed to help companies analyze and manage the lifecycle impact of their products and services. The company was formed initially to provide companies with an analytic software tool. It has since grown to include a range of related products and services.

Business to Consumer

New ventures that target the consumer abound and are referred to as **business to consumer** or "B2C" ventures. There are many ways that entrepreneurs can create value for consumers in both the service and product categories. People have a seemingly insatiable desire not only for functional products and services that help them meet their daily living needs, but also for fashionable, adventurous, whimsical, or simply entertaining products and services. For example, think about the enormous numbers of consumers who flock from around the globe to visit Disney World. Disney created a fantastic park, no doubt about it, but it serves no true human need other than the desire for entertainment and diversion from the cares of daily life.

© Roca, 2012. Used under license from Shutterstock, Inc.

Consumer products and services are in some ways more difficult to develop because of the great variety of ways in which value can be created. We saw in the section above that there are really only three ways to create value for businesses: help them make more money, save them money, or help them comply with prevailing social norms. Below is a non-comprehensive list of the ways in which entrepreneurs can serve consumers:

1. Functional: Tools, Furniture, Appliances
2. Entertainment: Amusement Parks, Comedy Clubs, Sports Teams
3. Adventure: Travel, Skydiving, Paintball
4. Fashion: Clothing, Shoes, Jewelry
5. Transportation: Automobiles, Boats, Bicycles
6. Health: Nutrition, Exercise, Fitness Gear
7. Communication: Telephones, Cable Television, Email
8. Shelter: Housing, Camping, Hotel/Motel
9. Food: Fast Food, Gourmet Food, Health Food
10. Beverages: Bottled Water, Soft Drinks, Alcoholic Beverages
11. Art: Galleries, Original Works, Performance
12. Literature: Books, Blogs, Libraries
13. Music: Concerts, Online Radio, Instruments

And the list could go on for likely hundreds of different categories, including some that have not even been invented yet.

Creating products and services for consumers is competitive, and most entrepreneurs that have been successful with consumer products counsel against being a **single-product venture**. It is fine to *launch* a venture around a single consumer product, but it is difficult to *grow* a company around a single product. The reason for this is well known to those who have competed in the consumer product space. If a product is successful, it can rapidly grow through multiple distribution channels, including the big retailers such as Walmart. However, that very success can also prove a venture's undoing. Other companies that sell products through Walmart and the other big retailers will likely not be far behind with an offering that competes directly with yours if your product is successful. While you may have patents and other intellectual property rights to prevent outright copying, there are many ways to get around these barriers. So while a single consumer product venture might enjoy success over the short term, it is also likely to see its revenues decrease as the market becomes more competitive. The moral of the story is, if you desire to start your own consumer products company, you should have a number of potential product ideas that you can bring to market in succession and that are consistent with the brand image that you're developing. With such a strategy, you can build your company brand and consumers will begin to look for that brand when deciding which products to purchase.

Consumer services range from the necessary to the nearly ridiculous. Necessary services include things like healthcare, food, and shelter. The nearly ridiculous include such consumer services as The Poop Happens LLC a doggy-do removal service.[10] Consumer markets are competitive, as we noted, but the demand for a wide range of personal services is scaling upward in our busy culture. For example, there have been a number of startups that focus on **personal concierge services**, providing individuals with everything from grocery pickup to travel planning. According to Sara-Ann Kasner, president and founder of the National Concierge Association, "The concierge business is exploding right now. There has been tremendous growth."[11] Personal concierges and industry analysts say there is plenty of room for even more growth.

THE IDEA GENERATION PROCESS

Knowing the various ways that aspiring entrepreneurs can create a venture is just the beginning of your idea generation process. Once you decide what type of venture you would like to create—B2B or B2C, product or service—then you must decide what value you can, in fact, create for the markets you've chosen to explore.

We've developed a five-step process that you can use to refine your emerging business concept.

1. Determine your target market
2. Decide what product or service to bring to the market
3. Decide on the appropriate business model
4. Determine how you will bring the product or service to the market
5. Consider how you intend to scale the business over time

Determine Your Target Market

It is much easier to start a new venture if you have some idea of who your **target market** will be and where it is.[12] Your target market doesn't determine the entire addressable market opportunity for your venture's products or services, but it does give you an important starting point. Every business has to start with the first customer, and it is far easier to get your first customer if you identify your target market, study its needs and idiosyncrasies, and tailor your offerings to that market.

We will discuss target market identification and analysis in far greater detail in Chapter 5. For now, simply be aware that you need to identify a target market, preferably one with which you have some familiarity and connections. Many aspiring entrepreneurs underestimate the difficulty of reaching their intended target market. Having inside connections to potential customers or to reliable distribution channels can lessen the time it takes to get to profit and cash flow break-even. For example, when I (TND) launched my company in India to provide editorial services to major publishers, I already had high-level connections among potential clients. It was far easier to get meetings with decision makers based on the relationships I had already built. There is little doubt that without these contacts it would have taken far longer for my company to scale to profitability.

Decide What Product or Service to Bring to Market

You may already have a rough idea of the product or service that you'd like to take to your target market. Be careful, however, not to simply rest with your initial intuitions about what your customers want. Product (or service) development is best understood as an iterative process.[13] That means you may cycle through multiple revisions of your product or service concept before it is ready for the market. A good way to iterate and develop your product over time is to show it to selected members of your target market and ask for their reaction. For example, Jim Holley, an inventor and patent holder of baby products brought his first product to market after more than a year of **iteration**. His first product was a baby bottle called "U Mix." U Mix was a unique design that held the fluid in one part of the bottle and the dry formula powder in another. When the baby was ready to feed, the bottle was rotated to enable mixing of the fluid and dry formula. Holley intercepted mothers in grocery aisles with his product prototype as one technique to gather highly relevant feedback. He listened to their feedback and revised his product over and over until it was ready for mass distribution.[14]

The iteration process does not need to end once you have entered the marketplace with your products. In fact, in order to keep a competitive edge in the modern economy, many analysts recommend continuous innovation as a core business strategy.[15] **Continuous innovation** means making ongoing improvements to the products you already have in the marketplace and inventing new ones to extend your brand and develop additional streams of revenue.

Decide on the Appropriate Business Model

A **business model** is simply the way a business makes money.[16] There are probably as many different business models as there are entrepreneurs. Companies make money in a variety of ways, and often it takes a bit of creativity to determine which business model will be right for your venture. For example, many of the social media companies that are based on user-generated content (such as Twitter, Facebook, and others) don't have any obvious business model. Registration is free, usage of the respective platforms is free, and there are no charges for uploading your own content. So how do these social media ventures make money? In part, they collect private user data and sell that data to other companies that can use it. This is a controversial part of their business models.[17] Some of these sites also sell advertising or sell the rights to market directly to their members. Many people are skeptical that the registered users on these various social media platforms can be "monetized." Yet, their extremely high valuations (Facebook, for example, has been valued at $50 billion) suggest that others believe a viable and scalable business model eventually will be discovered.

We will be returning to the concept of a business model throughout this text, but the following is a very short and non-comprehensive list of some possible business models that you might use to monetize your products or services:

1. Pay as you go: This model is probably the most well known. It simply means that your products and services are offered at a price, and your customers purchase them as they use them.

2. Freemium: This approach focuses on providing a base set of your products and services for free and an enhanced set at a reasonable price.

3. Billable hours: This business model is used by consulting firms and other professional service providers, such as attorneys. This model bills clients on an hourly basis for services rendered, often with a minimum fee or "retainer" as part of the business model.

4. Advertising based: This model is often used by Internet companies that do not charge for the content they offer. The goal is to aggregate users and sell advertising based on the number of daily and monthly visitors.

5. Subscription pricing: Subscription pricing provides a one-time fee for customers to get access to products (usually, information products) and/or services for a fixed period of time.

6. Distributor or reseller: A distributor business model doesn't actually make anything, rather it aggregates products from companies that do, and sells these products to end users.

7. Retailer/Wholesaler: These are familiar business models where the goal of the entrepreneur is to aggregate and hold products for end users and make them available as needed.

8. Landlord or lease holder: This business model is based on holding title to particular assets (such as office space) that others want to use but not purchase.

9. Broker: A broker doesn't buy or sell, but rather facilitates the transaction between buyer and seller. Ebay is an example of a successful e-commerce venture that is based on this broker model.

This brief list is not comprehensive, but it should give you a good start in thinking about how your products/services actually will be sold in the marketplace and how they can attract sufficient customers to generate a profit.

Determine How to Bring Your Product to Market

Bringing the product to the market is a more involved and complex process than many aspiring entrepreneurs think. It is complex because there are a vast number of unknowns that entrepreneurs will encounter regardless of how much prior market research they've conducted. Customers will, more often than not, respond in unexpected ways. For example, a venture that launches a product might discover that it is wildly popular with customers. While this may seem like a great outcome, it can be damaging to the venture if it doesn't have adequate supply to meet the demand. Frustrated customers may be lost forever, and the problem often spreads as bad word of mouth about inability to deliver product overwhelms its popularity.

Going to market is also a function of where the market is in relation to the venture. If the market is the local neighborhood, as it would be in a restaurant, it may be enough simply to put out a sign and announce that you are open for business. On the other hand, if you want to attract customers worldwide, there may be much more complexity and expense in announcing your existence and value proposition. Many aspiring entrepreneurs have learned too late that simply putting up a website is not enough to generate sufficient sales. A full-blown strategy for courting, acquiring, and maintaining customers should be part of your thinking about your new venture idea.

Consider How to Scale the Business

Finally, but certainly not least of importance, is the ability to scale your venture. **Scaling** simply means creating a value-producing system that is able to meet increasing customer demand over time. Entrepreneurs seek to scale their ventures to meet customer needs and also to create a venture that throws off a lot of cash and attracts potential buyers. Remember, one major difference between the entrepreneur and the small business owner is that the small business owner typically stays with the same business throughout his or her lifetime. They may also pass on the business to children or other heirs. The entrepreneur, in contrast, builds a venture to create value for customers and also to create enterprise value. Enterprise value is the value of the venture itself to external parties that may want to acquire it. The greater the scale of the venture, typically, the greater is the value of the enterprise as a whole.

There are many types of business that scale very well and relatively easily. Many Internet ventures, for example, scale well and enable global distribution, especially those businesses that are primarily based on information dissemination or user-generated content. Such ventures typically only need to scale their server farms to manage the increasing Internet traffic. In contrast, an artist who produces original artwork will find it difficult to scale because each piece takes time to produce. There are only a finite number of hours in each day and work year, so the artist who produces and sells original works will find it very difficult to scale. One artist who has addressed and overcome that challenge is Mickey Baxter-Spade. Mickey's company, Artistic Voyage, is able to sell multiple versions of her original artworks through a process known as giclée. A giclée is a precise reproduction of an artist's painting with the qualities of an original. A giclée gives the impression of an original painting due to the unique printing process, the high-quality art paper or canvas, and the increased color range.[18]

The Opportunity Register

Ideas are easy to come by, and many aspiring entrepreneurs never do make it past the idea stage. One of the major reasons they don't get past the idea stage is that they don't develop their ideas sufficiently to enable them to be turned into ventures. This happens because many aspiring entrepreneurs lock into a single idea and believe they must do all in their power to turn THAT idea into a venture. What the aspiring entrepreneur doesn't know that the expert knows all too well is that most ideas will fail as new ventures. To hedge against the risk of failure that attends a single idea, the expert entrepreneur knows that every good venture is based on a multitude of ideas that have gone through multiple and even continuous rounds of iteration and improvement.

As an aspiring entrepreneur yourself, there is no time like the present to begin to create your own list of ideas—we call it the **opportunity register**.[19] An opportunity register is simply a notebook or computer file that you will return to again and again as new ideas come to you and as you modify the ideas that you've already recorded. Exhibit 3.2 provides an example of an opportunity register.

Using the tools of the entrepreneurial method that you will be learning throughout this book, you can engage the process of constant evaluation and refinement of your business ideas. You should take care to record your ideas in enough detail that you will be able to give them a thorough analysis. A looseleaf folder is often best for an opportunity register in that you can add pages to each idea as needed. Each idea in your opportunity register should include:

1. The date on which the idea was initially entered. Each update to the idea should also include a date.

2. The context of the original idea and all future revisions. For example, if you are revising an idea, record what led to the revision. It may be that you received some important feedback from a trusted source. Record the source and the nature of the feedback.

3. As your idea matures over time, you should consider whether there is any intellectual property that you will need to protect. For example, new inventions evolve over time and eventually may result in some truly novel insights that can and should be patented. Patents are often granted to individuals who can demonstrate they had the idea first. One way to establish your priority in an idea is to file a patent, but that can be expensive. A far less costly, and yet legitimate, alternative is to make a copy of the page of your notes with the patentable insight and mail the copy to yourself. Don't open the envelope when the letter arrives. The official date stamp on the envelope from the post office will suffice for establishing an authoritative date on which you created the novel insight.

Field	Your Input
Business Concept: Short description	
Possible upside: What might the concept generate in revenue or profit terms?	
Related Trends	
Relevant Data: This is a place to jot down any material numbers or information that you may have.	
Obstacles and Barriers: What might stop you from grasping the opportunity?	
Position: What competences, skills, or resources might make this a good opportunity for you?	
Competition: Who is likely to contest this opportunity and what are they likely to do?	
Sources: Where did you get your information?	
Timing: How long is the window of opportunity? How quickly must you pursue it?	

EXHIBIT 3.2 Opportunity Register

Source: McGrath, R.G., and I. MacMillan, *The Entrepreneurial Mindset* (Boston: Harvard Business School Press, 2000).

It's also important for aspiring entrepreneurs to work with **deliberate speed** in the development of their ideas.[20] It is exceedingly rare for potent new ideas to be generated and developed in a complete vacuum. More likely than not, any good idea that you have is already being developed by someone else somewhere else in the world. We use the term "deliberate speed" because it is also important to recognize that many ventures fail because they don't develop the basic business concept and business model enough before going to market. Going to market too early can be very expensive, but getting to market too late can mean losing out to competitors. It is better to learn all you can about your markets and customers before launching than to do all this learning with an operating company. Yet, it is inevitable that you will learn as you go, and so it is essential to recognize the need continuously to return to your opportunity register even after venture launch. Listening to your customers and building the feedback into subsequent releases of your products or refinement of your services better to meet customer needs is vital to your success.[21]

Of course, an opportunity register doesn't constitute a new venture. To launch a new venture, you'll eventually have to choose which of the ideas that you've been developing is the best one to start with. Notice that we're saying "the best one to start with." It's possible that you'll be able to develop several of your ideas through your new venture or build several ventures around several ideas. Still, you need to start with a single idea—preferably the one you feel most confident about developing into a successful venture.

In the next chapter, we will be examining in greater detail some of the techniques you can use to evaluate your idea. Here, we focus merely on your need eventually to decide on a single idea to launch your venture.

Far too often, aspiring entrepreneurs have a lot of ideas that they'd like to build into a new venture, but they are unaware that they must focus on a single idea to start. Expert entrepreneurs know well that developing a single idea into a going concern is a difficult challenge. Attempting to develop more than one idea during the venture launch process is almost certainly a recipe for failure. You increase your chances for success if you choose the idea that you think is the most likely to have a ready market and for which you have most of the necessary resources. But be prepared to learn as you enter the market and gather feedback from your customers. Listen for feedback on the prices you charge, the features and benefits that you offer, customer response to your value proposition, and other things relevant to your success. You will also need to keep an eye on competitors during this time, to gauge their potential responses to your market entry.

In the next chapter, we'll discuss effectual analysis of your venture concept. This involves understanding the need to create a good "fit" between who you are, who you know, the resources you currently control and the venture concept. Lack of such a good fit is one of the primary reasons that new ventures fail.

Nontraditional Idea Sources

If your search for a venture idea is not going well, you may be able to find inspiration via some nontraditional sources. In this final section of this chapter, we will introduce you to some of these nontraditional idea sources. Remember, however, that we highly recommend, and analysis of expert entrepreneurs supports this point, that you build a business that is a good fit with who you are. Nonetheless, some of us are less adept at the idea generation process than others and can benefit from inspiration from nontraditional sources. Below is a short list of some nontraditional sources of inspiration that you may want to investigate.

READ ALTERNATIVE LITERATURE: The long history of the sciences and the arts has proven that good ideas in one domain often can be translated and transferred to another domain. For example, in the computer sciences extensive work has been conducted on mimicking the human brain via software algorithms. One of the more promising lines of research in this area is referred to as "neural networks." These are networks of interconnected and parallel processing circuits that can do some of the things that the human brain can do. As it turns out, neural networks have application to the world of high finance. Many leading investment houses today use neural network technologies to mimic the behavior of securities trading 24/7 around the world.[22]

In order for you to be able to transfer ideas from a domain outside your disciplinary expertise, you need to dive into the literature. If you are a business major steeped in the literature of finance, accounting, management, and marketing, you may find inspiration from reading evolutionary theory, cosmology, or art history. Steve Jobs was famous for the innovative and often beautiful products he created via his multiple ventures, Apple, Pixar, and Next. In his biography, Jobs stated that his ability to create one insight after another was because he was always seeking to remain on the intersection between technology and the liberal arts.[23]

VISIT STRANGE PLACES AND DO STRANGE THINGS: Experience is a great teacher. There are some things that simply cannot be learned by reading about them. Imagine a book that explains to you how to ride a bike and how you will feel when you ride down hills with the wind in your hair. Is it possible, do you think, to learn to ride a bike through reading a book, or to understand the thrill of the wind in your hair by reading about how good it will feel?

In order to stretch your world and develop new ways of understanding how people live and work, you'll need to get outside of your normal comfort zone. We're not recommending that you take more risk than you're willing to take, but it is very unlikely that you'll find some unique niche in the wide world of human affairs without venturing beyond your routines. You may engage in some world travel to witness the types of things that people struggle with in foreign lands. You may want to investigate what they eat, how they live, and their sources of entertainment. More than one entrepreneur has discovered novel products in foreign lands that sold well when imported to the home market.[24]

We're also not advocating that you do these things without prior forethought about what you'd like to learn. It is one thing to take irresponsible trips and do irresponsible things with no fore-thought about learning valuable lessons. It is quite another to take deliberate action intended to stretch your thinking and help you learn new and potentially valuable things. We are advocating that you use new experiences to refine the ideas in your opportunity register, and that you build on this experience over time to continue to refine and improve your venture ideas. As the follow-ing Mini-Case highlights, the team at Signal Snowboards in Huntington Beach, California, uses a variety of techniques to stimulate their thinking about new snowboard design.

MINI-CASE

Signal Snowboards Fires up the Creative Juices of its Team

The best perk from having your very own snowboard factory? You get to play. The team at Signal Snow-boards have made playing part of their idea generation process.

It's a hot afternoon in July, and Signal founder and CEO Dave Lee and his team are testing a paintball gun on a mannequin. The plan is to mount the gun to a board for an epic snowboard-paintball battle scheduled the following week on Mount Hood in Oregon. The entire process, along with battle day, is being filmed for the second season of "Every Third Thursday," an online video series that Lee started last year to "build freak boards with random materials" and explore the creative boundaries of snowboard construction.

You won't see these boards in the store, but Lee says "Every Third Thursday" ideas all have potential produc-tion points, and the industrial focus differentiates Signal from the competition. "We're making something fun, but we try things because we want to put them into production boards, whether it's looking at new shapes or how materials work with one another," he says. "People are interested in the behind-the-scenes making of a snowboard, and we've helped make the factory cool again."

Source: Adapted from Signal Snowboards Every Third Thursday, http://signalsnowboards.com/every-third-thursday; and J. Wang, "Snowboard Upstarts Break New Ground," *Entrepreneur.com*, http://www.entrepreneur.com/article/220697, accessed January 19, 2012.

MEET THOUGHT LEADERS: Thought leaders are people who are on the leading edge of ideas and innovations in a particular discipline. Where do you meet people like this? They are often times featured on television, especially via cable networks like the Discovery Channel. Stephen Hawking, for example, is a well-known thought leader who is often featured talking about cosmic questions. Many thought leaders also appear at leading conferences. The Consumer Electronics Show is an annual draw for people to see and hear from leaders in consumer technologies. The South by Southwest Conference in Austin, Texas, is also a major conference for thought leaders in technology and design. The Internet is also a rich source of access to thought leaders in nearly any category of human achievement. Below is a short list of websites that you may want to visit.

- TED (www.ted.com)

- The Edge (www.edge.org)

- Stanford University's eCorner (www.ecorner.stanford.edu)

- Fora TV (www.fora.tv)

Sometimes the ability to think different about products and services is referred to as thinking outside the box. What that means is that most people think in recurring patterns and often cannot think different without an external stimulus. This phenomenon is true for most of us, including some of the world's most accomplished scientists. Research into how science evolves demonstrated that most think about the problems they're trying to solve in terms of well received paradigms. Oftentimes in the history of science, the established paradigms actually blocked progress. Those who held fast to standard ways of thinking about problems were not the ones to create the revolutionary breakthroughs. In fact, the history of science is replete with rebels who dared to think differently, who oftentimes were vilified in their era, but who are today recognized as the giants of their discipline.[25]

In what ways is your way of thinking about the world stuck in old paradigms? How can you persuade yourself to think different about the world and the people in it? We have given you a few starting points in this chapter, but it truly is up to you to follow through and create the next great entrepreneurial venture.

SUMMARY OF LEARNING OBJECTIVES

1. **Identify** the four different venture types that aspiring entrepreneurs can choose among. *Entrepreneurs can choose to launch their venture focusing either on delivering either products or services, and they can also choose between business to business (B2B) or business to consumer (B2C) customers.*

2. **Develop** venture ideas using a five step approach. *The five-step approach to developing venture ideas begins with (1) identifying a target market. Entrepreneurs need to identify an initial market to help generate early sales. (2) Develop a product or service idea for that market. (3) Decide on an appropriate business model. The business model is defined as "the way the business makes money." (4) Determine how to bring the product or service to the market. This decision must take into account how customers will learn about and decide to purchase a venture's products and/or services. (5) Consider how the business will scale over time. In the event that the entrepreneur's products or services are popular, the venture must be prepared to meet that demand by scaling its ability to deliver value.*

3. **Weigh** the potential advantages and disadvantages of launching a B2B or B2C venture. *B2B ventures have the advantage that businesses usually have more money than consumers. Businesses also have a more limited range of value propositions. B2B ventures must either help clients increase sales, reduce costs, or manage compliance with community norms. B2C ventures have far more potential ways to provide value to customers, including entertainment, fashion, and adventure among many others. B2C ventures rarely succeed over the long haul if focused on a single product.*

4. **Create** an opportunity register to keep track of your venture ideas and refine them over time. *An opportunity register is a good way to keep track of your new venture ideas and to help them evolve over time. Expert entrepreneurs know that most successful venture ideas are not hatched all at once, but rather are refined and improved over time through a process of iteration. Feedback from the potential target market is a critical part of successful iteration and new product development.*

5. **Understand** the variety of business models and decide which of them might be right for your venture. *The business model is defined as "the way the business makes money." There are many ways that a business can make money, and the predominant strategy may change over time. For example, some Internet companies provide free access to their online content when they launch, and then begin to charge customers for continuing access once they learn to rely on the venture's offerings.*

QUESTIONS FOR DISCUSSION

1. What are the four venture types that the aspiring entrepreneur can choose among? Explain the various advantages/disadvantages of each type.

2. Why does an aspiring entrepreneur need to identify a target market as part of the idea generation process? What are some factors an aspiring entrepreneur should consider when identifying a target market?

3. What is meant by the term *business model*? Identify at least four business models and discuss the types of businesses that may use them.

4. How can an aspiring entrepreneur force themselves to think outside of their normal ways of thinking? Which of the ways discussed in this book would work the best for you? Explain.

5. What are the three ways that a new venture can create value for business customers? Explain each of these.

6. What are some of the ways that a new venture can create value for consumers? Provide an example of each type.

7. What is an *opportunity register*? How can an opportunity register help an aspiring entrepreneur develop ideas for a new venture?

8. What does it mean to say that developing a new venture product or service idea is an *iterative process*? How does one go about iterating a new venture idea?

IN-CLASS EXERCISE

This exercise is designed to introduce students to the process of iteration as it applies to a new venture idea. Iteration was defined in the chapter as a process of gathering feedback on a new venture concept, especially from people who represent the venture's target market.

The exercise is intended to be conducted over two class sessions and will focus on refining an idea for a new venture. The instructor will serve as the guide through a brainstorming process and will help facilitate the iteration through at least two distinct value propositions.

The object of this exercise is to help students think realistically and holistically about the new venture concept so as to give it the greatest chance of succeeding and the best chance of being scalable.

We suggest basing this exercise on the prospect of launching a new student-centered restaurant/bar on or near the campus. The restaurant/bar should be something with a distinct name, ambience, and cachet that may lend itself to franchising across the nation. The exercise should proceed as follows:

1. The instructor should introduce the exercise to the class, emphasizing that the goal is to create a unique restaurant/bar concept that has the potential to scale nationally. In other words, try to avoid getting trapped into creating a simple beer hall.

2. List concept ideas on the board in random fashion as the students shout them out. No idea is too weird or outrageous to be considered.

3. This next challenge is the most difficult. Try to get consensus on no more than ten ideas that will be used to generate a first draft of the restaurant/bar concept.

4. Once you have the ten dominant and most popular ideas, try to conceive a name that will capture the essence of those ideas. The name should be distinctive and enable the venture to be franchised nationally (i.e., avoid reference to local artifacts and landmarks).

5. Now that a name and basic concept has been established, the objective will be for the students to go out and talk to fellow students about the idea. Each student in the class should talk to at least five others (ask them to record the names) to help in the iteration process.

6. At the next class period, have students discuss the feedback they received from their fellow students. In a thirty-student classroom, you can collect feedback from as many as 150 others.

7. Finally, based on this feedback, iterate the original idea and poll the class afterward to determine whether there is consensus that the revised idea is superior to the original.

KEY TERMS

Business model: The way a business makes money.

Business to business (B2B): A venture organized to deliver products and/or services primarily to business customers.

Business to consumer (B2C): A venture organized to deliver products and/or services primarily to consumers.

Continuous innovation: Making ongoing improvements to the products you already have in the marketplace and inventing new ones to extend your brand and develop additional streams of revenue

Deliberate speed: The need to iterate new venture ideas quickly, but not too quickly so that you miss some important information or feedback that would make your offering better.

Iteration: The process of refining your new venture ideas over time based on information and feedback.

Opportunity register: Where you keep your new venture ideas and refine them over time as you gather new information and feedback.

Personal concierge services: A rapidly growing business sector that focuses on providing highly individualized services to consumers, for example, buying groceries for someone too busy to visit the store themselves.

Scaling: Creating a value-producing system that is able to meet increasing customer demand over time.

Single-product venture: A venture that aspires to succeed based on only a single product or service offering. Generally, this is discouraged.

Target market: The set of customers, business or consumer, who are the most likely to purchase your venture's offerings.

ENDNOTES

[1] Fiet, J.O., and P.C. Patel, "Entrepreneurial Discovery as Constrained, Systematic Search," *Small Business Economics,* 30(3(2008): 215–229.

[2] Gimpl, M.L., "Obtaining Ideas for New Products and Ventures," *Journal of Small Business Management,* 16(4)(1987): 21–26.

[3] Kutaula, P.S., "Funcastle: Creating a Business Opportunity from a Design Consultancy Assignment," *Design Management Review,* 19(3)(2008): 23–29.

[4] Bienstock, C.C., M.L. Gillenson, and T.C. Sanders, "The Complete Taxonomy of Web Business Models," *The Quarterly Journal of Electronic Commerce,* 3(2)(2002): 173–182.

[5] Burnaz, S., and P. Bilgin, "Consumer Evaluations of Brand Extensions: B2B Brands Extended into B2C Markets," *Journal of Product & Brand Management,* 20(4)(2011): 256–267.

[6] Information obtained at the Sysco website: www.sysco.com. Retrieved on January 20, 2012.

[7] Duening, T.N., and R. Click, *The Essentials of Business Process Outsourcing* (Hoboken, NJ: John Wiley & Sons, 2005).

[8] Click, R., and T.N. Duening, *Business Process Outsourcing:* The Competitive Advantage (Hoboken, NJ: John Wiley & Sons, 2004).

[9] O'Neil, G.D. Jr., J.C. Hershauer, and J.S. Golden, "The Cultural Context of Sustainability Entrepreneurship," *Greener Management International,* 55(2009): 33–46.

[10] For more on "bubba teeth" see, for example: http://www.partycity.com/product/bubba+teeth.do

[11] From: Entrepreneur.com, "How to be a Personal Concierge." http://www.entrepreneur.com/article/37930. Accessed on January 2, 2012.

[12] Lehoczky, E., and D. Bortz, "Litmus Test Your Biz Idea," *Entrepreneur,* 40(9)(2011): 34.

[13] Carlson, C.R., and W.W. Wilmot, *Innovation: The Five Disciplines for Creating What Customers Want* (New York: Random House, 2006).

[14] Holley, J., *The Startup Experience: Inventing and Bringing Products to Market* (Colorado Springs, CO: Businesses2Learn, LLC, 2011).

[15] Ries, E., *The Lean Startup: How Today's Entrepreneurs Use Continuous Innovation to Create Radically Successful Businesses* (New York: Crown Publishing Group, 2011).

[16] Weill, P., T.W. Malone, V.T. D'Urso, G. Herman, and S. Woerner, "Do Some Business Models Perform Better than Others? A Study of the 1000 Largest U.S. Firms," MIT Sloan School of Management Working Paper No. 226. Accessed at http://ccs.mit.edu/papers/pdf/wp226.pdf on January 3, 2012.

[17] Dwyer, C., "Privacy in the Age of Google and Facebook," *IEEE Technology & Society Magazine,* 30(3) (2011): 58–63.

[18] Spade, M.B., *The Startup Experience: Experience Starting a Creative Arts Company* (Colorado Springs, CO: Businesses2Learn, LLC, 2011).

[19] McGrath, R.G., and I. MacMillan, *The Entrepreneurial Mindset* (Boston: Harvard Business School Press, 2000).

[20] Cohen, D., and B. Feld, *Do More Faster: TechStars Lessons to Accelerate Your Startup* (Hoboken, NJ: John Wiley & Sons, 2010).

[21] Cooper, B,. and P. Vlaskovits, The Entrepreneur's Guide to Customer Development: *A Cheat Sheet to the Four Steps to the Epiphany* (Cooper-Vlaskovits, 2010).

[22] Huang, W., K. Keung, Y. Nakamori, S. Wang, and L. Yu, "Neural Networks in Finance and Economics Forecasting," *Information Technology & Decision Making,* 6(1)(2007): 113–140.

[23] Isaacson, W., *Steve Jobs* (New York: Simon & Schuster, 2011).

[24] Albergotti, R., "The NFL's Top Secret Seed," *Wall Street Journal,* January 20, 2012.

[25] Kuhn, T., *The Structure of Scientific Revolutions* (Chicago: University of Chicago Press, 1970).

EFFECTUAL EVALUATION OF YOUR VENTURE IDEA

Learning Objectives

As a result of studying this chapter, students will be able to:

- **Assess** your unique talents and understand how they are important to your entrepreneurial success.

- **Leverage** your passion as an important part of your ability to endure entrepreneurial challenges.

- **Understand** that value creation is the purpose of business.

- **Learn** how to create a compelling value proposition for your venture.

- **Leverage** the resources that you currently control and learn how to aggregate those you don't currently control.

- **Leverage** your unfair advantage and create a sustainable competitive advantage in your industry.

- **Recognize** the barriers to entry in your industry and learn various tactics for overcoming them.

INTRODUCTION

By now, it should come as no surprise to you that we advocate that venture idea generation should begin with who you are and what resources you currently control. This entire book is intended to help you think about your entrepreneurial life as a very personal thing. Undoubtedly, as you become more and more adept at the entrepreneurial method, you will also expand the range of venture

types with which you can become successful. In the early days, however, it is best to focus on your personal talents and those things that you do particularly well in comparison to your peers.

In this chapter we are going to explore a number of strategies that the aspiring expert entrepreneur can use to evaluate viable ideas for possible ventures. The strategies that you can use to develop viable ideas for a venture, as we mentioned, begin with yourself. No doubt you already have a fairly well-developed concept of who you are and where your talent lies. Despite this general sense of self-knowledge that most of us feel intuitively, there is much work that you can do to get a more insightful grasp of your real talents and skills. We will explore several techniques that you can use to get a realistic and objective view of your talents.

Expert entrepreneurs have also learned that it is important to be passionate about the ventures they create. We will examine your personal motivation and reasons for becoming an entrepreneur. You probably already know that it can be difficult to succeed with a startup venture. Statistics concerning the success rate of new ventures are often cited, with the rather depressing figure of 10 percent commonly cited. While the actual failure rate of startups is much different (see Exhibit 4.1), it is still likely that you will experience failure at some point in your entrepreneurial career.[1] To many people, a 50 percent chance of failure can be quite daunting. In addition to the personal impact of

EXHIBIT 4.1 Statistics on Startup Failure Rates are Sobering.

Year	Percent of Ventures Failed
Year 1	25 %
Year 2	36 %
Year 3	44 %
Year 4	50 %
Year 5	55 %
Year 6	60 %
Year 7	63 %
Year 8	66 %
Year 9	69 %
Year 10	71 %

Source: Derived from Kauffman Foundation Index of Entrepreneurial Activity.

failure, there can be consequences for one's family, finances, and social standing. These challenges that are a real part of becoming an entrepreneur are often cited by many as the reasons they avoid entrepreneurship.

Next, you'll be introduced to the concept of **value creation**. According to the entrepreneurial method the fundamental purpose of business is to create value. While that seems like a straightforward and obvious statement, it is astonishing how little emphasis value creation receives in most business books and classrooms. The entrepreneurial method is based on the belief that value creation is the fundamental purpose of a business in the same way that the scientific method believes that knowledge creation is the fundamental purpose of the sciences. Notice that universities, for example, often stray from their fundamental purpose by virtue of managing large sports programs, building extensive research laboratories focused on obtaining government grants, and sponsoring myriad campus programs that are primarily social activities.

Businesses often lose track of value creation as a fundamental purpose, focusing instead on short-term goals such as profit maximization, increasing shareholder value, or something similar. What they fail to understand is that these are *results,* not purposes. By focusing on creating value for an increasing number of customers a business will, as a result, increase profits and shareholder value. Apple under the leadership of Steve Jobs is a perfect example of a company that focused on creating value.[2] Under Jobs's leadership, Apple maintained an intense focus on creating "insanely great products." As a result, it has become the most valuable technology company in the world and its many shareholders have done extremely well. New ventures that build value creation into their DNA are more likely to succeed in the long run than those that are created for short-term profit gains.

We will also introduce you to some techniques that you can use to target and assess the market potential of a new venture. While the ultimate test of the market potential for any new venture comes after the venture has launched, there are some guidelines that expert entrepreneurs use to make a rough assessment of market potential. The more often you practice these assessment techniques, the better you will get at them. While they aren't always going to be 100 percent accurate, they will tell you whether you want to spend additional time exploring the possibility of launching or investing in a new venture. One technique, for example, is to identify one or two likely target markets for a new venture. It is not difficult; using a variety of readily available online tools, to get a fairly good idea of how large is the market that can be addressed by the venture's products and/or services. We will explore a variety of such techniques that you can master to help you get a rough estimate of the market potential of a new venture idea and, thus, whether it is worth your while to pursue the venture further.

In the last two sections of this chapter, you will be encouraged to examine your venture's unfair advantage and the barriers to entry that exist in the industry that you intend to enter. Your unfair advantages are those things that provide your company with a competitive edge in the market. It may be some piece of intellectual property that you've created, it may be unique talents possessed by your team, or it may be many other things. It is important to analyze your unfair advantage to determine whether it is a sufficient advantage around which to build a competitive venture.

Let's turn first to something that is very important for all entrepreneurs to assess: Their unique talents.

LEVERAGE YOUR TALENTS

Your talent is reflected in the types of things that you learn and develop easily compared to other things and compared to your peers. For example, you've probably heard of child prodigies that excel in mathematics, playing musical instruments, or something else. One generally accepted definition of prodigies is someone who, by the age of roughly 11, displays expert proficiency or a profound grasp of the fundamentals in a field usually only undertaken by adults.

Prodigies possess unique talent in the areas in which they are excelling. Learning to become expert in that area is relatively easy to them, compared to other things. For example, child prodigy Amadeus Mozart was playing exhibitions for royalty at a very young age. He had a domineering father who insisted that he practice incessantly, which contributed to his development. Still, had Mozart elected to spend his time in other pursuits, such as drawing or sculpture, it is unlikely that he would be known to us today. His intense focus, and intense practice, in the area of his unique talent led him to produce standout work in his brief musical career.[3]

You may not be a prodigy, but it is near certain that you have some talents that enable you to stand out among your peers. Many people make the mistake of neglecting to build their skills around their greatest talents because performing in their area of talent "comes easy to them." In fact, many of the messages that you've received in your formal education may have directed you to spend more time on those things that you don't do well. In an effort to help everyone come up to the same level of achievement, well-meaning teachers often require students to spend far more time working on those things they don't do well. As an entrepreneur, focusing on the things that you don't do well is a recipe for failure. Focusing on and building skills in the areas in which you are naturally talented is not a guarantee of success, but it does increase your chances to succeed.[4]

Fortunately, there are a number of things you can do to help you analyze your strengths. There is a wide range of free online resources that you can use to understand not only what your strengths and weaknesses are, but also how you compare to others in your peer group. Below is a short list of such resources that you can use to get a better handle on your own personal resources:

Myers-Briggs Personality Type Indicator

The purpose of the **Myers-Briggs Type Indicator® (MBTI®)** personality inventory is to make the theory of psychological types described by Carl Jung understandable and useful in people's lives. The essence of the theory behind the MBTI is that much seemingly random variation in behavior is actually quite orderly and consistent, due to basic differences in the ways individuals prefer to use their perception and judgment.[5]

Perception involves all the ways of becoming aware of things, people, happenings, or ideas. Judgment involves all the ways of coming to conclusions about what has been perceived. If people differ systematically in what they perceive and in how they reach conclusions, then it is only reasonable for them to differ correspondingly in their interests, reactions, values, motivations, and skills. You can take versions of the MBTI test through multiple free online sites. Here are a few:

- www.humanmetrics.com
- www.personalitypathways.com
- www.similarminds.com

You can also take the actual and complete MBTI assessment through paid Internet sites such as www.mbticomplete.com.

Much work has also been done in recent years regarding what are referred to as **multiple intelligences**. In Chapter 3, we discussed the work of Harvard's Howard Gardner with respect to the five minds for the future. Gardner is also well known for his extensive work on multiple intelligences.[6] Gardner has argued that human beings differ vastly one from another, and much of this difference can be attributed to their varying capacities in eight different intelligence categories:

1. *Linguistic intelligence* involves sensitivity to spoken and written language, the ability to learn languages, and the capacity to use language to accomplish certain goals. This intelligence includes the ability to effectively use language to express oneself rhetorically or poetically; and language as a means to remember information. Writers, poets, lawyers, and speakers are among those that Howard Gardner sees as having high linguistic intelligence.

2. *Logical-mathematical intelligence* consists of the capacity to analyze problems logically, carry out mathematical operations, and investigate issues scientifically. In Howard Gardner's words, it entails the ability to detect patterns, reason deductively, and think logically. This intelligence is most often associated with scientific and mathematical thinking.

3. *Musical intelligence* involves skill in the performance, composition, and appreciation of musical patterns. It encompasses the capacity to recognize and compose musical pitches, tones, and rhythms. According to Howard Gardner, musical intelligence runs in an almost structural parallel to linguistic intelligence.

4. *Bodily-kinesthetic intelligence* entails the potential of using one's whole body or parts of the body to solve problems. It is the ability to use mental abilities to coordinate bodily movements. Howard Gardner sees mental and physical activity as related.

5. *Spatial intelligence* involves the potential to recognize and use the patterns of wide space and more confined areas.

6. *Interpersonal intelligence* is concerned with the capacity to understand the intentions, motivations, and desires of other people. It allows people to work effectively with others. Educators, salespeople, religious and political leaders, and counselors all need a well-developed interpersonal intelligence.

7. *Intrapersonal intelligence* entails the capacity to understand oneself, to appreciate one's feelings, fears, and motivations. In Howard Gardner's view, it involves having an effective working model of ourselves and being able to use such information to regulate our lives.

8. *Naturalistic intelligence* designates the ability to discriminate among living things (plants, animals) as well as sensitivity to other features of the natural world (clouds, rock formations). Naturalistic intelligence enables people to enjoy the natural world and to make choices for preserving the natural world that are not necessarily "economically rational" choices.

As we have been stressing in this chapter, effectual analysis involves understanding not only what opportunities for venture creation exist, but which of those opportunities is right for you. Understanding that you have varying natural levels of talent in these differing intelligences allows you to analyze which of them seem to be your true talents. You probably have an intuitive understanding of which of these are stronger for you, but there also are online resources you can use to provide additional feedback. Several free online resources include:

- www.mypersonality.info/multiple-intelligences

- www.literacyworks.org/mi/assessment/findyourstrengths.html

- www.mindtools.com/pages/articles/newISS_85.htm

Of course, whatever you determine to be your greatest strengths in terms of your intelligences doesn't limit the range of ventures you may want to start. It DOES tell you, however, what type of alternative talent you may need to recruit to your cause to make sure you have the right people to help you achieve your goals.

Finally, we will mention one other category of personal traits that will be important to your eventual success as an entrepreneur: **emotional intelligence**. Emotional intelligence is a perspective on human beings that recognizes that much of our lives are dominated by emotions.[7] Emotional reactions to events and challenges are often difficult to understand. Why do some people shrink at the thought of giving a public speech? Why are some people heroic in the face of dangerous circumstances? Why do some people manage stress better than others? The answers to these and many other questions involving human emotions have to do with emotional intelligence.

In essence, emotional intelligence is simply the ability to recognize emotions in yourself and others and to respond appropriately to those emotions. For example, stress is an inevitable part of being an entrepreneur. Do you recognize when you're stressed? What do you do to manage your stress? Expert entrepreneurs have learned through experience that managing stress is critical to success. Each person is different with respect to his or her personal capacity to work long and hard hours. The expert entrepreneur knows that productivity declines with rising levels of stress. As such, the expert entrepreneur finds ways to reduce stress through such means as exercise, eating right, getting adequate sleep, and other things.[8]

As with the MBTI and multiple intelligences, there are a number of free online resources for you to assess your emotional intelligence. Some of these are:

RESEARCH LINK

The Emotional Intelligence of Entrepreneurs

This web-based exploratory study collected self-assessment data of emotional competencies on successful young entrepreneurs. The participating entrepreneurs reported that they demonstrated higher levels of self-confidence, trustworthiness, achievement orientation, service orientation, empathy, change catalyst, and teamwork and collaboration in comparison to other competencies in the questionnaire. In addition, these competencies seemed qualitatively higher when compared to the norm in the overall population. These findings may be of interest to entrepreneurs as they consider how to enhance their leadership skills.

- http://testyourself.psychtests.com/testid/3038

- www.queendom.com

- www.eiconsortium.org

While we know of few expert entrepreneurs who actually spend a lot of time taking online assessments, we believe that aspiring entrepreneurs can save themselves years of trial and error learning by becoming more self-aware. Many expert entrepreneurs who came of age in the prior century did not have access to free online tools to help them get a better handle on their personal strengths and weaknesses. As such, they had no choice but to learn many painful and often expensive lessons through trial and error. You are learning about entrepreneurship in an entirely new era. Today, there are many resources available to you to help you get a sense of who you are, and what types of value you are uniquely positioned to create and bring to the marketplace.

LEVERAGE YOUR PASSION

To ensure that you have the staying power and resilience to weather some of the entrepreneurial storms you are sure to encounter, you have to be passionate about the type of venture you intend to build. Passion is not just a function of what you do well—your talent—but also of what you would like to do. Talent can be applied in many ways to achieve financial and other types of success. Many social entrepreneurs use their talent to build ventures that are not focused on making money, but rather on solving some major social problem. Of course, many social entrepreneurs, such as Tom's of Maine, end up doing very well financially. Yet, if you speak to the founders of such ventures, it is usually the chance to solve major social problems that is their primary passion.

How do you determine your passion? It is likely that you have a strong idea of what you are passionate about, but we've developed a thought experiment that is designed to help you get a better handle on it.

© George Dolgikh, 2012. Used under license from Shutterstock, Inc.

Imagine that you just won the lottery and your bank account has recently grown by $50 million. That is probably enough money to make you financially comfortable for the rest of your life. The question that we pose to you is: What would you do after the money was placed into your account? Most people, if they are really honest with themselves, will react the same way. They will quit their jobs and de-stress their lives. Many envision going off to a warm beach, living the high life, which may include some excessive eating and drinking. And that is certainly understandable.

Of course, most people soon tire of lounging on the beach and staying away from challenges and adventures that make life worth living. We suspect that, as a college student, you also want new challenges and opportunities in your life. The real question, then, is not what would you do immediately after you won the lottery. The real question to ask is, After the period of de-stressing and coming to terms with your new wealth, what would you do next? You see, now that you no longer have to worry about your financial situation, you really can do anything you want to do (within legal limits, of course). You can pursue your passion. If you can determine what THAT is, you can learn to leverage it in your current situation even though you don't currently have $50 million in your bank account (we're guessing).

However, it is important to note that your passion is not enough to help you build a venture. After all, if you are passionate about something that no other person on earth is interested in, you are unlikely to be able to create marketable products and/or services. Some scholars recommend that rather than focusing on leveraging your passions, you should focus on solving really big problems.[9] More specifically, you should focus on solving problems that affect you in a personal way. For example, in her book *Passion & Purpose,* Umaimah Mendhro recounts her story of fleeing a war-torn Pakistan with her family and how the experience of dodging bullets to escape led her to found her company The Dream Fly, an initiative that creates connections across communities in conflict.[10] Focusing on working on big problems that affect you personally will no doubt draw upon your passions, but they will be drawn upon in a very practical way. Remember, we have said from the beginning of this text that the essence of entrepreneurship is to create value for other people. You certainly will create value if you help to solve some of the world's biggest problems.

FOCUS ON VALUE CREATION

Value creation is the purpose of business and the essential ingredient that is the same across all entrepreneurial ventures. There are probably as many ways to create value as there are people on the planet. Consider the Turkish fisherman who sets out each morning into the Black Sea to catch bass. He brings the fish he catches back to the open air market near the boat docks where housewives, professionals, and others eagerly scan the day's catch for a tasty dinner meal. The shoppers on the dock constitute the market for Black Sea bass. The individuals constituting that market find value in the fisherman's ability to catch the bass to the extent that they do not want to go out and catch their own. The market will also be interested in whether the bass provided by the fisherman are of adequate quality. Prices for the bass will reflect the quality of the catch and the extent to which the market has other Black Sea bass or substitute product choices.

For his part, the fisherman has a business venture that consists of setting out daily to bring fish back to his market. His resources are his boat and fishing gear, fishing know-how, and retail market space. On their own, none of these resources would provide the market with the bass that it needs. It is the entrepreneurial activity of the fisherman to organize and deploy these resources that leads to the creation of value for the bass-eating market.

Let's take this example of value creation to another domain. Consider the case of three individuals in Menlo Park, California, who set out to create a new type of Internet company. Menlo Park is located in the heart of Silicon Valley, which has been the birthplace of some of the most rapidly growing technology companies in history. These three individuals were veterans of technology companies, having been principals in the online payment service known as PayPal. From their garage in Menlo Park in December 2005, the entrepreneurs created one of the fastest growing companies of all time. Aggregating the resources that centered on the Internet and plain old know-how, the three entrepreneurs founded YouTube.

By July 2006, YouTube reported that more than 100 million videos were being watched every day, with as many as 50,000 videos being added to the site each day. In October 2006, a mere ten months after it was founded, YouTube was acquired by Google for $1.65 billion.[11]

These stories illustrate that "value" has myriad definitions and that entrepreneurs can develop successful ventures with widely different **value propositions**. A value proposition is the story that a venture tells its market about what value it intends to create and provide. For example, the value proposition for YouTube is: "Broadcast yourself." That simple statement, while not necessarily appealing to everyone, is the foundation of the online video-sharing rage. The value proposition for the fisherman might be something like: "The freshest Black Sea bass."

Value propositions are important for a venture. They help not only to communicate to the market about what the venture intends to provide, but they also help guide decision making. For example, the value proposition for well-known consumer products company Procter & Gamble is "Touching lives, improving life."[12] This value proposition tells P&G scientists and product developers how to structure their investment of research and development resources. P&G introduces hundreds of new products to markets around the world each year. The firm's value proposition guides decision making so that consumers do not get confused about the firm's intent and offerings.[13]

LEVERAGE YOUR RESOURCES

Entrepreneurs must be resourceful. Most startups arise out of unfunded ideas and claw their way to success over time. As a venture grows, resource accumulation and effective resource management become important to growing the venture. We will discuss techniques for resource accumulation and management in greater detail in Chapter 8. Here, we simply want to highlight the need for the aspiring entrepreneur to conduct a thorough inventory of resources currently controlled and those that will be needed to launch the venture.

For example, expert entrepreneurs are very familiar with the adage "cash is king." What that means is that entrepreneurs carefully must preserve and manage the venture's cash. In the early days of most ventures, there is little cash flow and what cash is available likely comes from the entrepreneur and close associates. This precious cash has to be managed carefully for the venture to be able to survive long enough to achieve breakeven.

Most expert entrepreneurs have learned how to stretch the entrepreneurial dollar a long, long way. They do so through a variety of techniques, including leasing instead of buying, using home office space instead of expensive commercial space, using e-mail and other forms of marketing instead of purchasing expensive collateral material, and many others. Let's begin our discussion of resources by examining the one thing that never seems to be enough of—capital.

Capital Resources

Entrepreneurs are nearly always pre-occupied with the acquisition of capital resources. For most, there is never enough cash. The strategies involved in acquisition of capital to launch and operate a technology venture are discussed at length in Chapter 6. Here, we intend only to emphasize the importance of capital to the new venture and the various sources of capital that are available in the early stages of the venture (see Exhibit 4.2).

In the early stages of most ventures, the only source of capital is the technology entrepreneur's own personal resources, and perhaps those of family and friends. Later, as the venture begins to establish an intellectual property portfolio and, hopefully, revenue, other funding sources begin to open up. **Angel capital** is available in most major cities, and most angel investors have clear objectives of the types of ventures they want to invest in and how much capital they are interested in putting at risk. The Angel Capital Association (ACA) is a nationwide organization in the United States that lists most of the angel groups and their interests.

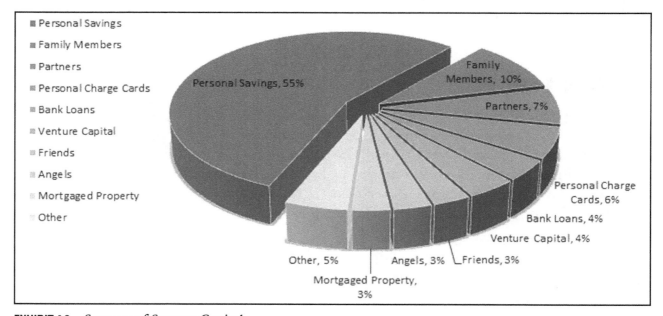

EXHIBIT 4.2   Sources of Startup Capital

Venture capital becomes available to ventures after they have achieved certain milestones and become poised for rapid growth. This is often the stage where the founding entrepreneur is also in need of additional expertise in managing and operating a high-growth venture. Venture capital firms normally invest large amounts of capital and usually are also heavily involved in managing the company thereafter.

The aspiring entrepreneur can also take advantage of debt financing and should seek to develop banking relationships early on. Providers of debt capital typically look to the venture's cash flow when deciding on whether to lend, but that is not always the case. Developing a banking relationship before capital is required can pay off in the future. Some banks provide **Small Business Administration (SBA) loans** that are backed by federal guarantees.

Other sources of new venture financing include grants, such as the **Small Business Innovation Research** (SBIR) and **Small Business Technology Transfer** (STTR) programs of the federal government. These can be sources of substantial capital, but they also come with strings attached.

The aspiring entrepreneur has little options for capital in the early days of a venture other than the proverbial "FF&F"—friends, family, and fools. That is, most early stage ventures are funded by the aspiring entrepreneurs, their family and friends, and "fools" who don't mind taking excessive risk with their money. Of course, we don't literally mean such people are fools, but there is ample evidence to indicate that investments in early stage ventures are, more often than not, completely lost. [14]

Expert entrepreneurs have become adept at finding ways to fund a venture in its early stages. Credit cards, second mortgages, and other techniques are often used to provide some quick cash in the early days. The objective is for the venture to be able to hang on long enough for it to achieve sufficient cash flows from operations to fund itself. As that milestone is being achieved, that is, as a venture demonstrates its market viability, other sources of capital may become available to assist. Ventures that never or rarely seek investor or loan capital are said to use a technique referred to as **bootstrap financing**. That is, the venture funds itself only through internal cash flows from revenue. The following Mini-Case highlights how Michael Dell used bootstrap financing to launch Dell Computer.

MINI CASE

Dell Computer Launched via Bootstrap Financing

Bootstrap financing was an integral part of the early life of Dell Computer Corporation. The company started with Michael Dell's $1,000 investment. Dell hired an engineer on contract to design his first computer. He moved his business from his two-bedroom condominium to a 1000-square-foot office and hired a few people to take orders over the telephone and a few more to fill them. Manufacturing consisted of three employees working at a 6-foot table. Handwritten orders were pinned to a clothesline. Dell's business generated income from the start, with monthly sales between $50,000 and $80,000 in upgraded PCs, kits, and add-on components. As Dell reinvested most of his substantial profit, the need for bootstrapping diminished. Michael Dell's novel idea of bypassing the middleman and selling custom-built PCs directly to customers made Dell Computers into one of the world's largest computer corporations, employing more than 100,000 people worldwide.

Source: Adapted from Tomory, E.A., "Bootstrap Financing: Four Case Studies of Technology Companies," *International Journal of Management Cases*, 13(3)(2011): 531–538.

Human Resources

The human resources we refer to here are top-level executives and board members—the talented people that add significant value to the venture and that often are referred to as **human capital**. Human capital is the talent and resourcefulness that you are able to aggregate around yourself and your venture idea. The myth of the "lone wolf" entrepreneur is just that—a myth. Expert entrepreneurs are exceedingly good at attracting talented people to help them achieve success with their ventures. They are able to recruit talented executives and employees that will be able to not only perform based on their unique talents, but they will also be able to adapt to the swiftly changing environment of the entrepreneurial venture.

In addition to executive officers and employees, the entrepreneur may want to establish a **board of directors** and/or an **advisory board**. The difference between the two boards is primarily centered on **fiduciary responsibility**. Fiduciary responsibility means responsibility to shareholders for the effective management of the venture. The board of directors has it; the advisory board doesn't. Recruiting well-qualified candidates to a venture's board of directors and/or advisory board can be an important factor in success.[15] Board members bring talent that the entrepreneur may not personally possess and often are able to bring additional value to the team, such as:

- Access to potential clients
- Knowledge of the industry and/or target market
- Experience in scaling a venture to meet increasing demand
- Access to capital sources
- Credibility and visibility within the industry

Human resources are vital to your venture success. Once you recognize that, you become more adept at identifying and recruiting talented people to your cause.

Organizational Resources

Organizational resources are those items that are required for people to do their jobs. This includes the normal tools of office work, such as desks, chairs, copy machines, and other things that people normally expect. Maximum productivity requires the normal tools for getting work done. New ventures often are operating on very tight budgets in the early stages, and these items can be expensive.

Notice, however, that we did NOT say these standard office items need to be top of the line. Often, new ventures are launched in the homes and/or garages of founders. Still, workstations should be set up, and opportunities for focused work should be created. For most office furniture and equipment, good deals can be found where there have been bankruptcies or liquidations of other ventures. In addition, most office furniture and equipment can be rented or leased. These can be less expensive short-term financing options, but might cost more in the long run.

Another organizational resource is office space. Office space can be a major hurdle for young ventures as many office buildings often require long-term commitments. Good office buildings in major cities will normally require the entrepreneur to sign a three-year lease. In addition, as early-stage ventures often have difficulty with cash flow, they will on occasion have trouble paying the monthly rent. Landlords know this, and they attempt to ward off problems with lease payments through several well-known tactics. One tactic landlords often use to lessen the risk of leasing office space to early-stage ventures is to require that the founders provide a personal guarantee on the lease. That means the founders will be required to continue making lease payments even if the business fails.

Technology Resources

The modern worker is accustomed to using a wide range of technology gadgets and tools to get work done. New ventures must provide these tools to compete with others in their industry and to attract the talented workers who expect these tools to be part of their work environment. In most new ventures, it is requisite that each employee will be outfitted with his or her own personal computer, which may also include a desktop workstation and a separate laptop computer. In addition, today's mobile workforce also expects to be outfitted with the tools required for the virtual office, including smart phone devices, computers, tablet computers, and other things.

The entrepreneur will need to determine which tools are required for the unique products and services offered by the venture, and the unique work processes that are required to produce them. As with the organizational resources discussed above, the requisite technology resources can also be obtained via lease, lease to own, or financing options. Companies such as Dell computer have divisions that cater to emerging ventures, offering each of these options as a means of limiting cash outflows in the short run. Of course, in the long run such options cost more, but to the small venture the preservation of precious cash in the near term may outweigh the long-term costs.

The technology required to operate a new venture likely will include various software applications as well. If the venture is ready for sales, it may want to investigate various sales force automation and customer relationship management packages. These are often available online and have a wide variety of purchasing options. From a straight-up commercial off-the-shelf software option to individual and enterprise licenses, these software tools can help the emerging venture appear bigger than it is and help it become more efficient.

LEVERAGE YOUR UNFAIR ADVANTAGE

In order to succeed over the long haul in entrepreneurship, it is very helpful to have an unfair advantage over your competitors and potential new entrants. The unfair advantage may simply be a unique talent that you or someone on your team possesses and that no one else does. Or, it may be due to **intellectual property** that you've created and protected. Patents are a common form of intellectual property that entrepreneurs use to develop an unfair advantage in a market. Once a patent is issued, no one else can use the same approach to address a market need as the patent holder for a finite period of time. This is as large an unfair advantage as can be granted by law and provides the patent holder with a virtual monopoly until the patent expires.

Another approach to developing an unfair advantage is based on the **resource-based theory (RBT)** of competitive advantage.[16] RBT has been applied to entrepreneurial ventures, but it has its origins in understanding large corporations. In the latter context, the theory holds that large organizations form to create and sustain some type of competitive advantage over rivals based on the resources they control and manage. The resources that provide advantage are those that have the following four characteristics:

- They are rare.
- They are valuable.
- They are difficult to copy.
- They have no ready substitutes.

When applied to entrepreneurial ventures, these various attributes of resources are exploited to develop a startup with a sustainable competitive advantage from the beginning.[17] The entrepreneur uses insight into these various characteristics of resources currently controlled to exploit a new venture opportunity.

Resources are rare if they are not widely available to potential competitors. Examples of rare resources for ventures include things like patents or trade secrets, access to inexpensive labor pools, and specialized knowledge possessed by only a few individuals.

Valuable resources help the venture implement its strategy effectively and efficiently. In other words, valuable resources help a venture exploit opportunities and minimize threats. Examples of valuable resources to a startup venture may include real property and its location, capital equipment, key people with unique talents and skills, and cash.

Ventures that possess rare and valuable resources will have an advantage over other ventures if those resources are difficult to replicate or copy. Several factors may conspire to make it difficult for ventures to copy each other's key resources, including unique historical conditions, complex social relationships (such as exclusive contracts), and ambiguous cause and effect so that the key resources are difficult to identify amidst a variety of factors.

Finally, non-substitutable resources are strategic resources that cannot be replaced by commonplace resources. For example, an expert system may replace a manager's knowledge about running an efficient operation. However, it may be far more difficult for a venture to find a commonplace substitute for the charismatic leadership that may be provided by a founding entrepreneur. There are many instances of the latter. Perhaps no better example exists than computer companies that have attempted to use commonplace resources to substitute for the charismatic leadership of a Steve Jobs, Bill Gates, or Michael Dell. For the most part, these iconic leaders of the computer age have been difficult if not impossible to replace.

Competitive Strategy Model

Michael Porter's competitive strategy model offers several alternative strategies new ventures can adopt to establish an unfair advantage.[18] According to Porter's model, ventures can develop **distinctive competence** in three ways: differentiation, cost leadership, and niche (see Exhibit 4.3). The goal of developing distinctive competence is to establish a unique position in the market, preferably a position that provides a **sustainable competitive advantage**

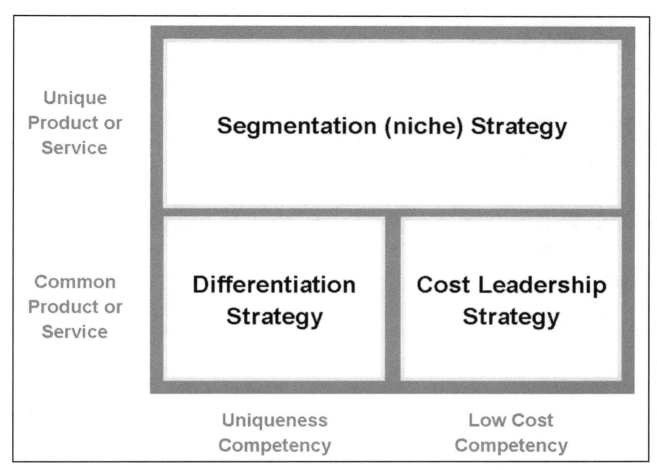

EXHIBIT 4.3 Michael Porter's Competitive Strategy Model

over others already in the market or those who potentially may enter. A sustainable competitive advantage is one that is based on unique knowledge, insight, or property.

DIFFERENTIATION: In an effort to distinguish its products, a firm using the differentiation strategy offers a higher-priced product equipped with more product-enhancing features than its competitors' products. Using this strategy, firms seek a premium price for their products and attempt to maintain high levels of customer loyalty. The firm markets and sells the product to a relatively small group of customers who are willing to pay a higher price for the premium features. This strategy (sometimes called a premium strategy) leads to relatively high-cost, low-volume production, with a high gross profit margin per item. Often advertising or marketing adds a perception of luxury that creates demand for the product due to the psychological value of buying and using it. Mercedes Benz automobiles, Ben & Jerry's ice cream, and Godiva chocolates are marketed under a differentiation strategy.

COST LEADERSHIP: In contrast to the differentiation strategy, the cost leadership strategy means low costs, low prices, high volume, and low profit margins on each item. With this strategy, a cost leader attempts to attract a large number of customers with low prices, generating a large overall profit by the sheer volume of units sold. Examples of cost leaders are Dell Computer and Hyundai. It's difficult, though not impossible, to be both lower cost and differentiated relative to competitors.

NICHE STRATEGY: The niche strategy involves offering a unique product or service in a restricted market (usually a geographic region). For example, Dallas-based Southwest Airlines has targeted the point-to-point, low-fare traveler since its beginnings. Many airlines have attempted to compete with Southwest in its niche, but usually meet with failure. Continental Airlines, for example, tried to compete with Southwest by introducing a new point-to-point service it called "Continental Lite." However, Continental learned a painful and expensive lesson by trying to compete in this niche at the same time as it maintained its traditional hub-and-spoke system. Continental Lite failed because the company didn't have the infrastructure to compete head to head in Southwest's niche.

These various approaches to developing distinctive competence have been debated and discussed by strategists, consultants, and scholars. Some have suggested that these three choices are not sufficiently refined—that there are other choices. For example, strategy scholars have suggested refining Porter's three strategic choices into five.[19] Exhibit 4.4 shows how they suggest this should be achieved:

This model expands on Porter's by differentiating the market opportunity between one that with a narrow focus and one with a broad focus. The five competitive strategies in this model are defined as:

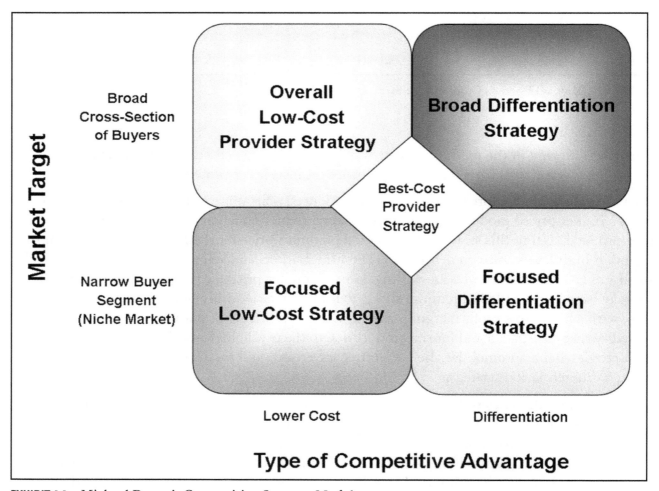

EXHIBIT 4.4   Michael Porter's Competitive Strategy Model

1. **Low-cost provider strategy:** Ventures using this approach strive to achieve overall lower costs than rivals and appeal to a broad spectrum of customers, usually by underpricing rivals. This was Dell's strategy in its early days, and today it is the strategy deployed by flat-screen television makers, such as Vizio.

2. **Broad differentiation strategy:** This strategy is based on differentiating the venture's offerings from rivals in ways that will appeal to a broad spectrum of buyers. One example of a company that uses this approach is Intel. Intel appeals to a broad spectrum of buyer's through its "Intel Inside" advertising campaign. Intel builds products for average users, power users, and business users. Each of these markets has learned to look for the "Intel Inside" logo on computer purchases.

3. **Best-cost provider strategy:** This strategy focuses on giving customers more value for their money by incorporating good-to-excellent product features at a lower price than rivals; the target is to have the lowest prices compared to rivals offering products with comparable attributes. This was the approach adopted by Hyundai on entering the U.S. market. Its cars were very low priced compared to domestic rivals. Hyundai's advertising emphasized that its cars had all the same features and the longest product warranty in the business. After spending years building its brand in the United States with very low-cost vehicles, in 2008 Hyundai pursued upper-scale buyers by introducing a new model, Genesis, that was marketed against Lexus, Mercedes, and BMW models.

4. **A focused low-cost strategy:** Ventures pursuing this strategy concentrate on a narrow customer segment and compete by having lower costs than rivals in this segment. For example, ventures that locate operations near their market can reduce costs involved in transporting goods to that local market. Those cost savings can be passed on to consumers as lower prices, without compromising quality and feature sets.

5. **A focused strategy based on differentiation:** This strategy concentrates on a narrow buyer segment and ventures that use it compete by offering customized attributes that meet their tastes and requirements better than rivals. This strategy is used by companies like TutorVista, an online tutoring service that utilizes experts around the world to tutor high school students on their studies. TutorVista is able to connect people with specific expertise to students who can use their services in a highly customized and personalized manner.[20]

The strategies discussed in this chapter are generic and offer a starting point for those who are interested in building a technology venture. However, it should also be noted that technology entrepreneurs are notorious for innovation—not only in products and services, but also in strategies. The various strategic frameworks discussed above will no doubt be eclipsed in the coming years with variations that are only dimly recognized today. Savvy technology entrepreneurs will be aware that strategy is always changing, and they will be attuned to understanding existing strategies and adept at inventing new ones.

BARRIERS TO ENTRY

Every startup has to consider all of the costs and other challenges it will face as it attempts to enter the competitive market. These costs and challenges are commonly referred to as **barriers to entry.** Every industry has its own particular barriers to entry, but some have far greater barriers than others. For example, if an aspiring entrepreneur wanted to enter the oil drilling industry based on novel insights about where oil is to be found, the barriers could be tremendous. Drilling for oil is a costly and risky undertaking. Even if the aspiring entrepreneur elects to hire a third-party company to conduct the drilling, there will be upfront expenses and the inevitable risk that the driller will find nothing but a dry hole.

© dotshock, 2012. Used under license from Shutterstock, Inc.

On the other hand, some industries do not have extensive barriers to entry and enable startups to enter the market with relatively little upfront investment. Jesse Schwarz was an aspiring entrepreneur in the early 2000s when he opened up a chicken restaurant using recipes from his native Mexico. Unfortunately, Jesse did not have experience in the restaurant industry and the venture failed within thirty days. Down to his last $10,000, Jesse decided to invest in learning how to create an Internet business. He learned all he could via free resources that he found on the web and launched a website that helps customers identify and select among various high-speed Internet service providers. Jesse's simple business model does not require him to provide those services himself, he simply helps customers decide and then refers them to the actual service providers. The service providers pay Jesse for these high-quality leads. Today, Jesse's website generates revenue in excess of $50,000/month, with less than $5,000/month in expenses.[21]

Some important barriers to entry that you will need to consider prior to launching your venture include:

- Capital
- Time to breakeven
- Production
- Market access
- Dominant brands

Capital

Some industries enable greater access to capital than others. For example, most venture capital companies are organized to invest primarily in a narrow range of industries. In other words, venture capital firms tend to specialize in industries for which they have the capacity to add value not only through monetary investments but also through knowledgeable partners. Some industries have heavy concentrations of venture capital interest. Exhibit 4.5 indicates where that interest was concentrated in 2010. A total amount of $22 billion was invested in the various industries noted in the graphic.

Exhibit 4.5 U.S. Venture Capital Statistics 2009–2011

Year	2009	2010	2011
Invested capital (US$M)	$24,084	$29,595	$32,557
Investment rounds	2,714	3,033	3,209
Median round size (US$M)	$5.0	$4.3	$5.0
Number of VC-backed IPOs	8	46	45
IPO capital raised (US$M)	$904	$3,255	$5,358
Median time to IPO (years)	7.9	8.1	6.5
Number of VC-backed M&As	416	560	477
Median M&A valuation (US$M)	$25.0	$40.4	$70.7
Median time to M&A (years)	5.6	5.4	5.3

Source: Derived from Venture Capital Association, 2011 Annual Report.

Of course, the distribution of venture money will change from year to year, but some industry sectors are traditionally more active than others. Technology usually have more interest of investors than, say, the restaurant industry. Aspiring entrepreneurs should conduct research to understand access to capital in their industry.

Time to Breakeven

Some industries have very long periods until the venture reaches profit and/or cash flow breakeven, and some are relatively quick. Large, capital-intensive industries such as automobile manufacturing or construction may take years before the entrepreneur achieves breakeven. Others, such as many Internet ventures or personal services companies, take far less time. The aspiring entrepreneur needs to develop an understanding of how much time may be needed to achieve breakeven before launching the venture. If that amount of time exceeds the aspiring entrepreneur's financial capacity to sustain the desired lifestyle, the industry may not be a good fit.

Production

For ventures that are product focused, the aspiring entrepreneur must take into consideration how those products will be manufactured and assembled and delivered to customers. The entire supply chain should be examined to determine whether all the necessary pieces are in place to manage production and meet customer demand. Of course, managing global supply chains is far simpler today with modern

© sevenke, 2012. Used under license from Shutterstock, Inc.

telecommunication capacities, but there are many variables to consider. Today, many product-based ventures are choosing to outsource their manufacturing to China and other nations with low-cost labor pools. This helps keep production costs low, but it also can lead to quality issues, problems with timely delivery of product to U.S. shores, and intellectual property concerns.[22] For example, American Electric Vehicle (AEV) is a small company that produces electric buses. AEV's electric buses are produced in China, and therein lies the problem. The buses are large and difficult to ship to the United States. In 2011, AEV was attempting to raise capital, but the only finished product that it held title to was still in China. Although the firm has video of the buses, it will need to spend the money to have some of its buses shipped to their U.S. headquarters.[23]

Market Access

In the previous chapter we talked about identifying your target market. Knowing *who* your market is only part of your challenge as an aspiring entrepreneur. You'll also need to know *where* it is and how your venture will be able to reach your customers. For example, Bloomin is a Colorado-based company that specializes in making products made out of seed paper. Seed paper is just what it sounds like, it is paper that is embedded with plant seeds. The company makes greeting cards and other items from the seed paper. Over the past decade, the small company discovered that its products were in high demand in foreign markets. The challenge concerned how to reach those markets. Fortunately, Bloomin found that most of the foreign markets that were interested had dependable distributors that would help them acquire shelf space in appropriate retail outlets. The use of international distributors has been a big winner for Bloomin as it now distributes its products in twelve foreign countries.[24]

Dominant Brands

A market that is dominated by brands that have broad recognition and loyalty among customers can be a daunting market to enter for an aspiring entrepreneur. Think about dominant brands such as Coke and Pepsi. Going head to head against such brands can be quite a challenge for a new entry. Of course, a large company such as Walmart can develop its own brand of cola, Sam's Cola, and compete successfully because it also has a well-known brand that has substantial customer loyalty. A startup venture doesn't have such a luxury. It would be far better for the small startup to differentiate in manner that does not require head-to-head competition. Think about the many energy drink products that have entered the market to steal market share from the big cola brands, without taking them on directly.[25]

SUMMARY OF LEARNING OBJECTIVES

1. **Assess** your unique talents and understand how they are important to your entrepreneurial success. *Your unique talents are vital to success in entrepreneurship because of the competitive nature of modern business and the need to create compelling value for customers. The only way you can accomplish that is by leveraging your natural talents.*

2. **Leverage** your passion as an important part of your ability to endure entrepreneurial challenges. *Passion is important to success in entrepreneurship as you will need to rely upon your emotional commitment to your goals to overcome the challenges associated with launching new ventures. Your passion is not sufficient for your success, but leveraging your passion is necessary for long-term success in entrepreneurship.*

3. **Understand** that value creation is the purpose of business. *The fundamental purpose of business is to create value for other people. Your venture should focus on creating and delivering value to customers.*

4. **Learn** how to create a compelling value proposition for your venture. *Your value proposition communicates the value your venture creates to customers and potential customers alike. Your value proposition should be compelling, truthful, and attractive to customers.*

5. **Leverage** the resources that you currently control and learn how to aggregate those you don't currently control. *Expert entrepreneurs have learned that startups need a variety of resources to achieve success. Capital resources, human resources, organizational resources, and technology resources are just some of the resources you'll need to be successful with your startup venture.*

6. **Leverage** your unfair advantage and create a sustainable competitive advantage in your industry. *Launching a new venture is never easy, but your path to success is made a bit easier if you have an unfair advantage over competitors. Unfair advantage can be realized through unique talent, intellectual property, brand loyalty, and other things.*

7. **Recognize** the barriers to entry in your industry and learn various tactics for overcoming them. *Barriers to entry are the obstacles that any new venture will face when entering an industry. Some industries have relatively high barriers to entry (e.g., the oil industry) and others have relatively low barriers (e.g., opening a new restaurant).*

QUESTIONS FOR DISCUSSION

1. Try some of the Myers-Briggs assessment tools recommended in the chapter. What do you think of the results you obtained? Discuss.

2. Try some of the assessments that measure your emotional intelligence. What do you think of the results? What kinds of things do you need to improve upon?

3. Do the thought experiment on determining your passion. What do you think you would spend your life doing if you were not concerned about money? Explain.

4. What is a value proposition? Think about some value propositions of key brands that you respond to. What is it about the value proposition that compels you to purchase the product and/or be loyal to the brand?

5. What types of resources are important to the entrepreneur in launching the startup venture? Explain how an entrepreneur can aggregate the needed resources in a cost-effective manner.

6. What are the sources of capital for a startup venture? Explain how you would leverage these sources if you were starting a venture today.

7. What is meant by the term "unfair advantage"? Identify several sources of unfair advantage that the entrepreneur can leverage.

8. Describe the barriers to entry for a new venture in the automobile industry. How can they be overcome? Describe the barriers to entry for a new online shoe store. How can these barriers be overcome?

IN-CLASS EXERCISE

Fun with the MBTI Assessment

For this exercise, students should be asked to take one or more of the free MBTI assessments recommended in this chapter. Students should write up a one-page summary of what they learned from the assessment and be prepared to discuss in class. In particular, their summary should address:

1. The four-letter outcome of the MBTI assessment.

2. Do they agree with or dispute the categories that the assessment identified as dominant for them? Why?

3. What are the students' key areas of strength (i.e., natural talent) and what are the areas of weakness?

Students should bring their essays to class and be prepared to discuss their findings and interpretation. The instructor should survey each student for the four-letter classification he or she obtained from the assessment. Keep track of how many students are in each category. Have those with similar categories discuss what they think their strengths are and why. Have them also discuss what they think their weaknesses are and why. Do the students in similar categories report similar strengths and/or weaknesses? Discuss these findings.

KEY TERMS

Advisory board: A board that does not have fiduciary responsibility, but rather is convened to add value in other ways, such as key contacts, industry knowledge, and executive experience.

Angel capital: Capital available to startup ventures from high-net-worth individuals.

Barriers to entry: The barriers to enter an industry that a startup venture will experience. Every industry has its own particular barriers to entry, but some have far greater barriers than others.

Board of directors: A formal board of directors for a company with actual fiduciary responsibility to shareholders for the effective management of the company.

Bootstrap financing: New ventures that finance their growth through internally generated funds are said to grow via bootstrap financing.

Distinctive competence: A venture's unfair advantage that is based on Michael Porter's competitive strategy model.

Emotional intelligence: The need to understand and be able to manage one's own emotional reactions and predispositions.

Fiduciary responsibility: Responsibility to shareholders for the effective management of the venture.

Human capital: Talent and resourcefulness that you are able to aggregate around yourself and your venture idea.

Intellectual property: The knowledge-based assets your venture has created such as patents.

Multiple intelligences: From the work of Harvard's Howard Gardner, who proposes that intelligence is not a single "thing," but rather there are multiple ways to interact intelligently with the world.

Myers-Briggs Type Indicator® (MBTI®): An assessment tool based on the work of psychologist Carl Jung that provides insight into one's natural talents.

Resource-based theory: A theory that says a venture's unfair advantage stems from resources it controls that are rare, valuable, difficult to copy, and non-substitutable.

Small Business Administration (SBA) loan: Loans made by banks to small businesses that are backed by the federal government of the United States.

Small Business Innovation Research (SBIR) grants: Grants made by the federal government to qualified small businesses working on federally supported technologies.

Small Business Technology Transfer (STTR) grants: Grants made by the federal government to qualified small businesses in a very narrow category of favored technologies.

Sustainable competitive advantage: A venture's unfair advantage that can be sustained over time.

Value creation: The purpose of business. Businesses are organized to create value for other people.

Value proposition: The way a venture describes the value it creates to customers and potential customers.

Venture capital: Capital available to high-growth ventures that is managed by a venture capital firm.

ENDNOTES

[1] Haltiwanger, J., R. Jarmin, and J. Miranda, *Business Dynamics Statistics Briefing: High Growth and Failure Rates of Young Firms* (Kansas City. MO: The Kauffman Foundation, 2009).

[2] Isaacson, W., *Steve Jobs* (New York: Simon & Schuster, 2011).

[3] See the movie *Amadeus* for an excellent portrayal of Mozart the genius and Mozart the tragic figure.

[4] Read, S., and S.D. Sarasvathy, "Knowing What to Do and Doing What You Know: Effectuation as a Form of Entrepreneurial Expertise," *Journal of Private Equity,* 9(1)(2005): 45–62.

[5] The Myers-Briggs Foundation. www.myersbriggs.org.

[6] Gardner, H., *Intelligence Reframed: Multiple Intelligences for the 21st Century* (New York: Basic Books, 2000).

[7] Goleman, D., *Emotional Intelligence* (New York: Bantam Books, 1995).

[8] Kariv, D., "The Relationship Between Stress and Business Performance Among Men and Women Entrepreneurs," *Journal of Small Business & Entrepreneurship,* 21(4)(2008): 449–476.

[9] Segovia, O., "To Find Happiness, Forget about Passion," *HBR Blog Network,* January 13, 2012.

[10] See: www.thedreamfly.org.

[11] Farzad R., "A Deal that Paid for Itself," *Business Week,* October 30, 2006, p. 38.

[12] See www.pg.com.

[13] Stringer, S., "Connecting Business Needs with Basic Science," *Research Technology Management,* (2008, January/February): 9–14.

[14] Braunschweig, C., "The Near Death of Early Stage Investing," *Venture Capital Journal,* 43(5): 4–6.

[15] Shultz, S.F., "Developing Strategic Boards of Directors," *Strategic Finance,* 11(2003): 1–4.

[16] Barney, J., "Firm Resources and Sustained Competitive Advantage," *Journal of Management,* 17(1991): 99–120.

[17] Dollinger, M.J., *Entrepreneurship: Strategies and Resources* (Upper Saddle River, NJ: Prentice-Hall, 1999).

[18] Porter, M., *Competitive Strategy: Techniques for Analyzing Industries and Competitors* (New York: Free Press, 1998).

[19] Thompson, A.A., Jr., A.J. Strickland, and J.E. Gamble, *Crafting & Executing Strategy: The Quest for Competitive Advantage,* 15th ed. (Burr Ridge, IL: McGraw-Hill, 2007).

[20] Prahalad, C.K., and M.S. Krishnan, *The New Age of Innovation: Driving Co-Created Value Through Global Networks* (New York: McGraw-Hill, 2008).

[21] Duening, T., *The Startup Experience: Experience Starting an Internet Marketing Company* (Colorado Springs, CO: Businesses2Learn Publishing, 2011).

[22] Adler, C., "Little Trouble in Big China," *Fortune Small Business,* 14(2)(2004): 56–61.

[23] See: American Electric Vehicles, www.aevehicles.com.

[24] Duening, T., *The Startup Experience: Experience an Exporting Business* (Colorado Springs, CO: Businesses2Learn Publishing, 2011).

[25] Strenk, T., "Revved Up," *Beverage World,* 127(6)(2008): 44–45.

GETTING TO KNOW YOUR MARKET, CUSTOMERS, AND INDUSTRY

Learning Objectives

As a result of studying this chapter, students will be able to:

- **Assess** the addressable market for a venture's offerings.

- **Identify** a target market using demographic, geographic, psychographic, sociographic, and controllable marketing element variables.

- **Assess** the venture's industry and its stage of maturity.

- **Assess** the wants, needs, and desires of the target market.

- **Adapt** your venture's offerings based on the feedback of your customers.

- **Learn** how to apply disruptive innovation and Blue Ocean Strategy as part of your venture's innovation strategy.

INTRODUCTION

Expert entrepreneurs know from experience that large market opportunities are better than small market opportunities. Large markets have room for multiple competitors and are easier for new ventures to enter than crowded and small markets. Large markets also present growth opportunities that smaller markets don't accommodate.

Assessing the size of a market is not always a simple task. Markets are fluid, changing, and they are constantly growing or shrinking. Think about how the market for personal computers (PCs) has changed over time. Not long ago that was one of the hottest markets on the planet with many new companies appearing all around the world. Today, the PC market has been dramatically reduced for a number of reasons, and there are far fewer PC manufacturers today than there was a mere decade ago.[1]

© Yuri Arcurs, 2012. Used under license from Shutterstock, Inc.

Your challenge as an aspiring entrepreneur is to learn how to assess your market opportunity. That assessment is not simply a matter of measuring the current market size, but also of assessing its future growth potential. In this chapter, we'll explore some basic techniques that you can use to identify your target market and assess its likely growth trajectory into the future. Of course, no single assessment will provide an absolute answer, but if you use a variety of approaches to understanding where the market is going, you can achieve a more reliable forecast.

Recall that in Chapter 4 we identified "value creation" as the purpose of business. Entrepreneurs usually are more intimately aware of the need to create value than are managers of large corporate entities. In part this is true because entrepreneurs can't pay the bills without creating value and pleasing customers. Your customers are the ultimate judge of the value you are creating. Many aspiring entrepreneurs believe strongly in the products or services they've created, only to find that customers simply aren't interested. Entrepreneurs who don't adjust to negative customer reaction, believing customers are just wrong or stupid, are likely to fail. Expert entrepreneurs have learned that listening to customers and adjusting one's products or services to meet their needs and tastes is critical to success.

Getting to know your customers involves a wide range of techniques. Some of these techniques are quantitative and provide opportunities for data analysis and discovery. Others are qualitative, focusing primarily on listening to what customers have to say. Each of these approaches to understanding your customers are valuable to the growing venture. We'll introduce you to several important techniques that expert entrepreneurs use to ensure they are delighting their customers.

It is also necessary for the aspiring entrepreneur to get a handle on the industry in which the venture will be competing. Industries have well-defined lifecycles, and entrepreneurs must be aware of which phase of the lifecycle their industry is currently traversing. We will introduce you to the industry lifecycle and explore its various phases. We'll also explore some techniques that the aspiring entrepreneur can use to identify the industry in which they are competing and to determine its current lifecycle phase. We will also introduce different strategies for competing effectively in the different lifecycle phases.

Finally, we will examine some techniques that entrepreneurs use to change their venture's offerings based on the information they've collected about their markets, customers, and industry. This process of gathering information and adapting offerings is often referred to as "innovation." We strongly believe in the need for ventures of all sizes to constantly be innovating to meet changing market needs. Note, however, that we are not endorsing innovation for its own sake. We believe that all innovation should be directed to customer value creation. This chapter will look at several different approaches to innovation, including disruptive innovation and Blue Ocean Strategy.

Of course, as we have been saying from the outset of this book, the entrepreneurial method is based in large measure on non-predictive control. That is, regardless of the amount of time you spend conducting research before you actually launch your venture, it is highly likely—near certain—that you will not have perfect information. The purpose of assessing your market, customers, and industry is to develop a mindset of moving ever closer to getting things right, but never quite reaching perfection. This approach to research, data collection, and analysis ensures that you and your venture team will never rest on your laurels. Even if your venture may get some critical things right and make customers very happy, change is a constant in business and that happy state of affairs is likely to change. Relentlessly pursuing more and better understanding of your markets, customers, and industry will ensure that your venture remains on the forefront and will not be left in the dustbin of history like so many companies that become overly complacent and refuse to adapt to change.

Let's begin this chapter by examining some techniques that you can use to assess your venture's market opportunity.

ASSESS YOUR MARKET

Assessing the market potential for a new venture begins with identifying its **target market**. A target market is nothing more than the set of customers that is most likely to purchase the venture's products or services. For example, if the entrepreneur was launching a new mobile phone service, the target market would be the people who potentially would want and could afford the new service.

Of course, identifying a target market is slightly more complicated than that. In the case of the mobile phone service, the target market is not simply "all people likely to purchase the service." That would use too broad a brush to identify a true target market. The entrepreneur behind the mobile phone service needs to identify his or her target market in more precise terms. For example, the phone service may be specifically set up for business users. In that case, the users would want the variety of features necessary for daily business communications, including voice, data, and other features. On the other hand, the service might target young people. In that case, popular features might include such things as text messaging, online games, and shopping deals.

The process of **market segmentation** is extremely important.[2] Expert entrepreneurs use market segmentation to identify a target market. The difference between the market and a venture's target market is profound. The **total addressable market** (TAM) for a product or service is everyone in the world who would purchase a product or service similar to your offerings. Your target market, on the other hand, consists of the subset of your TAM that can be made aware of the venture's products and services and that can potentially be persuaded to purchase those offerings. The target market is defined as some fraction or portion of the TAM. The proportion of the TAM that you are able eventually to win is referred to as your **market share**.

Once the target market has been correctly defined, it is much easier to develop a marketing strategy and the appropriate combination of product, distribution, promotion, and price to reach that market effectively. The target market that a venture sells into is known as the **served addressable market (SAM)**.

The first step in determining the venture's target market is to segment the overall market. This is a process of identifying various subsets of the TAM, then determining which of these is going to provide the greatest opportunity for the venture's products and services. The venture's market can be segmented using a variety of criteria. Entrepreneurs need to think very hard about their target market in order to ensure the best use of limited marketing resources.[3] There are several common ways to think about the market for a new venture, including:

- Demographics
- Psychographics
- Geography
- Sociographics
- Controllable marketing elements

Demographics is the term used to refer to readily identifiable characteristics of an individual or a group. These characteristics include many of the variables that are covered in U.S. Census data. Some examples of demographic characteristics for B2C markets include:

- Age
- Income
- Gender
- Race
- Ethnic background
- Marital status
- Home ownership
- Educational background

Many marketing groups closely monitor data on these characteristics. Products as diverse as movies and soft drinks are marketed to specific groups, based on detailed demographic information.

In B2B marketing, demographic data can be collected on firms in categories such as:

- Age of the firm
- Market size served
- Total sales
- Operating income
- Number of employees

There are many companies that specialize in providing demographic statistics compiled from government agencies and private studies by firms such as Gartner Group, Forrester Research, or E-Marketer.com. Demographic data can be just as important to ventures that market products and services to industrial customers as it often is to ventures that market directly to consumers.[4]

Another criterion that entrepreneurs use to segment markets and identify a target market is geographic location of the market. Geographic location, as might be guessed, concerns where the customers are physically located. A market's psychological profile refers to the activities, interests, opinions, attitudes and values of the people that comprise a market segment. Understanding these characteristics of a market segment is an important part of developing a volume strategy regardless of whether the target market is chosen for psychographic reasons.[5]

Psychographics is used to refer to group or individual characteristics that are less readily observable. Terms such as "attitude," "taste," or "values" are used to refer to these variables. They are terms that refer to psychological states or tendencies associated with individuals and/or groups. For example, a psychographic profile of college males might include their "preference" for sports, beer, and loud music. While this does not describe all college males, someone who had a product that would appeal to a group within that psychographic profile might try the college male market.[6]

Finally, **sociographics** refers to the tendency for people to identify with a particular cause or social group.[7] Many firms have developed distinctive competencies in recent years by marketing directly to individuals based on their social values. Tom's of Maine is a good example of a company that uses this approach. Tom's of Maine makes products that it sells to people who prefer to buy organic or so-called "natural" products. Tom's promises its customers that its products are developed using "pure and simple ingredients from nature." This message carries enormous appeal to people within a specific sociographic community and gives Tom's of Maine substantial pricing power.[8]

Segmenting based on **controllable marketing elements** refers to the potential to leverage communication and distribution channels. For example, some products are easily marketed through television shopping networks. This type of marketing appeals to a segment of the overall market, which is predictable to a high degree. The people who manage home shopping can usually determine with a high degree of accuracy whether a product is a fit for that type of marketing and how well it likely will do in terms of net sales.

Based on this segmenting process, the entrepreneur can determine which of various segments should be the venture's target market. In addition, the process of segmentation provides details about important target market characteristics. With this information, the entrepreneur can determine the most effective way to bring the products and services to market and the most effective means for positioning the products and services in the context of any competitors that may already be pursuing the same segment.

ASSESS YOUR CUSTOMERS

Getting to know your customers intimately is a key to success in the competitive world of entrepreneurship. Providing them with value is the core of your efforts, but you should consider how it's possible to go far beyond that. Zappos founder Tony Hsieh has written a book titled *Delivering Happiness*.[9] Hsieh built Zappos from the ground up on the simple principle of delivering happiness to customers. He took the rather mundane category of shoes and created an e-commerce platform that now delivers a wide range of consumer products—and happiness—to customers around the world. Exhibit 5.1 highlights Hsieh's principles for achieving exceptional customer service.[10]

The customer service that Zappos provides is something that all aspiring entrepreneurs should study and emulate. Developing a deeper knowledge of your customers will enable you to provide them with better overall services. Tony Hsieh knew that many customers find the shopping experience with other online retailers to be less than desirable. No doubt you have also had experiences where you simply weren't able to get in touch with anyone from the online retailer to provide support or to help you solve your problems. Zappos makes sure its customer service reps provide customers with what they want by measuring and incentivizing the right things.

BULLET BREAKOUT

Customer Service Dos and Don'ts from Zappos

- Do make customer service a priority for the entire company.

- Do empower your customer service representatives to solve customer problems.

- Do fire those customers who are impossible to please or who are abusive toward your employees.

- Don't base customer service on metrics such as call times, or upsell success, and don't use scripts to respond to customer problems.

- Don't make it difficult for customers to talk to actual people.

- Do view the costs of handling customer problems as a marketing investment.

- Do celebrate customer service success and share stories throughout the company.

EXHIBIT 5.1.

Source: Adapted and reprinted with permission from "The Innovator's Dilemma: When New Technologies Cause Great Firms to Fail" by Clayton M. Christensen. Harvard Business Press, 1997. Copyright © 1997 by Harvard Publishing; all rights reserved.

In setting out to create value for your customers, it is vitally important to know that going beyond the obvious features and benefits can provide a huge competitive edge. Steve Jobs famously obsessed about the details of each of the products he developed through Apple Computer and Pixar. His attention to design details went so far as to include the layout of the circuit boards inside the various electronic products he oversaw while CEO of Apple.[11] Note that NO ONE WOULD EVER SEE the circuit boards except for the Apple engineers who were building them, but Jobs knew that attention to details is contagious, and it must be a discipline instilled throughout the company and encompass all elements of the company's offerings.

The most powerful technique you can use to get into the minds of your customers is actually to find them and speak with them. This technique is often referred to as the **intercept interview**. That is, you will literally intercept potential customers in their natural environments and talk to them about your product or service. You may have encountered intercept interviewers at shopping malls or in various retail settings.[12] Many of the interceptors that you meet in retail stores are not focused on gathering information; they are simply trying to get you to try their product. If you've been to a grocery store such as Whole Foods or the grocery department in a Costco, you likely have encountered friendly people with food samples. We are not talking about this type of intercept interview.

What we are talking about is a far more involved process of critical information gathering. You want to know as many of the details as you possibly can about how your customers perceive your product or service and what is important to them when making the purchasing decision. To learn those types of details about your customers requires a systematic approach that involves asking the right questions and listening carefully to the answers.

The **semi-structured interview format**, a technique used in social science research, is another tool for helping entrepreneurs identity unknown unknowns or **unk-unks**—the things they don't know they don't know.[13] Although entrepreneurs often do market research by designing surveys that they distribute electronically, that approach can be problematic because in the early stages of exploring a venture entrepreneurs may be asking questions about the wrong product, the wrong pricing model, and/or the wrong potential market segment. Also, entrepreneurs enamored of their own idea may ask leading questions while doing market research or focus on their idea more than on customer needs. The semi-structured interview format avoids these pitfalls. It features open-ended questions and short prompts that encourage respondents to elaborate.

The semi-structured interview provides an opportunity to ask questions beyond the standard list. In other words, the interviewer is empowered to follow the interview wherever it is leading in an attempt to explore additional insights the customer may have. This approach is more time consuming then a standard interview or online survey, but it is an excellent tool for uncovering the dreaded unk unks.[14]

Some entrepreneurs conduct their own intercept interviews so that they are in direct contact with the people for whom they are creating value. There is nothing more important for an entrepreneur than to be in direct contact with his or her customers. Of course, everyone in the organization should be empowered to listen to and serve customers, but direct contact by the CEO is not only vital to long-term success, but it also sends the right message to customers and employees alike.

Discovering Your Unk Unks

In January 2005, Kenn Jorgensen and Cassian Drew, two British entrepreneurs who were passionate about rock climbing, wanted to know if their sport could be adapted for use in exercise facilities. Indoor climbing walls already existed, but they were used by serious climbers in urban areas as substitutes for outdoor rock formations that weren't easily accessible. What if a new kind of low-impact, high-tech exercise regime could be created that was done on climbing walls just a few feet off the ground in ordinary fitness studios with ordinary ceilings, invigorating music, and a spirited instructor—but with walls equipped with climbing holds?

"A surefire winner," said one of their rock climbing buddies. "Not a chance," said a female fitness enthusiast who worked out three times a week in a nearby gym. Jorgensen and Drew decided they needed to confirm or refute what they thought they knew about their innovative idea: bringing climbing concepts to fitness studios. More crucially, though, they set out to try to discover the unknown unknowns—the "unk unks," as such unknowns have long been called in engineering and project management circles. In other words, they sought to identify things *they didn't know they didn't know* that could derail the new venture they were considering.

Source: Adapted from J.W. Mullins, "Discovering Unk-Unks," *MIT Sloan Management Review*, 48(4)(2005): 17–21.

Trade Shows

Trade shows are another great place to get feedback on your products and services. There are trade shows in practically every industry. Some are extremely large and well attended; others are focused on very narrow niche areas and attract fewer participants. It really doesn't matter how many people attend a trade show, however, because you will know the participants at the show are interested in your industry.[15]

© Dariusz Gudowicz, 2012. Used under license from Shutterstock, Inc.

Many entrepreneurs attend trade shows but don't necessarily purchase a booth to display their products and services. Instead, they simply bring along samples and talk to show attendees about what they've created. Trade shows can be fantastic for gathering feedback, gaining key contacts, and learning about the direction of your industry and your market. Some trade shows are held annually in major cities, and they are not that difficult to find. Trade shows generally are organized and operated by trade associations. Trade associations provide a great starting point for entrepreneurs who want to learn more about an industry and its addressable market.

Focus Groups

Focus groups are another technique many entrepreneurs use to identify the features and benefits that are of most interest to their target market. Focus groups are groups of potential customers gathered for the express purpose of providing feedback about the venture's offerings in a structured setting. Entrepreneurs who are not experienced in organizing and managing focus groups should work with professionals who know what they're doing. From the outside, a focus group may appear to be little more than asking questions of a group of people. But the nature of the group, the structure of the questions, and many other variables will determine whether the collected data are useful or misleading. Consultants who have experience in selecting people for a focus group, designing appropriate questions, and analyzing data are likely to produce better, more actionable results than if the entrepreneur, trying to save a few dollars, acted independently. For example, here are some common mistakes that entrepreneurs make when running their own focus groups:

- Asking leading questions

- Populating the focus group only with people favorably disposed to their offerings

- Reacting emotionally to negative or critical feedback

- Failure to have clear goals and objectives

- Avoiding listening to obnoxious focus group participants

Focus groups are difficult to manage, but the results of these direct customer interactions can be invaluable to the young company. As we've stated, we recommend that the aspiring entrepreneur consider working with an independent third party to ensure the focus group achieves its intended goals. In the case that you prefer to conduct your own focus groups, the Bullet Breakout below provides some tips for success.

BULLET BREAKOUT

Tips for Successful Focus Groups

- You never can do too much planning for a focus group.

- Manage the recruitment process actively to be sure to get the right people in the groups.

- Don't prejudge the participants based on physical appearance.

- The best focus group moderators bring objectivity and expertise in the process to a project.

- Achieving research objectives does not guarantee a successful focus group project.

- The moderator and the client should coordinate their efforts at all stages of the process for the research to achieve its objectives.

- Most client organizations conduct more focus groups than are necessary to achieve the research objectives.

- One of the most important services a moderator can provide is a fast report turnaround.

- Client observers should be thoroughly briefed about the research objectives before the session starts.

- The most valuable service a moderator can provide is objective conclusions based on the interpretation of the research, without regard for what the client wants to hear.

Source: Derived from Thomas Greenbaum, "10 Tips for Running Successful Focus Groups," Groups Plus, Fairfield County, CT; http://www.groupsplus.com/pages/mn091498.htm; accessed on February 13, 2012.

Surveys

In addition to conducting focus groups, entrepreneurs can use other techniques to get in direct touch with their customers. For example, many companies use a variety of different types of surveys to gather feedback. You've probably encountered surveys as they now seem to be a standard part of nearly every commercial transaction. Hotels, retailers, restaurants, and many others use surveys to gather feedback from customers. You've probably also noticed that many of these surveys are designed primarily to gather *positive* feedback. Retail clerks and others often remind you that if you give them a perfect score on the survey you might be eligible for a prize or guide your responses to the positive in some other way. This is *not* what you want to learn as an entrepreneur. Sure it's nice to receive positive feedback on the things you are doing, but you can't get better with only positive feedback. Entrepreneurs intent on building lasting value over time must seek out and be prepared to act upon *negative* feedback from customers.

Surveys are popular because they are relatively easy to implement, collect information, and analyze that information. Surveys can be implemented in several forms:

- Paper surveys
- Telephone surveys
- Surveys sent through the mail
- Online surveys

There are definite techniques that you can use to design surveys that will provide you with the type of constructive feedback from customers that will help you grow your business. The process of conducting the survey can be implemented as follows:

- Preparing survey questions
- Choosing the distribution method of a survey
- Disseminating the survey
- Collecting and analyzing the data

Competitor Observation

Competitor observation is another technique that many entrepreneurs find useful in assessing their customers. Randy Price, for example, is a successful owner of the Rocky Mountain Restaurant Group. Randy founded and owns multiple restaurants in a variety of culinary and price formats. When asked about how he stays in touch with the restaurant industry and where customer tastes are headed, he said that he visits a lot of restaurants when he travels. In fact, Randy calls this technique "culinary espionage." He literally takes pen and paper with him to note the items on the menus, how people are reacting to the food and ambiance, and other factors. Randy uses these observations not only to conceive of new restaurant concepts, but also to improve the ones that he already is using.[16]

You should be conducting ongoing competitor analysis anyway, so why not review objectively and truthfully how customers are responding to their offerings? This requires going into the field and listening to customers talk about and interact with your competitors' products. As you observe customers using competitor products, you have to maintain your objectivity, because in this setting you are not selling, you are gathering information. For example, try to observe some of the following:

- How customers respond to the packaging and shelf space allocated to competitor offerings

- How long customers take on average to make a purchase decision

- The average emotional reaction customers seem to have to competitor offerings

- Who is the primary decision maker for purchasing competitor offerings (e.g., head of household, wife, husband, child, other?)

- Negative reactions can you observe regarding competitor offerings

Ask Employees

Employees, especially so-called **customer-facing** employees are excellent sources of feedback from your customers.[17] Your venture will have some employees who regularly provide customer interaction. These are your customer-facing employees. Customer-facing employees work in jobs such as checkout clerks, help desk personnel, sales, or customer service. It is important to empower these employees to gather customer feedback and to share it with the venture's top decision makers.

Don't make the common mistake that many novice entrepreneurs make when they react negatively to hearing any bad news. Ventures that succeed are open to and even thrive on bad news. You are more likely to meet the long-term needs of your customers by listening to them when they have a complaint than by listening to them only when they have positive things to say.[18] Additionally, by demonstrating concern for your customers, you may be able to retain them despite any unhappiness they may have with your venture's offerings.

Because many customer-facing employees are often among the lowest-paid employees in a company, their advice and comments are too often overlooked. Don't make that mistake either. Make sure that your customer-facing employees realize how valuable they are to the success of the venture and encourage them to remain focused on customer delight.

ASSESS YOUR INDUSTRY

There are several techniques the aspiring entrepreneur should use to assess the industries they intend to enter. A good first step is to narrow down the industry category by determining which Standard Industrial Classification (SIC) Code defines your industry. An **SIC Code** is a number used to specify what industry a particular company belongs to. The Standard Industrial Classification

(SIC) code system was replaced by the **North American Industry Classification System (NAICS)** in 1997. The NAICS is the standard used by federal statistical agencies in the United States to classify business establishments for the purpose of collecting, analyzing, and publishing statistical data related to the U.S. economy. SIC and NAICS codes can be obtained at the following websites:

- SIC Codes: U.S. Occupational Safety & Health Administration (OSHA); www.osha.gov/pls/imis/sicsearch.html

- NAICS Codes: U.S. Census Bureau; www.census.gov/epcd/naics02/

When entering search terms to identify your appropriate code, you may want to try some variations. Singular words are usually better than plural words, but there are exceptions. For example, on the OSHA site, "florist" doesn't bring up any results while "florists" delivers six different code categories.

Once you know your venture's SIC and NAICS code numbers, you can research other companies that operate under the same code. However, because competitors are varied, you might need to investigate several related codes as well. For example, if you're a florist (SIC 5992), competitors may include grocery stores (SIC 19800) and online retailers like 1800Flowers.com (SIC 5990).

With your NAICS and SIC codes identified, you can conduct more in-depth industry research. Industry information is abundant, but many companies charge fees for the information they've gathered and analyzed. Fortunately, there are a number of free resources that you can use to begin your industry research:

- Your university library will have databases such as:
  - Business Source Premier
  - Business and Company Resource Center
  - Factiva
  - Hoovers Online
  - Reference U.S.A.
- Edgar.com
- Current Industrial Reports (from the U.S. Census Bureau)
- IBIS World
- Standard & Poor's Net Advantage
- Encyclopedia of American Industries
- Investext
- Datamonitor Industry Profiles
- Dun & Bradstreet Key Business Ratios

Another technique for assessing your industry is to analyze its health. Industry health refers to whether the industry is marked by innovation, growth, and dynamism, or whether it is in decline. The maturity of an industry in part is a reflection of its health. An emerging industry is often characterized by rapid growth and frequent and dramatic changes. On the other hand, an industry that has peaked and is on the decline will have less opportunity for growth. The future prospects of an industry are linked to customer trends and buying patterns. For example, future prospects of the cola industry are strong, but it is a mature industry and likely inhospitable to new ventures. Industries typically progress through five lifecycle stages:

Introduction Stage: This is the stage where alternative product design and positioning is rapidly occurring among a wide range of competitors. These competitors are not only creating the new products/services, they also literally are establishing the range and boundaries of the industry itself. For example, the early pioneers of e-commerce had to find out through experience what types of products would sell online. There were many early failures, as new startups attempted to sell everything from books to dog food. The boundaries of the e-commerce industry were mostly set between the years 1995–2005, although there remains some fuzziness at the outer extremes. In other words, new ventures entering Internet-based industries today will need to conform, in large part, to existing business models.

Growth Stage: The growth stage of an industry can be an exciting time for entrepreneurs. Growth in an industry usually occurs once the new products/services are well known and accepted among customers, and the demand begins to soar as new customers enter the market. Many technology products offer great examples of how this phenomenon works. In the early days of the PC, for example, sales were relatively slow as many people, including many business customers, could not foresee how they would use the new devices. However, as more and more people began to use PCs, and as businesses began to realize advantages over competitors by being early adopters in their industry, demand began to soar. The growth phase for the PC industry was a time of many new venture launches, as entrepreneurs sought to fill every conceivable gap in market coverage by existing companies.

Maturity Stage: In this phase, companies settle on what is referred to as the dominant design (supply chains, production techniques, etc.), and the existing competitors tend to develop very similar cost structures. In this phase, the barriers to entry become very high for new ventures. For example, the automobile industry worldwide is very capital intensive and most competitors use similar production techniques. It is very difficult for a newcomer to enter the automobile industry. The only place this is occurring is in the emerging markets, such as India and China, where the rising economies are allowing many more people to purchase automobiles. In the maturity phase of the industry lifecycle growth is no longer the main focus. Companies still competing in the industry mostly battle for relative market share. A good example of a mature industry is the popular soft drink known as Cola. Coke and Pepsi are the main competitors, and each strives for market share through a wide range of marketing campaigns. The basic formulas, serving sizes, and taste of these products haven't changed in decades, but there is still opportunity to garner market share through marketing.

Decline Stage: During the decline phase of an industry lifecycle revenues are declining and the industry as a whole may disappear in favor of something completely new. Think of the many companies that were in the horse-drawn wagon industry at the turn of the 20th century. Very few have survived to modern days, replaced slowly but inevitably by the rise of the automobile industry. Today, the PC business is being supplanted by mobile computing, hospital emergency rooms are being supplanted by urgent care centers, and cable television is threatened by Internet TV.

© Warren Goldswain, 2012. Used under license from Shutterstock, Inc.

Entering an emerging industry that doesn't have an established market often means that the new venture will need substantial capital to sustain itself during the market-building period.[19] Many entrepreneurs in emerging industries overestimate the customer response to their product or service and underestimate the amount of cash they will need to develop a market that is large enough to sustain the business. For example, many of the early Internet companies overestimated the market potential of e-commerce because they believed their online presence created a worldwide market. In reality, many of these "dot-com" ventures failed because they did not have the cash to develop a loyal customer base. Today, as the e-commerce industry matures and people become more comfortable with online buying, many business models that were abandoned just a few years ago are now successful.

A growth industry is one that has achieved critical mass in terms of market size and now has enough active customers to sustain a growing number of competitors. A growth industry presents a new set of challenges for the entrepreneur. During the emerging industry stage, the major issue confronting the entrepreneur is whether enough cash could be generated to survive day by day. During the growth stage, the challenge is whether the company can scale itself quickly enough to capture a significant market position. Despite the growth in the industry, many new ventures fail during this phase of the industry lifecycle because they attempt to grow faster than their systems, skills, and available capital allow. When that happens, a company may wind up losing customers due to lack of available product, poor customer service, or poor product/service quality.

Steady or only slowly growing industry-wide revenues characterize the mature stage of an industry. This is the stage in which a few well-established brands dominate the industry, and control much of the market share. Despite the lack of growth in the industry, the mature stage can be attractive to a new venture because of its stability.[20] Entering a growth phase industry means that innovation could make a large difference between winners and losers. During the mature phase, innovation is less important than outright execution. Customers in a mature industry have well-established buying patterns and preferences. It's usually very difficult to get customers to switch their buying habits based on a product/service innovation. What will matter more to customers in this phase is execution—delivery of the product or service in a manner that meets customer needs.

An industry that is in decline is characterized by falling industry-wide revenues, consolidation of competitors, and falling prices and profit margins.[21] Declining industries tend to eliminate competitors who are least efficient in their delivery of products and services. The falling prices and smaller profit margins mean that loose operations are likely to experience cash flow problems. One consequence of that is employee layoffs and/or declining salaries and bonuses. A declining industry is not all bad, however. Many entrepreneurs are very proficient at building businesses in declining industries. Some seek out distressed companies and purchase their assets at a fraction of their former value. Entrepreneurs skilled at "turnarounds" are able to reverse the course of the distressed company and return it to a profitable enterprise. If the entrepreneur is successful, the revitalized company can then be sold to an established competitor for a profit.

The main point of understanding the stage of the industry lifecycle is that no phase is "better" than any of the others from the perspective of whether profits can be made. The point is that the entrepreneur needs to understand the industry lifecycle phase in order to develop an appropriate business strategy.[22]

Another variable to examine in your industry analysis is the relative size of the industry. Industry size is characterized by the total revenues generated by all of the competitors in the industry. You can determine the size of your industry in a number of ways. Many industries have what are called **trade associations**. Trade associations are organizations—usually nonprofit organizations—designed to promote and conduct research on an industry. Trade associations can be very useful resources for aspiring entrepreneurs to learn more about their industry, and their markets and customers. Most trade associations provide their industry members with extensive and ongoing research into vital indicators of the health and status of the industry and its customers. Some of this research is offered for free, but often only summary information is provided free of charge. Still, the summary information can be very useful for the insights you can gain into the industry. You can find the websites of trade associations via the online database called Associations Unlimited.

Another industry variable that aspiring entrepreneurs should explore is the future prospects of the industry. It's one thing to know the historical background of an industry, as told by the revenue numbers from the past. It's another thing altogether to forecast where an industry is going and how large (or small) it's going to get. Forecasting industry trends can be done in several ways. A direct means of forecasting is to plot industry size over the past five to ten years on a graph, then extrapolate the graph forward. Another, perhaps more reliable, method is to examine what industry analysts are saying about an industry's growth potential.

Both the industry lifecycle phase and the future growth prospects of an industry can be investigated and reasonably determined. The best place to find this high-level information is through what are called "industry analysts." Analysts work for a variety of firms, but most are associated with securities brokerage companies. The analysts conduct ongoing research into an industry to provide securities sales professionals with quality information. Much of this information is public. The following websites provide you with a starting point for conducting your own industry research:

- Global Industry Analysts (wwwstrategyr.com/)
- IDC (www.idc.com)

In addition to these general industry analyst websites, you can find specific research into your industry by using the generic name of your industry in an Internet search. For example, if you are in the retail industry you may want to use a standard Internet search engine and enter the keywords "retail industry analyst." This should produce a number of useful links that will take you to websites hosted by investment banking firms, independent research firms, and others. Some of these reports can be downloaded for free as the companies that are featured in the reports often want the analyst perspectives to be made available to the retail investing public.

REFINING YOUR OFFERINGS

Once you have collected information from potential users about their preferences regarding your venture's offerings, you are now ready to analyze the information. Analysis is critical because not all the information that you gathered from the various sources is useful. You have to sift through the information to determine which of the variables will have the greatest impact on your venture

and its offerings. For example, if you are getting feedback that your prices are too high, the tendency may be to lower prices. That may be the wrong reaction. Another approach would be to increase the perceived value of your offerings. Customers will usually assess the "fairness" of prices subjectively, based on the information they have at the time of their purchase decision. These subjective judgments involve the perceived value of the offerings they are considering to buy. If customers do not perceive the full value of your offerings, they will automatically believe that they are priced too high. Lowering your price in response to customer complaints that prices are too high would unnecessarily reduce your margins if you can increase customer perceived value. A simple solution might be better, more descriptive packaging, selling products through more reputable retailers, or adding a "money back guarantee."

Analysis of the information you gather regarding your markets, industry, and customers should be ongoing and systematic. For example, Conor McCluskey, CEO of BombBomb, a video e-mail company, uses constant feedback and analytics to improve his company's sales success and customer retention rates.

Your venture will go through many changes on the way to its final outcome—all ventures do. To help assure that the final outcome is successful, it is imperative that you analyze the feedback that you've been receiving from your customers and adapt your products, services, features, and benefits accordingly.

One technique that is gaining favor among marketing professionals is referred to as **conjoint analysis.** That is a technical-sounding term, to be sure, but what it means is that customers often don't make purchasing decisions based on a single, isolated, benefit or feature of your offerings.[23] Rather, they look at several such features and benefits, jointly, to make a decision. For example, when you are buying a new car, you look at many features and benefits, including perhaps reliability, affordability, gas mileage, warranty, color, interior, handling, and many others. Every time you purchase a car, you likely are going to have to make some tradeoffs on these variables. If you want high performance, for example, you are likely to sacrifice gas mileage (unless you purchase a Tesla Roadster, in which case you sacrifice affordability).

Conjoint analysis cannot be taught in the few remaining pages of this chapter, and it would not be in your interest to attempt to learn the techniques of this approach here. Rather, this technique can be addressed by a consulting firm or marketing expert skilled in its application. You may want to learn how to do conjoint analyses internally, or hire an employee who has the skills, but that is not necessary. A good marketing firm familiar with the needs and concerns of new ventures will be able to assist in setting up techniques that enable you to assess how the features and benefits of your offerings should be arranged to maximize sales.

Another way to adapt your products to customer feedback, especially when you are unsure if you are getting the changes exactly right, is to use a **test market**. Test markets allow you to try new offerings or modifications of current offerings in a limited way.[24] Limiting the test market to a specific geographic region or specific subset of customers protects the integrity of your existing products and your company's brand. The test market may not like what you have offered, and that will be useful information to know. At the same time, your standard offerings continue to be marketed and additional feedback gathered to try again.

Many ventures use focus groups prior to actually releasing a new product or product innovation to a test market. This provides additional opportunity to gauge customer reaction and increase the chances of a successful release. Still, there is usually nothing better than experimenting with new offerings in a test market so that you gather information from customers in their natural setting. You are likely to have different data to work with between your focus group and test market. If the data are in any way confusing or ambiguous it is quite common for ventures to iterate their new product testing in the same way that you iterated your new venture ideas and as we discussed in Chapter 3. Iteration is more difficult, of course, if you need to redesign a new product prototype each time, but if you are experimenting with service offerings, prices, or simple design elements the process can be done fairly quickly. The Mini-Case below illustrates how one company refined its product offering using an online or "virtual" focus group service.

MINI CASE

Ontolo Leverages Crowdsourcing to Improve its Product

Ben Wills is the founder of Ontolo.com, which supplies a suite of automated link-building tools and data-prospecting services targeting search engine optimization (SEO) consulting firms. After three years in business, Wills knew that the time was right to expand his business by adding new features and tools to help clients. The problem was, he didn't know what additions and enhancements his customers wanted most. He also was not sure how to solicit and collect customer feedback effectively.

To solve these problems, Ontolo signed up to work with Napkin Labs, a crowd-sourcing platform that allow companies to create online consumer "labs." The labs are branded environments that function like online, virtual focus groups. The Ontolo Feedback Community Lab encouraged clients to help shape the ongoing evolution of its product, complete with a suggestion box, voting mechanism, and a scoring system for replies. "We want our customers to tell us what we don't know," said Wills. "There are so many parts of our business where we can really use their help. This community is going to facilitate the feedback we need."

Source: Ankeny, J.,"Listen In,"*Entrepreneur*, 39(12)(2011): 50–51.

Nothing that we are saying in this final section should indicate that you have a lot of time to iterate and experiment with your products and services. Quite the opposite is true. Today's competitive global economy requires that your venture constantly innovate and speed new ideas, products, and services to the marketplace. **Speed to market** is often regarded as one of the major sources of sustainable competitive advantage in the highly interconnected global marketplace.[25] Just a few years ago the U.S. market was relatively isolated from global competitors, but that state of affairs is no longer the case. In fact, the U.S. market is not necessarily the most coveted of the global markets. Emerging economies in Asia, Latin America, and even on the African continent are ripe for products and services tailored to the paticular needs of the people living in those places.

© dotshock, 2012. Used under license from Shutterstock, Inc.

The final concept we want to discuss in this chapter is **innovation.** Innovation is a term that refers to the changes that you make to your venture's products and services over time. In other words, your venture's offerings no doubt will evolve over time and, hopefully, they will evolve in a manner that is preferred by your customers. Many companies today focus on innovation as a core competency and strive to stay ahead of their competition by refusing to allow their offerings to become obsolete.

The so-called **innovator's dilemma** is that companies oftentimes need to disrupt their own marketplace with new offerings that address unmet needs in a category that they aren't currently serving.[26] Harvard scholar Clayton Christensen has identified a tendency for firms to ignore the fact that their industry often has customers who are not being served—he calls them **overshot customers**. In other words, many firms pursue their high end customers and ignore those who need their products or services but cannot afford the higher prices and/or they don't need rich feature sets. **Disruptive innovation** describes a process by which a product or service takes root initially in simple applications at the bottom of a market and then relentlessly moves "up market," eventually displacing established competitors.[27]

For example, Intel is well known for the high end, and expensive, computer chips that it makes for top-of-the-line PCs and mainframes. However, to its credit, Intel realized that there was space opening up on the lower end of the product spectrum for lower-priced computer chips. Such chips would have to tradeoff some performance in order to reach the lower price point. Intel, not wanting to send the wrong message about its company and its brand, innovated a new line of chips that it called Celeron that competed in a different space than its high-end Pentium chips.

Finally, we want to discuss one more innovation strategy that is referred to as **Blue Ocean Strategy.**[28] The Blue Ocean Strategy is an approach to product/service innovation that seeks to carve out a new market space where no one is currently competing. The contrasting red ocean is red because of all the blood that is being spilled by competitors fighting for market share in an increasingly crowded ocean. A blue ocean is one that is created anew by the entrepreneur and that doesn't currently have any incumbent competitors to compete with.

Southwest Airlines is a good example of a company that established a blue ocean strategy. Back in the 1970s when Southwest was created, the airline industry was highly competitive and highly standardized. Every major carrier based its scheduling and flights on the so-called "hub-and-spoke" system. That is, airlines would have a major hub airport out of which they operated, and would pick up additional passengers at the "spokes," other major airports. In this way, airplanes were routed around the nation, making multiple takeoffs and landings everyday as they hopscotched across the country. Southwest decided to use a different, point-to-point strategy where aircraft literally flew back and forth all day between secondary airports in major cities. What this offered passengers was greater convenience in scheduling air travel, fewer connections in getting from one place to another, and, because of Southwest's focus on service, much better customer service than was typical in the industry. Southwest didn't compete against the incumbents; it created an entirely different means of air travel.

Another good example of a Blue Ocean Strategy is Cirque de Soleil. This company is famous for the elaborate, ornate, and highly choreographed shows it conducts in major venues around the world. The performers delight crowds with aerial acrobatics that are not available anywhere other than perhaps a circus. And that is just the point. The founders of Cirque de Soleil knew that many people would be fascinated to see the high wire and death-defying acts of a circus, but they didn't like the rather low-brow venues and atmosphere of a traditional circus. So they eliminated many of the standard elements of a circus, such as animal acts, clowns, and roving cotton candy sales, and upgraded other things such as the artistry of the performances, the venues in which performances are held, and the price of admission.

Exhibit 5.2 is a template that you can use for innovation in your venture's offerings. It is a four-quadrant analysis of the current state of the offerings in the industry and how they can be changed to create a blue ocean.

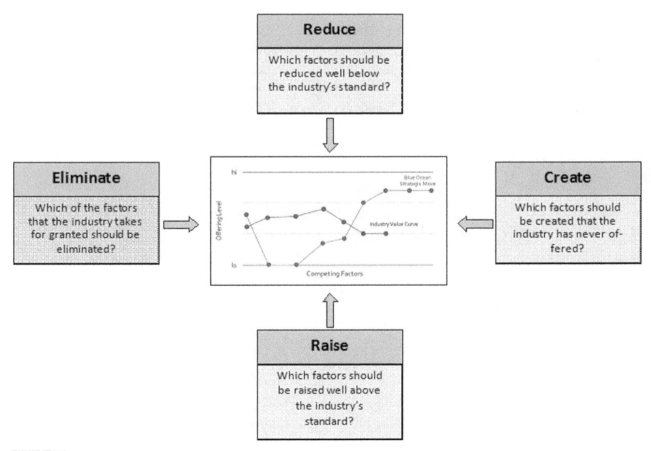

EXHIBIT 5.2

In the case of Cirque du Soleil, the application of the above technique would look something like Exhibit 5.3.

There is much work to be done for your new venture, whether you are just getting started or are working on revising successful product offerings. The entrepreneur should never rest on his or her laurels. You are better advised to listen to your customers and analyze their needs using a variety of tools, including those of disruptive innovation and Blue Ocean Strategy as you grow your venture.

<table>
<tr><td></td><td>Reduce
Fun & humor
Thrill & danger</td><td></td></tr>
<tr><td>Eliminate
Star performers
Animal shows
Aisle concession sales
Multiple show arenas</td><td>CIRQUE DU SOLEIL.
</td><td>Create
Theme
Refined environment
Multiple productions
Artistic music & dance</td></tr>
<tr><td></td><td>Raise
Unique venue</td><td></td></tr>
</table>

EXHIBIT 5.3

Source: W.C. Kim and R. Mauborgne, Blue Ocean Strategy: How to Create Uncontested Market Space and Make the Competition Irrelevant (Cambridge, MA: Harvard Business School Press, 2005).

SUMMARY OF LEARNING OBJECTIVES

1. **Assess** the addressable market for a venture's offerings. *The total addressable market (TAM) for your venture's offerings is all the potential customers for your offerings. Your addressable market is some subset of that and constitutes your target market.*

2. **Identify** a target market using demographic, geographic, psychographic, sociographic, and controllable marketing element variables. *Target markets can be segmented by demographic factors such as age, disposable income, gender, and others; by geographic region in which the customers are located; by psychographic factors such as interests, predispositions, and desires; sociographic factors such as ethnic heritage, community groups, and others; and/or by controllable marketing elements that enable you uniquely to reach a particular set of customers.*

3. **Assess** the venture's industry and its stage of maturity. *The maturity of an industry is very relevant for a new venture. There are four primary stages of industry development: emerging, growth, mature, and decline. It doesn't matter, really, what stage your industry is in, what matters is that you develop the appropriate strategy to succeed in that stage.*

4. **Assess** the wants, needs, and desires of the target market. *This chapter identified a number of techniques that entrepreneurs can use to get in touch with customers. Focus groups, surveys, interviews, and others should be used continuously to adapt products, prices, features, and benefits to the evolving needs of the venture's customers.*

5. **Adapt** your venture's offerings based on the feedback of your customers. *New ventures should analyze the feedback received from customers to determine which features are most important. Conjoint analysis is one technique that enables companies to assess what feature sets are most important to customers.*

6. **Learn** how to apply disruptive innovation and Blue Ocean Strategy as part of your venture's innovation strategy. *Disruptive innovation describes how new ventures can enter a market with well-established incumbents by targeting customers that have been overshot with the current offerings. Blue Ocean Strategy analyzes and industry by what can be reduced, what can be eliminated, what can be enhanced, and what can be added to create an entirely new industry or market space.*

QUESTIONS FOR DISCUSSION

1. What is the target market for Walmart? What is the target market for Nieman-Marcus? How do these two retailers differ? Would a Walmart shopper be comfortable at Nieman-Marcus? Explain your response.

2. Name a company that you think targets the 18- to 24-year-old male demographic. Name one that targets the 14- to 18-year-old female demographic. How do these companies differ? Why?

3. What psychographic factors do you think underlie the sale of Budweiser beer? What psychographic factors underlie the sale of Michelob? Explain why these might be different.

4. Explain what Tony Hsieh, founder of Zappos, means by "Delivering happiness." How does that phrase help Zappos be successful?

5.   What is meant by the term "unk unks"? How can a new venture entrepreneur uncover some of the unk unks in his or her industry? How can an entrepreneur prepare for the unkunks he or she is likely to encounter?

6.   How might an entrepreneur use trade shows to get to know customers? Focus groups? Competitor observation?

7.   How can an entrepreneur determine the NAICS code that is appropriate for his or her industry? What competitive information can be gained once an appropriate NAICS code is identified?

8.   What are the four stages of an industry lifecycle? What stage is best for the aspiring new venture? Explain.

9.   How can the entrepreneur use trade associations to learn more about his or her industry?

10.   Explain how a new and/or growing venture should use innovation to evolve its offerings. What is disruptive innovation? What is meant by "Blue Ocean Strategy"?

IN-CLASS EXERCISE

For this exercise students will use the Blue Ocean Strategy to analyze and industry and attempt to come up with a new venture idea that would exploit the Blue Ocean.

The instructor should divide the class into four roughly equal groups. Each of the four groups will take one quadrant of the basic Blue Ocean approach. That is, one group will focus on elements that can be eliminated from the industry, another will focus on elements that can be reduced, another on elements that can be eliminated, and finally the fourth group will focus on those elements that can or should be enhanced.

The instructor may want to run this exercise with a variety of different industries sequentially and give student groups different Blue Ocean quadrants to work on each time. For starters, we suggest the following industries as targets for analysis:

1.   Higher education
2.   Public transportation
3.   On-campus food service
4.   Textbooks
5.   Online retail
6.   Cable television

Of course, you may want to choose your own industries, but these are some that students are likely to have strong opinions about.

Finally, the instructor should record the recommendations of each of the groups and then have a discussion with the entire class about how they might be combined to create a new, Blue Ocean, offering.

KEY TERMS

Blue Ocean Strategy: An approach to product/service innovation that seeks to carve out a new market space where no one is currently competing. The contrasting red ocean is red because of all the blood that is being spilled by competitors fighting for market share in an increasingly crowded ocean.

Controllable marketing elements: A market segmentation technique based on a venture's ability to control marketing techniques allowing access to that market.

Conjoint analysis: A market research technique that investigates which combination of your venture's offerings is favored by customers and to what extent.

Customer-facing employees: Employees who have direct contact with customers.

Disruptive innovation: A process by which a product or service takes root initially in simple applications at the bottom of a market and then relentlessly moves "up market," eventually displacing established competitors.

Focus groups: Groups of potential customers gathered for the express purpose of providing feedback about the venture's offerings in a structured setting.

Innovation: A term that refers to the changes that you make to your venture's products and services over time.

Innovator's dilemma: Companies oftentimes need to disrupt their own marketplace with new offerings that address unmet needs in a category that they aren't currently serving

Intercept interview: A technique for gathering customer feedback whereby the entrepreneur or someone employed by the entrepreneur literally intercepts potential customers in a shopping environment to get their feedback on the venture's offerings.

Market segmentation: The process of dividing a venture's total addressable market into meaningful submarkets, including a target market.

Market share: The proportion of a venture's TAM that it has captured and is presently serving.

North American Industry Classification System (NAICS): The standard used by federal statistical agencies in the United States to classify business establishments for the purpose of collecting, analyzing, and publishing statistical data related to the U.S. economy.

Overshot customers: Many firms pursue their high end customers and ignore those who need their products or services but cannot afford the higher prices and/or don't need rich feature sets—the overshot customers in the industry.

Psychographics: A technique for analyzing markets based on the psychological profile of customers.

Semi-structured interview: An interview technique that allows the interviewer to deviate from a script to elicit insights from customers designed to reveal unknown unknowns (unk unks).

Served addressable market: The customers that a venture is serving with its offerings.

Sociographics: A technique for analyzing markets based on the social profile of customers.

Speed to market: The need for modern ventures to focus on getting products into the market quickly because of intense global competition.

Standard industrial classification (SIC) code: A number used to specify what industry a particular company belongs to. The Standard Industrial Classification (SIC) code system was replaced by the North American Industry Classification System (NAICS) in 1997.

Target market: A target market is the set of customers that is most likely to purchase the venture's products or services

Test market: A market in which a venture attempts a limited rollout of a new product or modification of an existing product to gauge market reaction.

Total addressable market (TAM): All the potential customers in the world who might be interested in purchasing the venture's offerings.

Trade association: Organizations—usually nonprofit—designed to promote and conduct research on an industry.

Trade shows: Most industries have major national and/or international trade shows where industry competitors and service providers gather.

Unk unks: The unknown unknowns that can affect a venture.

ENDNOTES

[1] Copeland, M.V., "The IPad Changes Everything." *Fortune,* 161(4)(2011): 150–153.

[2] Eva K. Foedermayr, "Market Segmentation in Practice: Review of Empirical Studies, Methodological Assessment, and Agenda for Future Research," *Journal of Strategic Marketing,* 16(3) (July 2008): 223–265.

[3] Spence, M., and L.H. Essoussi, "SME Brand Building and Management: An Exploratory Study," *Journal of Marketing,* 44(7/8)(2010): 1037–1054.

[4] Powers, Thomas L., and Jay U. Sterling, "Segmenting Business to Business Markets: A Micro-Macro Linking Methodology," *Journal of Business & Industrial Marketing,* 23(3)(2008): 170–177.

[5] Lam, Michael D., "Psychographic Demonstration," *Pharmaceutical Executive* (January 2004): 78–82.

[6] Berner, R., "How Unilever Scored with Young Guys," *BusinessWeek,* 3934(2005): 39.

[7] Morton, Linda P., "Segmenting Publics: An Introduction." *Public Relations Quarterly* (Fall 1998): 33–34.

[8] Ottman, J.A., "Environmental Branding Blocks Competitors," *Marketing News,* 32(17)(1998): 8.

[9] Hsieh, T., *Delivering Happiness: A Path to Profits, Passion, and Purpose* (New York: Business Plus, 2010).

[10] Hsieh, T., "Zappos CEO on Going to Extremes for Customers," *Harvard Business Review,* 88(7/8) (2011): 41–45.

[11] Isaacson, W., *Steve Jobs* (New York: Simon & Schuster, 2011).

[12] Frost-Norton, T., "The Future of Mall Research: Current Trends Affecting the Future of Marketing Research in Malls," *Journal of Consumer Behaviour,* 4(4)(2005): 293–301.

[13] Mullins, J.W., "Discovering Unk-Unks," *MIT Sloan Management Review,* 48(4)(2005): 17–21.

[14] Loch, C.H., M.E. Solt, and E.M. Bailey, "Diagnosing Unforeseeable Uncertainty in a New Venture," *Journal of Product Innovation Management,* 25(1)(2008): 28–46.

[15] Torres, N.L., "Tricks of the Trade." *Entrepreneur,* 36(8)(2008): 78–80.

[16] Duening, T.N., *The Startup Experience: Experience Starting a Restaurant* (Colorado Springs, CO: Businesses2Learn, LLC, 2011).

[17] Markey, R., F. Reichheld, and A. Dullweber, "Closing the Customer Feedback Loop," *Harvard Business Review,* 87(12)(2009): 43–47.

[18] Wirtz, J., S.K. Tambyah, and A.S. Mattila, "Organizational Learning from Customer Feedback Received by Service Employees," *Journal of Service Management,* 21(3)(2010): 363–387.

[19] Forbes, D.T., and D.A. Kirsch, "The Study of Emerging Industries: Recognizing and Responding to Some Central Problems," *Journal of Business Venturing,* 26(5)(2011): 589–602.

[20] Verreyenne, M.L., and D. Meyer, "Small Business Strategy and the Industry Lifecycle," *Small Business Economics,* 35(4)(2010): 399–416.

[21] Baptista, R., and M. Karaoz, "Turbulence in Growing and Declining Industries," *Small Business Economics,* 36(3)(2011): 249–270.

[22] Ganco, Martin, and Rajshree Agarwal, "Performance Differentials Between Diversifying Entrants and Entrepreneurial Start-Ups: A Complexity Approach." *Academy of Management Review,* 34(2)(April 2009): 228–252.

[23] McKelvie, A., J.M. Haynie, and V. Gustavvson, "Unpacking the Uncertainty Construct: Implications for Entrepreneurial Action," *Journal of Business Venturing,* 26(3)(2011): 273–292.

[24] Cadbury, N., "When, Where, and How to Test Market," *Harvard Business Review,* 53(3)(1975): 96–105.

[25] Wang, J., "Speed to Market," *Entrepreneur,* 39(8)(2011): 90.

[26] Christensen, C., *The Innovator's Dilemma: When New Technologies Cause Great Firms to Fail* (Boston: Harvard Business School Press, 1997).

[27] Christensen, C., *How Disruptive Innovation Will Change the Way the World Learns.* (New York: McGraw-Hill, 2008).

[28] Kim, W.C., and R. Mauborgne, *Blue Ocean Strategy: How to Create Uncontested Market Space and Make the Competition Irrelevant* (Boston: Harvard Business School Press, 2005).

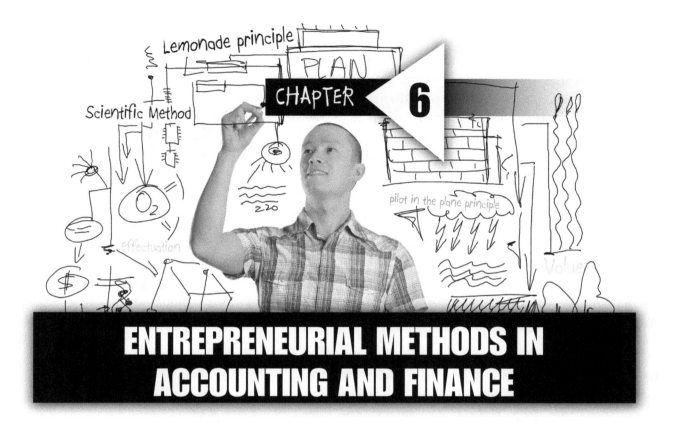

CHAPTER 6

ENTREPRENEURIAL METHODS IN ACCOUNTING AND FINANCE

Learning Objectives

After studying this chapter, students should be able to:

- **Perform** in the role of financial manager for a startup venture.

- **Develop** financial pro forma forecasts, including assumptions.

- **Project** cash flows and estimate capital needs over time.

- **Develop** a startup venture financial plan.

- **Analyze** financial statements using ratio analysis techniques.

- **Develop** credit and collections policies to ensure adequate cash flows.

INTRODUCTION

Every venture needs capital (money) to start, operate, maintain itself, and grow. Money, preferably in the form of cash, fuels the venture. To be successful, a venture must take in more cash than it needs to operate. That cash must be generated either via sales, or it must come from external investors and/or lenders. Businesses need money to purchase or lease equipment; build up inventory; and pay the utilities, employees' wages, taxes, and rent. Without cash, a business cannot survive. A well-funded venture can

be *unprofitable* for a while until it builds a customer base and moves toward profitability. However, without the *cash* needed to pay its creditors, employees, and others it cannot last very long at all.[1]

No venture, no matter how large or how small, is isolated from the need for sound financial management. Often, when firms get too large and lose track of important details of their day-to-day financial condition, they encounter problems that may take months or even years to fix—and some cannot be fixed at all. The bankruptcy of large financial firms such as Bear Stearns, Lehman Brothers, and AIG during the credit crisis of 2008 has placed a new emphasis on financial control and reporting. These firms had long histories, well-respected brands, and were, prior to their bankruptcies, worth billions of dollars. The fact that they went bankrupt should highlight the need to pay attention to the financial health of the venture at all times.

In this chapter, we define accounting and finance and describe the role of the accountant and the financial manager through launching, operating, and growing a new venture. Entrepreneurs don't need to be professional accountants or financial wizards, but they must know how accounting works and how to manage the financial affairs of the venture. Often, this includes working with others who are professional accountants or financial managers. Still, the entrepreneur does not want to outsource entirely these vital functions. We will examine accounting and finance in this chapter from the perspective of the "need-to-know" elements of the entrepreneurial method.

Next, we will explore the basic financial statements that are used both to estimate how the venture will perform in the future and to analyze how it actually does perform. There are four fundamental financial statements that all entrepreneurs need to understand and utilize to manage their ventures: sales forecast, income statement, cash flow statement, and balance sheet. The entrepreneur should be concerned with these statements not only in regard to how they reflect the operating history of the venture, but also as forward-looking or **pro forma financial forecasts** of where the venture is headed. In this chapter, we will focus on the forecasting application of these financial statements.

We will also explore in this chapter how to analyze financial statements to determine whether a venture is achieving its goals and to provide insight into what is working and what is not working. Many expert entrepreneurs develop deep insights into how their venture is performing from a financial perspective. This involves analyzing performance over time and comparing one period to another, and also via comparing the venture's financial performance with other firms in the industry. Several key ratios are often used to ensure that such comparisons are useful in evaluating the venture's actual performance.

Finally, we review some techniques for managing a venture's cash and finances, including accounts receivable, inventory, credit and collections policies, and several other items. Many novice entrepreneurs learn too late that setting up appropriate cash management policies at venture launch can help preserve precious cash and limit decision-making problems. Too often new ventures are overly eager to begin to perform work and book revenue without putting enough thought into how they will collect actual cash payments. It seems reasonable to expect, in theory, that clients will pay their bills on time, but in reality entrepreneurs often find out after much pain that that is not always the case. In this chapter, we stress the need for the young venture to have as many professional-level cash management policies, procedures, and contract forms in place prior to launch.

Let's begin the chapter by examining the function of accounting and how it influences venture performance.

ACCOUNTING FOR ENTREPRENEURS

Busy entrepreneurs and business people sometimes deride accounting as being little more than "bean counting." However, expert entrepreneurs will attest that a basic understanding of accounting principles is an essential entrepreneurial tool.[2] In a sense, accounting is the language of business. Anyone who aspires to launch and operate a technology venture must, to some degree, speak that language. Businesses run on their numbers, and accounting plays an important role in recording and validating the numbers that drive business decisions. The American Accounting Association defines **accounting** as "the process of identifying, measuring, and communicating economic information to permit informed judgments and decisions by users of information."[3] The Mini-Case below highlights a situation where an entrepreneur did not pay attention to his accounting and suffered the consequences:

MINI-CASE

A Banker's Advice on Financial Records

If your goal is to qualify for a bank or SBA loan in the future, you will need a good financial management system. Bank loan officer Kate Lister recalled the time she was handed a credit file on a shoe store chain and asked to review the owner's latest loan request. On the surface, it looked like an entrepreneurial success story. Based on the performance of his first shoe store, the bank had loaned the owner the money he requested to expand.

Lister quickly realized, however, that the new loan request wasn't going to be easy because the shoe store owner hadn't "cleaned up" his line of credit. A line of credit is intended to fund a temporary mismatch of cash coming in and cash going out—but if it maxes out and stays that way, there's a problem. The owner was apparently unaware of the problem because he didn't keep good financial records.

The owner couldn't clean up his line of credit, it turned out, because he'd used the money to fund new stores, not for smoothing cash-flow troughs as he should have. Technically, this put him in breach of his loan agreement. As a result, the bank downgraded his credit, put him on a watch list, and forced him to track his performance on a weekly basis. If he didn't close the unprofitable stores and get his financial controls in order, the bank would call the loan.

The lesson here is that the banker is the last person you want to uncover a flaw in your business operations. Regular and effective financial reports as well as proper checks and balances would have prevented this entrepreneur from facing impending doom. An experienced business accountant would have spotted the trouble, too.

Source: Adapted from Lister, K., "What the Banker Found," *Entrepreneur* (October 2010).

Over the years, accounting has become increasingly standardized, but there are always new and unexpected transaction types that must be understood in accounting terms. It's important for entrepreneurs to realize that accounting, although based on rules, is an evolving discipline. In general, accounting practitioners adhere to what is known as **generally accepted accounting principles (GAAP).** The Financial Accounting Standards Board (FASB) develops the principles in GAAP. The FASB consists of seven board members who issue statements and guidelines regarding accounting practices. As new financial reporting and measurement systems arise, FASB board members consider how business transactions should be recorded.

Accounting can be divided into two categories: financial accounting and managerial accounting. These types of accounting differ primarily by virtue of the people they are designed to serve. **Financial accounting** is intended primarily for use by external decision makers such as investors, creditors, and the Internal Revenue Service. **Managerial accounting** is mainly used by internal decision makers such as company managers. In this chapter, we will be concerned primarily with financial accounting.

Accounting information is useful to a venture's managers, investors, creditors, advisors, and others. Current investors use it to review the performance of the company in which they have interest and to determine whether to maintain, increase, or liquidate their investment.[4] Potential investors use accounting information to help them make investment decisions. Creditors use financial information to evaluate credit applications and to make decisions about candidates for loans. In most cases, when making a loan decision, lenders will look at a firm's historical financial records (usually, at least three years). Most lenders focus on **cash flow** when making a loan decision to ensure that the firm has sufficient **liquidity** to make principal and interest payments.[5]

The venture's top officers are the most frequent users of its accounting information. They must have reliable information to make decisions about allocating resources, cutting expenses, and investing in growth. Entrepreneurs also use accounting information to assess the consequences of alternative business strategies. In addition, accounting information can be used to compare actual financial results with expectations.[6]

The Accounting Cycle

A primary purpose of accounting is to communicate the results of business transactions. The **accounting cycle** is a sequence of six steps used to keep track of what has happened in the business and to report the financial effect of those events. The steps in the accounting cycle are depicted in Exhibit 6.1.

The accountant first analyzes business transactions to determine which should be recorded and at what amount. Typically, accountants record only transactions that can be measured and verified with some degree of precision. For example, the purchase of a truck for making deliveries to customers can accurately be measured and easily be verified via a document called a "title." However, an event like the resignation of a key employee, also a business transaction, would not be recorded. Although such an event may represent an economic loss to a company, it is difficult to determine accurately what the amount of the loss would be.

Accounting transactions are recorded chronologically in a **journal**. A journal may be either a book (in a manual accounting system) or an electronic file (in a computerized accounting system). Each entry contains the date of the transaction, its description, and debit and credit columns. Transactions are recorded in the firm's general journal or in specialized journals. A general journal is a book or file in which transactions are recorded in the order they occur. As businesses expand, they may adopt specialized journals to record particular types of business transactions (for example, credit sales or capital expenditures).

EXHIBIT 6.1   The Accounting Cycle

Businesses need to know the balances of various financial statement elements (assets, liabilities, owners' equity, revenues, and expenses) at any point in time. **Accounts** are used to summarize all transactions that affect a particular financial statement component. A business maintains separate accounts for each of its assets, liabilities, equities, revenues, and expenses. All transactions affecting an account are posted (recorded) from the general journal or specialized journals to the account. All the accounts of a business are summarized in the **general ledger**.

The final steps of the accounting process involve preparing financial statements. **Financial statements** present a company's financial position, results of operations, and flow of cash during a particular period of time. The financial statements that are prepared via the accounting process include the income statement, balance sheet, and statement of cash flows. They can be prepared for any time interval (e.g., daily, weekly, monthly), but they are *always* prepared annually according to the venture's fiscal year. Investors, creditors, company managers, and others interested in a firm's financial position all rely heavily on financial statements. In preparing these statements, accountants check the balance sheet to determine whether their entries balance. If not, adjustments are made to how the numbers have been entered until a balance is achieved and the books can be closed.

The basic **accounting equation** indicates a company's financial position at any point in time. On its framework rests the entire accounting process. According to the accounting equation, a company's assets equal its liabilities plus owners' equity, thus:

$$Assets = Liabilities + Owner's\ Equity$$

This is easy enough to understand if you realize that all of the assets of a venture are owned either by the owners themselves, by creditors who have claims on the assets, or some combination of the two. Later, you will be introduced to the concept of the venture's debt-to-equity ratio. This is simply an indicator of how much debt the venture is carrying compared to the equity position of the owners. A debt to equity ratio of 1.0, for example, would indicate the venture has equal parts debt and equity ownership of the venture. Depending on the type of venture, this ratio will vary. It's important to know the standard for your industry and how your venture matches up to that standard.

Any recorded business transaction can be analyzed in terms of its effect on the accounting equation. Also, business transactions must be recorded to maintain the equality of this equation. This equality is reflected in the balance sheet, one of the financial statements a firm is required to prepare. These are some terms and concepts that businesses use to keep records:

- **Assets** are anything of value owned by the business and used in conducting its operations. Examples include cash, investments, inventory, accounts receivable, and furniture and fixtures.

- **Liabilities** are debts owed by the business to its creditors, including obligations to perform services in the future. Liabilities include accounts payable and notes payable (e.g., when a firm uses credit to purchase machinery), wages payable to employees, and taxes payable.

- **Owners' equity** represents the claims of the owners against the firm's assets.

- **Revenues** are inflows of assets resulting from the ongoing operation of a business. Businesses generate revenues by sales of goods and services, interest earned on investments, rents, royalties, and dividends.

- **Expenses** are costs incurred to produce revenues. Expenses include the costs of goods sold (the goods or services that the firm used to generate revenues), salaries, utilities, taxes, marketing, and interest payments. Revenues and expenses are components of owners' equity. Revenues result in an increase, while expenses result in a decrease in owners' equity. Net income, or the bottom line, is the excess of revenues over expenses. Investors, creditors, and company managers closely watch net income, a chief barometer of business performance.

Working with Accountants

Most entrepreneurs don't spend their time actually doing the venture's accounting. Rather, they generally hire an experienced certified public accountant (CPA) to manage the venture's accounting. Most cities have multiple CPA firms that work with small to medium-sized companies and who will tailor their pricing and billing to match the budgets of these smaller ventures.

Entrepreneurs should search for and select a CPA with experience in their industry. The rules that govern accounting are constantly changing, and some industries experience more rapid changes than others. A good CPA will know the rules that apply within a particular industry and will use them aggressively, yet ethically, to the best advantage of the venture. A good way to find an accountant qualified to work with a particular company in a particular industry is to ask others for referrals. The best accountants usually acquire most of their new clients via referrals, which is an endorsement of their capabilities and service quality.

Accountants serve to record and report the financial transactions of the venture. They are responsible for assuring that the venture conforms to the accounting rules of its industry. The finance function, by way of contrast, uses accounting statements to determine whether the venture has adequate capital, whether the capital it has is being used efficiently, and whether additional capital needs to be obtained. This is the role of the financial manager.

Alternatively, for those entrepreneurs who do not want to outsource their accounting to an external company, there are sophisticated software tools that help them manage their finances. These tools can, at least in the early stages of the venture, provide substantial support in establishing accounts and the venture's journals and general ledger.[7]

Regardless of the method used to set up and manage a venture's accounts, the research is very clear that entrepreneurs who develop financial controls into the venture early on are more likely to succeed than those who do not.[8]

FINANCE FOR ENTREPRENEURS

Because a venture must have a sufficient supply of cash to operate, the area of cash management requires special attention. Entrepreneurs must determine the venture's cash needs for both the short and long term, and then find sources to provide the necessary cash. Cash management within the firm is the entrepreneur's responsibility.

© Yuri Arcurs, 2012. Used under license from Shutterstock, Inc.

As a discipline within a business school, **finance** is the study of how to manage money—either from a personal perspective or from a business perspective. At the personal level, finance is concerned with household wealth management, including things like savings accounts, mortgages, mutual fund investments, and others. Within a business, finance is the functional area charged with locating and acquiring capital for the business, managing capital in a disciplined manner, and determining the best uses of capital given the strategies and goals of the venture. There are vast differences between personal finance and business finance. And there are substantial differences between corporate finance and entrepreneurial finance. The latter, of course, will be our primary concern in this chapter.

The **financial manager** is the individual responsible for the venture's finance function. It is common for large firms to use the title of chief financial officer (CFO) to refer to the person in charge of a firm's financial affairs. Many entrepreneurial ventures do not formally appoint a financial manager, but the financial management tasks must still be performed. In entrepreneurial ventures, one of the managers or owners often will handle these tasks. The tasks assigned to the person responsible for financial management include:

- Business plan development
- Risk management and insurance
- Benefits and compensation
- Equipment leasing and financing
- Facility and real estate needs analysis
- Budget development
- Tax planning
- Expansion planning
- Cash flow management
- Owner compensation planning
- Commercial real estate financing and planning
- Financial system design and implementation
- Business sale preparation

Another option available to early stage ventures that cannot afford a full-time CFO is to work with a firm that provides **virtual CFO** services.[9] These firms work with early-stage ventures in a manner similar to accounting firms. A virtual CFO firm will assign one of its financial experts to work with the client venture. In turn, the client is billed for services normally at an hourly or monthly rate. Often, the venture will list the individual performing virtual CFO duties as the "acting CFO" in its business plan and investor documents, and/or it may list the retained firm in those documents.

Entrepreneurial finance differs from corporate finance in several important ways. The first and most obvious difference is that of scale. Corporate finance is concerned with the management of large amounts of capital. It includes such activities as investing the firm's capital to ensure that the business is earning optimum returns and that its capital is not sitting idly in a non-interest-bearing savings account. The second major difference is the relative time spent on activities associated with financial management. The corporate financial manager spends considerable time thinking about how to invest the company's money and about where and how to acquire capital for large projects and investments. The entrepreneurial financial manager spends far more time acquiring capital and relatively little time investing.[10]

To be effective, the financial manager in the entrepreneurial venture should develop and follow a financial plan.[11] A sound financial plan will minimally require the following tasks to be performed:

- Estimate month-by-month flow of funds into the venture.

- Estimate month-by-month flow of funds out of the venture.

- Compare monthly inflows to monthly outflows.

- If excess funds exist, plan how to use these funds for growth or investing

- If funds are short, adjust inflows or outflows and/or look for other sources of funding

- If other funding sources are needed, analyze alternatives to find the most efficient source

- Establish a system routinely to monitor and evaluate the results of this process

Over time, a venture's financial plan can become very complex, with investors, creditors, suppliers, and customers all adding or subtracting cash. These inflows and outflows of cash must be tracked diligently. The monthly expenses that a business incurs to operate, regardless of where the funds come from, are commonly referred to as the venture's **burn rate**. Investors and lenders will all examine a venture's burn rate and its cash on hand to determine how long it can operate. For example, if a venture's burn rate is $30,000/month and it has $300,000 in the bank, it can operate for another ten months before more cash will be required.

In addition to the monthly burn of cash, the future growth strategies and cash requirements of the venture have to be considered. The venture's financial manager must work with the financial statements produced by the firm's accountant to monitor the burn rate. The financial manager must also work with the executive team to understand the strategic objectives of the venture and the amount of capital that will be required to achieve those objectives in the future.

Often, entrepreneurial ventures need to raise cash from outside sources to achieve sufficient sales to be able to operate without external capital. Raising capital can be considerably more challenging for some types of ventures than for others. For example, bio-pharmaceutical and medical device companies may require large injections of capital before they reach cash flow breakeven.[12] This unique challenge requires diligence and persistence on the part of the entrepreneur.[13] It also requires developing relationships with investors and/or lenders *before* capital is required. Smart entrepreneurs cultivate potential investors in advance of their actual capital requirements. That is, the entrepreneur should develop key relationships with investors and lenders in advance so that they can develop an understanding of the business and a sense of trust for the management team.[14] This will provide a slight edge in the fundraising process over first-impression meetings when capital is critical to carry on operations.

Financial Forecasting

A venture's cash needs will change over time, and having sufficient capital for continued operations can become an issue even for long-established ventures. To avoid such problems, a venture must plan its cash flow. A detailed financial plan helps ensure the long-run success of the venture. Entrepreneurs are usually required to estimate how the venture will perform financially in the future. This is done through four basic financial statements:

1.   The Sales Forecast
2.   The Income Statement
3.   The Cash Flow Statement
4.   The Balance Sheet

These basic financial statements (often referred to as "pro forma financial statements") are normally required as part of a complete business plan.[15] Investors and lenders will almost always require that entrepreneurs provide financial projections for three years or more into the future.[16] Note that the process of estimating future financial performance is different from what accountants do. Accountants record actual performance and allocate the cash flow from transactions to the various financial statements. The process of estimating future cash flows is usually not a job done by the venture's accounting firm. Rather, it is the job of the financial manager to estimate sales, expenses, cash needs for growth, and *future* performance. Later, we'll examine how financial managers use the actual financial statements prepared by accountants to analyze *past* performance. Here, we examine the four statements in the context of estimating how the venture will perform in the future. We begin with the sales forecast.

THE SALES FORECAST: The finance function in a business is responsible for acquiring the funds the business needs to operate and succeed. Sound financial management involves determining how much money is needed for various time periods and the most appropriate sources of funds. The most obvious source of funds for a venture is the revenue generated by the business through sales of its products and services. However, as stated earlier, sometimes a venture cannot generate adequate cash inflows from sales to operate and grow. This is especially true of startup ventures, and may also occur during the venture's high-growth phase. To determine the amount of external financing needed, financial managers estimate the revenues the venture can expect on a month-to-month basis, and subtract all of the expected costs.

The primary tool for estimating a venture's cash inflows from selling activities is the **sales forecast**. The sales forecast is the foundation of the various financial statements that entrepreneurs use to for their venture's pro forma financial projections into the future because the numbers generated in the sales forecast flow into the other financial forecast statements. A sales forecast consists of the following basic components:

*   Units of sale
*   Pricing for each of the various units

- Volume of sales for each unit in each accounting period
- Variance in sales volume between accounting periods due to exigencies such as:
  - Market penetration rates (referred to as **ramp rate**)
  - Seasonality (variations in sales patterns based on seasons)
  - Marketing investments (variations in sales due to marketing investments)
- Total (or "gross") sales (this line will be carried to the top line of the income statement (revenue) without change

Exhibit 6.2 provides a basic template for a sales forecast. Many entrepreneurs use Microsoft Excel to generate these statements from scratch, but there are commercially available software packages as well as free shareware and Excel templates available on the Internet. Notice the template is divided into monthly accounting periods, which is standard. Notice also that the template contains the basic components listed above. Each cell of the template is formula driven, other than those that establish price and ramp rate. These must be based on reasonable assumptions.

All **assumptions** used to develop the pro forma financial statements should be listed on a separate document. Your assumptions page should include justification or rationale for every number that you enter that is not a direct result of a formula in the spreadsheet, and it should include justification or rationale for each formula. Investors and other stakeholders want to know how you derived your fundamental numbers and formulas.

The formula-driven nature of the sales forecast enables the entrepreneur to run through various "what if?" scenarios to see the effects on gross sales of changes in assumptions about price, ramp rate, or both. This enables you to conduct what is referred to as **sensitivity analysis**. A sensitivity analysis targets several key variables and examines how different values for these key variables affect the viability of the venture. In other words, this type of analysis enables the entrepreneur to determine the sensitivity of the venture's business model to variations in these key variables.

The entrepreneur must first determine the venture's basic units of sale. The price of each of these various units is recorded as an assumption in the sales forecast. The ramp rate of sales per item is also recorded as an assumption for each unit of sale and for each accounting period. That is, the ramp rate may change from period to period as market penetration proceeds and/or as seasonal factors take effect. Entrepreneurs must think hard about how slowly or quickly their offerings will be adopted by the market. The ramp rate should be justifiable—that is, it should be based on research rather than guesswork.[17] Anyone interested in looking at the venture's financial projections will want to know why the assumed ramp rate was used.

In addition, to pondering how many units of each item the venture will sell, the entrepreneur must think hard about how long it will take to sell each new unit. The length of time required to obtain a new sale is referred to as the **sales cycle**. The sales cycle will vary from industry to industry. For example, getting physicians to adopt a new medical instrument or pharmaceutical will likely take longer than getting consumers to purchase a new computer game. Experienced entrepreneurs know that it is far easier and less expensive to sell more products to existing customers than it is to acquire new ones. Selling more to existing customers creates **recurring revenue**. Recurring revenue is even better if the customer is set up to purchase continuously and automatically. For example, consider your mobile phone service provider. Essentially, the provider is selling you service every month. And, if you are like many customers, it automatically debits your credit card or checking account to get its payment.

EXHIBIT 6.2 The Sales Forecast

Year 1

Item	Month 1	Month 2	Month 3	Month 4	Month 5	Month 6	Month 7	Month 8	Month 9	Month 10	Month 11	Month 12	Total	%
Product A Unit Sales	50	50	101	201	402	804	1,206	1,809	2,714	4,070	6,105	9,158	26,670	
Product A Revenue	$500	$503	$1,005	$2,010	$4,020	$8,040	$12,060	$18,090	$27,135	$40,703	$61,054	$91,581	$266,699	65.0%
Product B Unit Sales	0	0	0	100	175	245	294	323	356	391	430	473	2,788	
Product B Revenue	$0	$0	$0	$2,995	$5,241	$7,338	$8,805	$9,686	$10,654	$11,720	$12,892	$14,181	$83,512	20.4%
Product C Unit Sales	0	0	0	0	0	0	0	1000	1000	1000	1000	1000	5,000	
Product C Revenue	$0	$0	$0	$0	$0	$0	$0	$12,000	$12,000	$12,000	$12,000	$12,000	$60,000	14.6%
Product A Ramp Rate	0.000%	0.500%	100.000%	100.000%	100.000%	100.000%	50.000%	50.000%	50.000%	50.000%	50.000%	50.000%		
Product B Ramp Rate	0.000%	0.000%	0.000%	0.000%	75.000%	50.000%	10.000%	10.000%	10.000%	10.000%	10.000%	10.000%		
Product C Ramp Rate	0.000%	0.000%	0.000%	0.000%	75.000%	40.000%	20.000%	10.000%	10.000%	10.000%	10.000%	10.000%		
Product A Price	$10.00	$10.00	$10.00	$10.00	$10.00	$10.00	$10.00	$10.00	$10.00	$10.00	$10.00	$10.00		
Product B Price	$29.95	$29.95	$29.95	$29.95	$29.95	$29.95	$29.95	$29.95	$29.95	$29.95	$29.95	$29.95		
Product C Price	$12.00	$12.00	$12.00	$12.00	$12.00	$12.00	$12.00	$12.00	$12.00	$12.00	$12.00	$12.00		
GROSS SALES	$500	$503	$1,005	$5,005	$9,261	$15,378	$20,865	$39,776	$49,789	$64,422	$85,946	$117,762	$410,212	100.0%

Often entrepreneurs will develop multiple sales forecasts, reflecting worst case, base case, and best case scenarios. The projections developed in the sales forecast flow into the other financial statements. The gross sales figures on the bottom line of the sales forecast flow through to the income statement as the top line or gross revenue. The Bullet Breakout box has some additional suggestions for crafting a sales forecast.

► BULLET BREAKOUT ◄

Tips for Developing a Sales Forecast

- **Develop a unit sales projection.** Start by forecasting unit sales per month. Not all businesses sell by units, but most do, and it's easier to forecast by breaking things down into their component parts.

- **Use past data if you have it.** Whenever you have past sales data, your best forecasting aid is the most recent past.

- **Use factors for a new product.** Having a new product is no excuse for not having a sales forecast. Nobody who plans a new product knows the future—you simply make educated guesses. Break it down by finding important decision factors or components of sales. If you have a completely new product with no history, find an existing product to use as a guide. For example, if you have the next great computer game, base your forecast on sales of a similar computer game.

- **Break the purchase down into factors.** For example, you can forecast sales in a restaurant by looking at a reasonable number of tables occupied at different hours of the day and then multiplying the percent of tables occupied by the average estimated revenue per table.

- **Be sure to project prices.** The next step is prices. You've projected unit sales monthly for 12 months and then annually, so you must also project your prices.

Source: Adapted from Tim Berry, "Creating a Sales Forecast," *Entrepreneur.com*, accessed on February 17, 2012.

THE INCOME STATEMENT: Operating costs (usually referred to as "expenses") for a venture are projected or recorded on what is referred to as the **income statement.** The income statement reports the gross sales of the venture as *revenue* on its top line. All of the expenses associated with operating the venture are recorded and subtracted from revenue in each accounting period (monthly and annually) to generate bottom line profits or losses.

Costs associated with operating a venture can be divided into categories of variable and fixed. **Variable costs** are those that vary directly with production and output. For example, a venture that makes electric automobiles will need to increase production as demand for its products increases. Increasing production will require that the firm purchase additional raw materials, energy to run the plant, and other items whose costs will vary directly with the increased production. In the language of accounting, variable costs are listed on the venture's income statement as "Cost of Goods Sold."

Fixed costs, by definition, do not vary directly with production. For example, the car manufacturer will use the same factory and equipment to produce more or less cars over a period of time. It will also use the same labor and other items that are referred to in the venture's income statement as **General and Administrative (G&A) expenses**. Sometimes, these costs are also referred to as **overhead**. Note that it's possible the venture will need to hire more people and/ or build new plants to handle its increased output. These costs are still "fixed" in that they don't vary directly with the increased output. Once the factory is built, for example, its cost remains fixed on the venture's income statement across accounting periods.

A template for a basic income statement (also often referred to as the "profit and loss statement" or, simply, "P&L") is provided in Exhibit 6.3.

The result of subtracting G&A expenses from gross profit is a line item typically entered as **EBIT** or **EBITDA**. These abbreviations stand for "earnings before interest and taxes" and "earnings before interest, taxes, depreciation, and amortization." Depreciation is a non-cash expense that accounts for wear and tear on the venture's capital assets (e.g., machinery, real estate). Amortization is the interest paid on loans. Depreciation and amortization are considered business expenses and can be subtracted from a venture's revenue.

The amount of money that is left after all expenses are subtracted from revenue is the venture's net income. Net income represents the venture's taxable income. The amount that remains after taxes is the venture's profit. This is what the venture's officers can now decide to reinvest into the venture as retained earnings or distribute to shareholders as dividends.

THE CASH FLOW STATEMENT: A very important financial statement to entrepreneurs is the **cash flow statement**. The cash flow statement shows the flow of cash into and out of a business during a period of time. You may have heard the expression that, to the entrepreneur, "cash is king." What that means is cash is required to pay bills and to invest in venture growth. This statement also highlights the difference between cash and profits.

Profits can be shown on an income statement without the venture having received any cash at all. For example, according to the rules of accounting, a venture can record that a sale has occurred and book revenue on the income statement even though no cash has been transferred. This would be common for credit transactions, where a sale is made to a customer who promises to pay at some future date. Until that future date arrives, the venture's income statement will indicate revenue and profit on the transaction, even though no cash has been received. That is why it is vital for the entrepreneur to monitor the actual cash position of the venture. Only cash can be used to pay bills.

The cash flow statement monitors the inflow and outflow of cash from the venture's operating, investing, and financing activities. Cash flow from **operating activities** measures the cash results of the firm's primary revenue-generating activities. **Investing activities** include buying fixed assets, buying stock in other companies, and selling stock held as an investment in another company. **Financing activities** include issuing new stock, paying dividends to shareholders, borrowing money from banks, and repaying amounts borrowed. The statement of cash flows also shows the net change in cash for the period. Exhibit 6.4 is a template for a basic cash flow statement.

As a summary of the effects on cash of all the firm's operating, financing, and investing activities, the statement of cash flows allows entrepreneurs to see the results of past decisions. The statement may, for example, indicate a great enough cash flow to allow the firm to finance projected

EXHIBIT 6.3 The Income Statement

													Year 1		
Revenue	Month 1	Month 2	Month 3	Month 4	Month 5	Month 6	Month 7	Month 8	Month 9	Month 10	Month 11	Month 12			
Total Revenue	$500	$503	$1,005	$5,005	$9,261	$15,378	$20,865	$39,776	$49,789	$64,422	$85,946	$117,762	$410,212		
COGS															
Raw Materials	$200	$201	$402	$2,002	$3,705	$6,151	$8,346	$15,910	$19,916	$25,769	$34,378	$47,105	$164,085	95.20%	
Shipping	$75	$10	$20	$100	$185	$308	$417	$796	$996	$1,288	$1,719	$2,355	$8,269	4.80%	
Total COGS	$275	$211	$422	$2,102	$3,890	$6,459	$8,763	$16,706	$20,912	$27,057	$36,097	$49,460	$172,354	100.00%	
GROSS PROFIT	$225	$291	$583	$2,903	$5,372	$8,919	$12,102	$23,070	$28,878	$37,365	$49,848	$68,302	$237,858		
%	45.00%	58.00%	58.00%	58.00%	58.00%	58.00%	58.00%	58.00%	58.00%	58.00%	58.00%	58.00%			
G&A															
CEO	$3,500	$3,500	$3,500	$3,500	$3,500	$3,500	$3,500	$3,500	$3,500	$3,500	$3,500	$3,500	$42,000	25.74%	
Sales Salary	$2,000	$2,000	$2,000	$2,000	$2,000	$2,000	$2,000	$2,000	$2,000	$2,000	$2,000	$2,000	$24,000	14.71%	
Burden	$1,045	$1,045	$1,045	$1,045	$1,045	$1,045	$1,045	$1,045	$1,045	$1,045	$1,045	$1,045	$12,540	7.69%	
G&A Allocated Rent	$2,500	$2,500	$2,500	$2,500	$2,500	$2,500	$2,500	$2,500	$2,500	$2,500	$2,500	$2,500	$30,000	18.39%	
Travel	$2,500	$2,500	$2,500	$2,500	$2,500	$2,500	$2,500	$2,500	$2,500	$2,500	$2,500	$2,500	$30,000	18.39%	
Insurance	$400	$400	$400	$400	$400	$400	$400	$400	$400	$400	$400	$400	$4,800	2.94%	
Professional Services	$300	$300	$300	$300	$300	$300	$300	$300	$300	$300	$300	$300	$3,600	2.21%	
Telephones	$500	$500	$500	$500	$500	$500	$500	$500	$500	$500	$500	$500	$6,000	3.68%	
Office Supplies	$500	$500	$500	$500	$500	$500	$500	$500	$500	$500	$500	$500	$6,000	3.68%	
Office Equipment	$300	$300	$300	$300	$300	$300	$300	$300	$300	$300	$300	$300	$3,600	2.21%	
Postage/Courier	$50	$50	$50	$50	$50	$50	$50	$50	$50	$50	$50	$50	$600	0.37%	
Total	$13,595	$13,595	$13,595	$13,595	$13,595	$13,595	$13,595	$13,595	$13,595	$13,595	$13,595	$13,595	$163,140	100.00%	
EBITDA	($13,370)	($13,304)	($13,012)	($10,692)	($8,223)	($4,676)	($1,493)	$9,475	$15,283	$23,770	$36,253	$54,707	$74,718		
Depreciation	$0	$0	$0	$0	$0	$0	$0	$0	$0	$0	$0	$0	$0		
Interest	$0	$0	$0	$0	$0	$0	$0	$0	$0	$0	$0	$0	$0		
Taxes	$0	$0	$0	$0	$0	$0	$0	$2,842	$4,585	$7,131	$10,876	$16,412	$41,846		
NET INCOME	($13,370)	($13,304)	($13,012)	($10,692)	($8,223)	($4,676)	($1,493)	$6,632	$10,698	$16,639	$25,377	$38,295	$32,871		

EXHIBIT 6.4 The Cash Flow Statement

		Year 1										
	Month 1	Month 2	Month 3	Month 4	Month 5	Month 6	Month 7	Month 8	Month 9	Month 10	Month 11	Month 12
Cash Flow from Operations												
Income from Operations	($13,370)	($13,304)	($13,012)	($10,692)	($8,223)	($4,676)	($1,493)	$6,632	$10,698	$16,639	$25,377	$38,295
Add Depreciation	$0	$0	$0	$0	$0	$0	$0	$0	$0	$0	$0	$0
Net Cash from Operations	($13,370)	($13,304)	($13,012)	($10,692)	($8,223)	($4,676)	($1,493)	$6,632	$10,698	$16,639	$25,377	$38,295
Cash Flow from Investing												
(Increase) Decrease Machinery	$0	$0	$0	$0	$0	$0	$0	$0	$0	$0	$0	$0
Net Cash from Investing	$0	$0	$0	$0	$0	$0	$0	$0	$0	$0	$0	$0
Cash Flow from Financing												
(Decrease)Increase LTD	$0	$0	$0	$0	$0	$0	$0	$0	$0	$0	$0	$0
(Decrease)Increase LTD	$0	$0	$0	$0	$0	$0	$0	$0	$0	$0	$0	$0
(Redemption) Issuance Common Stock	$100,000											
Net Cash from Financing	$100,000	$0	$0	$0	$0	$0	$0	$0	$0	$0	$0	$0
Net Increase (Decrease) in Cash	$86,630	($13,304)	($13,012)	($10,692)	($8,223)	($4,676)	($1,493)	$6,632	$10,698	$16,639	$25,377	$38,295
Beginning Cash	$0	$86,630	$73,326	$60,314	$49,622	$41,399	$36,723	$35,230	$41,862	$52,560	$69,199	$94,577
Ending Cash	$86,630	$73,326	$60,314	$49,622	$41,399	$36,723	$35,230	$41,862	$52,560	$69,199	$94,577	$132,871

needs itself rather than borrow funds from a bank. Or management can examine the statement to determine why the firm has a cash shortage, if that is the case. Investors and creditors can use the statement of cash flows to assess the firm's abilities to generate future cash flows, to pay dividends, and to pay its debts when due, as well as its potential need to borrow funds.

THE BALANCE SHEET: The **balance sheet** lists everything a company owns and everything it owes at a specific moment in time. It shows where all of the venture's money has come from (sources of capital) and what it has been used for. In the end, a balance sheet must balance because all of the sources of money to the venture must equal the uses of that money. The previous financial statements discussed earlier all represent how the venture performs over time.

© Ingvar Bjork, 2012. Used under license from Shutterstock, Inc.

The balance sheet, by way of contrast, is a "snapshot" of the financial health of the venture at a particular moment. Balance sheets normally are prepared at the end of each month and at the end of each fiscal year.

The sources of money for a venture include owners and creditors. Creditors have loaned money to the venture and have thus created liabilities for it. That is, the venture is liable for paying back the money it has borrowed, plus interest. Owners have invested their own money into the venture, or they have allowed the venture's earnings to be retained rather than drawing them out in the form of dividend payments. As equity is understood, the venture "owes" its owners their pro rata share of the accumulated equity (invested capital plus retained earnings).

A template for a balance sheet is provided in Exhibit 6.5. As depicted, the balance sheet has two sides: one lists all of the venture's assets (what it owns) and the other lists its liabilities and equity (what it owes). The basic equation that represents the balance sheet is:

$$Assets = Liabilities + Equity$$

The assets side of the balance sheet represents how the venture has used its capital. The other side represents where the capital came from. If everything has been accounted for properly, the two sides will be equal and are said to "balance."

In Exhibit 6.5 both assets and liabilities are listed in decreasing order of liquidity. **Liquidity** refers to the readiness with which an asset can be converted to cash, or to the urgency with which a liability requires cash. On the asset side, the most liquid asset, of course, is the cash the venture holds in its bank accounts. Accounts receivable is listed next. This is the amount of money that is due to the venture from sales to customers—sales that have been made on credit. Additional items on the asset side include inventory and fixed assets. These are usually the least liquid of a venture's various assets.

Liabilities usually begin with accounts payable. These are listed first because they represent the vendors that provide the venture with supplies and materials needed to operate and produce. If these bills go unpaid, the venture may be unable to meet customer demand. Second on the list of

EXHIBIT 6.5 The Balance Sheet

YEAR 1	
Assets	
Cash	$132,871
Equipment	$0
Less Depreciation	$0
Total Equipment	$0
Total Assets	**$132,871**
Liabilities	
Notes Payable	$0
Less Principal Paid	$0
Equity	
Owner's Equity	$100,000
Retained Earnings	$32,871
Total Liabilities + Equity	**$132,871**
Correction	$0

liabilities is what is referred to as "accruals." **Accruals** are simply expenses associated with transactions that are not entirely complete at the close of an accounting period. For example, suppose a monthly accounting period ends on a Wednesday, but a venture pays its employees on Friday. The accrued salaries for those employees must appear on the end-of-month balance sheet, which is developed on Wednesday. If those accrued wages were not recorded in the end of month balance sheet, the actual liabilities of the venture would be misstated. Current liabilities are defined as those requiring payment within one year, and long-term debt consists of the venture's obligations to lenders.

The equity in the venture consists of two items: that which has been directly purchased by investors as common stock and that which represents the retained earnings. Money retained by the venture is considered to be a contribution by the owners. That is, the owners decide whether to take earnings out of the venture in dividend payments, or they leave it in the venture as retained earnings to fuel future growth.

FINANCIAL STATEMENT ANALYSIS

Financial statement analysis compares (or finds relationships in) accounting information to make the data more useful or practical. For example, knowing that a company's net income was $50,000 is somewhat useful. Knowing also that the net income for the previous year was $100,000 is more useful. Knowing the amounts of the company's assets and sales is better yet. To this end, several types of financial statement analysis have been developed. Here, we discuss two of the primary techniques entrepreneurial financial managers use to analyze the venture's financial statements: breakeven analysis and ratio analysis.

Breakeven analysis is normally done for two different variables: profit and cash. Profit breakeven occurs when the venture sells enough of its goods and services to cover its operating costs. Cash breakeven occurs when the venture is able to collect sufficient cash from sales of its goods and service to cover all of its outgoing cash payments. Each is calculated differently. The profit breakeven point is calculated using the income statement, and the cash breakeven point is calculated using the cash flow statement.

In Exhibit 6.6, the profit breakeven point can be seen to occur around the time the venture is selling 25,000 units per year. It is the point where the venture estimates that its sales will bring in greater revenue than its variable and fixed costs, combined.

The cash flow breakeven point for a venture generally occurs after the profit breakeven point—sometimes many months after. That is because the venture may make at least a portion of its sales using credit terms. The lag between profit breakeven and cash breakeven is the time it takes to collect the accounts receivable. There may also be some portion of payments that never all collected, increasing the time lag between profit breakeven and cash breakeven.

Ratio analysis examines the logical relationships between various financial statement items. Items may come from the same financial statement or from different statements. The only requirement is that a logical relationship exists between the items. Ratios are very important to investors and other stakeholders in evaluating the financial health of the venture. Comparing company ratios to industry standards can indicate areas in which the company is successful—and those in which the company is below standard. Using ratios enables a venture to compare itself to others in its industry, regardless of the size of the comparable firms.[18] For example, a small medical devices venture may compare itself to firms such as Medtronic or Smith-Kline.

Credit managers, bankers, and financial and investment analysts use several hundreds of different ratios to analyze the health of a venture. Only a handful of these ratios are useful in interpreting

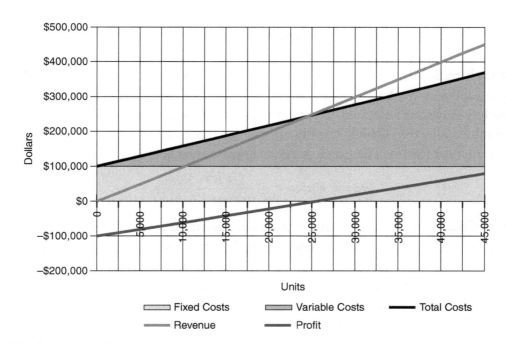

EXHIBIT 6.6 Breakeven Analysis

a venture's financial standing, and many more may give misleading information. The ratios presented here—liquidity, activity, profitability, and debt—are some of the so-called **key ratios** that are in common use. Industry standards on certain key financial ratios can be found for most industries through trade associations, investment analyst reports, or from leading business publications. Trends in a company's performance are also easily spotted by comparing ratios from the current period with ratios from earlier periods.

It is important to note that different industries have distinct standards for ratio adequacy. What is an adequate ratio for a company in one industry may not be adequate for a different company in another industry. Beware of judging a ratio solely on the basis of a universal standard; ratios should be viewed against industry norms. For instance, the banking industry and manufacturing industry would differ significantly in terms of current assets. Banks carry an enormous amount of liquid current assets, whereas manufacturing firms have a much more even division of current and long-term assets. So a comparison of a bank and a manufacturing firm in terms of any ratio that contains current assets would not be realistic.

There are four basic types of ratio analysis commonly used to determine the financial health of a venture. They are:

Liquidity Ratios: A firm's ability to pay its short-term debts as they come due is measured by liquidity ratios. Liquidity is a measure of how quickly an asset can be converted to cash. Highly liquid firms can more easily convert assets to cash when needed to repay loans. Less liquid firms may have trouble meeting their obligations or obtaining loans at low cost. Two common liquidity ratios are the current ratio and the quick (acid-test) ratio:

- The **current ratio,** which is current assets divided by current liabilities (two balance sheet items), indicates a firm's ability to pay its current liabilities from its current assets. Thus, the ratio shows the strength of a company's working capital. Current ratio is expressed using the following equation:

$$Current\ Ratio = \frac{Current\ Assets}{Current\ Liabilities}$$

- The **quick ratio,** also called the acid-test ratio, divides quick assets by current liabilities. It measures more immediate liquidity by comparing two balance sheet items. Quick assets do not include inventory because to convert inventory to cash, merchandise must be sold and a receivable collected. **Quick assets** are cash or those assets the firm expects to convert to cash in the near future. The quick ratio is expressed in the following equation:

$$Quick\ Ratio = \frac{Quick\ Assets}{Current\ Liabilities}$$

Activity Ratios: How efficiently the firm uses its assets to generate revenues is measured by activity ratios. These ratios indicate how efficiently a firm uses its resources. A common activity ratio is accounts receivable turnover. Accounts receivable turnover is the number of times per year that the average accounts receivable is turned over (collected). An income statement item (net sales) is compared with a balance sheet item (accounts receivable). We calculate this ratio by dividing net sales by average net accounts receivable as shown below:

$$Accounts\ Receivable\ Turnover = \frac{Net\ Sales}{Average\ Net\ Account\ Receivable}$$

The allowance for doubtful accounts is first deducted to arrive at net accounts receivable. Average net accounts receivable is computed by adding the accounts receivable amounts at the beginning and end of the year and then dividing by two.

Profitability Ratios: A company's overall operating success—its financial performance—is measured by **profitability ratios.** These ratios measure a firm's success in terms of earnings compared with sales or investments. Over time these ratios can indicate how successfully or unsuccessfully management operates the business. Two common profitability ratios are return on sales and return on equity.

- **Return on sales** measures a firm's profitability by comparing net income and net sales, both income statement items. It is computed by dividing net income by net sales:

$$Return\ on\ Sales = \frac{Net\ Income}{Net\ Sales}$$

- **Return on equity (ROE)** measures the return the company earns on every dollar of shareholders' (and owners') investment. Investors are very interested in this ratio; it indicates how well their investment is doing. We compute return on equity by dividing net income (an income statement item) by equity (a balance sheet item).

$$Return\ on\ Equity = \frac{Net\ Income}{Equity}$$

Debt Ratios: Companies measure their ability to pay long-term debts by debt ratios. These ratios try to answer questions such as (1) Is the company financed mainly by debt or equity?, and (2) Does the company make enough to pay the interest on its loans when due? Potential investors and lenders are very interested in the answers to such questions. Two ways to answer them are the debt-to-equity ratio and the times-interest-earned ratio.

- The **debt-to-equity ratio** measures a firm's leverage as the ratio of funds provided by the owners to funds provided by creditors, both balance sheet items. Total debt includes current liabilities and long-term liabilities. The debt-to-equity ratio demonstrates the risk incurred by the owners of the firm. The higher the debt-to-equity ratio is, the greater the chance that the firm will be unable to meet its obligations.

$$Dept\ to\ Equity = \frac{Total\ Dept}{Equity}$$

- Creditors need to know whether a borrower can meet interest payments when they come due. The **times-interest-earned ratio** compares cash received from operations with cash paid for interest payments. It measures how many times the firm earns the amount of interest it must pay during the year.

$$Times\ Interest\ Earned = \frac{Income\ Before\ Interest\ and\ Taxes}{Interest\ Expense}$$

FINANCIAL MANAGEMENT

The entrepreneurial venture's financial manager is responsible for maintaining the proper flow of funds into and out of the venture. They manage the use of funds and find the appropriate sources of funds as required. They also invest excess funds to earn additional income for the company. In performing these duties, the financial manager has to estimate the venture's startup costs, manage its working capital, develop capital budgets, and develop appropriate financial controls.

A common mistake made by new ventures is failing to plan for sufficient **startup capital** (the money needed to start a business) assuming that revenue will provide the cash needed to operate and grow. Insufficient capital is a problem not only for new ventures, but it can also be a problem for long-established firms.

Startup costs can be projected and managed by creating a startup budget. When seeking initial capital to launch the venture, the entrepreneur should ensure that sufficient capital is raised to cover these startup costs, and the costs of operating until breakeven or until additional capital is raised. A template for the startup budget is provided in Exhibit 6.7. Note that the categories of costs listed are somewhat generic, and any given venture may have quite different associated startup costs.

If a firm's current liabilities (obligations that must be paid within a year) are subtracted from its current assets, the result is the value of working capital. **Working capital** represents the amount of capital available for the day-to-day running of the firm. Sufficient working capital is obviously important to the effective management of a firm's operations.

In managing current assets, the financial manager needs to concentrate on three assets: cash, accounts receivable, and inventory. The primary concern with cash is that it should never be left idle; it should always be working. Funds not immediately needed should be invested and earning interest. At the very least, an interest-earning checking account should be used.

Accounts receivable are really promises of cash from customers of the firm. Until this cash is in hand, the firm has only the promise. One task of the financial manager is to speed up the

EXHIBIT 6.7 Example of a Startup Budget

Startup Expenses	
Legal	$50,000
Stationery etc.	$2,000
Brochures	$0
Consultants	$3,000
Insurance	$3,000
Rent	$9,300
Research and development	$0
Expensed equipment	$0
Custom CAD software	$5,700
Logo design	$1,000
Management salaries	$56,000
Other	$0
Other	$0
Other	$0
Total Startup Expenses	**$130,000**

collection of accounts receivable as much as possible. This, of course, must be done without offending customers and with the understanding that, in many cases, providing credit is necessary to generate sales.

In managing accounts receivable, the financial manager needs to date accounts receivable so that overdue accounts are flagged immediately and appropriate action is taken. The financial manager also wants to speed up the conversion of received payments into cash in the company's account. When received at the office, they must be processed and then sent to the bank. This means that the cash may not be credited to the company's account for two more days. To speed this up, many companies use electronic transactions to enable their customers to deposit money directly into a bank account.

Many ventures also elect to enable their customers to use credit cards to make payments. Credit cards speed their time to the receipt of cash, but at a price. Companies that use credit cards must pay a small part of each transaction to the credit card company—usually between 3 and 5 percent. Banks also require a special account, called a **merchant account,** to process credit card transactions. Most banks charge a monthly and annual fee to maintain a merchant account. For many firms, these fees are worth their expense because they facilitate the timely receipt of cash.

Credit and Collections Policies

© CandyBox Images, 2012. Used under license from Shutterstock, Inc.

The venture must develop credit and collections policies, and it must execute those policies consistently to maximize revenue. In fact, a venture's credit and collections policies and procedures can have dramatic effect on revenue. For example, a credit policy that is overly lenient allows customers to take ownership of a product or service without cash being transferred to the business. Credit is based on the assumption that the customers will pay later, usually with an interest charge. An overly lenient credit policy may attract a lot of customers. The problem is, some of these customers are credit risks—they will not pay what they owe, or they will pay only at their own pace. Such a lenient credit policy can result in a lot of "sales," but it can be very damaging to the cash flow stream of the growing venture.

The decision about how to use credit as a component of a venture's sales strategy is an important one, especially for companies that sell big-ticket items. Credit must be extended to customers for goods such as housing and automobiles. Without credit most customers would not be able to afford such purchases. The challenge for big-ticket businesses is not whether to extend credit to customers, but on what terms credit will be offered.

Granting credit without an established collection policy has ruined many businesses. Collection policy refers to the system for collecting from customers who do not pay on time. Accounts receivable is the term used to refer to payments due from customers. Accounts receivable (also known simply as "receivables") arise as a result of selling inventory or services on credit terms that allow delivery prior to the collection of cash. Inventory is sold and shipped, an invoice is sent to the customer, and cash is collected at a later date. The receivable exists for the time period between the sale and the receipt of cash. The Bullet Breakout below provides some pointers to an effective credit regime in an entrepreneurial venture.

▶ BULLET BREAKOUT ◀

Suggestions for an Effective Credit Regime

- **Have policies:** Even if you have a full-time experienced credit manager on staff, you need to set policies for extending credit and making collections.

- **Keep it legal:** You need to be sure that anyone making credit decisions on your company's behalf understands the legal issues involved. For example, when determining credit eligibility, you need to be sure that factors such as race, sex, or ethnic origin are not considered.

- **Use the phone:** When monies owed you are overdue and the amount is in excess of a few dollars, your best bet for collection activity is via the phone. Phone calls are simply much more effective than letters.

- **Keep it positive:** Always keep a positive, upbeat attitude when you are pursuing collections, whether through written correspondence or over the phone. Maintaining a positive, but firm, rapport with people who owe you money is the most effective means toward possible payment.

- **Size is no guarantee:** Just because a customer is large doesn't mean it can pay its bills. So, especially if you are considering extending credit to a large company, run a credit check first.

- **Tier credit decisions:** For small credit requests, set up criteria so that a lower-level clerk can quickly make a decision. For large credit requests, have a credit manager or accounting manager make the decision. For very large credit requests, have your top financial person make the decision. And for the largest requests, you, the owner of the business, should become involved.

- **Keep salespeople away from credit decisions:** Salespeople are invariably too loose with credit. Pay very little attention to their credit recommendations, no matter how much seniority or experience they have.

Receivables exist because most industries, with the exception of retail, offer their customers payment terms other than cash on delivery. A company that refuses to offer credit terms will lose some customers because they will purchase their goods from competitors who do offer such terms. Credit terms are quoted in a variety of ways, such as:

- Net 10
- Net 30
- 2% in 10 days, net 30

The first term requires payment in ten days from the invoice date. The second term requires payment within thirty days from the shipment date. And, the third set of terms offer a bonus for early payment. It offers 2 percent discount from the invoice amount if it is paid within ten days of the invoice date. Beyond the ten days, up to thirty days, the customer pays 100 percent of the invoice. The discount is an incentive to the customer to pay early.

The existence of receivables indicates that the company, instead of collecting cash, invested cash into receivables that, in effect, are loans to customers. If a company gives thirty-day terms, it should collect its receivables in thirty days. One method of measuring the quality of receivables is to compare the actual collection period to the stated terms. The average actual collection period is known as **Days Receivable** and can be calculated as follows:

Days Receivable = Actual Accounts Receivable/Sales Per Day, where

Actual Accounts Receivable = Average levels of receivables on the balance sheet during the period being evaluated.

Sales per Day = Annual sales/360

Aging of accounts receivable identifies problem customers and also allows the firm to manage its credit policies based on industry standards. If the venture's accounts receivable are abnormally long, it must work harder at collecting. If, on the other hand, accounts receivable are abnormally short, it may be able to increase sales by easing its credit policies.

Once a business understands the concept of Aging and Days Receivable, it is easier to understand other aspects of collection. There is one universal maxim that every entrepreneur should understand: *The longer an account goes unpaid, the more difficult it becomes to collect.* No account, with the exception of government or certain medical claims should be uncollected for more than ninety days. After the original billing goes out, a notice should be sent once the due date has past. Notices should be sent out at thirty, sixty, and ninety days. During this time, phone calls should be attempted to reach the party. If no arrangements are made and there has been no response, then there are a few options. They include:

- **Pre-Collect Notice:** A pre-collect notice is a notice sent by a collection agency to the "debtor" (if the firm doesn't pay, it ceases being called "client" or "customer") stating, "We are monitoring this account, please make arrangements to pay or we'll take the account over." The debtor then has the opportunity to pay the business directly, or to deal with the collection agency.

- **Collection Agencies:** Generally, collection agencies focus on collecting past due accounts for businesses. They are considered by law to be "third-party collectors." This means they must follow state and federal laws in the collection of a debt. One of the laws they must follow is the Fair Debt Collection Practices Act or FDCPA. Depending on the state, there may also be certain state laws that apply.

- **Court:** According to the FDCPA, a legal debt collector may sue consumers for the purpose of obtaining court judgments for debts but, **only in the judicial district where the consumer resides or signed the contract,** except that an action to enforce a security interest in real property that secures the obligation must be brought where the property is located.

Despite the occasional need to take action to motivate a customer to pay, retaining the customer as a client must always be a consideration. If the customer doesn't have a regular history of late paying, the venture may want to be tolerant of overdue payments. On the other hand, it may be wise for the venture to "fire" those customers who are routinely late in paying and who must be contacted repeatedly to honor their obligations.

Inventory Management

Inventory is an investment in future sales. Until sold, however, inventory represents a cash use for the technology venture. The financial manager needs to continuously review inventory levels to pinpoint any excess inventory and work with production and marketing to alleviate the condition. Of course, understanding inventory's importance to sales, the financial manager also works with production and marketing to make sure sufficient inventory is available to satisfy customer needs.

Many inventory models use computer programs and company information to determine the best level of inventory for different levels of sales. These models also help determine the best time to order additional inventory and the amount of inventory to order. The auto industry has begun working more closely with its suppliers to reduce the lead time needed for deliveries. The goal is to achieve just-in-time (JIT) deliveries, or deliveries of materials that arrive at the plant just when they are actually needed for production.

Inventory needs are further complicated by the fluctuations in demand that occur in various businesses. A retail business such as Walmart will have to build up its inventory for the Christmas season when sales are brisk, and then hold down inventory levels in January and February when sales are slower. A farmer must purchase his inventory of seed and fertilizer all at one time but can expect no income from his crops until they are harvested. While a vegetable canner will have to purchase the vegetables for canning when the vegetables are harvested, that is, all at one time of the year, sales of that inventory will be stretched over the entire year. A detergent manufacturer, on the other hand, will experience a relatively stable product demand and material supply and therefore will experience much less fluctuation in inventory needs than the other firms mentioned.

Purchase of Capital Assets

Although capital assets such as land, buildings, and equipment often have to be purchased by a firm at startup, these same assets must be periodically replaced and upgraded. And as business increases, additional assets may be required. A firm may need to open a second plant, purchase another delivery truck, or buy additional machinery. The company may also want to plan for the future by purchasing land for expansion when the real estate market is most favorable. All of these represent major expenditures and therefore major uses of company funds. If these expenditures are not planned for, the company may have to borrow unnecessarily or at high interest rates, or the firm may have to forgo the purchase of new equipment, expansion of the plant, or purchase of delivery equipment.

Payment of Debt

Most firms need to borrow money at some time or another. They may borrow to make major purchases or to get over a particularly tight cash period during the year; however, the financial manager has to consider the payment of interest and principal on any outstanding debt as a use of funds and needs to add this debt service into the calculation for funds usage.

Payment of Dividends

Dividends are payments made to the firm's shareholders as a form of earnings on their stocks. Although stock usually does not require the payment of dividends, most firms pay dividends to keep their stock attractive to potential investors and to show that the firm is financially sound. As a use of funds, the payment of dividends must be planned for.

Capital Budgeting

Capital budgets represent the funds allocated for future investments of the firm's cash. These may be plant expansion, equipment improvement, acquisitions, or other major expenditures. The process of **capital budgeting** involves comparing and evaluating alternative investments.

Capital investments are generally long-term investments and therefore involve long-term sources of funds. When evaluating different capital projects, the financial manager looks not only at the amount of money required to do the project but also at the incremental cash flow the project will produce. These cash flows are looked at to determine when the project will have paid for itself (generated sufficient cash to pay for the initial investment) and what the long-term rate of return will be.

Determining the long-term rate of return can be difficult because it depends on factors such as customer response, competitive reactions, the state of the economy, and other environmental factors. Therefore, benefits are difficult to gauge in advance. Managers generally look at the most likely circumstances and try to estimate returns based on these. However, this approach does not always work.

SUMMARY OF LEARNING OBJECTIVES

1. **Perform** in the role of financial manager for a startup venture. *The entrepreneur has to perform multiple roles in the venture, one of which is to serve as the venture's chief financial officer. While part of the financial manager role can be outsourced or delegated, the entrepreneur is often required to be deeply involved in the venture's financial affairs and health.*

2. **Develop** financial pro forma forecasts, including assumptions. *As a result of studying this chapter, you should be able to develop financial forecasts for your venture, including the sales forecast, income statement forecast, cash flow forecast, and balance sheet forecast. You should also be able to create a list of the assumptions that you used to generate the numbers and formulas in your forecasts.*

3. **Project** cash flows and estimate capital needs over time. *To the entrepreneur "cash is king." That means the entrepreneur must pay special attention to the way cash flows into and out of the venture. The cash flow statement forecast provides a handy way for the entrepreneur to project future cash needs. For example, a venture cannot have negative ending cash as that would mean bills are not getting paid. As such, anytime that appears on the cash flow projections the entrepreneur knows that external sources of cash must be tapped to cover the negative cash position. In general, the rule is that the entrepreneur needs to raise at least twice the worst negative cash position in a cash flow forecast.*

4. **Develop** a startup venture financial plan. *The financial plan for a startup venture generally should extend three years into the future. In addition to the pro forma forecasts, the entrepreneur should also analyze the funds that will be needed to launch the venture. A startup budget includes all the costs that the venture will incur before it begins operations.*

5. **Analyze** financial statements using ratio analysis techniques. *One of the ways to track the financial health of your venture is to generate key ratios that allow comparison with other firms in the industry. The key ratios to track will differ by industry, but there are a few—including those covered in this chapter—that are common to most ventures. The entrepreneur should track these common ratios and those indicative of financial health within the venture's particular industry.*

6. **Develop** credit and collections policies to ensure adequate cash flows. *One painful lesson that many novice entrepreneurs learn too late is, "the longer a debt goes unpaid the harder it will be to collect." It is important for new ventures to develop credit and collections policies in advance of engaging in business transactions. Having the necessary accounting paperwork and credit and collections policies in place prior to commencing operations will reduce the likelihood of delivering products or performing services for which you don't get paid.*

STUDY QUESTIONS

1. Explain the role of accounting in new venture operations. What is the accounting equation? Can you explain the components? Explain the accounting cycle.

2. How does accounting differ from finance? Who performs the role of "financial manager" in the startup technology venture?

3. Define the four fundamental financial statements that are used to estimate the future performance of the venture. Explain how each statement is used to manage the venture over time.

4. What is the role of the new venture's financial plan? What data should the financial plan track? What type of useful information can be extracted from the plan?

5. How is it possible that a venture could reach its profit breakeven point sooner than its cash flow breakeven point?

6. Explain the role of ratio analysis in managing the new venture's financial plan. Define the different ratio types and the role they play in managing the venture.

7. How should the technology entrepreneur manage the venture's accounts receivable? Provide some specific details.

8. Explain the difference between variable and fixed costs. How can the technology entrepreneur minimize variable costs during times of rapid growth?

9. What are the basic elements of a sales forecast? Explain each and how they interact with one another.

10. Define the terms assets, liabilities, equity, revenue, and profit. How does profit differ from cash?

IN-CLASS EXERCISE

For this exercise the class should be divided into teams of four to six individuals. The task will be to develop a one-year sales forecast for a simple business model as defined below. The exercise is designed to focus on the underlying assumptions that each group uses to develop its sales forecast.

The Business Model

The business model for this exercise is selling hamburgers at a stand located near the college campus. The units of sale and prices should be as follows:

1. Hamburger: $2.00
2. Hot Dog: $1.75
3. Soda: $1.25
4. Chips: $1.25

THE ASSIGNMENT. Each team should specify the underlying assumptions that form the basis of its sales forecast. The assumptions that each team should specify include but are not limited to:

1. Location
2. Foot traffic at the location
3. Average number of customers/day
4. Average sale/customer
5. Hours of operation

The exercise can be completed in class or as a homework assignment. Each team should develop a spreadsheet and list of assumptions. Each team should present its spreadsheet to the rest of the class and be prepared to discuss and defend the assumptions.

KEY TERMS

Accounting: The process of identifying, measuring, and communicating economic information to permit informed judgments and decisions by users of information.

Accounting cycle: The series of steps taken, from a business transaction through entering the transaction in the general ledger for the business.

Accounting equation: The basic accounting equation that equates a business's assets to its liabilities and equity combined, commonly expressed as:

$$Assets = Liabilities + Owners'\ Equity$$

Accounts: Accounts are used to summarize all transactions that affect a particular financial statement component.

Accounts receivable: Accounts receivable refers to promises by customers to pay for sales that have occurred at some point in the past.

Accruals: Accruals refers to realizing accounting charges in the present for expenses that will be paid at some future date.

Activity ratios: Ratios that measure how efficiently the firm uses its assets to generate revenues.

Aging: Aging refers to the length of time it takes, on average, for a venture to collect its accounts receivable.

Assets: Assets refers to anything the business uses to perform its functions and that are owned by the shareholders of the venture.

Assumptions: Your assumptions page should include justification or rationale for every number that you enter that is not a direct result of a formula in the spreadsheet, and it should include justification or rationale for each formula.

Balance sheet: The report that lists everything a company owns and everything it owes at a specific moment in time.

Breakeven analysis: Breakeven analysis is used to determine the number of units the venture needs to sell to reach profitability and/or become cash flow positive.

Burn rate: The amount of cash that a venture uses each month to pay for operations.

Capital budgeting: The process of comparing and evaluating alternative investments.

Cash flow: The flow of actual cash into and out of a venture.

Cash flow statement: The statement that shows the flow of *cash* into and out of a business during a period of time

Current ratio: The ratio that indicates a firm's ability to pay its current liabilities from its current assets.

Days receivable: The average collection period for a company's accounts receivable.

Debt ratios: Ratios that measure the company's ability to pay long-term debts by debt ratios.

Debt to equity ratio: The ratiothat measures a firm's leverage as the ratio of funds provided by the owners to funds provided by creditors, both balance sheet items.

EBITDA or EBIT: Earnings before interest, taxes (EBIT), depreciation, and amortization (EBITDA) is used to identify how effectively a venture operates prior to the deduction of interest, taxes, etc., which are not operating expenses.

Expenses: Costs incurred to produce revenues.

Finance: The study of how to manage money—either from a personal perspective or from a business perspective

Financial accounting: Accounting that is intended for use by a venture's external decision makers.

Financial manager: The individual responsible for the venture's finance function.

Financial statements: Standard statements that are used to record revenue, expenses, and profits and losses of a venture. They include an income statement, cash flow statement, and balance sheet.

Financing activities: Revenue generated by a business through investing excess cash in other businesses as well share sales or dividend payments to shareholders is referred to as financing activities.

Fixed costs: Those costs associated with operating a venture that do not vary directly with output. These are also referred to as "overhead."

General and Administrative (G&A) expenses: This term refer to the fixed costs or "overhead" associated with an operating venture.

General ledger: The repository of closed transactions that have occurred during an accounting period (e.g., monthly, annually).

Generally Accepted Accounting Principles (GAAP): The accounting principles established by the Financial Accounting Standards Board and to which all companies in the United States must comply.

Income statement: The financial statement that records both revenue and expenses for the venture across accounting periods; sometimes called the profit and loss statement.

Investing activities: The income and expenses associated with a venture generated by investing its excess cash into assets that are not associated with its primary business (e.g., an interest bearing savings account).

Journal: Where day-to-day transactions of a venture are recorded.

Key ratios: Particular financial ratios that companies in an industry generally track to gauge their relative health compared to their peers.

Liabilities: Debts owed by the business to its creditors, including obligations to perform services in the future.

Liquidity: Refers to the ability of a venture to meet its near-term financial obligations.

Liquidity ratios: A firm's ability to pay its short-term debts as they come due is measured by liquidity ratios.

Managerial accounting: Accounting that is used primarily by a venture's internal decision makers.

Merchant account: A type of bank account that accommodates credit card transactions.

Operating activities: The income and expenses generated by a venture during the course of its normal business activities.

Overhead: Fixed costs associated with an operating venture. Generally, this is referred to as the General and Administrative (G&A) expenses on the income statement.

Owner's equity: The claims of the owners against the firm's assets

Profitability ratios: Ratios that measure a firm's success in terms of earnings compared with sales or investments.

Pro forma financial forecast: Forward-looking financial forecasts usually including the sales forecast, income statement, cash flow statement, and balance sheet, and usually forecasting at least three years of venture performance.

Quick assets: Cash or those assets the firm expects to convert to cash in the near future.

Quick ratio: Also called the acid-test ratio, this ratio divides quick assets by current liabilities. It measures more immediate liquidity by comparing two balance sheet items

Ramp rate: The rate of market penetration that is an assumption built into the sales forecast.

Ratio analysis: Analysis that examines the logical relationships between various financial statement items. Items may come from the same financial statement or from different statements

Recurring revenue: Revenue that is generated by selling products/services to existing customers on a regular basis.

Return on sales: Measures a firm's profitability by comparing net income and net sales, both income statement items.

Return on equity: Measures the return the company earns on every dollar of shareholders' (and owners') investment

Revenues: Inflows of assets resulting from the ongoing operation of a business.

Sales cycle: The amount of time required to sell products or services to a new customer.

Sales forecast: The foundation of the various financial statementsthat entrepreneurs use both to project their venture's financial performance into the future.

Sensitivity analysis: An analysis that targets several key variables and examines how different values for these key variables affect the viability of the venture.

Startup capital: This term refers to the capital (cash) a venture needs to get started.

Times interest earned ratio: This ratio compares cash received from operations with cash paid for interest payments.

Variable costs: Costs associated with a venture that vary directly with increased output.

Virtual CFO: Virtual CFO services provide chief financial officer service to ventures on a contract basis. This enables ventures to have CFO input into management without the need to hire an expensive employee.

Working capital: The amount of capital available for the day-to-day running of the firm.

ENDNOTES

[1] Brush, C.G., "Pioneering Strategies for Entrepreneurial Success," *Business Horizons,* 51(1) (2008): 21–27.

[2] Ballou, B., and D.L. Heitger, "Kofenya: The Role of Accounting Information in Managing the Risks of a New Business," *Issues in Accounting Education,* 23(2)(2008): 211–228.

[3] Carmichael, D.R., R. Whittington, and L. Graham, *Accountant's Handbook: Volume One: Financial Accounting and General Topics* (Hoboken, NJ: John Wiley and Sons, 2007).

[4] Baldenius, T., and X. Meng, "Signaling Firm Value to Active Investors," *Review of Accounting Studies,* 15(3)(2010): 584–619.

[5] Carter, S, E. Shaw, W. Lam, and F. Wilson, "Gender, Entrepreneurship, and Bank Lending: The Criteria and Processes used by Bank Loan Officers in Assessing Applications," *Entrepreneurship: Theory and Practice,* 31(3)(2007): 427–444.

[6] Toms, S., "Accounting for Entrepreneurship: A Knowledge-Based View of the Firm," *Critical Perspectives on Accounting,* 17(2/3)(2006): 336–357.

[7] Bressler, L.A., "How Entrepreneurs Choose and Use Accounting Information Systems," *Strategic Finance,* 87(12)(2006): 56–60.

[8] Davila A., and G. Foster, "Management Control Systems in Early-Stage Startup Companies," *Accounting Review,* 82(4)(2007): 907–937.

[9] Campian, M., "Part Time CFOs: A Concept Worth Considering," *Small Business Association of Michigan (SBAM Focus)* (May 2008): 10–12.

[10] Berman, K., and J. Knight, *Financial Intelligence for Entrepreneurs: What You Really Need to Know About the Numbers* (Boston: Harvard Business School Press, 2008).

[11] Shane, S., *The Illusions of Entrepreneurship: The Costly Myths that Entrepreneurs, Investors, and Policy Makers Live By* (New Haven, CT: Yale University Press, 2008).

[12] Baeyens, K., T. Vanacker, and S. Manigart, "Venture Capitalists' Selection Process: The Case of Biotechnology Proposals," *International Journal of Technology Management,* 34(1/2)(2006): 28–46.

[13] Schrager, J.E., "Strategies and Techniques for Venture Investing," *Journal of Private Equity,* 7(2)(2004): 1–2.

[14] Timmons, J.A., and D.A. Sander, "Everything You (Don't) Want to Know About Raising Capital," *Harvard Business Review,* 67(6)(1989): 70–73.

[15] Sahlman, W.A., "How to Write a Great Business Plan," *Harvard Business Review,* 75(4)(1998): 98–108.

[16] Mason, C., and M. Stark, "What Do Investors Look for in a Business Plan? A Comparison of the Investment Criteria of Bankers, Venture Capitalists, and Business Angels," *International Small Business Journal,* 22(3)(2004): 227–248.

[17] Reynolds, P.L., and G. Lancaster, "Predictive Strategic Marketing Management Decisions in Small Firms: A Possible Bayesian Solution," *Management Decision,* 45(6)(2007): 1038–1057.

[18] Patrone, F.L., and D. Dubois,"Financial Ratio Analysis for the Small Business,"*Journal of Small Business Management,* 19(1)(1981): 35–40.

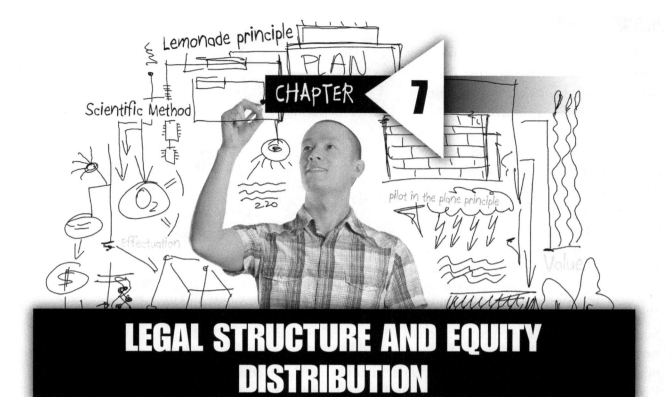

LEGAL STRUCTURE AND EQUITY DISTRIBUTION

Learning Objectives

After studying this chapter, students should be able to:

- **Examine** a business as an entity that is separate and distinct from participants in the enterprise.

- **Understand** the role of business partners in a business.

- **Define** limited liability.

- **Differentiate** between various forms of legal entity for structuring a business.

- **Describe** the formalities of maintaining a limited liability status.

- **Characterize** the nature of equity interest and its various forms.

- **Understand** distribution of equity interest among founders of a venture.

- **Appreciate** the role of employee stock options.

INTRODUCTION

Starting a new venture is difficult even for expert entrepreneurs. Imagine the challenges that face the first time or novice entrepreneur. Most first-time entrepreneurs are not short of passion, vision, and dreams of a better future. Usually they have those vital elements of entrepreneurial success in abundance. What they too often lack, however, is the necessary expertise, credibility, and resources that they will need to complement their vision and passion. In order to aggregate all of the key skills, resources, and other things needed for success entrepreneurs must usually recruit others to their venture.

So, how are skills, expertise, and credibility recruited into a venture? In general, the entrepreneur has two choices. The needed components of success can be acquired via strategic alliances with other businesses, or by hiring individuals with the needed skills, expertise, or credibility. People who are recruited to a venture will require some type of compensation for their services. The entrepreneur can pay them as employees or, more typically in startups, the people who supply the needed skills, expertise, and/or credibility are brought into the venture by giving them the opportunity to share in its success. These individuals become business partners, where they are provided an ownership or **equity interest** in the venture in lieu of all or part of the compensation that they might otherwise command in the open market. The relative ownership interests of the various business partners, of course, depend upon their relative contributions to the venture.

This chapter begins by examining the issues that are associated with owning and managing a venture. Many people who are entering entrepreneurship for the first time are particularly concerned about issues concerning their personal liability with respect to operating a venture. This is an important issue, and there are some considerations that every entrepreneur must address. For example, some types of business forms do not separate the business from the person or persons operating it. In such instances, liabilities incurred by the business are the responsibility of those who own the business. Business entities that don't separate the owners from the business are known as unlimited liability entities. In other words, the owners' personal assets may be at risk for liabilities incurred by the business. Fortunately, there are relatively easy-to-form and maintain legal structures that limit the liability of the owners and will provide separation between business and personal assets. We will discuss limited and unlimited liability and how you, as an entrepreneur, can ensure that you understand your options.

Next, we examine the various legal structures that you can choose for your business. As we mentioned, some of these structures have unlimited liability associated with them and some have limited liability. There are also a number of other issues associated with choice of legal structure. For example, some of the structures allow for the issuance of stock, and others don't. There are also different tax treatments for the various legal structures, and your choice of structure will affect both your personal and corporate taxes.[1] We will discuss the various types of business legal structures in this chapter and the issues that surround deciding on one or another structure.

Finally, we examine issues surrounding equity (ownership) distribution and how that affects your ability to recruit and retain motivated partners and employees to your venture. The venture's founders must decide how to divide ownership based on their relative current and future inputs to the company. This is often a delicate, yet vital, early decision for the venture. Giving away too much equity means someone with little to contribute has large influence on future decisions and directions of the venture. Giving away too little may mean that someone who is important to the venture's success may not be satisfied and elect to exit the venture. We will discuss equity distribution and strategies for getting it right throughout the life of the venture. Let's begin this chapter by examining ownership and liability issues.

OWNERSHIP AND LIABILITY ISSUES

A startup venture is typically owned by one or more individuals or entities, each making a contribution to or an investment in the business in return for equity interest (percentage of ownership). The individuals or entities that initially form the venture are generally referred to as the **founders**. In general, the individuals or entities that own the venture are referred to as the **principals** or owners. Individuals or entities that make contributions to the business after it has been formed are referred to as **investors** or **lenders**.

In the United States, a business entity can take the form of any one of a number of different legal structures, including:

- Sole Proprietorship
- General Partnership
- Limited Partnership
- Limited Liability Company (LLC)
- Corporation (C-Corporation or S-Corporation)

The choice of any one of the legal structures above can affect the business in many ways, including the potential risk to owners, potential for business growth, availability of benefits, taxation of the business entity along with its principals, and the types of exit strategies available. One of the primary considerations to make when selecting a particular form of business legal structure is the liability of the principals. Some legal structures limit the liability of the principals, and some do not. We turn to that discussion next.

Limited vs. Unlimited Liability

Certain forms of business entities, such as **sole proprietorships** and **general partnerships**, are considered to be the "alter ego" of the owners. These are **unlimited liability** companies since each owner of the entity (sole proprietor or partner) can be held personally liable for the entire amount of the venture's debts, obligations, and/or liabilities. All personal assets are at risk to satisfy the debt, obligation and/or liability. Furthermore, the personal assets of each owner of an unlimited liability entity are at risk not only with respect to the debts, obligations, and/or liabilities that they create through their individual actions, but also those created by an employee or partner even without any personal involvement or knowledge.

This problem with unlimited liability entities has been recognized and state governments in all fifty states have created other types of business entities that avoid this problem. These include entities that provide a legal existence that is separate and apart from the individuals participating in the venture, or they limit the liability of the participants to their investment in the venture. These entities, referred to as **limited liability** entities, include **corporations**, **limited liability companies (LLC)**, and **limited partnerships (LP)**. These legal forms limit the principals' liability exposure to the particular assets each contributed to the venture and shields their personal assets.

Why would the government want to shield the personal assets of an entity's owners from the debts and obligations of the entity? The reason for the existence of limited liability entities is to promote commerce. Certain types of ventures tend to require substantial infusions of capital and other resources well beyond the means of the typical entrepreneur. In order for those types of businesses to be created and sustained, the resources of investors must be brought to bear. The infusion of investor capital can take a number of different forms, including purchase of an equity position in the company. However, unless the venture takes the form of a limited liability entity, merely purchasing or otherwise acquiring an equity interest in the venture would make all of the investor's personal assets available to satisfy the debts and obligations of the venture.

Under unlimited liability conditions, it would be difficult to find investors, and if found, they would be extremely expensive; the percentage of ownership would have to reflect the amount of risk assumed by virtue of the investment. This is particularly true with respect to wealthier investors since potentially exposing their entire wealth to satisfy the debts of a venture would create a disproportionate risk.

© Alexander Sherstobitov, 2012. Used under license from Shutterstock, Inc.

In general, the most important reason for establishing a venture as a limited liability entity is to protect the assets of principals and managers from the consequences of any financial or legal misfortune of the business. So long as these entities are properly formed, are compliant with all necessary formalities, and individuals observe a general fiduciary duty of loyalty and care to the venture in conducting its affairs, they are shielded from personal liability to third parties arising from those business affairs.

Limited liability status, often referred to as the **corporate veil**, is almost always disregarded by courts for criminal acts of the officers, shareholders, or directors of a company. There are also circumstances under which limited liability entity status will be ignored, and liability imposed on the business owners, even in the absence of personal culpability. The imposition of liability on the owners of a limited liability entity is often referred to as **piercing the corporate veil**. The issue typically comes up in the context of a lawsuit against a business when it does not have sufficient assets to satisfy the damage claims. Some reasons for piercing the corporate veil include:

- Undercapitalization of the venture
- Failure to observe entity formalities such as properly incorporating
- Commingling of personal and business assets
- Insolvency at the time of a transaction
- Siphoning of funds by those owning or controlling the entity
- Absence of corporate records

There are also instances where personal liability for corporate debt is imposed by statute, such as in cases involving employers' tax withholding obligations, wage and retirement benefits, environmental liability and violations of the federal securities laws. Personal liability may also arise because of contractual obligations, such as when a shareholder signs a personal guaranty or fails to adequately identify that he or she is signing on behalf of the company.

With these considerations in mind, the technology entrepreneur is ready to make an informed choice about the legal form for the new venture. We turn to that discussion next.

LEGAL STRUCTURE

Each form of business entity has distinct characteristics that come with advantages and disadvantages, depending upon specific circumstances. In order to determine the optimum form of entity for a particular business venture, here are some factors to take into consideration:

- The potential risks and liabilities entailed in the venture: Limited liability entities limit the owner's exposure to the assets contributed to the venture.
- Owner's: Certain forms of organization have limits on the number of owners, and the nature of those owners.
- Capital growth needs and strategy: Certain forms of organization are more amenable than others to raising capital from multiple sources.
- Management structure: Certain forms of organization are more flexible than others.
- Tax implications: Tax laws vary dramatically between the various types of entity structures.
- Regulatory burden: Securities laws have a greater impact on some forms of entity than others.
- Administrative burden, formalities, and expenses involved in establishing and maintaining the various business structures: Some forms require that documents be prepared and filed with a designated state agency and/or via written agreements between the participants.
- Survivability: Some entities terminate upon certain events.

- Privacy: Certain business and financial information regarding certain entities are required to be made public.

- Exit strategy and liquidity needs: Certain structures provide more flexibility for the participants as to liquidity and/or withdrawal.

As mentioned earlier, legal form choices for a new venture run from sole proprietorships to full-blown corporations. Let's explore each form in detail, and weigh in on the various advantages and disadvantages of each.

Sole Proprietorships

The most basic business legal form is the sole proprietorship. A sole proprietorship is created by default any time an individual owns a business without going through the specific formalities required to create a **statutory entity**. A sole proprietorship can operate under the individual owner's name or under a fictitious name. Most jurisdictions require that fictitious names be registered. A sole proprietorship does not have separate legal status from the owner.

For liability, as well as tax purposes, a business operated as a sole proprietorship is the alter ego of the proprietor. A proprietor is personally responsible for the debts and obligations of the business, as well as for the actions of employees.[2] If the sole proprietor sells someone an interest of less than 100 percent of the business, the business by default becomes a general partnership. Of course, if you launch your business as a sole proprietorship that *does not* mean you are not able to change the legal structure. In fact, many people conduct business originally under the sole proprietorship form, but change the structure to a limited liability structure once they get serious about it.[3]

A sole proprietorship is owned and managed by one person (or for tax purposes, a husband and wife). From the perspective of the Internal Revenue Service (IRS) a sole proprietor and his or her business are one tax entity. Business profits are reported and taxed on the owner's personal tax return and taxed at the personal income tax rate.

Setting up a sole proprietorship is easy and inexpensive since no legal formation documents need be filed with any governmental agency. Once a fictitious name statement is filed in jurisdictions that require one and other requisite basic tax permits and business licenses are obtained, the enterprise is ready for business.

When a business is operated as a sole proprietorship, essentially all income generated through the business is self-employment income and subject to the self-employment tax. The primary and significant downside of a sole proprietorship is that it is an unlimited liability entity—its owner is personally liable for all the business debts. Given that fact, why would anyone operate a business as a sole proprietorship? The unfortunate answer is that most of the time they are simply unaware of the unlimited liability. However, someone might choose to operate as a sole proprietorship because of the relative ease of, and lack of expenses entailed in, establishing the business.

Typically, the sole proprietor owns a small service or retail operation, such as a roadside produce stand, hardware store, bakery, or restaurant, that frequently caters to a group of regular customers. The owner normally provides the capital needed to start and operate the business through personal savings or borrowed money. The sole proprietor is usually an active manager, employing only a few people and working in the business every day. He or she controls the operations, supervises the staff, and makes the decisions. The managerial ability of the owner usually accounts for the success or failure of the business.

ADVANTAGES: Many people desire to be their own boss, write their own paycheck, and set their own working hours. A sole proprietorship accomplishes this goal and takes it a step further. As mentioned above, the owner of a sole proprietorship *is* the business. If something should happen to the owner, the business immediately ceases to exist. From a tax perspective, the owner pays taxes on all earnings from the sole proprietorship at the personal income tax rate. The advantages of a sole proprietorship go beyond being your own boss. They also include the following:

- **Ease of Starting.** A sole proprietorship is the easiest way to start a business. Most states require no legal forms to be filed. Some do recommend registering the firm name with the state or county clerk office, especially when using an assumed name (i.e., when operating other than under the proprietor's name). This form is usually called a **"DBA"** or **"doing business as,"** and usually entails a small filing fee.

- **Control.** The sole proprietor has sole control of the business. That means the owner is in charge of marketing, sales, customer relations, and maintenance. As the singular owner of the firm the sole proprietor doesn't have to have board meetings or meet with shareholders to make changes to the business plan.

- **Sole Participation in Profits and Losses.** Because the sole proprietor has no outside investors, he or she is the only one to participate in the profits and losses of the business.

- **Use of Owner's Abilities.** The sole proprietor has the satisfaction of running her business and making as much money as her abilities will allow. The limits of her personal income are bounded only by her own skills and business savvy.

- **Tax Breaks.** A major, advantage of the sole proprietorship is that the business itself pays no income tax. The company's profits and losses are reported on the owner's personal tax return.

- **Secrecy.** Since there are no shareholders in a sole proprietorship other than the owner, there is no need for disclosure of business information. Companies with more than one shareholder are required to disclose financial performance, governance decisions, and information about financing and shareholder rights.

- **Ease of Dissolving.** If the sole proprietor decides to dissolve her business for any reason, there are no legal complications. As long as she had paid all the outstanding bills, her decision would be all that was needed to close the company.

DISADVANTAGES: If the sole proprietorship had only advantages, a person organizing a business would have little to consider. But the realities of business are never so simple or certain. Sole proprietorships also have a number of disadvantages, including the following:

- **Unlimited Liability.** The law provides that the sole proprietor's total wealth may be used to satisfy claims against the business. For the business owner, this means almost everything she owns could be sold to pay any debts or legal claims against the business.

- **Difficulty in Raising Capital.** For most sole proprietors, their investment in the business is limited to their personal wealth. The amount the business owner can borrow to operate the business is limited by that personal wealth. If the owner has a large estate, there would be little problem borrowing money. Generally, however, businesses requiring large amounts of capital are not formed as sole proprietorships.

- **Limitations in Managerial Ability.** The sole proprietor must have or must obtain all the know-how needed to manage the business. Operating a business requires planning, organizing, controlling, marketing, financial, motivational, and other skills. Rarely does an individual have this range of needed expertise.

- **Lack of Stability.** Death, illness, bankruptcy, or retirement of the owner terminates the proprietorship. The sole proprietor's assets could be sold to others, but the original business, as organized, would cease to exist.

- **Demands on Time.** Sole proprietors often work 60 to 80 hours a week, especially when the business is new.

- **Difficulty in Hiring and Keeping Highly Motivated Employees.** The sole proprietor is the business. Where can another self-motivated, high-energy employee go in the business? Workers with their own visions and goals and a high drive to succeed often have to quit the sole proprietorship to find opportunities for personal growth.

Exhibit 7.1 provides a summary of the advantages and disadvantages of the sole proprietorship form of business.

EXHIBIT 7.1 The Advantages and Disadvantages of the Sole Proprietorship

Sole Proprietorships	
Advantages	**Disadvantages**
Ease of starting	Unlimited liability
Control	Difficulty in raising capital
Sole participation in profits and losses	Limitations in managerial ability
Use of owner's abilities	Lack of stability
Tax breaks	Demands on time
Secrecy	Difficulty in hiring and retaining employees
Ease of dissolving	

Partnerships

Partnership law in the United States has been derived from the **Uniform Partnership Act** (UPA), originally introduced in 1914 by the National Conference of Commissioners on Uniform State Laws. The more recent Revised Uniform Partnership Act (RUPA) was approved in 1994, bringing the law of partnerships in line with modern business practices and trends while retaining many of the valuable provisions in the original act. It was amended in 1997 to provide limited liability for partners in a limited liability partnership (LLP).[4]

Section 6 of the Uniform Partnership Act defines **partnership** as "an association of two or more persons to carry on as co-owners of a business for profit."[5] The law regards individuals as partners when they act in such a way as to make people believe they operate a business together. A partnership can be based on a written contract or an oral agreement. Other than the difference in the number of owners, a partnership is similar in many respects to a sole proprietorship. In a partnership the co-owners share everything, including the risk, hard work, assets, and profits. Some of today's large corporations, including Sears, Procter & Gamble, and Lever Brothers, began as partnerships. Partnerships account for 8 percent of U.S. businesses and 6 percent of the total revenue.

About 1.8 million partnerships of various types exist in the United States, including more than 16 million people who are in the role of "partner." The three major partnership types are general partnerships, limited partnerships, and joint ventures. A **general partnership** is a business with at least one general partner who has unlimited liability for the debts of the business. A limited partnership has at least one general partner and one or more **limited partners**. Finally, the **joint venture** is a special type of partnership established to carry out a special project or to operate for a specific time period. Let's look at each type separately.

General Partnership: Regardless of the percentage of the business they own, general partners have authority to act and make binding decisions as owners of the business. Each general partner is liable for all the debts of the business. Partners generally share profits and losses according to a plan specified by an agreement between or among them.

© szefei, 2012. Used under license from Shutterstock, Inc.

With the authority to act as an owner, each general partner can engage the partnership in binding agreements. Unless a partnership agreement prevents a general partner from making such agreements, the partnership is responsible for all actions of each owner.

Limited Partnership: All partnerships must have at least one general partner. A limited partnership includes one or more general partners and one or more limited partners. The general partners arrange and run the business, while the limited partners are investors only. The limited partner investors receive special tax advantages and protection from liability. Limited partners legally may have no say in managing the business. If this requirement is violated, the "limited" status is dissolved.

Limited partnerships are usually found in service industries or in professional firms such as real estate and dentistry. They are also used extensively to enable various international arrangements. In some states, a special notice must be filed in the county or district where the limited partnership has its offices.

Joint Venture: Sometimes a number of individuals and businesses join together in order to accomplish a specific purpose or objective or to complete a single transaction. For example, they may wish to purchase a building in downtown Phoenix and resell it for a profit. This would be called a joint venture.

A joint venture in the United States or abroad is something less than the ordinary partnership, which continues as a business. There is some confusion among the courts as to whether a joint venture is a partnership. We think there are enough similarities to categorize it as such. For instance, one of the joint venture partners acting within the scope of his or her authority may bind the other partner(s) in the joint venture. Also, the liabilities of the parties to a joint venture are similar to the liabilities of the partnership. For many entrepreneurs, this business form is used to establish international operations. Working in a joint venture with an international partner can make it easier to enter foreign markets.[6]

As you can see, there are a variety of partnership forms to choose among. Entrepreneurs should select the form that best enables the venture to achieve its business goals. As with the sole proprietorship, partnerships have a number of advantages and disadvantages. Let's examine the advantages of a partnership next.

ADVANTAGES

- **Greater Access to Capital.** In the sole proprietorship, the amount of capital available to the new enterprise is limited to the personal wealth and credit of the owner. In a partnership, the amount of capital may increase significantly. A person with a good idea but little capital can look for partners with the capital and/or credit standing to develop and market the idea.

- **Combined Managerial Skills.** In a partnership, people with different talents and skills may join together. One partner may be good at marketing; the other may be expert at accounting and financial matters. Combining these skills could provide a greater chance of success.

- **Ease of Starting.** Because it involves a private contractual arrangement, a partnership is fairly easy to start. It is nearly as easy to start as a sole proprietorship. The cost of starting a partnership is low; it usually involves only a modest legal fee for drawing up a written **partnership agreement**, which is not necessary but highly desirable.

- **Clear Legal Status.** Over the years, legal precedents for partnerships have been established through court cases. The questions of rights, responsibilities, liabilities, and partner duties have fairly well-established legal precedents. Thus the legal status of the partnership is clearly understood: Lawyers can provide sound legal advice about partnership issues.

- **Tax Advantages.** The partnership has some tax advantages over other forms. In a partnership, as in a sole proprietorship, the owners pay individual taxes on their business earnings, but the partnership, as a business, does not pay income tax.

DISADVANTAGES

- **Unlimited Liability.** Each general partner is liable for a partnership's debts. Suppose Tom and Greg's partnership fails. A bad deal that Tom had made left the partnership with outstanding bills of $25,000. This amount must be paid by the partnership, or through liquidation of one or both partners' personal assets. If the partnership has no assets, and Tom lacks the personal assets to pay his share of the debt, Greg would be legally obligated to make up the difference, including through the use of personal assets. This is a major reason for choosing partners carefully.

- **Potential Disagreements.** Decisions made by several people are often better than those made by one. However, having two or more people deciding on some aspects of the business can be dangerous.[7] Power and authority are divided, and the partners will not always agree with each other. Also, decision making becomes more time consuming because agreement must be reached before action can be taken. If the disagreement grows into irreconcilable differences, breaking up the partnership can be an expensive and painful process.[8]

- **Investment Withdrawal Difficulty.** A person who invests money in a partnership may have a hard time withdrawing the investment. The money is tied up in the operation of the business. The partnership agreement generally specifies how or when partners may be able to recover their investments. In general, the criteria for getting money back out are stringent since cash is a precious resource to a new enterprise.

- **Limited Capital Availability.** The partnership may have an advantage over the sole proprietorship in the availability of capital, but it does not compare to a corporation in ability to raise capital. In most cases, partners have a limited capability and cannot compete in business requiring large outlays. The amount of capital a partnership can raise depends on the personal wealth of the partners and their credit ratings. It also depends on how much partners are willing to invest.

- **Instability.** If a partner dies or withdraws from the business, the partnership is dissolved. A new partnership or some other form of business organization must be legally established.

Exhibit 7.2 provides an at-a-glance view of the various advantages and disadvantages of a partnership.

EXHIBIT 7.2 Advantages and Disadvantages of a Partnership

Partnerships	
Advantages	Disadvantages
Greater access to capital	Unlimited liability
Combined managerial skills	Potential disagreements
Ease of starting	Investment withdrawal difficulty
Clear legal status	Limited capital availability
Tax advantages	Lack of stability

The Limited Liability Company

The limited liability company (LLC) is a relatively new legal form that has now been adopted in all fifty states and has become a very popular form of business entity.[9] In essence, the LLC provides all the benefits of a partnership, but limits the liability exposure of each owner to the amount of their investment. Further, unlike a limited partnership where the limited partner cannot participate in management of the company, anyone can participate in the management of an LLC and still have limited liability protection.

When two or more people go into business together, they've automatically formed a general partnership; they don't need to file any formal paperwork. By contrast, to form a limited liability company (LLC), business owners must file formal **Articles of Organization** with their state's LLC filing office (usually the Secretary or Department of State) and comply with other state filing requirements. The LLC can have an unlimited number of investors, who in the parlance of the LLC are known as **members**. Generally, the filing fee is between $50 and $300, depending on the state. Usually the website that includes your state's legal forms will also enable you to search whether your preferred firm name is already in use. If not, granting the LLC is typically perfunctory and occurs within minutes if you file online, or within weeks if you prefer to file via mail. The LLC is also required to prepare an **operating agreement**, which is similar to a partnership agreement.

The operating agreement sets the rules for governing the company (such as the rules for investor meetings, if any) as well as the rights and responsibilities of the members. Thus, it states the members' understanding of who is responsible for contributions of capital and how much, who is to receive distributions and how much, who is to be allocated the various tax attributes of the company such as profits, losses, gains and credits, and under what circumstance the company will dissolve, among others. The operating agreement is not filed with any state agency, but is rather kept by a designated member of the LLC or an assignee, such as an attorney.

Aside from formation requirements, the main difference between a partnership and an LLC is that partners are personally liable for any business debts of the partnership—meaning that creditors of the partnership can go after the partners' personal assets—while members (owners) of an LLC are not personally liable for the company's debts and liabilities.

© Lyao, 2012. Used under license from Shutterstock, Inc.

There is one similarity between LLCs and partnerships, however. They both offer **pass-through taxation**, which means that the owners report business income or losses on their individual tax returns; the partnership or LLC itself does not pay state or federal income taxes. Significantly, the LLC provides the opportunity flexibly to allocate the profits and losses of the venture. That is, it is up to the owners to decide how to allocate the profits or losses among themselves. For example, if the venture makes nice profits, it is possible that one of the founders is better able to pay the taxes on those profits. As such, that individual may have a larger portion of the profits allocated for tax purposes. Note that this allocation occurs *regardless of whether* cash is actually distributed. Most startups elect to keep any profits in the venture for future growth. The allocation of the tax implications of those profits must occur despite this. Thus, if the venture makes a lot of money and that money is retained in the venture, it is possible to allocate the tax implications of that profit in a flexible manner. Of course, anyone who accepts more than his or her pro-rata share of tax liability may expect some type of compensation for doing so. This may be in the form of additional stock or stock options.

ADVANTAGES. There are many advantages to a Limited Liability Company. Combining the best features of both partnerships and corporations, the main advantages of an LLC are the following:

- **Limited Liability:** The investors in an LLC enjoy limited liability for the commitments and actions of the company. That means their personal assets are not at risk as long as the company does not engage in fraudulent business practices. They are liable up to the amount of their percentage ownership of the company's assets.

- **Pass-Through Taxation:** As with sole proprietorships, partnerships, and S-corporations, the LLC is not separately taxed. Profits and losses of the LLC "pass through" to the owners to be taxed at the individual income tax rate.

- **Flexible Allocation of Profits/Losses:** The LLC structure allows for flexible allocation of profits and losses. In other words, the tax liabilities associated with the venture's operations can be allocated flexibly according to the needs and wishes of the principals.

- **Investors Can Manage:** Unlike a limited partnership, which does not allow limited partners to manage, the LLC allows any shareholder to also be a manager without risking limited liability status. This advantage is significant, especially to the founders of a company who want to contribute funds and be part of the active management team.

- **Unlimited Membership:** The LLC has no restrictions regarding the number of individuals who may participate as shareholders. In most states, the S-corporation restricts the number of investors to thirty-five individuals. An LLC can have as many "members" as necessary.

- **Ease of Organizing:** Organizing an LLC is usually a simple matter, requiring only the filing of Articles of Organization with the appropriate state Secretary of State. Usually, LLC owners can file this paperwork without the aid of an attorney for less than $500.

DISADVANTAGES. The disadvantages of an LLC are due primarily to its relatively recent adoption by state legislatures. With the LLC form now less than a decade old, many people still don't understand it well, and courts have only begun to form a record of common law. The latter is important because well-established common law makes for a more predictable legal environment. For example, most cases involving small corporations are settled out of court because the attorneys can determine from common law the likely outcome of an expensive trial. With the LLC and its limited history of common law the outcome of legal disputes is less certain. Other disadvantages of the LLC form of business include:

- **Difficulty in Raising Money:** The LLC does not allow for the issuance of shares of stock. Rather, individuals who invest in an LLC are known as "members." Many seasoned and savvy investors are less comfortable with this form of investment, preferring to have actual stock certificates on file with their attorneys.

- **No Continuity of Life:** An LLC does not have a reliable continuity of existence. The Articles of Organization must specify the date on which the LLC's existence will terminate.

Unless otherwise provided in the articles of organization or a written operating agreement, an LLC is dissolved at the death, withdrawal, resignation, expulsion, or bankruptcy of a member (unless within ninety days a majority in both the profits and capital interests vote to continue the LLC).

- **Limited Transferability:** No one can become a member of an LLC (either by transfer of an existing membership or the issuance of a new one) without the consent of members having a majority in interest (excluding the person acquiring the membership interest) unless the articles of organization provide otherwise.

Exhibit 7.3 highlights the various advantages and disadvantages of the limited liability company.

EXHIBIT 7.3 Advantages and Disadvantages of a Limited Liability Company

Limited Liability Companies	
Advantages	Disadvantages
Limited liability	Difficult to raise money
Pass through taxation	No continuity of life
Investors can manage	Limited transferability
Unlimited membership	
Ease of organizing	

Corporations

A corporation is an artificial legal entity typically chartered by a state. A corporation is usually formed to operate a business. Once chartered, the corporation is completely separate from its owners, has its own life, is liable for its own debts, and must pay its own taxes.

There are actually two types of corporations that the entrepreneur can choose between. The more commonly known of the two varieties is the so-called C-corporation. This type of legal entity is better known because it is the legal structure for many of the largest companies in the world. Most public companies—those traded on the major stock exchanges—choose this form because of the well-established laws that govern the structure worldwide, and for the multiple options it offers for raising capital.

The main difference between a C-corporation and other business structures is that a C-corporation files and pays corporate income taxes directly. This is because a C-corporations is considered a separate legal entity from its shareholders and must pay taxes on income left over after business expenses.

There are a number of instances in which it is beneficial for the entrepreneur to choose this legal form. If the entrepreneur plans to retain profits to finance growth, repay debt, or make other capital expenditures, the C-corporation form could make sense. This is because C-corporations can take advantage of corporate income tax rates, which are sometimes lower than personal tax rates. For profitable companies, C-corporation status has the ability provide greater flexibility in terms of planning and controlling federal income taxes. C-corporations also can deduct the cost of certain fringe benefit packages.

On the other hand, the C-corporation is taxed twice on its profits—once as a corporation, and a second time when those profits are dispersed as dividends or upon liquidation. This effect is known as **double taxation** and is one of the major disadvantages of a C-corporation. The C-corporation also has advantages for fund raising as it is the only business form that is allowed to sell both **common** and **preferred stock**. Common stock is often non-voting and has restrictions on transfer and redemption. Preferred stock usually includes voting rights and is usually treated preferentially if the company is sold or liquidated.

Special rules and regulations permit what is referred to as the S-corporation to use non-corporate tax rates at the request of the shareholders. This allows the shareholders to be treated as individual taxpayers. In other words, the income or loss of the corporation passes through to the individual shareholders as if they were partners. To qualify as an S-corporation, a business must meet the following requirements:

- It must be incorporated within the United States.

- It can only sell shares of common stock.

- All shareholders must be residents of the United States.

- Shareholders must be natural persons, estates, or trusts.

- No shareholder can be a partnership or a corporation.

- Some states limit the number of shareholders.

- No more than 20 percent of its income can come from passive activities (such as owning shares of stock in another corporation).

Like other forms of ownership, the S-corporation has advantages and disadvantages. The primary advantage is that the shareholders' tax brackets can result in tax savings. If a corporation expects to lose money in the first years of operation and if the shareholders will have income from other sources, the S-corporation is preferred. Here the losses passed through from the S-corporation can shelter the shareholders from income tax. (Losses are limited to specific amounts.) The primary disadvantage is that the tax law governing the S-corporation is very complex. Tax and legal advice is strongly recommended before and after making the S-corporation choice.[11] The best time to terminate "S" status is when the S-corporation begins to produce very high levels of taxable income. Thus, owner(s) must be alert and up-to-date on the flow of taxable income. Corporations can change legal form from S-corporation status to C-corporation status fairly easily, but there are costs involved.

ADVANTAGES. The power and presence of corporations in American business suggest that this form has certain advantages over other forms of business ownership.

- **Limited Liability.** A person investing funds in a corporation receives shares of stock and becomes an owner. In a corporation, the liability for the shareholder equals the amount of funds invested. Thus, if the business is forced to liquidate, each owner loses only the amount of money he or she has invested.

- **Skilled Management Team.** The board of directors has the duty of hiring professional managers, and the owners delegate their power of operating the business to these managers. Professional managers are trained and experienced career executives. They may own shares of stock in the business but usually not enough to control the corporation.

- **Transfer of Ownership.** Shareholders have the right to sell their shares of a corporation's stock to whomever they please, barring a legal restriction on some closed corporations. These shares of ownership can be sold whenever the shareholder desires and at the price the buyer is willing to pay. Thus, shareholders can freely buy and sell shares of stock. The investment flows easily and is not frozen. This right to sell shares of stock gives corporations the ability to attract large numbers of shareholders.

- **Greater Capital Base.** As previously stated, the size of a proprietorship or partnership is limited to the amount of capital that one or several people have available and are willing to invest. Corporations, however, can attract capital from a large number of investors by selling shares of stock.

- **Stability.** State law varies, but a corporation can usually be chartered to operate indefinitely. Shareholders' deaths, retirement, or sale of stock need not dissolve the business. The corporation's policies may be altered by the sale of large blocks of stock, but the business will go on. Nor will the death or retirement of the president of the board or the chief executive officer stop the corporation from doing business.

- **Legal-Entity Status.** A corporation can purchase property, make contracts, or sue and be sued in its corporate name. These characteristics distinguish it most clearly from other forms of business organization. As Justice Thurgood Marshall of the U.S. Supreme Court stated, a corporation is "an artificial being." This legal status allows the shareholders to have limited liability.

DISADVANTAGES. As was true with the other forms of business organization, the corporation has some disadvantages.

- **Difficulty and Expense of Starting.** Starting a corporation involves applying for a charter from a state. Each state has its own set of laws; these must be considered before deciding where to incorporate. An attorney should be hired to complete legal forms. Attorney fees and state charter fees must be paid. The chosen state then reviews the application and issues a charter that specifies various restrictions on operations.

- **Lack of Control.** The individual shareholder has little control over the operations of the corporation except to vote for a slate of individuals for the board of directors. The buying and selling of shares of stock is the only real control an owner has.

- **Multiple Taxation and Fees.** In addition to an annual franchise tax in the state of incorporation, an annual payment is required by most states for the right to operate as a corporation. No such fees are charged to a proprietorship or partnership. Some states levy a corporate income tax on those monies earned within the state. At the federal level, the corporation has to pay taxes on its profits. Small corporations are taxed at 15 percent for income up to $50,000; income $50,000-$75,000, 25 percent; income over $75,000, 34 percent. The shareholders must also pay income tax on the dividends they receive through ownership.

- **Lack of Secrecy.** A corporation must provide each shareholder with an annual report. In a closed corporation, the few reports circulated usually won't get into the hands of non-owners. But when a large number of reports are issued, the reports become public knowledge. These reports present data on sales volume, profit, total assets, and other financial matters. Public disclosure enables competitors and other outsiders to see the corporation's financial condition.

- **Lack of Personal Interest.** In most large corporations, management and ownership are separate. This separation can result in a lack of personal interest in the success of the corporation. If the managers are also shareholders, personal interest is enhanced. It is assumed that employees who are also owners will work harder for the success of the business, but the accuracy of this assumption isan individual matter. Most managers have pride in their work and want any business they are involved with to succeed.

- **Credit Limitations.** Banks and other lenders have to consider the limited liability of the owners of a corporation. If the corporation fails, its creditors can look only to the assets of the business to satisfy claims. For partnerships, the creditors can rely on personal assets of the partners to pay off business debts.

Exhibit 7.4 summarizes the various advantages and disadvantages of the corporation.

EXHIBIT 7.4 Advantages and Disadvantages of Corporations

Corporations	
Advantages	**Disadvantages**
Limited liabillity	Difficult and expensive to start
Skilled management team	Lack of control
Transfer of ownership	Multiple taxation and fees
Greater capital base	Lack of secrecy
Stability	Lack of personal interest
Legal entity status	Credit limitations

Nonprofit Corporations

There are more than 1.1 million nonprofit organizations that employ about 12 million people in the United States. Many organizations are **nonprofit corporations;** that is they are not profit-seeking enterprises. The nonprofit sector includes universities and other schools, charities, churches, volunteer organizations, credit unions, country clubs, government organizations, cooperatives, and a number of other organizations.

Actually, the term "nonprofit" can be misleading. The nonprofit has to make a profit in order to continue to operate. No organization can run without making a profit, or without at least making enough money to cover expenses. The nonprofit corporation differs from the for-profit corporation primarily in that the former is prohibited by law from distributing earnings (paying dividends) to owners. Whereas the organization can make a profit, pay its expenses, and grow, these profits cannot be provided to owners in the manner of a for-profit enterprise. The nonprofit exists because the founders believe that the firm provides something of value (e.g., help to the homeless, research, education) that is not being provided well or at all by other enterprises. Donations, dues, and the sale of goods or services provide the funds to pay employees and finance operations.

Exhibit 7.5 provides a handy summary of the various legal forms discussed in this chapter.

EXHIBIT 7.5 Summary of Business Legal Forms		
Type of Entity	Main Advantages	Main Disadvantages
Sole Proprietorship	Simple and inexpensive to create and operate Owner reports profit or loss on his or her personal tax return	Owner personally liable for business debts
General Partnership	Simple and inexpensive to create and operate Owners (partners) report their share of profit or loss on their personal tax returns	Owners (partners) personally liable for business debts
Limited Partnership	Limited partners have limited personal liability for business debts as long as they don't participate in management General partners can raise cash without involving outside investors in management of business	General partners personally liable for business debts More expensive to create than general partnership Suitable mainly for companies that invest in real estate
Regular Corporation (C-Corporation)	Owners have limited personal liability for business debts Fringe benefits can be deducted as business expense Owners can split corporate profit among owners and corporation, paying lower overall tax rate	More expensive to create than partnership or sole proprietorship Paperwork can seem burdensome to some owners Separate taxable entity
S Corporation	Owners have limited personal liability for business debts Owners report their share of corporate profit or loss on their personal tax returns Owners can use corporate loss to offset income from other sources	More expensive to create than partnership or sole proprietorship More paperwork than for a limited liability company, which offers similar advantages Income must be allocated to owners according to their ownership interests Fringe benefits limited for owners who own more than 2 percent of shares

Nonprofit Corporation	Corporation doesn't pay income taxes Contributions to charitable corporation are tax deductible Fringe benefits can be deducted as business expense	Full tax advantages available only to groups organized for charitable, scientific, educational, literary, or religious purposes Property transferred to corporation stays there; if corporation ends, property must go to another nonprofit
Limited Liability Company	Owners have limited personal liability for business debts even if they participate in management Profit and loss can be allocated differently than ownership interests IRS rules now allow LLCs to choose between being taxed as partnership or corporation	More expensive to create than partnership or sole proprietorship State laws for creating LLCs may not reflect latest federal tax changes
Limited Liability Partnership	Mostly of interest to partners in old-line professions such as law, medicine, and accounting Owners (partners) aren't personally liable for the malpractice of other partners Owners report their share of profit or loss on their personal tax returns	Unlike a limited liability company or a professional limited liability company, owners (partners) remain personally liable for many types of obligations owed to business creditors, lenders, and landlords Not available in all states Often limited to a short list of professions

EQUITY AND EQUITY DISTRIBUTION

Equity is simply another term for an ownership interest in a business. Equity financing should be distinguished from debt financing. Debt financing, taking out a loan or selling bonds to raise capital, involves paying interest to a lender for the use of the lender's money. The cost of debt financing is typically finite, and the lenders will not share in any appreciation in the value of the business. However, in the short-term, repayment of the loan can place constraints on the startup venture's cash flow; both principal and interest must be repaid, and repayment is required regardless of whether the company is successful. The requirement to make periodic payments to service debt can make it difficult for the startup venture to manage its cash flow.

Equity financing entails selling part of the ownership of the company. Equity financing is more flexible than debt financing with respect to cash flow concerns. There are typically no short-term repayment requirements, and equity investors share the risk. However, equity investors also share in any appreciation in the value of the business. And, while profit interests can be separated from governance and control, any time equity investors are added, there is some loss of independence on the part of the pre-investment ownership team.

Equity and Stock

The particular terminology used to denominate equity varies depending upon the particular legal structure of the entity. As noted earlier, equity interests in partnerships and LLCs are typically referred to in terms of ownership percentages or **units** corresponding to a percentage of ownership. When a corporation is created, its Articles of Incorporation authorize it to issue up to a designated total number of **authorized shares** of stock. The original number of authorized shares is largely arbitrary, but it should be selected carefully based on the venture's financial plan and future fundraising objectives. The number of authorized shares can be changed, but only through a vote by the venture's shareholders. From the authorized pool of shares, the venture then can issue shares to founders and investors. It is the **issued shares** that constitute the ownership structure of the venture. That is, a shareholder's percentage of ownership of the venture is calculated as the proportion of shares held compared to total shares that have been issued. Most ventures will reserve a portion of the authorized shares in the total company's treasury for later use. The shares held in reserve are called **unissued shares**.

It is also important to note that not all stock is created equal. A venture's Articles of Incorporation can be crafted to permit it to issue different classes of shares, each having a specific designation and unique preferences, limitations, and/or rights. These share classes are usually associated with financing rounds, and are often designated as Class A, Class B, and so on; or as Series A, Series B and so on. The Articles of Incorporation either specify the particulars of each class of shares, or delegate the authority to the board of directors. In general, the preferences and relative rights of classes of shares relate to voting, payment of dividends, and distribution of corporate assets on dissolution. Limitations of a class of shares typically relate to restrictions on transferability. Shareholders of private ventures normally do not want to leave it up to shareholders to decide to whom they may transfer their shares. Transferability is usually governed by **buy-sell** clauses in the shareholder's agreement.

In the next sections we discuss two types of stock, common and preferred, that are commonly used to represent ownership interests and rights in a corporation.

Common Stock

Common stock refers to the baseline of ownership in a corporation and a right to a portion of profits from that company. Many ventures do not specifically define common stock. Instead, they refer to classes of stock having different characteristics without ever specifically categorizing any particular class or classes as common stock. The designation for common stock tends to vary from company to

© Mike Flippo, 2012. Used under license from Shutterstock, Inc.

company often depending upon whether a special class of stock is issued to the founders. If only one class of stock is issued, it will be common stock. As used in this text, the term *common stock* means a class of stock that does not have any preference over another class of stock. Common stock is normally the last in line when dividends are paid, and in the event of liquidation. In the event of liquidation, creditors, bondholders, and preferred stockholders typically are paid first and common stockholders are entitled only to what is left.

Owners of common stock usually have voting rights to elect the members of the board of directors who oversee the management and operations of the company. Different classes of stock may have different voting rights, as will be discussed. Profits of the company may be paid out in the form of dividends to the common stockholders. However, dividends on common stock are not guaranteed and usually only occur when the company is profitable. The amount and timing of dividends are determined by the board of directors.

Owners of common stock get the benefits of increases in value as the company grows. On the other hand, the value of their ownership interest decreases if the company is unsuccessful. So ownership in common stock may provide the greatest upside potential to investors, but it may also provide the greatest risk of loss if the business does not succeed.

Preferred Stock

Technically, any stock that has any sort of advantageous characteristic over other classes of stock is referred to as preferred stock. Preferred stock typically has provisions over and above common stock that:

- Provide a specific dividend on a periodic basis (e.g., monthly, quarterly, semiannually, or annually)

- Classify the stock as senior to other classes of stock in the order of distribution (i.e., payments are made to the preferred stockholder before dividends are paid to the other classes or when there is a distribution upon liquidation)

- Indicates that preferred shareholders have limited or no voting rights.

Preferred stock tends to be a more conservative investment than common stock; it is not as volatile. Investors purchase preferred stock for the dividends. Unlike a dividend on common stock that is paid out to shareholders essentially at the discretion of the board of directors, dividends on preferred shares often are a fixed amount regardless of the earnings of the company. In some cases, the right to those dividends can accrue on a periodic basis. While payment of dividends on preferred classes of stock are not guaranteed *per se*, they are guaranteed to be paid before payment made to any junior classes of stock.

Preferred stock can include a wide range of advantages, also referred to as "sweeteners." A few of these advantages are discussed below.

Founder's Stock

Founder's stock is used to refer to stock issued to the founders of the corporation. There is, however, no universal definition of founder's stock in terms of its characteristics. If the corporation issues a single class of stock, founder's stock is simply common stock issued to the founders. However, founder's stock can sometimes be a separate class of stock with its own specific characteristics. For example, the company founders may issue two classes of stock: Class A stock, which has one vote per share, and Class B stock, which has 10 votes per share. The founders would offer the Class A stock to investors, and issue the Class B stock to themselves, with the intent that the super-voting rights would ensure that they retain decision-making control of the company. In addition to the super-voting privilege, there have been a number of characteristics proposed for founder's stock, including:

- The right to convert shares into any other class of stock when that class of stock is offered to investors

- Liquidation preferences at a designated amount such as actual monies invested by the founders, a specified percentage of the founders holdings, or the valuation of the company prior to a successive round of financing

- Making the founder's stock preferred participating

Often, when part of the founder's contribution to the venture is **sweat equity**, founder's stock is subject to **vesting** in accordance with a predetermined, usually time-based, schedule or formula. Actual ownership of stock does not transfer until the vesting condition is met.

Of course, there tends to be a tension between having a special class of founder's stock with protective characteristics and the ability to attract future investors for subsequent financing rounds. In many instances, when a special class of founder's stock is in place, investors will attempt to negotiate away the founder's preferences as a precondition to invest.

It is important that founders keep the tax consequences of receiving stock in return for services. As a general proposition, such stock is considered income to the founder. Under the U.S. tax law, the founder has the option to recognize income (the difference between fair market value of and the price paid for the stock) either when the stock is issued or when the stock vests. However, if the founder/employee elects to recognize the value of the stock as income when the stock is issued, an **83(b) election** must be filed with the IRS no later than thirty days after the stock is issued. Since the value of the stock is likely to increase over time, it is generally beneficial for a founder/employee to make an 83(b) election. The 83(b) election starts the one-year capital gain holding period and phrases ordinary income (or alternative minimum tax) recognition to the issue date.

Equity Distribution in the Startup Venture

We have discussed the various legal structures that a business can take and different forms of equity. We now return to the interrelational dynamics of the creation and growth of the business. When one or more founders form a business, each makes a contribution to the business in return for some consideration. Initial contributions by principals are

© Monkey Business Images, 2012. Used under license from Shutterstock, Inc.

typically made in return for, at least in part, an equity interest. The particular form of that equity interest depends upon the particular legal structure selected for the venture. The question we now address is: How should the equity be distributed among those individuals or entities?

When the business is founded by more than one person (or entity), the perceived relative values of the contributions that each makes (or will make) to the venture are typically reflected by the relative percentages of ownership. The issue is simplified if each of the founders makes a strictly monetary contribution to the venture in return for their equity interest. In that case, the relative percentage of ownership is easily determined. Each principal would hold an ownership interest equal to the ratio of the amount of money contributed by the individual to the total money contributed.

To the extent that founders make non-monetary contributions to the venture, the venture can provide separate compensation, other than equity, for such contributions. For example, one or more of the founders will often be involved in the management and operation of the business. In that case, the individual will provide those services as an employee or independent contractor and will be separately compensated. Most often, the venture pays a salary or fee for those services. However, compensation can also be in the form of trade, for example, the services are exchanged for an equivalent fair market value of services or product from the business. Likewise, a founder can also provide resources or intellectual property (IP) to the entity for compensation other than equity. In that case, the founder provides the IP or resources in the role of an independent entity (e.g., a lessor or licensor) and is compensated with something other than equity, such as a lease or royalty payment. The following Mini-Case focuses on a startup that paid for engineering services with royalties on future sales of the product.

MINI CASE

FAB Light Pays for Prototype with Royalties

Linda Pond's FAB Light startup didn't have the funds it needed to build its product—an LED light for coolers, toolboxes, or tackle boxes. The company had a rough prototype of the product, and it also had a good relationship with a local engineer who had the skills the company needed. To complete product development, Pond entered an agreement with the engineer. The agreement would pay him a portion of sales once the product hit the retail shelves. By deferring product development costs in this way, Pond saved approximately $60,000, which allowed the venture to funnel its $40,000 in cash into patent fees, product materials, and travel. In the first four years of sales, the company sold more than 136,000 FAB Lights through major retailers such as Walmart and Target.

Source: Adapted from Goodman, M., "Delayed Gratification," *Entrepreneur* (March 2012): 78; and from www.lindaleepond.com/fablight.

Despite these alternative compensation options for non-monetary contributions, such contributions often are compensated with equity. When non-monetary contributions must be figured into the equity distribution equation the determination of relative ownership percentage is more complicated. For example, when non-monetary contributions are made for equity in the business, the relative value of that contribution must be determined. In many instances, this value can be difficult to determine. Non-monetary contributions can take any number of other forms:

- Intellectual property

- An intangible right or relationship, such as a contractual right (e.g., the right to purchase property or a purchase order from a potential customer)

- Sweat equity (providing time and effort without drawing a "salary" or at a reduced "salary"; services provided at market rates are not a contribution to the venture)

- Resources (facilities, distribution, R&D, management)

- Credibility (e.g., credit, reputation) or access to sources of capital (network)

Facebook hired graffiti artist David Choe to paint some murals on the walls of the company's startup headquarters in Palo Alto. As the Mini-Case highlights, Choe made out very well when he elected to accept stock options in lieu of cash for payment for his creative work.

MINI-CASE

Artist Goes from Rags to Riches From Facebook Stock Options

Graffiti artist David Choe is hands-down one of the most surprising success stories to come out of the Facebook initial public offering. Choe was hired by then Facebook president Sean Parker to paint a mural at Facebook's first office in Palo Alto in 2005. When the mural was finished, Parker gave Choe the option of taking cash or stock options. At the time, Facebook was only a year old and only open to college and high school students. There was no "like" button, no revenue from advertising and no hype of a $5 billion dollar IPO.

Instead of taking cash, Choe took a chance and opted for the stock options. Choe was added on as an "adviser" to the company and received 0.1 to 0.25 percent in stock options. After you do the math, Choe's share is worth about $200 million. That's a mind-blowing figure, if you also consider that Choe has been homeless since painting that fateful mural.

Source: Adapted from C. Ngak, "Facebook Graffiti Artist David Choe, From Homeless to Millions," *CBS News TECHTALK*, February 3, 2012.

When the business is founded by more than one entity, the perceived relative values of the contributions that each makes or will make to the venture are typically determinative of the relative percentages of ownership. However, in many instances those standard valuation techniques are not applicable to non-monetary contributions. In fact, quite often with startup ventures the issue of relative value of contributions is simply a matter of the negotiation skills of the contributors. Factors tending to influence the valuation of a non-monetary contribution include:

- The relevance of the contribution to the venture. For example, there is often a premium for contributing the idea around which the venture is built.

- The intrinsic or demonstrable merit of the contribution. For example, consider the negotiating position of an inventor with an unproven idea as compared to that of an inventor that already has a working prototype.

- Favorable assessments by independent third parties.

- Legal exclusivity or protections. For example, consider the negotiating position of an inventor with an unproven idea as compared to an inventor with a patent.

- Uniqueness of the contribution.

- Demonstrable expertise in the technology or processes that form the basis of the venture.

- Relevant experience and track record.

- Relevant contacts and network.

- Reputation and goodwill.

- Efforts already taken that increase the likelihood of success of the venture

In practice, pure force of personality and skills in negotiations often tend to play a significant and sometimes definitive role in determining the relative equity positions of the founders.

Employee Stock Options

Employee stock option (ESO) plans are a flexible tool used by many companies to reward employees for performance and attract and retain a motivated staff. In effect, options preserve cash for the business while giving employees a stake in the success of the company. The popularity of ESO plans has seen remarkably steady growth since the 1980s. ESO plans became particularly popular during the days of the dot.com boom and, indeed, for a period of time, were an expected component of a compensation package for employees of high-technology companies. Today, ESO plans continue to be a relatively popular method of compensating employees and garnering loyalty for the employer. One survey estimates that over 11.2 million employees are participants in such plans.

In essence, an ESO plan is a contract between employer and employee that gives the employee the right to buy a specific number of shares in the company at a specified price, referred to as the **strike price**, over a specified period of time, referred to as the **exercise period**. When the employee exercises the option, he or she will get the benefit of the difference between the fair market value of the stock at the time of exercise and the strike price. In a typical ESO plan, there are specific provisions regarding the employee's eligibility to earn options under the plan and various restrictions on how the option is exercised and transferability of the stock after the option is exercised. Several common provisions and restrictions are explored below.

In the context of an employee stock option, vesting is a process or condition that must take place before an option can be exercised by the employee. For example, an ESO plan may require uninterrupted employment for a specified period of time (or some other length of service) before the employee is "vested." The vesting condition is most frequently the passage of time, but it may also be other things, such as the occurrence of an event or a milestone in the growth of the company. ESO plans may incorporate simple or elaborate vesting schedules. A typical vesting schedule for employees of a technology startup is incremental over four years, with the employee having no exercisable rights until he or she has remained with the company for at least twelve months at which point the right to exercise the option on the first 25 percent of the shares vests, and approximately 2 percent vest each month thereafter. No further vesting occurs after an employee leaves the company.

SUMMARY OF LEARNING OBJECTIVES

1.   **Understand** a business as an entity that is separate and distinct from participants in the enterprise. *The entrepreneur can set up a legal structure for their venture that separates the venture from the entrepreneur's personal assets. This type of limited liability entity enables the entrepreneur to operate the business and raise capital without risking his or her personal assets. Of course, the entrepreneur must operate the business in "good faith" and avoid fraudulent or negligent behavior to retain the limited liability status.*

2.   **Understand** the role of business partners in a business. *Business partners include the founders, investors, and others who by virtue of some contribution are granted an ownership position in the venture via the distribution of equity.*

3.   **Define** limited liability. *Limited liability is a legal status enjoyed by ventures that have registered with the state as an LLC or corporation. This status separates the assets of the venture from the personal assets of each of the principals (owners).*

4.   **Differentiate** between various forms of legal entity for structuring a business. *There are two basic business forms: unlimited liability entities and limited liability entities. The unlimited liability entities consist of the sole proprietorship and the general partnership. The limited liability entities consist of the limited partnership (which must include a general partnership to operate the venture), the limited liability company and the corporation (including both S-corporations and C-corporations).*

5.   **Describe** the formalities of maintaining a limited liability status. *To maintain limited liability status as a limited partner, the limited partner must refrain from assisting in the management and strategic decision making of the venture. This is referred to as an "arms length" relationship with the venture. To maintain limited liability status with LLC or corporation legal structures requires the principals to operate in good faith. This simply means that the principals are managing the venture openly, honestly, and, to the best of their knowledge, within the limits of legally allowable activities.*

6.   **Characterize** the nature of equity interest and its various forms. *Equity interest in a venture can be held in terms of "membership shares" in the case of an LLC, common stock in the case of an S-corporation, or common or preferred stock in the case of a C-corporation.*

7.   **Understand** distribution of equity interest among founders of a venture. *Equity interest in a venture is, at the founding, determined by the relative contributions of the founders (as judged by all the founders). Equity interest for investors is determined by their investment amount relative to the overall value of the venture as determined by mutual agreement between the investor and the owners. Equity interest for employees could be determined according to stock options and the terms that are offered for their on-the-job performance.*

8.   **Appreciate** the role of employee stock options. *Employee stock options can be used to provide incentives to employees to help the company grow and achieve its goals. Stock options provide opportunities for employees to become shareholders in the company based on their performance and length of tenure. Since they are motivated by the potential for ownership, they will help grow the venture to make their ownership percentage more valuable.*

STUDY QUESTIONS

1.   What are the risks of operating a business as a sole proprietorship?

2.   What are the advantages associated with operating a technology venture as a limited liability company?

3. Define the significance of making a business a "limited liability entity."

4. Who is responsible for the wrongful acts of a businesses employee? Under what circumstances would be employee be personally liable? Under what circumstances would the owners of the business be personally liable?

5. How does an entrepreneur determine which form of entity to adopt for his or her business?

6. Under what circumstances is it most beneficial for a company to self-fund or obtain debt financing to reach a particular milestone?

7. Describe what is meant by the term "Employee Stock Option plan." How can an entrepreneur use such a plan to build a new venture?

8. How can a technology entrepreneur use a vesting schedule to motivate employees?

9. What are the responsibilities of a corporation's board of directors? How can a technology entrepreneur ensure compliance with statutes governing the corporate entity?

10. Explain the difference between common and preferred stock. What are some potential features that can be added to preferred stock offerings?

KEY TERMS

83(b) election: A special tax status election that pertains to an Employee Stock Option plan whereby taxation of the value of the underlying shares can be deferred to a future date.

Articles of organization: The formal documents that govern the operations of a business entity that is organized as an LLC.

Authorized shares: A designated maximum total number of equity shares that a corporation is authorized to issue in its articles of incorporation.

Buy-sell clause: A clause within a business entity's formal agreement that limits the conditions under which ownership interest can be bought and sold.

Common stock: Baseline ownership interest in a corporation and a right to a portion of profits from that company.

Corporate veil: The limited liability protection enjoyed by principals of a statutory business entity that operates in good faith.

Corporation: The legal form of business entity that provides limited liability status to principals and also allows issuance of stock certificates. Corporations can be organized as subchapter S-corporations or as subchapter C-corporations.

DBA or "doing business as": A sole proprietorship or partnership that operates under a name other than the name of the owner(s) must file a DBA with the county clerk of courts in the county in which the headquarters is located.

Double taxation: A disadvantage of the C-corporation legal form is that profits may be taxed once as corporate profits and a second time as individual income when profits are distributed to owners as dividends.

Employee stock option (ESO): A contract between employer and employee that gives the employee the right (but not the obligation) to buy a specific number of shares in the company at a specified price (the grant, strike, or exercise price), over a specified period of time (the exercise period).

Equity: Another term for ownership interest in a business.

Equity interest: An ownership interest in a business enterprise.

Exercise period: The time period during which an employee may exercise an option to buy shares under an employee stock option plan.

Founders: The individuals or entities that initially form a business.

Founder's stock: Stock issued to the organizers of a business.

General partnership: The form of (unlimited liability) business entity created when the profits and losses of a business enterprise are shared between more than one individual, unless the formalities for creating a statutory entity have been followed.

Investors: Individuals or entities that provide capital to a venture in exchange for an ownership interest.

Issued shares: Shares authorized to a venture that have actually been distributed to principals (founders and/or investors).

Joint venture: A special type of partnership established to carry out a special project or to operate for a specific time period.

Lenders: Individuals or entities that provide capital to a business entity and expect repayment and interest over a specified period of time.

Limited liability: Forms of business entities that limit liability of the protected principal to the particular assets that the principal contributed to the venture and shielding the principal's other assets. These entities include, for example, corporations, limited liability companies (LLCs), and limited partnerships (LPs).

Limited liability company (LLC): A statutory entity formed by filing Articles of Organization, owned by members, and managed by either by the members or by one or more manager (who may or may not be a member).

Limited partner: A partner in a limited partnership who has limited liability to the extent of his or her contribution to the venture.

Limited partnership (LP): A statutory entity having one or more general partners and one or more limited partners. The general partners are responsible for managing the partnership. The limited partners are essentially passive investors and have limited liability.

Members: The owners of an LLC.

Nonprofit corporations: Nonprofit corporations are organizations that do not seek to make and distribute profits to owners.

Operating agreement: The official formative document for an LLC.

Pass-through taxation: Taxation on business entities that allocates profits and losses to principals to be taxed at the individual income tax rate.

Partnership: An association of two or more persons to carry on as co-owners of a business for profit.

Partnership agreement: An agreement among the partners in a general partnership.

Pierce the corporate veil: Circumstances under which limited liability entity status will be ignored, and liability imposed on the business owners, even in the absence of personal culpability, merely by virtue of their equity interests.

Preferred stock: Stock in a class that has any sort of advantageous characteristic over other classes of stock, typically a liquidation preference and/or a dividend preference.

Principals: Also known as owners, the individuals or entities that own a business (although there is specific terminology associated with the principals of different types of business entities).

Sole proprietorship: The form of (unlimited liability) business entity created when a single individual owns a business without going through the specific formalities required to create a statutory entity.

Statutory entity: A business that is formally registered within a particular state; it will receive limited liability protection (such entities take either LLC, LP, or corporate form).

Strike price: The pre-specified price at which shares allocated in an Employee Stock Option plan may be purchased from the company.

Sweat equity: Equity interest earned in a venture in exchange for labor contributions.

Uniform Partnership Act: The original act, introduced in 1914, that provides guidance for the legal responsibilities and limits of general partnerships. The Act was revised in 1994 as the Revised Uniform Partnership Act.

Units: Equity interests in a venture as blocks of shares.

Unissued shares: Authorized shares held in reserve by a corporation.

Unlimited liability: The condition under which a business and its owner(s) are considered to be one and the same, and where the non-business assets of the owner(s) are liable in the event of business failure or legal action against the business.

Vesting: A process or condition that must take place before a right can be exercised by, or actual ownership is transferred to, a beneficiary.

EXERCISES

In-Class Exercise

This in-class exercise is designed to give students a sense of what it feels like to distribute equity and decide legal structure. Groups of five students should be identified at random and asked to determine the equity structure for a startup software venture. They are to allocate equity among the five "founders" according to their ability to contribute value to the growing venture. After 15–20 minutes, each team should report out on how they allocated their equity among themselves.

Outside of Class Exercise

For this exercise, students are to visit their state's Secretary of State website to determine how to incorporate in that state. Each state has different procedures, fees, and options for new ventures to incorporate. To find your Secretary of State website you will probably need to do a Google search using appropriate key words.

For this assignment, students are to write a two-page summary of their findings, paying particular attention to the following:

- Does your state allow for online corporate registration? How long does that process take?

- What fees are involved in establishing your own LLC? S-corporation? C-corporation? Limited partnership?

- Conduct a name search for your venture concept. Is your business name available? What are some nearby business names? Will that be a problem for your branding?

- What other business services are provided at the Secretary of State website?

ENDNOTES

[1] Darby, J.B. III, "Right From the Start: Tax Strategies for Structuring a Startup Business," *Venture Capital Journal*, 43(4)(2003): 40–41.

[2] Fleischman, G.M., and J.J. Bryant, "C Corporation, LLC, or Sole Proprietorship? What Form Is Best for Your Business?"*Management Accounting Quarterly*, 1(3)2000: 1–8.

[3] Ellentuck, A.B., "Converting a Sole Proprietorship Into an LLC, "*Tax Adviser*, 36(10)(2005): 647–648.

[4] Berry, E., "Death by a Thousand Cuts or Storm in a Teacup? The Reform of Limited Partnership Law," *Journal of Business Law*, 6(2011): 578–596.

[5] Uniform Partnership Act, National Conference of Commissioners of Uniform State Laws.

[6] Hsiu-Li, C., and Y. Huang, "The Establishment of Global Marketing Strategic Alliances by Small and Medium Enterprises," *Small Business Economics*, 22(5)(2004): 365–377.

[7] Thomas, P., "As Partnership Sours, Parting Is Sweet," *Wall Street Journal-Eastern Edition* (July 6, 2004): A20.

[8] Harris, R.A., "The Passionate World of Business Divorce: Some Tips for Counsel," *Dispute Resolution Journal*, 59(2)(2004): 40–43.

[9] Petravick, G., and C. Trouthan, "Has the LLC Replace the S Corporation as the Entrepreneur's Entity of Choice?" *Business Entities*, 9(6)(2007): 18–27.

[10] Opiela, N., "According to Form: Choosing the Right Business Entity," *Journal of Financial Planning*, 17(7)(2004): 36–41.

[11] Barlas, S., "Free at Last," *Entrepreneur*, 29(12)(2003): 26.

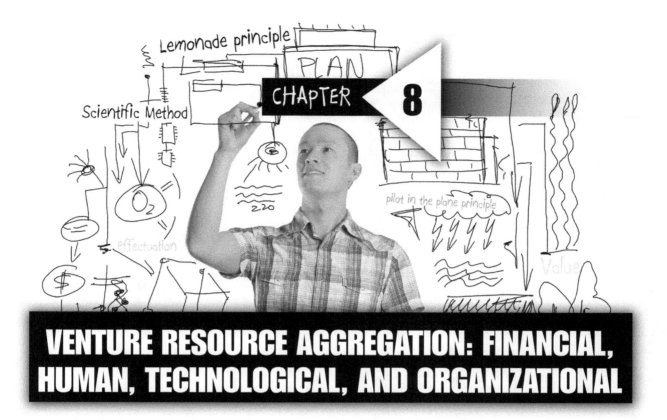

VENTURE RESOURCE AGGREGATION: FINANCIAL, HUMAN, TECHNOLOGICAL, AND ORGANIZATIONAL

Learning Objectives

After reading this chapter, students should be able to:

- **Understand** the difference between equity and debt financing.

- **Network** effectively as a means of gathering needed resources.

- **Raise** capital in compliance with the Securities and Exchange Commission rules.

- **Create and effectively leverage** a board of directors and/or an advisory board.

- **Calculate** equity ownership positions, dilution, and basic valuations.

- **Estimate** startup costs and the basic technological and organizational resources needed to launch a venture.

INTRODUCTION

Launching a venture doesn't happen in an instant, but rather is a process that requires energy, discipline, and determination. Of course, there will be a moment in time when your business is officially "launched," but there are a large number of milestones that must be achieved prior to that auspicious moment. The period prior to the actual launch of your venture is termed the "pre-launch" or "startup" period. Expert entrepreneurs realize that this is a critical time in the venture's life-

cycle. It's important to launch your venture with resources that are adequate for you to achieve your goals.

Throughout this text, we have discussed many of the challenges you will face in launching and operating a venture. In this chapter, we focus only on the resources that you may need to aggregate in order to launch and grow your venture. We will assume that you already have a product or service concept in mind and that you desire to build a business around those offerings. Of course, depending upon the type of business that you intend to open, the types and magnitude of resources you need will vary. Still, the entrepreneurial method includes a number of effective actions that you can take regardless of the type of venture you intend to operate.

For example, one of the most common pre-launch activities for entrepreneurs is fundraising. While most ventures start out with $25,000 or less in capital, many first-time entrepreneurs find that they need some external capital to feel confident that they have enough to launch the venture.[1] We will discuss the various sources of capital for the new and growing venture, and also provide some insights into the fundraising process itself. While startup capital can be difficult to find and to acquire, there are sources that entrepreneurs can tap into. Knowing where the capital sources are and who they are can lessen the pain that is often associated with the fundraising process during the early stages of the venture.

Expert entrepreneurs recognize that fundraising doesn't end with the launch of the venture. In fact, some of the most serious and intense fundraising occurs after the venture has launched and begins to grow. As the venture begins generating revenue and its market opportunity becomes clearer, other types of investors, including venture capital investors and angel investors, may become interested. In this chapter, we will focus primarily on sources of startup financing, but the tips and techniques that we discuss regarding the fundraising process are generally applicable throughout the venture's lifecycle.

Of course, the startup venture requires more than just capital resources to launch. In addition to capital the startup venture will likely require other people besides the entrepreneur. Whether these other people are recruited to the venture as employees, advisors, or some other type of stakeholder, they can be instrumental to the venture's success.[2] Rare is the lone entrepreneur able to build and scale a venture beyond a small business.[3] Sole proprietorships are the most common type of venture in the United States, but we are talking about entrepreneurial ventures that focus on growth, scalability, and exit. To achieve the type of growth that will enable the entrepreneur to scale and exit the venture will undoubtedly require the assistance of other people.

In addition to people, the startup venture likely also will need physical resources, tools, and equipment to succeed. Physical resources include mundane things like office space and office furniture. These mundane things are necessary for most ventures, and some ventures go far beyond these basic needs. The tools and equipment that a venture will need to succeed also varies by venture type. Many Internet ventures require very few tools beyond computers and can be started in a garage or basement. Other venture types are exceedingly resource intensive. For example, if you intend to startup a restaurant, you'll need equipment such as ovens, food lockers, pots and pans, and many other things. Our discussion later in this chapter will focus on equipment and tools that most any type of business will need to get started. We will highlight a few specific types of businesses to give you an idea of the extent to which necessary startup equipment and physical space can impact your startup budget.

A critical pre-launch activity for the entrepreneur is networking.[4] Networking will be critical to recruiting the talent that you will need to round out the operating team, to raising the capital that you will need to fuel the venture's growth, and to generating a level of "buzz" about the venture. In this chapter, we'll discuss some techniques entrepreneurs use to maximize networking effectiveness. We'll also discuss some of the pitfalls of networking and how they can be avoided. Let's begin by exploring the sources of financing for new ventures.

FINANCING THE VENTURE

The entrepreneur has a variety of funding sources. Despite this variety of sources, however, capital for new ventures is of only two types: Equity or debt. The distinction is important and presents another challenge to the entrepreneur in a growing venture. **Equity capital** is capital that is raised in exchange for an ownership (equity) stake in the venture. **Debt capital** is capital that is raised in exchange for a promise of repayment with interest.

Equity financing is provided to a venture with no expectation of payments in the short term and with the anticipation that the long-term returns may be substantial. Debt financing, by way of contrast, is provided to generate a stream of interest payments. Usually, entrepreneurs who obtain debt financing are expected to begin paying back the principal, with interest, immediately. With no expectation of large future returns, the motivations behind debt financing differ significantly from those that underlie equity financing. Exhibit 8.1 is a rough illustration of the different types of financing that will be available to a venture during its various stages of growth.

There are advantages and disadvantages to each type of capital. The entrepreneur at each stage of the venture's development must weigh financing options in light of the venture's goals and objectives. During the early stages of a venture's life, referred to as the **seed capital stage**, it is very doubtful that any type of debt capital will be available. Debt capital is usually provided to firms that have a substantial likelihood of being able to repay the loan with interest—which is rarely the profile of a new startup venture. The startup venture also has limited opportunities for equity capital, and usually must rely upon funds from the founders or from the proverbial **friends, family, and fools (FFF).** Startup ventures are thought to be very risky for investment

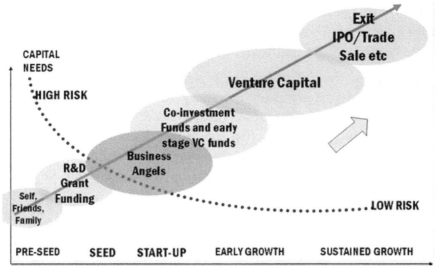

EXHIBIT 8.1 Stages of Venture Growth and Financing

purposes. Generally only the entrepreneur's friends and family will invest in the face of such high risks based on their personal knowledge and respect for the entrepreneur.[5] Alternatively, the entrepreneur may be able to convince some fools who are unaware of the risk or don't care about their money to invest in the startup venture.

During the **growth capital stage** of venture development, however, where market reaction to the venture's offerings has been proven, financing becomes a bit easier. Banks are more likely to lend capital to ventures that have proven and consistent cash flows, and equity investors are more interested in taking ownership of ventures that have prospects for future growth. Let's examine each type of financing in more detail, beginning with equity financing.

Equity Financing

Equity financing comes from individual investors, **angel investors**, or **venture capital investors**. Individual investors include friends and family who are not active private venture investors, but who may provide critical funds when other sources are unavailable to the entrepreneur. Angel investors are wealthy individuals who have risk capital they are willing to invest in select entrepreneurial ventures. Angels typically are sophisticated investors and have developed techniques for evaluating and selecting ventures for their capital.[6] Venture capital investors are professionals who invest their own and other people's money into promising new ventures that have the potential for very high rates of return. Venture capital can be exceedingly difficult to obtain and requires that the entrepreneurs find a good fit between their venture and the investing objectives of the venture capital firm from which they are seeking funds.[7]

Equity financing is attractive to entrepreneurs because equity does not require the venture to pay back the capital invested. In the United States, the **Securities and Exchange Commission (SEC)** governs all equity investments whether the venture associated with the equity transaction is public or private. Public companies are those listed on one of the major stock exchanges such as the New York Stock Exchange or NASDAQ. Public companies offer shares to investors in the public markets under the governance of the SEC. Public companies are required to produce and distribute quarterly reports (called 10-K reports) and annual reports revealing their audited financial performance. These requirements ensure that the investing public is aware of how the company is performing, providing reasons to invest or not.

The SEC has developed unique rules that enable private companies to sell shares to **accredited investors**. Accredited investors are those whom the SEC deems savvy enough to make informed choices about where and how to invest. Generally, the SEC defines an accredited investor as an individual who has more than $1 million in personal net worth, or who has income exceeding $200,000 per year. Private companies, such as a startup venture seeking funds from

© Dmitriy Shironosov, 2012. Used under license from Shutterstock, Inc.

friends, family, angels, or VCs, are not under the same comprehensive SEC rules. Nonetheless, private companies that desire to sell ownership interest (equity) to others must comply with SEC rules. Under the Securities Act of 1933, any offer to sell securities must either be registered with the SEC or meet an exemption. The SEC's **Regulation D** contains three rules providing exemptions from the registration requirements, allowing private companies to offer and sell their securities without having to register the securities with the SEC. These rules are the following:

Rule 504 of Regulation D: This rule provides an exemption from the registration requirements for some companies when they offer and sell up to $1,000,000 of their stock shares in any 12-month period. A company can use this exemption so long as it is not a **blank check company** and does not have to file reports under the Securities Exchange Act of 1934. A blank check company is a development stage company that has no specific business plan or purpose or has indicated its business plan is to engage in a merger or acquisition with an unidentified company or companies, other entity, or person. Also, the exemption generally does not allow companies to solicit or advertise their securities to the public, and purchasers receive **restricted securities**, meaning that they may not sell the securities without registration or an applicable exemption. Rule 504 does allow companies to sell securities that are not restricted under some special circumstances.

Rule 505 of Regulation D: This rule allows companies to decide what information to give to accredited investors, so long as it does not violate the antifraud prohibitions of the federal securities laws. But companies must give non-accredited investors disclosure documents that generally are the same as those used in registered offerings. If a company provides information to accredited investors, it must make this information available to non-accredited investors as well. The company must also be available to answer questions by prospective purchasers, and it must provide the following financial information. Prospective purchasers

- Can only offer and sell up to $5 million of its securities in any twelve-month period.

- May sell to an unlimited number of accredited investors and up to thirty-five other persons who do not need to satisfy the sophistication or wealth standards associated with other exemptions.

- Must inform purchasers that they received restricted securities, meaning that the securities cannot be sold for at least a year without registering them.

- Cannot use general solicitation or advertising to sell the securities.

In addition,

- Financial statements need to be certified by an independent public accountant.

- If a company other than a limited partnership cannot obtain audited financial statements without unreasonable effort or expense, only the company's balance sheet (to be dated within 120 days of the start of the offering) must be audited.

- Limited partnerships unable to obtain required financial statements without unreasonable effort or expense may furnish audited financial statements prepared under the federal income tax laws.

Rule 506 of Regulation D: This rule is considered a safe harbor for the private offering exemption of Section 4(2) of the Securities Act. Companies using the Rule 506 exemption can raise an unlimited amount of money. A company can be assured it is within the Section 4(2) exemption by satisfying the following standards:

- The company cannot use general solicitation or advertising to market the securities.

- The company may sell its securities to an unlimited number of accredited investors and up to 35 other purchases. Unlike Rule 505, all non-accredited investors, either alone or with a purchaser representative, must be accredited—that is, they must have sufficient knowledge and experience in financial and business matters to make them capable of evaluating the merits and risks of the prospective investment.

- Companies must decide what information to give to accredited investors, so long as it does not violate the antifraud prohibitions of the federal securities laws. But companies must give non-accredited investors disclosure documents that are generally the same as those used in registered offerings. If a company provides information to accredited investors, it must make this information available to non-accredited investors as well.

- The company must be available to answer questions by prospective purchasers.

- Purchasers receive restricted securities, meaning that the securities cannot be sold for at least a year without registering them.

Equity financing for a private venture will be governed by any one of these Regulation D offering rules. There usually are some costs involved with preparing an offering, and the costs are usually greater as larger funding amounts are sought. This is so because larger amounts of funding usually require the entrepreneur to talk to and distribute documents to more people. In addition, larger transactions often are more complex and require more legal work to structure a deal that is attractive to both former and new investors.

The costs associated with conducting a private equity offering are usually greater than applying for and receiving an equivalent amount of debt. The greater costs involved in an equity offering are part of the entrepreneur's deliberations when deciding on the type of financing to pursue.[8] Of even greater influence on this decision is the degree to which equity financing will **dilute the ownership positions** of the existing shareholders. Anytime a venture sells shares to raise capital, the ownership positions of the existing shareholders will be affected. The degree to which dilution occurs is a function of the venture's **valuation** at the time of the financing. Valuation refers to the dollar value that both current owners and new investors place on the venture as a whole at the time of the financing transaction.

A discussion of methods for determining a venture's valuation will be provided in Chapter 14 when we discuss exit strategies. Here we will simply note the effects of valuation on venture ownership. Suppose two individuals launch a technology venture, and they decide to split ownership equally between them with each now owning 50 percent of the company. They have invested their own funds to launch the venture, thus they currently have no other shareholders. Now, suppose they have developed their venture over a period of time and have received positive feedback from test markets. The two founder-entrepreneurs are ready to expand the company, but they need capital to do that. They decide that they need to raise $1 million. What effect will that amount of capital raised have on their respective ownership positions?

The answer is: It depends on the current valuation of the venture. Let's assume the entrepreneurs are able to convince investors that their company is worth $2 million. In the language of deal making this is referred to as the **pre-money valuation** of the venture. That is, this is what the venture, arguably, is worth prior to any investor money coming in. There are a number of factors to consider in establishing the value of a private company, but we will put off that discussion until later. For now, let's assume that the $2 million pre-money valuation is reasonable and agreeable to the investors. At this valuation, each of the founder-entrepreneur's 50 percent stake in the company is worth $1 million (50 percent of $2 million).

If the entrepreneurs are successful in raising the $1 million, the venture would have a **post-money valuation** of $3 million. Note that the post-money valuation is simply the pre-money valuation plus the amount that is raised. What is the dilutive effect of this raise? It's plain to see that the investors who put in the $1 million will own one-third of a venture that has a post-money valuation of $3 million. The two entrepreneurs, who previously owned 50 percent each, have been diluted by one-sixth to a stake of 33.3 percent each. Together, they maintain a controlling interest, 67 percent in the company, but they have been diluted. Note, however, that despite the dilution in the percentage of their ownership the dollar value of their shares remains $1 million (i.e., one-third of $3 million). Several tools for modeling a venture's valuation and dilution can be found at the following websites:

- www.ownyourventure.com/equitySim.html

- https://docs.google.com/spreadsheet/ccc?key...hl=en

- www.docstoc.com/docs/15116622/Equity-dilution-model

In summary, the main advantages of equity financing include:

- You will not have to keep up with costs of servicing bank loans or debt finance, allowing you to use the capital for business activities.

- Investors expect the business to deliver value and will help you explore and execute growth ideas.

- The right business angels and venture capitalists can bring valuable skills, contacts, and experience to your business.

- Investors have a vested interest in the business' success.

- Investors are often prepared to provide followup funding as the business grows.

The principal disadvantages of equity financing include:

- Raising equity finance is demanding, costly, and time consuming and may take management focus away from the core business activities.

- Potential investors will seek comprehensive background information on you and your business. They will look carefully at past results and forecasts and will probe the management team.

- Depending on the investor, you can lose a certain amount of your power to make management decisions.

- You will have to invest management time to provide regular information for the investor to monitor.

- There can be legal and regulatory issues to comply with when raising finance, e.g., when promoting investments.

Let's now turn our attention to debt financing and the various advantages and disadvantages of that type of capital for the startup venture.

Debt Financing

Debt financing is normally provided to entrepreneurs via an **institutional lender**, such as a bank. However, this may not always be the case. Some entrepreneurs structure deals where they take loans from private parties. While this is not a common practice, some estimates indicate that as many as 10 million people in the United States have accepted private loans from people they know.[9] Borrowing from family and friends

© Adam Gregor, 2012. Used under license from Shutterstock, Inc.

can provide easier terms than an institutional lender, including a longer repayment period and a lower interest rate. However, borrowing from family and friends has some risks that are dissimilar from institutional lenders.[10] For example, if the entrepreneur does not repay the loan within a reasonable amount of time, the trust of the family and/or friend lenders could be lost. Worse, if the entrepreneur defaults on repaying the loan, relationships may become strained, family ties could be severed, and lawsuits could be filed.[11]

It is important to carefully document the terms of the business loan between friends and relatives who lend money to a venture. This can help ensure that these individuals are less apprehensive about how their money is being used. It can also prevent messy or awkward situations in the event the venture has difficulties living up to the loan terms. If details regarding remedies for late payments and even for complete default are discussed and agreed to in advance, the impact of such eventualities can be lessened. The Bullet Breakout below provides a summary of tips for keeping relations when you borrow from relatives.

BULLET BREAKOUT

Requesting a Loan from a Family Member

When requesting a loan from a family member to launch a venture, it is wise to follow formal procedures in establishing the terms of the loan. Here are some tips on how to proceed:

- Establish a formal meeting when preparing to ask for a loan.

- Present a carefully organized business plan or proposal.

- If a loan is agreed to, make sure the parties document the terms in a promissory note. An attorney is not required, but it might be a good idea to seek professional legal advice.

- Items to address include: payment schedule; what happens if the business is sold; how the lender will be kept abreast of the venture's progress, including its losses and profits; what new initiatives, marketing strategies, or products are being implemented to grow and expand the business.

Institutional lenders, such as banks, can be a source of financing for new ventures. However, banks will require more documentation than friends and family normally require; they will also require that the venture be able to secure the loan by pledging an equivalent amount of **collateral**. That is, most institutional lenders reduce the risk of their loans by gaining a **security interest** in property owned by the borrower that is adjudged to be equivalent in value to the loan principal amount. Collateral can be any property owned by the borrower, including personal property.

It is also not uncommon for entrepreneurs to provide—or to be required to provide—a **personal guarantee** on the amount of the loan. This is done when the venture has few assets to use as collateral, but the entrepreneur has personal assets that will suffice. For example, some entrepreneurs will use their personal savings, home equity, or real estate as collateral for loans from a bank for business purposes. In the case of default, the bank would then be able to exercise its claim on the collateral in an effort to recover whatever portion of the loan remains unpaid.

In addition to pledging collateral in the amount of the loan's principal, institutional lenders also normally require that the entrepreneur begin to pay back the loan immediately, with an added interest charge.[12] Payments on a loan are normally made in monthly increments. The rate of interest charged to a startup venture for a loan will exceed the rate charged to large, well-established, companies. The latter receive preferential rates from banks—usually called the **prime rate**—because they are less risky borrowers than a startup venture. Startup ventures will receive a rate that is termed prime plus. That is, the rate will be some measure above the prime rate depending on the risk profile of the venture and, to some extent, its principals and the collateral they are able to pledge.

Most banks will have a similar prime rate, but they will vary significantly from one to another in the rates they charge to entrepreneur borrowers. For example, some banks specialize in originating real estate or construction loans. They will typically have loan officers who are familiar with these industries and will have experience in judging the risks involved in lending to this type of venture. In contrast, a bank that specializes in real estate lending may not be able to evaluate the risk involved in lending to a technology startup. It's important for the entrepreneur to conduct research prior to approaching a lender to determine whether it is capable of understanding the nature of the venture and its risks.

Loans made by institutions also require payback to occur over a certain period of time referred to as the **term of the loan**. Short-term loans will carry slightly lower interest rates than long-term loans, but they will also require larger monthly payments. Long-term loans are generally considered to be those that have a term of ten years or greater. Different lenders use different methods to calculate loan repayment schedules depending on their needs, borrowers' needs, the institution's interest rate policy, the length of the loan, and the purpose of the borrowed money. Normally, business loans are paid back on a monthly schedule in equal payments throughout the term of the loan.

Institutional lenders will also usually require that the startup venture adhere to certain **restrictive covenants** in order to remain in good standing on the loan. Restrictive covenants enable the lender to maintain some control of the venture by specifying performance targets. In the event these performance targets are missed, the lender would have the option to **call the loan**. That is, it can demand complete payment of the outstanding principal before the term of the loan is completed. Restrictive covenants are of two types: **positive covenants** and **negative covenants**. Positive covenants specify performance targets that must be attained in order for the borrower to remain in good standing. For example, a bank and borrower may agree to establish positive covenants targeting total sales, cash flow, profitability, or others. Negative covenants establish performance floors below which the venture may not fall in order to remain in good standing. For example, the bank and the borrower may agree that the venture may not fall below target figures in sales, cash flow, the ratio of debt to equity capital in the venture, and others.

Restrictive covenants are usually determined through negotiations between the lender and the borrower, but many lenders have lending guidelines that establish in advance the covenants that they must put into any lending agreement. Entrepreneurs must be aware of the covenants that banks require and determine whether they will impede the venture's ability to succeed. For example, many businesses are subject to fluctuations in sales based on business cycles and other factors. A restrictive covenant that did not account for these sales fluctuations may result in an unnecessarily premature decision by the lender to call the loan. In a time of decreased sales, such an action could be fatal to the startup venture.

Another type of loan facility that is exceedingly useful to the startup venture is the **line of credit** or **revolving loan.** A line of credit is simply an amount of money that is set aside by a lender for a business to use as needed. The borrower can draw down the line of credit for business expenses without having to fill out a loan application each time funds are required. This saves the lender and the borrower a lot of time. Lenders provide lines of credit using the same risk calculations as any other loan, and they will also usually require collateral in the amount of the credit line. Borrowers benefit from a line of credit in that they only need to pay back the amount withdrawn, and pay interest only on the withdrawn capital. In addition to the interest collected, most banks will charge an annual maintenance fee to provide a line of credit to a company.

Small Business Administration (SBA) Loans

Another type of loan commonly used by startups is the **Small Business Administration Loan**.[13] The name of this loan type is confusing to some. The Small Business Administration (SBA) is an agency of the United States federal government. However, the SBA does *not* originate loans made to ventures. An entrepreneur who wants to secure an SBA loan must do so through a commercial bank that provides such loans. The bank *originates* the loan, and the SBA *guarantees* payment on the loan up to a predefined percentage of the principal amount. In this way, the SBA provides a form of collateral and takes a good deal of risk out of the loan for the bank[14]. The following Mini-Case describes a case where a startup received an SBA loan in 30 days.

MINI CASE

Maryland Solar Solutions Funded by SBA

The recent economic recession has hit the construction segment especially hard. But when her growing construction firm started slowing down, owner Colette Hayward used the change to reexamine her business model and to follow her passion—clean, renewable energy.

Hayward envisioned a new company that would help bring solar energy to more consumers and small businesses in a sustainable way. Maryland Solar Solutions, Inc. was conceived as a complete "green" integrator that would not only help with the technical installation of solar panels but also the emerging, and often confusing, paperwork of getting government rebates and utility credits.

Hayward knew that she needed funding for the purchase of inventories and for working capital to accommodate the delays in attaining grants and utility credits. She also knew that her application for financing would not be an easy or straightforward process. While she did have an excellent personal credit score and could demonstrate fifteen years of profitable growth from her construction firm, she was applying for funding for Maryland Solar Solutions, Inc—a startup with no history. Traditional business loans were not an option.

So, Hayward carefully researched financing options through the SBA. She compiled a complete, thorough business plan with financial projections and requirements. Over a three-day period she submitted her loan request and documentation to several SBA lending institutions with the directive, "the fastest approval wins." She received the financing she needed within 30 days.

Source: Adapted from "Maryland Solar Solutions, Inc: Fast Funding to Grab Green Market Opportunity." Case Study: SBA Loans, Sun Trust Banks, Inc.

While the SBA provides a credible and useful debt facility for many entrepreneurs, an SBA loan also has significant disadvantages. SBA loans generally require more documentation and disclosure on the part of the small business than does a traditional loan. SBA loans also frequently have higher interest rates than would a loan provided directly by a commercial lender. Still, there are many advantages to getting an SBA loan, not the least of which is the fact that many startup ventures have no other options. The SBA has more loan programs than the primary ones listed above, including some that are designed specifically to support minority- and women-owned enterprises.

In summary, the advantages to debt financing for the entrepreneur include:

- When you borrow from a lender, you are obligated to make the agreed-upon payments on time. This may be a burden on your most precious resource—cash.

- In most cases, the principal and interest payments on a business loan are classified as business expenses, and thus can be deducted from your business income taxes.

- If the bank is charging you 10 percent for your loan, and the government taxes you at 30 percent, then there is an advantage to taking a loan you can deduct. After your tax deductions, you'll be paying the equivalent of a 7 percent interest rate.

Some of the major disadvantages to debt financing for the entrepreneur are:

- Your sole obligation to the lender is to make your payments. Unfortunately, even if your business fails, you still have to make these payments. And if you are forced into bankruptcy, your lenders will have claim to repayment before any equity investors.

- Even after calculating the discounted interest rate from your tax deductions, you may still be faced with a high interest rate. Interest rates will vary with macroeconomic conditions, your history with the banks, your business credit rating, and your personal credit history.

- It might seem attractive to keep bringing on debt when your firm needs money, a practice knowing as "levering up," but each loan will be noted on your credit rating. And the more you borrow, the higher the risk to the lender, and the higher interest rate you'll pay.

- Even if you plan to use the loan to invest in an important asset, you'll need to make sure your business will be generating sufficient cash flows by the time loan repayment starts. Also you'll likely be asked to put up collateral on the loan in case you default on your payments.

Now that we've explored the various sources of financing for new ventures, let's turn our attention to the actual process of fundraising.

FUNDRAISING TOOLS AND TECHNIQUES

Fundraising for a new venture is never a sure thing, but there are some tools and techniques that can improve the odds of acquiring needed capital. Of course, the first thing the entrepreneur needs to determine is how much money to raise. The capital that is needed to start the venture is different from the capital required to grow the venture. In general, startup capital should be enough to grow the venture either to the point at which its revenues exceed its costs, and therefore it can operate on its own, or to the point at which the venture will be attractive enough to investors and or bankers to acquire additional capital.

Figuring out startup costs is not difficult, but it does vary by industry. In general, entrepreneurs can develop a startup budget that reflects all of the costs necessary for equipment, office space, and other items. This should be done, as we stated above, for the time period until the venture reaches breakeven or becomes eligible for additional financing. Exhibit 8.2 provides a template for a startup budget.

Once you have your startup budget determined, it's time to think about the fundraising process itself. One of the primary tools of fundraising for the entrepreneur is the **business plan**. It is rarely possible to raise money outside of the friends and family network without a business

[Business Name]   # Business Startup Costs

FUNDING	Estimated	Actual	Under/(Over)
Investor Funding			
Owner 1	10,000	9,600	400
Owner 2	5,000	5,500	(500)
Other			-
Total Investment	15,000	15,100	(100)
Loans			
Bank Loan 1			-
Bank Loan 2			-
Non Bank Loan 1			-
Total Loans	-	-	-
Other Funding			
Grant 1			-
Other			-
Total Other Funding	-	-	-
Total FUNDING	15,000	15,100	(100)

COSTS	Estimated	Actual	Under/(Over)
Fixed Costs			
Advertising for Opening			-
Basic Website			-
Brand Development			-
Building Down Payment			-
Building Improvements/Remodeling			-
Tools & Supplies			-
Travel			-
Truck & Vehicle			-
Other 1 (specify)			-
Other 2 (specify)			-
Total Fixed Costs	-	-	-
Average Monthly Costs			
Advertising (print, broadcast and Internet)			-
Business Insurance			-
Business Vehicle Insurance			-
Employee Salaries and Commissions			-
Supplies			-
Telephone	63	65	(2)
Travel			-
Public Utilities			-
Website Hosting/Maintenance	24	15	9
Other 1 (specify)			-
Other 2 (specify)			-
Total Average Monthly Costs	87	80	7
x Number of Months	6		
Total Monthly Costs	522	480	42
Total COSTS	522	480	42
SURPLUS/(DEFICIT)	14,478	14,620	(142)

EXHIBIT 8.2   Template of a Startup Budget

plan. Angel investors will almost always ask to see the venture's business plan before investing. Venture capitalists and institutional lenders will always require a business plan. Entrepreneurs should develop and maintain a business plan at all times because most startup ventures are in near-constant fundraising mode. A good business plan will describe the venture and its technologies in terms the investor or lender can understand and evaluate.

Another tool that should be part of the entrepreneur's fundraising arsenal is the **executive summary**. The executive summary is an abridged version of the business plan, normally condensed down to a single page. Exhibit 8.3 is a common executive summary template that many startups use quickly to convey basic information about their ventures and funding needs.

CONFIDENTIAL – INTERNAL USE ONLY

INVESTMENT BANKING DEPARTMENT – DEAL OVERVIEW – CONFIDENTIAL WORKSHEET

Company Name

US Headquarters:

T: --.---
F: --.---
W: www.companywebsite.com
E: ceo@companywebsite.com

Company Highlights:

- Industry -
- Public/Private (Symbol)/Market Price$
- Intellectual Property/Contracts/Clients
- Previous capital raised in company $
- Shares Outstanding/Valuation

Management Team:

Mr. XYZ
Founder & CEO
Prior SVP with Ernst & Young

Mr. ABC
VP and CFO
Former president of public company 123

Mr. Sales manager
VP of Sales & Channel Partner Management
Former director of national sales for ATT

Mrs. International Dealmaker
VP of International Sales
Senior VP of International Sales - Honeywell

Strategic Partners:

- Key partner 1
- Key partner 2
- Key Partner 3

Major Clients:
- Large Client - 1
- Large Client - 2
- Medium Client – 3

Other Key Highlights:

Whatever:
LawFirm:
Accountant/Auditors:
Special Industry Partner:

Description

This is where you put in the overview of the target client company. Their products are purchased by resellers and wholesalers throughout the United States. The Company's service industries and target market clients service the broader business community in the following industries:

Media & Entertainment, Telecommunications & Data transport, Healthcare Technology, Financial Services Software

The Company will focus and endure its growth stage towards maintaining its competitive advantage, a defensible market position, unique products or services creating a paradigm shift in a particular industry to solidify its position within a particular market, industry, service or product.

Financing Needs – Investment Banking Assignment:

Financing Amount:	$17 - $20Million
Structure:	Equity
Orientation:	Growth Equity and recap a majority of debt.
Use of Proceeds:	$12M debt paydown, $8M Growth Equity/WC
Existing Debt:	$10Million with Sr Lender A, $2Million Mezz B
Other:	Company will likely put us on buy-side assignment within 6 – 12 months once growth kicks in to make strategic acquisitions.

What Makes this Company a great investment opportunity:
1. Excellent Financial fundamentals + several patents pending
2. Strong consistent growth for past 3 years + great client roster
3. Strong management team with long standing experience
4. Market conditions favorable for their industry
5. Additional buy-side acquisitions for additional growth.

What are the biggest hurdles the Company has to overcome?:
1. pending lawsuit with former employee
2. strong cyclicality to business – may be negative cashflow for 3 months during summer season
3. Client concentration with largest client is 40% of sales

Financial Highlights:

	2006	2007	2008
Revenue			
Gross Profit			
EBITDA			
Current Assets			
Long Term Assets			
Current Liabilities			
Long Term Liab.			

1   Confidential

EXHIBIT 8.3   Template of an Executive Summary

Equity financing is invested into a venture under terms specified in a **private placement memorandum(PPM)**. A PPM is a document that provides the equity investor with the full disclosure required by the U.S. Securities and Exchange Commission (SEC). The SEC governs all equity transactions in the United States. Exhibit 8.4 shows the first page of a typical PPM.

The PPM provides potential investors with details on the venture. It resembles the business plan in that it will describe the business, including its products and services, management team, financial projections, competitors, and the target market. In addition, the PPM goes far beyond the business plan in providing the investor with disclosure of the risks associated with an investment in the venture. Risks discussed in the PPM might include the potential for patent filings to be rejected by the patent office, misjudgment of the market potential of the venture's products and services, inability to raise sufficient capital in the future to operate, and many other contingencies. Most law firms that deal with startup companies will have a PPM "boilerplate" that can be edited and tailored to a specific venture.

Most early stage fundraising will divide the amount to be raised into **units**. For example, if a venture is raising $500,000 and selling its stock for $1.00/share, it does not want 500,000 individuals each purchasing one share. That would be an administrative nightmare. Instead, the venture would sell the $1.00/share stock in units of, say, $25,000. That means that anyone interested in investing would need to purchase at least 25,000 shares.

In addition to stating the amount that is going to be raised, the PPM also often specifies the minimum amount that needs to be raised in order for the venture to be able to use the funds. This is often referred to as the **min/max.** This concept can be understood most clearly from the perspective of the investor. If an investor puts money into a venture, he or she wants to be sure that the venture has a fair chance of success. However, if the venture raises only a small portion of what it needs, it may fail. The min/max specifies the minimum amount of money that is required for the venture to have a fair chance to succeed. The venture does not use any of the funds it raises until it achieves the minimum amount. Funds raised prior to reaching the minimum are held in trust in a bank account. Once the minimum has been raised, the venture is allowed to use the invested capital.

The final document to include in equity fundraising is the **subscription agreement.** A subscription agreement is a document that a potential investor signs, indicating an intent to invest at a certain amount. Even though a subscription document is not considered to be binding on the potential investor, it creates a psychological commitment on the part of the investor. For example, imagine that an entrepreneur completes a lengthy presentation to an angel investor in their office. The investor indicates an interest, but would prefer to look over the business plan and PPM before making a decision. If the entrepreneur walks out of the office with no signed commitment, the potential investor may not be interested enough to continue thinking about the deal. It is far more influential to have a signed agreement when conducting follow up conversations, including the penultimate conversation where the entrepreneur asks for the check, than it is merely to have a promise.

Entrepreneurs should also practice their investment "pitch," which is sometimes referred to as an **elevator pitch.** This term is used to conjure what it would be like to meet a potential investor in an elevator and, in the limited time available, describe the business in a manner that captures the investor's attention.[15] An elevator pitch should articulate the venture's offering (product and/

XYZ , LLC

PRIVATE PLACEMENT MEMORANDUM

10% Unsecured Promissory Notes

XYZ, LLC
2500 Anywhere Rd.
XYZ Estates, IL
Voice: (xxx) xxx-xxxx

This document is the Regulation D, Rule 506 Private Placement Letter Offering for Punta Cana, LLC offered to "Accredited Investors."

Date of this Memorandum is _____, 20___

Name of Offeree: _____   PPM No._____

IMPORTANT NOTICE ABOUT THIS MEMORANDUM

CONTACT US FOR MORE INFORMATION

EXHIBIT 8.4   Typical First Page of a PPM

Source: Obtained from PPM Source at http://www.ppmsource.com/samples/sample-cover-page, accessed on April 1, 2012.

or service), its business model (how it will make money), and the size of the opportunity. In a full investor presentation, the entrepreneur will need a slide deck (e.g. PowerPoint) that clearly articulates the business, the market, the value proposition, financial outlook, and the deal (including projected returns) for the investor. [16]

ALTERNATIVES TO DEBT AND EQUITY FINANCING

While the primary sources of capital for the startup venture are the sources of debt and equity discussed above, there are alternatives. Many technology ventures are able to get started and fund operations using government grants as their primary revenue source. Next, we look at two government grant programs available to the technology venture, and also at bootstrap financing,which relies on internal cash only to grow the venture.

One particular type of government grant that is commonly used by technology ventures is the **Small Business Innovation Research(SBIR)** program. The U.S. Small Business Administration's Office of Technology administers the SBIR program. SBIR is a competitive program that encourages small businesses to explore their technological potential and provides the incentive to profit from its commercialization. Since its enactment in 1982 as part of the Small Business Innovation Development Act, SBIR has helped thousands of small businesses to compete for federal research and development awards. Ventures must meet certain eligibility criteria to participate in the SBIR program:

- American-owned and independently operated

- For-profit

- Principal researcher employed by business

- Company size limited to 500 employees

Each year, eleven federal departments and agencies are required by SBIR to reserve a portion of their R&D funds for award to small business investments, including:

- Department of Agriculture

- Department of Commerce

- Department of Defense

- Department of Education

- Department of Energy

- Department of Health and Human Services

- Department of Homeland Security
- Department of Transportation
- Environmental Protection Agency
- National Aeronautics and Space Administration
- National Science Foundation

These agencies designate R&D topics and accept proposals. Following submission of proposals, agencies make SBIR awards based on small business qualification, degree of innovation, technical merit, and future market potential. Small businesses that receive awards then begin a three-phase program.

- Phase I is the startup phase. Awards of up to $100,000 for approximately six months support exploration of the technical merit or feasibility of an idea or technology.

- Phase II awards of up to $750,000, for as many as two years, expand Phase I results. During this time, the R&D work is performed and the developer evaluates commercialization potential. Only Phase I award winners are considered for Phase II.

- Phase III is the period during which Phase II innovation moves from the laboratory into the marketplace. No SBIR funds support this phase. The small business must find funding in the private sector or other non-SBIR federal agency funding.

Another grant program offered by the SBA is the **Small Business Technology Transfer Program (STTR)**. Central to this program is expansion of the public/private sector partnership to include joint venture opportunities for small business and nonprofit research institutions. The STTR program reserves a specific percentage of federal R&D funding to offer awards to small business and nonprofit research institution partners. The STTR program combines the strengths of both entities by introducing entrepreneurial skills to high-tech research efforts. The idea is that the small business partner is able to transfer from the laboratory to the marketplace the technologies and products developed within the nonprofit organization. As with the SBIR program, ventures must meet certain eligibility criteria to participate in the STTR program:

- American-owned and independently operated
- For-profit
- Principal researcher need not be employed by small business
- Company size limited to 500 employees

The nonprofit research institution partner must also meet certain eligibility criteria:

- Located in the United States
- Meet one of three definitions
- Nonprofit college or university
- Domestic nonprofit research organization
- Federally funded R&D center (FFRDC)

Each year, five federal departments and agencies are required by STTR to reserve a portion of their R&D funds to award to small business/nonprofit research institution partnerships:

- Department of Defense
- Department of Energy
- Department of Health and Human Services
- National Aeronautics and Space Administration
- National Science Foundation

These agencies designate R&D topics and accept proposals. Following submission of proposals, agencies make STTR awards based on small business/nonprofit research institution qualification, degree of innovation, and future market potential. Small businesses that receive awards then begin a three-phase program.

- Phase I is the startup phase. Awards of up to $100,000 for approximately one year fund the exploration of the scientific, technical, and commercial feasibility of an idea or technology.

- Phase II awards of up to $750,000 for as long as two years expand Phase I results. During this period, the R&D work is performed and the developer begins to consider commercial potential. Only Phase I award winners are considered for Phase II.

- Phase III is the period during which Phase II innovation moves from the laboratory into the marketplace. No STTR funds support this phase. The small business must find funding in the private sector or other non-STTR federal agency funding.

Another way that startup ventures finance their growth is through what is often referred to as **bootstrap financing**.[17] Here, the company uses its own sales and cash flows to invest in its growth. This type of internal growth is also referred to as **organic growth**. That is, the company grows only by virtue of its own ability to sell, control costs, and reinvest profits.

Bootstrap financing has the advantage of helping the firm steer clear of the dilutive effects of equity financing, and the debt burden effects of debt financing. The primary disadvantage of this type of financing is that it limits the venture's ability to grow rapidly. That could be a major disadvantage for ventures in highly competitive industries where acquiring market share is the key to long-term success.

In addition to financial resources, the startup venture will need a host of additional resources to launch and grow. We examine some of these additional resources beginning in the next section.

ACQUIRING OTHER RESOURCES

The entrepreneur will need a wide range of resources to effectively launch a venture, and even more to grow it successfully. Among the resources other than capital that will be required are human capital, organizational resources, and technology resources. Expert entrepreneurs have learned the techniques for acquiring these resources without using up a lot of the venture's precious cash. Let's examine the human capital resource needs of the venture first.

Human Capital

The human resources we refer to here are top level executives and board members—the talented people that add significant value to the venture and that often are referred to as **human capital**.[18] During the early stages of a venture, it may be necessary to recruit other executive talent to the venture. The original founder must choose carefully when selecting others who will join as founders/executives of the venture. In general, these early recruits will request a significant equity stake in the company and may also require a salary. The equity stake will dilute the founder's ownership interest, and the salary will be a drain on the venture's cash.

© Yuri Arcurs, 2012. Used under license from Shutterstock, Inc.

One way to avoid granting excessive equity to an individual brought on in the early stages of the venture is to establish a vesting schedule. The concept of vesting and how it affects venture ownership was discussed Chapter 7.

In addition to executive officers, the venture may want to establish a board of directors and/or an advisory board. The difference between the two boards is primarily centered on **fiduciary responsibility**—the board of directors has it, the advisory board doesn't. Fiduciary responsibility refers to the responsibility to deploy the resources of the venture in a manner that maximizes returns to the shareholders. Recruiting well-qualified candidates to a venture's board of directors can be an important factor in success.[19]

Advisory boards can be a useful addition to any type of venture. Entrepreneurs form advisory boards for a variety of business reasons.[20] Selecting advisory board members carefully and strategically can improve the venture's chances for success in a number of ways, including:

- Board members often will have expertise that the entrepreneur lacks, and that the entrepreneur cannot afford to acquire via a new employee.

- Board members may have deep experience in the venture's industry and may be able to provide important strategic insights that will help the venture grow.

- Board members may have significant contacts within the industry and may be able to accelerate the venture's path to profitability by opening doors and facilitating early sales.

Employees are another human capital resource that the entrepreneur may need to recruit to work in the venture. It's important during the early days of a venture to have a plan for leading and managing employees. For example, John Mackey of Whole Foods developed his venture concept from the ground up with a clear focus on how to recruit, retain, and motivate employees. As a result of his comprehensive human resource plan, Mackey can rely on his employees to fulfill the vision he has for his stores.

Organizational Resources

Organizational resources are those items that are required for people to do their jobs. This includes the normal tools of office work, such as desks, chairs, copy machines, and other things that people normally expect. Imagine showing up for work on day one of the launching of a new venture and finding that there were no desks or other office equipment or furniture. Maximum productivity requires the normal tools for getting work done. Startup ventures often are operating on very tight budgets in the early stages, and these items can be expensive.

Notice, however, that we did NOT say these standard office items need to be top of the line. Often, new ventures are launched in the homes and/or garages of founders. Still, makeshift workstations should be set up, and opportunities for focused work should be created. For most office new and equipment, good deals can be found where there have been bankruptcies or liquidations of other ventures. In addition, most office furniture and equipment can be rented or leased. These can be less expensive short-term financing options, but might cost more in the long run.

Another organizational resource is office space. Office space can be a major hurdle for young ventures as they often require long-term commitments. Good office buildings in major cities will normally require the entrepreneur to sign a three-year lease. In addition, as early stage ventures often have difficulty with cash flow, they will on occasion have trouble paying regular monthly bills. Landlords know this, and they attempt to ward off problems with lease payments through several well-known tactics. One tactic that is commonly used in early stage ventures is to require the lease applicant to submit a business plan as part of the application process. The landlord knows that a business without a plan is more likely to fail. Another tactic landlords often use to lessen the risk of leasing office space to early stage ventures is to require that the founders provide a personal guarantee on the lease. That means the founders will be required to continue making lease payments even if the business fails.

Technology Resources

The modern worker is accustomed to using a wide range of gadgets and tools to get work done. Most new ventures must provide these tools to compete with others in their industry and to attract the talented workers who expect these tools to be part of their work environment. In most ventures, it is requisite that each employee be outfitted with his or her own personal computer, which may also include a desktop workstation and a separate laptop computer.

The entrepreneur will need to determine which tools are required for the unique products and services offered by the venture, and the unique work processes that are required to produce them. As with the organizational resources previously discussed, the requisite technology resources can also be obtained via lease, lease to own, or financing options. Companies such as Dell computer have divisions that cater to the emerging venture, offering each of these options as a means of limiting cash outflows in the short run. Of course, in the long run such options cost more, but to the small venture the preservation of precious cash in the near term may outweigh the long-term costs.

The technology required to operate a new venture likely will include various software applications as well. If the venture is ready for sales, it may want to investigate various sales force automation and customer relationship management packages. These are often available online and have a wide variety of purchasing options. From a commercial off-the-shelf software option to individual and enterprise licenses, these software tools can help the emerging venture appear bigger than it is and help it become more efficient.

NETWORKING

Most entrepreneurs would agree that networking is an important part of their daily activities. **Networking** is defined as the art and practice of attending social events and connecting with individuals who may be able to assist with the entrepreneurial venture. Entrepreneurs use their networking skills for a variety of reasons: acquiring new business; finding new employees and other human resources; learning new ways of doing things that may be better than the old ways; and obtaining resources such as money, office space, second-hand telephone systems and many other things.[21]

© ioforo, 2012. Used under license from Shutterstock, Inc.

Entrepreneurs need capital, skills, knowledge, and labor to start new ventures. The entrepreneur provides some of these resources, and some are gathered from the entrepreneur's social network. The webs of contacts that help bring about success are the **social capital**. Over time, entrepreneurs accumulate social capital, which is essential for starting and growing new ventures.[22] An entrepreneur's social network has several characteristics. One of these characteristics is the size of the network. Entrepreneurs can enlarge their social network to gain access to crucial resources. Another characteristic of an entrepreneur's social network is **positioning**. Entrepreneurs can position themselves within the social network so as to shorten the pathway to crucial resources.

Networking is usually a deliberate act on the part of the entrepreneur to increase his or her social capital and to improve positioning within the **social network**. As mentioned, the research is fairly clear that social networking is an important part of an entrepreneur's business success. Fortunately, there are some straightforward techniques that the entrepreneur can use to be effective in networking.[23] The Bullet Breakout box lists eight such techniques.

BULLET BREAKOUT

Effective Networking

- **Make a great first impression:** When you meet someone for the first time, whether it is a male or female think "S.H.E. is the key." The acronym "S.H.E." stands for "Smile, Handshake, Eye Contact".

- **Remember names:** A good way to remember names is to repeat the name aloud followed by a social comment such as "It's nice to meet you."

- **Ask open-ended questions:** Open-ended questions tell people that you are interested in them, and they allow people to talk about themselves.

- **Be an active listener:** Active listening means paying attention to the person you are talking to and really understanding what he or she is saying. **Establish common ground:** From the base of common interests, a deeper relationship can be developed that may include business and friendship. To find common ground, use techniques 3 and 4 above.

- **Seek to help others first:** The most successful networkers think of the many ways they can help others before they help themselves.

- **Be able to describe how your venture helps others:** When you tell others about your business, tell them how it helps others.

- **Follow up:** Develop a system for recording information, including contacts and relevant notes, following a networking event. The notes you record could include such items as the common ground established with a contact, key dates and phone numbers, and names of people referred by contacts.

Source: Adapted from Joe Takash, "Networking Success: Discover the Tools You Need to Get to the Top," *Business Credit* (April 2004): 24–25.

The results of networking can occur in a few months or over several years—nothing is guaranteed, but the potential is unlimited. Once someone knows who the entrepreneur is, evaluates his or her work ethic, and determines what the individual can do, then entrepreneur becomes a contact for that person—and vice versa.

Entrepreneurs usually network with a purpose in mind, but not always. Sometimes it's important to network at specific types of events merely because the right people are attending. **Serendipity** is the term that refers to finding something that you need, but weren't necessarily seeking. Entrepreneurs often attend social functions and events that are linked to their industry based on the possibility of a serendipitous encounter.[24] They may meet someone who is looking for the products/services offered by the venture. They may meet someone who knows how to solve a difficult problem that the venture has been facing. Or they may meet someone who has a key contact with a customer they've been trying to land. The seasoned entrepreneur is always networking because a serendipitous encounter may happen anywhere, including on the airplane, at the symphony, during lunch, or standing on line at the baseball game.

Remember, a large part of networking is simply "being present" so that the contacts that are being made can be leveraged if and when they are needed. As part of networking, the entrepreneur should also readily be willing to offer support, advice, and contact information to others who are also seeking to build their network. In fact, some networking consultants advise that the primary objective of networking should be to gain an understanding of others' concerns and problems. Then the entrepreneur can make an assessment regarding whether the contact would have any interest in the solutions the venture offers. Most people waste the few moments they have with new and existing contacts by focusing on themselves. Better to spend most of that time asking questions and collecting information about them.[25]

Establishing key contacts is the goal of networking. Once those contacts have been established, the entrepreneur must develop the relationship for business purposes. Each party will have business interests that will occasionally overlap and present the opportunity for working together.

SUMMARY OF LEARNING OBJECTIVES

1. **Understand** the difference between equity and debt financing. *Equity financing is financing that is provided by investors who trade cash for an equity position (ownership stake) in a venture. Equity financing does not need to be repaid but does result in dilution of ownership for the founders of the venture. Debt financing is provided by individual or institutional lenders. The amount of the loan is called the principal and must be repaid usually with interest.*

2. **Network** effectively as a means of gathering needed resources. *Effective networking is essential for entrepreneurial success. It means going to events where other entrepreneurs, investors, and service providers congregate and communicating your venture's intentions, interests, and capabilities.*

3. **Raise** capital in compliance with the Securities and Exchange Commission rules. *The SEC allows private ventures to raise capital from accredited and non-accredited investors via Regulation D. Entrepreneurs seeking to raise capital must do so in compliance with the private equity rules laid out in Regulation D.*

4. **Create and effectively leverage** a board of directors and/or an advisory board. *A board of directors and/or an advisory board can be exceedingly valuable to a venture. An entrepreneur should select board members who are familiar with their industry, have contacts within the industry, can open doors to potential sales, and who may be able to invest in the venture.*

5. **Calculate** equity ownership positions, dilution, and basic valuations. *Entrepreneurs that need external capital to grow their ventures must be able to recognize the dilutive effects of taking investor capital and understand how to manage those effects through potentially multiple rounds of financing.*

6. **Estimate** startup costs and the basic technological and organizational resources needed to launch a venture. *Startup costs will differ depending on the venture type and growth objectives. Nonetheless, it is possible to estimate startup costs by listing out all of the resources that are necessary to start and to generate sufficient revenues that either exceed costs or position the venture for additional fundraising.*

STUDY QUESTIONS

1. Explain some of the key elements of effective networking. Why does the entrepreneur want to learn how to network effectively? What are some potential outcomes of effective networking?

2. Explain the major differences between equity and debt financing for a new and growing venture. What types of financing are most likely available to the startup venture?

3. Debt financing often includes restrictive covenants that are written into the terms of the loan. Explain what this means and also explain the implications of positive and negative covenants for the entrepreneur who uses debt financing.

4. Describe two alternatives to debt and equity financing. Explain how the entrepreneur can position a venture to leverage these types of financing.

5. Explain how the founders of a venture are diluted over time when new investors take equity positions in a venture. In your explanation, use the terms *pre-money valuation*, *post-money valuation*, and *dilution*.

6. How would you go about securing a loan from a family member as part of your new venture financing plan? Explain what you will need to do to close such a deal. How would you go about securing a loan from a bank? What do you need to close a deal with a banker?

7. What are the various ways the novice entrepreneur can benefit from human capital? What is the difference between and advisory board and a board of directors? How should the entrepreneur use an advisory board?

8. If you were hired to be an employee and shareholder of a startup venture for an e-commerce venture, what type of technology tools would you require to do your job? If you were hired for a restaurant venture? If you were hired for a new manufacturing venture?

9. What are some techniques that you can use as a new entrepreneur to minimize your startup costs? List them out and discuss whether the cost-minimizing tactics might affect the performance of a new venture.

10. What is the difference between a business plan and a private placement memorandum? What are the basic documents you'll need to raise equity capital from angel investors? What is an elevator pitch? What is its purpose?

KEY TERMS

Accredited investor: Those whom the SEC deems savvy enough to make informed choices about where and how to invest.

Angel investor: Wealthy individuals who have risk capital they are willing to invest in select entrepreneurial ventures.

Blank check company: A development stage company that has no specific business plan or purpose or has indicated its business plan is to engage in a merger or acquisition with an unidentified company or companies, other entity, or person

Bootstrap financing: Bootstrap financing refers to the use of internally generated funds from sales to finance the growth of the business.

Business plan: The plan that explains the business in detail to a variety of stakeholders. It is often referred to as the new venture's roadmap.

Call a loan: Most loan agreements with institutional lenders include terms by which the lender can immediately request payment on a loan's outstanding balance.

Collateral: Real property or other assets that are pledged to a lender to secure a loan.

Debt capital: Capital that is raised in exchange for a promise of repayment with interest.

Dilution:: Dilution of ownership occurs when entrepreneurs sell equity in their ventures to new shareholders.

Equity capital: Capital that is raised in exchange for an ownership (equity) stake in the venture.

Elevator pitch: A term used to conjure up what it would be like to meet a potential investor in an elevator and, in the limited time available, describe the business in a manner that captures the investor's attention. An elevator pitch should articulate the venture's offering (product and/or service), its business model (how it will make money), and the size of the opportunity.

Executive summary: An abridged version of the business plan, normally condensed to a single page.

Fiduciary responsibility: The responsibility to deploy the resources of the venture in a manner that maximizes returns to the shareholders.

Friends, family, and fools (FFF): Said to be the only type of financing available to a new venture during its seed stage of development.

Growth capital stage: The stage where additional financing beyond FFF becomes available, including angel capital, venture capital, and debt capital.

Human capital: The value added to the venture through the intelligence, ingenuity, and creativity of its people.

Institutional lender: An institutional lender is a bank or some other business that is in business to lend money.

Line of credit (also known as a **revolving loan**)**:** An amount of money that is set aside by a lender for a business to use as needed. The borrower can draw down the line of credit for business expenses without having to fill out a loan application each time funds are required.

Min/Max: In addition to stating the amount that is going to be raised, the PPM also often specifies the minimum amount that needs to be raised in order for the venture to be able to use the funds; this is referred to as the min/max.

Negative covenants: Restrictive covenants in a loan agreement that state what the loan recipient is to avoid.

Networking: The practice of meeting new people with the intent of discovering ways to help one another.

Organic growth: Organic growth refers to venture growth that is fueled entirely by the operations of the venture without using any external equity or debt financing.

Personal guarantee: Most lenders, in the absence of evidence of adequate collateral or cash flow, will require an entrepreneur personally to guarantee a loan amount, typically by pledging assets that he or she owns personally and that are not owned by the business.

Positioning: How the entrepreneur is regarded by others within a network of individuals.

Positive covenants: Restrictive covenants in a loan agreement that state what the loan recipient is to achieve and when it is to be achieved.

Post-money valuation: The value of a venture immediately after an investing transaction is completed.

Pre-money valuation: The value of a venture before an investing transaction is completed.

Prime rate: The rate of interest charged by institutional lenders to their most reliable clients.

Private placement memorandum (PPM): A document that provides the equity investor with the full disclosure required by the U.S. Securities and Exchange Commission.

Regulation D: The SEC's regulation thatcontains three rules providing exemptions from the registration requirements, allowing private companies to offer and sell their securities without having to register the securities with the SEC.

Restricted securities: Those sold to private investors that are restricted by the SEC such that they may not be sold without registration.

Restrictive covenants: Terms outlined in a loan agreement that restrict the recipient of the loan to certain performance standards agreed to by both parties.

Securities and Exchange Commission (SEC): The board that governs all equity investments whether the venture associated with the equity transaction is public or private.

Security interest: Most institutional lenders will require collateral in which they will take what is called a security interest in an amount roughly equivalent to the amount they will lend.

Seed capital stage: The earliest stage in the venture's life when only friends, family, and fools (FFF) are said to be interested in investing.

Serendipity: The eventuality of finding something useful that one was not necessarily intentionally seeking.

Small Business Administration (SBA) loan: A loan originated by an institutional lender (a bank) and guaranteed in part by the federal government.

Small Business Innovation Research(SBIR): A competitive program that encourages small businesses to explore their technological potential and provides the incentive to profit from its commercialization.

Small Business Technology Transfer Program (STTR): A competitive program that reserves a specific percentage of federal R&D funding to offer awards to small business and nonprofit research institution partners.

Social capital: The network of people that an entrepreneur builds up and upon which the entrepreneur can rely for advice and other forms of support.

Social network: The network of all individuals associated with an entrepreneur and his or her venture.

Subscription agreement: A document that a potential investor signs, indicating an intent to invest at a certain amount.

Term of a loan: The length of time specified in the loan agreement during which it is to be paid back.

Units: Discrete investment amounts used in most early stage fundraising.

Valuation: The dollar value that both current owners and new investors place on the venture as a whole at the time of the financing transaction.

Venture capital investors: Professionals who invest their own and other people's money into promising new ventures that have the potential for very high rates of return.

OUT-OF-CLASS EXERCISE
Attend an Investor Event

This may be a challenging exercise because investor events are not held in every community. However, there are now hundreds of angel investor groups in the United States, and there is likely to be one within driving distance. It is worth your while to get to know more about how such groups operate and where they are located.

For this assignment students are to attend an investor group meeting where the member investors actually are listening to entrepreneurs make their pitches for funding. Students should pay special attention to the financial projections that the entrepreneur makes and listen to the questions that address the projections.

The assignment is to write a two-page report on the meeting. In particular, make sure students address the following items:

- Who were the entrepreneurs that were presenting at the meeting? What were the names of their ventures?

- What did you think of the venture presentations? If you had some money to invest, would you invest in any of them?

- What issues arose in regards to the financial projections presented by the entrepreneurs?

- Did you spot any major issues in any of the financial projections? What were they? How did the entrepreneur explain the issue?

ENDNOTES

[1] Shane, S., *The Illusions of Entrepreneurship: The Costly Myths that Entrepreneurs, Investors, and Policy Makers Live By* (New Haven: Yale University Press, 2004).

[2] Stam, W., and T. Elfring, "Entrepreneurial Orientation and New Venture Performance: The Moderating Role of Intra- and Extra-Industry Social Capital," *Academy of Management Journal,* 51(1) (2008): 97–111.

[3] Branson, R., "Richard Branson on the Myth of the Lone Wolf Entrepreneur." *Entrepreneur.com* (2010), www.entrepreneur.com/article/217567, accessed on March 26, 2012.

[4] Baker, E., J. Onyx, and M. Edwards, "Emergence, Social Capital and Entrepreneurship: Understanding Networks from the Inside," *Emergence: Complexity & Organization,* 13(3)(2011): 21–38.

[5] Copeland, M.V., "How to Find Your Angel." *Business 2.0,* 7(2)(2006): 47–49.

[6] Degennaro, R.P., "Angel Investors: Who They Are and What They Do; Can I Be One Too?" *Journal of Wealth Management,* 13(2)(2010): 55–60.

[7] Wijbenga, F.H., T. Postma, A. van Witteloostuijn, and P.S. Zwart, "Strategy and Performance of New Ventures: A Contingency Model of the Role and Influence of the Venture Capitalist," *Venture Capital,* 5(3)(2003): 231–250.

[8] Willoughby, Kelvin W., "How Do Entrepreneurial Technology Firms Really Get Financed, and What Difference Does It Make?" *International Journal of Innovation & Technology Management,* 5(1) (March 2008): 1–28.

[9] Townes, Glenn, "Financing a Business with Loans from Family and Friends, "*The National Federation of Independent Business* (August 18, 2005).

[10] Collins, L., "Finding Funds, "*Engineering Management,* 16(5)(October 2006): 20–23.

[11] Bortz, D., "Keeping up Relations When Your Brother is Your Banker," *Money,* 41(3)(2012): 38.

[12] de Bettignies, J.E., and J.A. Brander, "Financing Entrepreneurship: Bank Finance versus Venture Capita,." *Journal of Business Venturing,* 22(6)(2007): 808–832.

[13] Wichman, H., Jr., K. Abramowicz, and H.C. Sparks, "SBA Helps Small Businesses Think Big," *Strategic Finance,* 90(4)(2008): 45–49.

[14] Box, R., "How to Land an SBA Loan," *Journal of Accountancy,* 211(3)(2011): 34–37.

[15] Pagliarini, R., "What Is an Elevator Pitch?" *American Venture* (June 2006): 31.

[16] Clark, C., "The Impact of Entrepreneurs' Oral 'Pitch' Presentation Skills on Business Angels Initial Screening Investment Decisions," *Venture Capital,* 10(3)(2008): 257–279.

[17] Goodman, M., "Boot-Strap Your Business," *Entrepreneur,* 39(12)(2011): 90–95.

[18] Ucbasaran, D., P. Westhead, and M. Wright, "Opportunity Identification and Pursuit: Does an Entrepreneur's Human Capital Matter?" *Small Business Economics,* 30(2)(2008): 153–173.

[19] Shultz, Susan F., "Developing Strategic Boards of Directors," *Strategic Finance* (November 2003): 1–4.

[20] Advani, A., "Put Your Advisory Board to Work," *Entrepreneur,* 37(6)(2009): 86.

[21] Bottles, Kent, "Focus, Exchange, and Trust Mark Successful Entrepreneurs," *Physician Executive* (March 200): 71–73.

[22] Davidsson, Per, and Benson Honig, "The Role of Social and Human Capital Among Nascent Entrepreneurs," *Journal of Business Venturing* (May 2003): 301–331.

[23] Baron, Robert A., and Gideon D. Markman, "Beyond Social Capital: How Social Skills Can Enhance Entrepreneur's Success," *Academy of Management Executive* (February 2000): 106–116.

[24] Cooper, Arnold C. et al., "Entrepreneurship," *Academy of Management Proceedings* (1992): 74–89.

[25] Cook, Charlie, "7 Secrets of Effective Networking." Retrieved from: www.charliecook.net/networking-secrets.html

CHAPTER 9

EXPLORING AND SERVING YOUR MARKET

Learning Objectives

After reading this chapter, students should be able to:

- **Understand** the concept of a *value proposition*. **Construct** a compelling value proposition for your business concept.

- **Understand** various strategies for setting prices for your venture.

- **Use** various techniques to serve and support customers.

- **Measure and track** a venture's customer service efforts.

- **Recognize** the value of customer service as part of a venture's offerings.

INTRODUCTION

In this chapter we will discuss the process of exploring your market. To this point in your entrepreneurial journey, you've been concerned with identifying your unique talents, developing a product or service that you'd like to bring to market, identifying a target market, and setting up the basic tools of your business. In this chapter we make the assumption that all of those pieces are in place and it's time to bring your products or services to the market. Some entrepreneurship and business texts address this topic by focusing on market research and analyzing market data. That may be the traditional approach taken by large companies that introduce new products or services to the market, but it is decidedly NOT the approach that expert entrepreneurs take. The quotes below reflect just some of the feedback that effectuation scholars received when they asked expert entrepreneurs how they approach the challenge of bringing new products or services to the market:

- "I don't believe in market research, actually, I just go sell it"

- "Traditional market research says, you do very broad-based information gathering, possibly using mailings. I wouldn't do that. I would literally target key companies and do a frontal lobotomy on them."

- "I think you have to be right in there, eyeball to eyeball into the reality of what the customer looks like"[1]

As you can discern from the above quotes, expert entrepreneurs are too impatient to wait until the market research has been conducted, analyzed, and interpreted before they begin to explore their markets. Expert entrepreneurs have learned that, for most entrepreneurial ventures at least, bringing new products to market is a discovery process, not a planning process. That is, there are far too many variables and far too little time to uncover all the unknowns. The expert entrepreneur prefers to learn through low-cost, targeted market exploration. The expert entrepreneur prefers to forge ahead with the best information available and listen to customers, observe their responses to the venture's offerings, and make adjustments on the fly. In many industries speed to market is a critical success factor, and the entrepreneur simply cannot wait to collect and analyze all the data.[2] In most industries, as we have alluded to, the number of variables and potential responses from customers are too vast to analyze effectively other than via direct experience.

In this chapter, we will explore a number of key components of market exploration. The first component that we will discuss is your venture's **value proposition**. Your value proposition is an articulation of what you are offering to your customers. That may sound simple, but getting your value proposition right can mean the difference between success and failure. You may think that your venture's products and services address a glaring need in the market. And you may be right. But if that product or service is not introduced into the market in a manner that clearly addresses how your customers prefer to use it, pay for it, benefit from it, and many other factors, you may not be able to generate sales. It is crucial to know how your customers think and what they really need. We will provide insights into how to develop a compelling value proposition for your company, some examples of both good and bad value propositions, and how to adjust your value proposition to true customer needs and wants.

Another challenge for entrepreneurs in bringing their products and services to market is setting the right price.[3] There are a number of perspectives on price setting, but it is important for you to remember that your market should be the primary driver of your pricing decisions. Entrepreneurs who allow their production and other costs to set their price often learn that the market is simply not willing to pay as much as it costs to bring the product or service to market. Of course, that would be an unsustainable business. You can't build a business based on a model where your costs exceed your market price. In the short run you might be able to get away with it, and many businesses do as a strategy to gain initial market share. Eventually, however, the entrepreneur must discover how to charge more to customers than it costs to bring the product or service to them. We will discuss various approaches to pricing strategy and examine different examples of these various strategies.

Finally, we will discuss the valuable role that effective customer service plays in the success of startup ventures. Customer service may seem like a straightforward part of any new venture, but entrepreneurs too often neglect this important component of their overall operations. In fact, customer service is often overlooked by established companies, as you have probably painfully experienced. Because each venture and its customers will differ in terms of what the appropriate customer strategies should be, your particular strategy is also part of the market discovery process. Thus, in this chapter we will outline some fundamentals regarding effective customer service and also provide some insights into metrics that you can use to make sure your venture is striving constantly to get it right. The following Mini-Case highlights the story of Nick Nardello, whose focus on customer service has made him the number one Wingstop franchisee in the United States.

MINI CASE

Nick Nardello's Focus on Customer Service Makes Him #1

Nick Nardello is an unlikely success story in the Wingstop restaurant business, but he's achieved the franchisor's highest sales ranking with more than $2 million in annual sales. Nick is an unlikely success because he started out in business as a hairdresser, and he came upon the Wingstop concept entirely by accident. When he started his Chicago-based franchise in 2002, things didn't go smoothly. In fact, Nick very nearly became insolvent because customers just didn't understand the idea of chicken wings as a primary menu item. But Nick persisted, and through his extreme focus on customer service, his restaurant reached the $1 million in sales mark by 2005. From the very beginning, Nick positioned his store as a community asset. Any local team—whether it was T-ball, basketball, softball, flag football, or bowling—could count on his sponsorship. "My business really branched out from that," Nick said. "From having one happy customer to that person telling ten others, it just spider-webbed like that," he said. In 2008 Nardello's Wingstop location became the highest-grossing store in the nation, pulling in more than $2 million. And he's maintained that level of sales ever since with his focus on customer satisfaction.

Source: Adapted from Daley, J., "Secret Sauce," *Entrepreneur*, 38(10)(2010): 136–144; and "Wingstop Honors Top Franchise Performers," www.wingstop.com/news_detail.aspx?footer=1&news_id=129, accessed on June 26, 2012.

We begin this chapter by exploring how you can develop a compelling value proposition for your new venture.

DEVELOPING YOUR VALUE PROPOSITION

Value propositions are important for a venture. As stated in the Introduction, your value proposition is what you tell your customers about your offerings and your company. Value propositions help not only to communicate to the market about what the venture intends to provide, but they also help guide the venture's decision making. For example, the value proposition for well-known consumer products company Procter & Gamble is "Touching lives, improving life." This value proposition tells P&G scientists and product developers how to structure their investment of research and development resources. P&G introduces hundreds of new products to markets around the world each year. The firm's value proposition guides decision making so that consumers do not get confused about the firm's intent and offerings.

New ventures can also benefit from having a well articulated value proposition to guide them through the stages of venture development. For example, Dell computer had a potent value proposition when it was founded in 1984 by Michael Dell, who at the time was a college student at the University of Texas. Mr. Dell founded his company on the belief that, by selling personal computer systems directly to customers, he could better understand customers' needs and provide the most effective computing solutions to meet those needs. Dell Computer built on this vision over the years and is now among the 500 largest companies in the United States, employing more than 70,000 people worldwide.

The first step in establishing your value proposition is to focus on your target market. You've already been exposed to the process of selecting a target market for your venture's offerings. We suggested then that you choose a target market with which you have some familiarity. You will need to have familiarity with your target market in order to establish a value proposition that adequately communicates to that market. For example, if you are planning to sell high-technology products to senior citizens, you may find they are not interested in technical descriptions of the product. Rather, they may be more interested in learning how simple the product is to operate and how much better it will make their lives. In contrast, if you were selling your technology products to hobbyists or enthusiasts, they may be more interested in the technical details of the product than in what it does.

Using the right language to express your value proposition is your first challenge. The next challenge is to say the right thing. Many novice entrepreneurs make the fundamental mistake of expressing their value proposition according to their own value system and understanding of their product. This personal value system, of course, may be vastly different than the value system and understanding of the customers that comprise the venture's target market. For example, the entrepreneur may be convinced that his or her product can save money for business clients. However, the business client may only be looking at the time and expense that is involved in installing the product or training people to use it. If the entrepreneur's value proposition only focuses on cost saving, the customer may never be persuaded to purchase the product.

$$(Value_s - Cost_s) > (Value_a - Cost_a)$$

where:

$Value_s$ = the value of your solution

$Cost_s$ = the cost of your solution

$Value_a$ = the value of the next best alternative

$Cost_a$ = the cost of the next best alternative

EXHIBIT 9.1

For those of you who like complex concepts boiled down to a simple equation, Exhibit 9.1 provides a useful way for understanding value.[4]

This equation makes clear that you don't necessarily need the lowest price in order to provide the greatest value to your customers. What really matters is the difference between the value provided and the price. If your customers can be convinced that you provide the greatest difference between value and cost, you have a chance of winning their business.

Getting the value proposition right is a discovery process, as we've stated. Expert entrepreneurs know that a few failed attempts at selling are potent sources of information. Rather than seeing the lack of a sale as a failure, the expert entrepreneur regards such instances as opportunities to learn and improve. An effective technique is to ask customers why they decided not to purchase your offering. There is no harm in seeking to understand better the concerns that are uppermost in their minds. Many will be happy to tell you where your offering fails to meet their expectations as long as they know you are only seeking information. If they perceive that you are simply trying once again to push a sale, they are less likely to be forthcoming with the information you are seeking.

So listen to your customers, even those who don't purchase from you, to refine and calibrate your value proposition. Eventually, you may find that your value proposition is appropriately worded for your target market and you are generating sales at a rate that meets your expectations. You may think that this is a great situation to be in and that you can now rest on your laurels. Of course it is a great situation, but you probably don't have time to rest. As an entrepreneur focused on growth, you probably now are interested in exploring new markets beyond your original target market, so you may need to undertake a new discovery process for your new customers.

Your original target market may have been a very specific **vertical market** that is working very well. A vertical market is a market that consists of customers in a particular and discrete industry. The fast food restaurant industry is an example of a vertical market. If you have been serving a particular vertical, eventually you may want to begin exploring a new vertical market that is similar to the market in which you've found success. For example, if you have been selling products or services to colleges or universities you may now want to consider how to break into community colleges or high school systems. You will need a different value proposition for each of these distinct vertical markets as each has distinct needs. Many entrepreneurs make the mistake of asserting the same value proposition for different markets. Some other common mistakes entrepreneurs make in developing value propositions include:

- Trying to be everything to everybody rather than focusing on a specific measure of value.

- Making big claims such as "world class" or "cutting edge" without backing them up with evidence or substance.

- Attacking competitors rather than responding to customer needs.

- Providing a technical or factual description without indicating its value to the customer.

- Focusing on being the lowest price solution without regard to what really matters to the customer.

There are basically three ways to create a value proposition. The first and perhaps most commonly used technique is to highlight the benefits of the product or service. This approach focuses on the benefits that the entrepreneur thinks are part of the products and services being offered. This approach is least concerned with actual customer needs and suffers from the disadvantage of what is called **benefit assertion**. This means that entrepreneurs may claim advantages for features that, in reality, offer no benefits to customers.[5]

The second approach to developing your value proposition focuses on favorable points of difference between your venture's offerings and the competition. This approach is intended to emphasize how your offerings differ from the competitors in a manner that makes your offerings more favorable to the customer. However, many entrepreneurs emphasize points of difference that are not valuable to customers. This common mistake is referred to as **value assumption**. To avoid this common error, it is imperative that you understand what is truly valuable to your customers. Don't emphasize points of differentiation if those points do not help the customer make a clear value assessment of your offering. Another common error entrepreneurs make when using this approach is to emphasize too many points of difference. This only complicates the buying decision for customers. To use this approach effectively, make sure you are emphasizing points of differentiation that have the greatest value to your customers.

The third approach to establishing a value proposition is to develop what is known as a **resonating focus**. Entrepreneurs can provide a resonating focus value proposition to their customers by emphasizing a few elements that matter the most to customers, demonstrate and document the value of this superior performance, and communicate it in a way that indicates a deep understanding of the customer's business. A resonating focus will highlight both **points of parity**—those elements of your offerings that are on par with the competition—and a few, important points of difference.

Exhibit 9.2 provides a handy means for understanding how these three different approaches to developing a value proposition are different.

The preferred method is to create a value proposition that centers on a resonating focus and articulates clear value for the customer. A compelling value proposition will readily indicate to the customer not only how your product compares to competitors, but why it will provide them with superior value overall.

VALUE PROPOSITION:	ALL BENEFITS	FAVORABLE POINTS OF DIFFERENCE	RESONATING FOCUS
Consists of:	All benefits customers receive from a market offering	All favorable points of difference a market offering has relative to the next best alternative	The one or two points of difference (and, perhaps, a point of parity) whose improvement will deliver the greatest value to the customer for the foreseeable future
Answers the customer question:	"Why should our firm purchase your offering?"	"Why should our firm purchase your offering instead of your competitor's?"	"What is *most* worthwhile for our firm to keep in mind about your offering?"
Requires:	Knowledge of own market offering	Knowledge of own market offering and next best alternative	Knowledge of how own market offering delivers superior value to customers, compared with next best alternative
Has the potential pitfall:	Benefit assertion	Value presumption	Requires customer value research

From "Customer Value Propositions in Business Markets," by James C. Anderson, James A. Narus and Wouter Van Rossum. *Harvard Business Review*, March 2006. Copyright © 2006 by Harvard Business Publishing; all rights reserved.Reprinted by permission.

EXHIBIT 9.2 Approaches to Building a Value Proposition

Source: Anderson, J.C., J.A. Narus, and W. van Rossum, "Customer Value Propositions in Business Markets," *Harvard Business Review*, 84(3)(2006): 90–99.

PRICING AND YOUR MARKET

One of the most straightforward business truths, yet one of the more difficult for the new entrepreneur to understand is: *The marketplace sets the price.* The entrepreneur's marketplace is made up of customers and competitors. Competitor pricing strategy is an overriding consideration in setting price because the competition presents customers with an alternative to paying the entrepreneur's price.

New entrepreneurs often set the price of their products/services by adding up all of the costs involved in bringing the product or service to market, and then adding a specific amount for profit (say, 15 percent). This is referred to as **cost-plus pricing**.[6] The problem with this approach is that customers don't care about an entrepreneur's costs—customers care about the price they have to pay for products and services and the value they receive for that price. If the entrepreneur uses the cost-plus pricing approach, one of two outcomes are likely: The price is set too high and the customer does not buy, or the price is set too low and each sale returns less profit to the business than is possible.[7]

There are several common misconceptions among new business owners about the reasons for setting a price. One common misconception among entrepreneurs is that the goal of pricing a product or service should be to increase sales volume. As most entrepreneurs learn, using price as a mechanism to drive sales volume can lead to problems. For example, sales of a product or service are likely to increase in proportion to price reduction. Following this logic, if the price is reduced to zero then sales volume will be at its peak. By using price to drive sales volume the entrepreneur can reach sales goals, but he won't be in business long if there is no profit.

Elastic and Inelastic Markets

An effective price strategy is one that is responsive to the type of demand present in the market. Economists recognize two basic types of demand in free markets: *elastic* and *inelastic*. An **elastic market** is one in which the overall demand in the market will expand if prices are lowered. An **inelastic market** is one in which demand will not respond to price changes. The most often cited example of an inelastic market is the market for salt. No matter the price of salt people simply will not buy more than normal—the consumption rate of salt is based primarily on physiological need and is highly inelastic to price changes.[8] A classic example of an elastic market is the airline business.[9] As competition escalates among carriers and ticket prices drop people tend to fly more frequently. The demand for air travel is highly elastic and very sensitive to price.

In an inelastic market, any increase in market share for one competitor has to be at the expense of one or more of the others. Therefore, any price cutting strategy in such a market is likely to be matched by the competition. This competitive reaction leads to what is known as **price wars.** Price wars are destructive to markets and are generally won by the organization with the strongest financing.[10] It is illegal in the United States to use price-cutting as a method of putting competitors out of business.

In an elastic market, the reduction of prices by a competitor has two potential consequences. First, it can lead to more buyers coming into the market, thereby expanding the market. Second, the reduction of prices can lead customers to buy the price cutter's product or service instead of the competitor products. In an elastic market, it must be expected that competitors will react to any substantial loss of customers caused by a reduction in prices. When prices in a given market reach the level that the market is no longer able to expand, then the price reduction must stop or a price war will develop.

Customer Acquisition Cost

There are a number of pricing strategies the startup venture can use to generate initial sales and, hopefully, begin to acquire loyal customers. Depending on the type of venture you are launching, **customer acquisition costs (CAC)** will vary. Customer acquisition costs are simply the costs that are involved in acquiring each new customer. For some venture types the CAC can be very high indeed. For example, ventures that attempt to break into a crowded industrial market may need to spend a lot of money and time in the initial selling process. Industrial buyers typically are slow to adopt new technologies, especially when the existing technologies are good enough and allow them to keep operating. New entries into such markets will likely be required to make multiple sales calls, provide free samples, and assist in the testing of the samples to enable comparison with existing products.

© aerogondo2, 2012. Used under license from Shutterstock, Inc.

By way of contrast, opening a new yogurt shop may not have extensive CAC. A yogurt shop owner may need to give away free samples, set up a booth at a local fair, or distribute flyers on windshields of cars in a parking lot. Obviously, the goal of any venture is to achieve a CAC figure that is less than the **lifetime value (LTV)** of each customer. Customer LTV is defined as how much a customer will spend with you for their lifetime (i.e., the total number of products they buy from you over time multiplied by the price of each product). For example, if it costs $100 to acquire a customer whose LTV is only $40, the business will be unsustainable. The business cannot sustain itself by losing $60 on each customer that it acquires. Starbucks, for example, uses the following approach to estimate the LTV of its customers

Step 1: Estimate how much each customer will spend per visit to a Starbucks store.

Step 2: Estimate how many visits each customer will make per week.

Step 3: Calculate the average customer value per week by multiplying the figure in Step 1 times the figure in Step 2.

Step 4: Estimate the average customer lifespan.

Step 5: Calculate the LTV of a customer by multiplying the figure in Step 3 by 52 (because there are 52 weeks in a year) and further multiplying the product of that equation by the average customer lifespan.

Using actual figures from Starbucks, it turns out that the average LTV for its customers is nearly $25,000. Thus, Starbucks must develop its business model to ensure that its CAC is less than $25,000.

Many novice entrepreneurs fall prey to the trap of underestimating the CAC in their industry.[11] This common trap results in a venture finding out too late that it doesn't have adequate startup capital to reach its breakeven point. Of course, it's always possible to go back to the capital markets for more money. However, that may be difficult given the business plan would have to reflect that the original breakeven milestone was not reached. The following Bullet Breakout highlights some techniques entrepreneurs can use to minimize CAC.

BULLET BREAKOUT

Tips for Minimizing Customer Acquisition Costs

- Create videos that answer every likely sales question and make them available to your customers on your website or via DVD.

- List the common sales objections that come up in the sales cycle and provide answers to these on the website.

- If your customers are going to compare you to the competition as part of their process, consider doing this for them, with a section of your site that has a comparison matrix with appropriate check marks.

- Try to develop a sales model that reduces the amount of actual customer contact required to close a sale.

It can be difficult to develop a good estimate of the CAC in your industry prior to startup. The most reliable method that you can use to estimate this cost is to investigate what others in your industry have experienced. This research should focus on the costs that were incurred when your competitors got started, not the costs they are currently incurring to acquire customers. Customer acquisition costs generally decline over time as the venture's visibility increases and customers are acquired via referral and word of mouth.

Startup Pricing Strategies

There are a wide range of options for pricing during the startup phase of your venture. We'll explore each of these strategies and discuss the various tradeoffs that attend each one.

FREEMIUM PRICING: This strategy is very common among web-based ventures. The strategy focuses on providing substantial value to customers for free. For example, Box.com is a web-based storage venture that provides customers 5 GB of free storage. That is a substantial free offering that enables the company to generate a large number of registered users. It also offers paid services that provide substantial additional value. Box knows that once it has registered users, it can continue to market products and services to those users, and perhaps monetize them in some other way such as by online advertisements. Of course, the freemium pricing model is risky because it assumes that, at some point in the unknown future, the venture will figure out how to monetize its registered users. This often turns out to be difficult as users get used to the free offerings.[12]

VALUE BASED PRICING: Under this approach, the entrepreneur prices offerings based on the value created for customers. This is usually the most profitable form of pricing.[13] The most extreme variation on this is "pay for performance" pricing for services in which the venture charges on a variable scale according to the results achieved. Let's say that the venture's offering saves the typical customer $1,000 a year. If the offering reliably produces that kind of cost savings, you the venture can charge a percentage of that savings since, if the cost savings in fact are realized, the offering is essentially free to the buyer.

PENETRATION PRICING: Penetration pricing is used by new ventures to achieve initial market share.[14] It focuses on using a low price, perhaps even a price below the CAC, in order to gain the initial set of loyal customers who can help spread the word about the venture's offerings. These initial customers are often referred to as **early adopters**. Early adopters are those who are most likely to try your new offerings. They often consist of enthusiasts, hobbyists, or people who are prone to experiment with new products. Once the early adopters have been captured via the penetration pricing strategy, and a word of mouth buzz has been initiated around the venture's offerings, prices can be raised.

PRICE SKIMMING: The price skimming strategy is different from penetration pricing in that price skimming charges high, rather than low, prices to the early adopters. Price skimming carefully identifies different market segments and attempts to sell to each segment at the maximum price each segment will allow. As each market segment is exhausted, prices are lowered to the highest price the next segment will allow. Apple uses a price-skimming approach for most of its new product releases. The company charges high prices initially to the enthusiasts who will gladly stand in long lines to buy the latest Apple product. Then, it gradually brings prices down to achieve greater market penetration in advance of the next product release. Exhibit 9.3 illustrates the price skimming approach for three distinct market segments designates as A, B, and C.

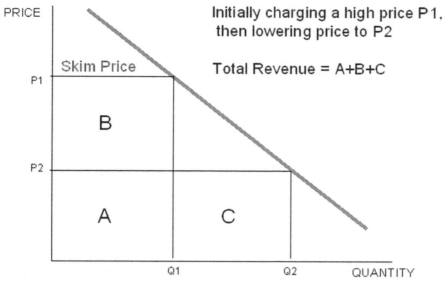

EXHIBIT 9.3 Price Skimming

BUNDLE PRICING: Bundle pricing focuses on providing customers with discounts if they purchase multiple products in a single transaction as opposed to purchasing the same products over multiple transactions.[15] McDonald's understood this when it created its "value meal" approach to pricing. Not only does bundling speed the ordering process at its restaurants ("I'll take a number 2"), but it also has raised the average ticket price as it bundles large versions of fries and drinks in the value menu.[16]

TARGET RETURN PRICING: This approach is sets prices for products and services based on a target rate of return on invested capital. For example, suppose that the founders of a product based venture have $10,000 invested. They want to recoup their investment in the first year, during which they project they will be able to sell 1000 units of their new product. As such, they will need to make a $10 profit on each unit sold during the first year to recoup their $10,000 investment.

Pricing and the Growing Venture

As the venture begins to gain customers and increases its visibility in the marketplace, different pricing strategies become available. While the growing venture does have expanded pricing options, it may have to return to startup pricing strategies as it releases new products or services. Of course, the growing venture also has a growing list of loyal customers that it can sell to. Selling to existing customers is a great way for ventures to avoid the customer acquisition costs that were discussed earlier, and yet increase sales. Selling additional products and services to existing customers generates what is referred to as **recurring revenue**. Expert entrepreneurs recognize the importance of recurring revenue and strive to achieve loyal customers that can be counted on for future sales. Not only does recurring revenue enable the venture to avoid CAC, but it also provides a more reliable stream of revenue that enables planning and investing in further growth.

A price increase that increases sales—or, at least, does not reduce sales—is a powerful tool for profit. Since an increase in price does not entail a rise in costs, the added revenue falls directly to the venture's profit line (the "bottom line"). Businesses that are able to raise prices without cost increases and without sacrificing sales possess what is called **pricing power**. Pricing power is the ideal situation where a business sells goods into a willing market at a price it determines and, at least to some extent, controls.[17]

One of the most important considerations in any price strategy is to protect the **core prices** of the business. Core prices are those associated with a company's most important sources of revenue. These sources of revenue are usually the most popular products or services, with the greatest margins and the best customers. Once again, the airline industry provides a good example of the concept of **core price protection**. The core customer for airlines is the business traveler. The business traveler usually travels on a fixed schedule that is not easily changed. In addition, the business traveler travels at company expense and is able to pay more than a recreational traveler. Finally, the business traveler usually wants to be home on weekends. As part of its pricing strategy, the airline industry often offers discounted fares and special promotions, but these are always limited by restrictions. The most common restrictions on round-trip fares include two-week advance purchase of tickets, and a Saturday night stay-over prior to using the return portion of the ticket. These restrictions preclude most business travelers from taking advantage of the discounted fares, protecting the core price.

Another common method that companies use to protect their core pricing is through product downsizing. In many markets, raw material price increases outstrip productivity gains, requiring companies to raise their prices to consumers to maintain stable gross margins. But, as we have seen, higher prices lead to reduced demand and lower sales volumes. Companies that sell products—say, cereal—that is sold by volume or weight can downsize the product and leave the price the same without affecting consumer demand. For example, a cereal maker that reduces a 14-ounce box of cereal to 12 ounces without changing the price on the box will not lose many customers. Research on consumer behavior has demonstrated that consumers are far more sensitive to changes in price than they are to changes in quantity.[18]

Discounting is the most widely used price strategy. Discounting protects core pricing by focusing only on certain items or certain customers. When the discounted prices are offered for a limited time period, it is usually called a sale.[19] Many firms use strategies such as an "End of Year Sale" or a "This Week End Only Sale." These and many other types of temporary discounts are designed to entice the buyer to "buy now."

Walmart has become the largest retailer in the United States by abandoning the core price concept and discounting all merchandise on a permanent basis. This strategy, known as "everyday low pricing" or EDLP, has been disruptive within the retail industry.[20] EDLP has violated the conventional wisdom to avoid cost-plus pricing. Walmart has succeeded in this approach by developing buying power over its suppliers. By driving the costs of the goods it buys below the costs competitors pay, Walmart is generally able to sell products at prices below those in the general marketplace. But Walmart's success is founded not only on its ability to drive down costs, but also on the way in which it "prices up." An observant

Walmart shopper will note that certain items are actually priced above the general marketplace. These items provide extra margin for the retailer.[21] The customer buys the product despite its above-market price because Walmart has created the perception that everything it sells is a bargain.

Discounting is not always aimed directly at increasing sales volume. Discounting is also used to dispose of obsolete or unwanted inventory.[22] Recognizing that some items in inventory are unlikely to sell at their standard price, many retailers liquidate that inventory by selling it at a discount. This enables the retailer to recover inventory space and to derive some value from the obsolete or unwanted items. Obsolescence occurs at different rates, depending on the products or services. An example of an industry that faces the inventory obsolescence problem regularly is automobile manufacturing. Each year, even before the new models are announced, dealers and manufacturers must review their inventories and decide when and by how much they will discount cars that have not been sold.[23]

Pricing and Finance Discounting

The U.S. economy has grown to its present size in large part based on the use of credit. Virtually all expensive products and services—houses, cars, and jewelry—are purchased on credit. Consumers, and even many businesses, could not participate in the marketplace without extended payment plans. The markets for housing and automobiles, for example, would be a fraction of their present size if customers had to pay cash for those products.

© Photobac, 2012. Used under license from Shutterstock, Inc.

The introduction of credit cards has expanded the number of goods and services bought on credit. Credit cards enable consumers to purchase less expensive items—such as CDs, groceries, and shoes—on credit. In fact, the use of "plastic" has grown so common that certain merchants have placed a minimum purchase requirement on the use of credit cards in their establishments.

Because the use of credit has become so pervasive credit terms have become an important part of price and volume strategy. Offering credit terms to consumers at a more advantageous rate than current market rates is, in reality, another form of price discounting. The furniture and appliance industries are examples of the use of interest rate discounting. A popular strategy in the furniture industry is to allow customers to buy the merchandise and pay no interest on the financing for one year or more. If the customer pays for the merchandise before the expiration of the interest-free period they are able to avoid paying any interest on the goods. However, if the customer fails to completely pay for the purchase within the interest-free period many merchants will then add a high interest rate—usually above market rates—to the remaining balance. This strategy provides consumers with an incentive to complete their payments during the interest-free period and provides the retailer with a premium if it is forced to wait longer than that period to receive payments.

Because of the downward pressure on prices exerted by discounters in the marketplace, many retailers have had to pressure their suppliers to lower their prices. As an alternative, some retailers ask suppliers for better credit terms. The effect of having a longer time period to pay for goods enables retailers to reduce investment in inventory, thus lowering costs. When costs are reduced, it is possible to pass the saving to the customer with a price reduction, or the retailer may keep the saving which will increase its profit.

When starting a new business, many entrepreneurs are tempted to set their prices below the general market. The intent of such a strategy is to attract customers by offering them a price advantage. The rationale is that the business is new and unknown and needs some advantage over competitors who have an established reputation and brand in the marketplace. Price is often regarded to be the advantage customers will respond to most readily. However, sometimes this price strategy will lead to the opposite reaction. American consumers generally believe that "there is no free lunch." This belief leads the consumer to be skeptical of unexplained pricing below market prices. Customer perception is an important factor in the success of any business. If the entrepreneur believes it is necessary to begin operating with a low price, it is better to advertise the market price and then provide a Grand Opening discount to customers. The promotional effects of such an offer will be discussed in the next chapter.

Pricing and Competition

Pricing strategy should never be executed without considering the reaction of competitors. The strength and speed of a competitor's reaction to a price change depends primarily on the effect the price has on the competitor's business. In an inelastic market the reaction will be swifter and stronger than in an elastic market. In an inelastic market any gain one participant makes must necessarily be at the expense of the others. Therefore, if a price strategy is effective and encroaches on the competitor's market share, there is likely to be a vigorous reaction.

In an elastic market a price change may bring new customers into the market. If that occurs, competitors may initially ignore the price change. However, if a price reduction strategy results in a rise in profits for the firm executing the strategy, competitors usually will drop their prices as well. When the price reduction proves that the market is sufficiently expandable to make the price-reduction strategy profitable for all participants, the lower price level tends to become established as the new market price.

The establishment of a lower price level in a marketplace is appropriate in industries where products are being manufactured for lower costs over time. In such situations the lowering of prices can be accomplished without reducing corporate profits regardless of whether the price reduction results in an increase in sales volume. When a price reduction is based on lower costs and the price move results in a larger number of buyers in the market, the strategy is a great success. Computers and other consumer electronic devices provide great examples of this cost/price effect.

The reverse side of the success of price reductions based on lowered costs and expanded market is also demonstrated in the computer and consumer electronics market. Technology advances have led to dramatic price reductions on computers and consumer electronics. When this pricing pattern is continued for an extended period, consumers become **price sensitive**. Once in this mode, they tend to shop for products based on low prices rather than **brand recognition** or other features. Discounters look for markets where consumers are price sensitive. They tend to drive prices down faster than the rate at which costs are reduced. The result is reduced margins for all participants in the marketplace, and reduced profits.

The airline industry is an example of the price reduction cycle in an elastic market. It has been well established in the United States that when prices for airline tickets drop more people fly. In the 1960s and 1970s, before the advent of discount or low cost airlines, the major air carriers were able to charge prices that allowed large margins and large profits. As the airlines became more profitable labor demanded its share of the earnings. The result was that labor costs

© chungking, 2012. Used under license from Shutterstock, Inc.

increased, especially the cost of pilots and mechanics. When low-cost airlines—such as Southwest—entered the market, they used price strategy as the principal method of competing with the major airlines.

The major airlines did not follow the price reduction strategy employed by the low-cost carriers. Instead, the majors decided to rely on their better system of routes and on their established relations with business flyers who were the most profitable segment of the business. These companies emphasized safety and convenience as the reasons to pay their higher prices.

The market for air travel proved to be highly elastic. As a result, the price spread between the majors and the low-cost carriers was tolerated for a number of years. However, as the low-cost airlines gained better routing and more scheduled flights, the major airlines began to feel the competitive pressure. The financially weaker of the majors began to lose money, and many went out of business.

All of these developments conspired to make air travel less expensive for the consumer. While this is good for the consumer it is hard on the airlines. Nonetheless, this example clearly demonstrates how important competition is to price strategy.

Price increases are equally subject to competitive pressures. The airline industry demonstrates this point as well. When several carriers attempted to add a modest fuel surcharge ($9–$10) to their ticket prices, the other airlines did not go along. The originators of the surcharge were forced to remove it from their pricing rather than allow their competitors to have even this small price advantage.

Pricing and Gross Margin

Entrepreneurs must monitor the effect of their pricing strategy on the firm's **gross margin**. Gross margin is defined as the difference between the selling price of a product or service and the amount the entrepreneur had to pay for the raw materials that make up that product or service (the "cost of goods sold"). It represents the amount of money a venture has left to pay its selling costs and general and administrative expenses associated with operating the business. After these latter two expense categories are covered, the remaining amount of money is the profit before tax for that business. Gross margin is expressed as a percentage of revenue, using the following equation:

$$\frac{\text{Revenue} - \text{Cost of Goods Sold}}{\text{Revenue}}$$

A price reduction usually results in a reduction in gross margin. This negative effect on gross margin is usually offset by an increase in sales volume that usually accompanies a price reduction. Increasing sales volume can lead to a reduction in the average **cost of goods sold** since suppliers will often provide discounts to clients that buy in large volumes. Additionally, in some businesses an increase in sales volume leads to efficiencies in labor or equipment use that helps ease the reduction of gross margin. Nonetheless, it is rarely the case that these savings totally offset the negative effect of a price reduction on gross margin.

SERVING YOUR MARKET

Expert entrepreneurs know that there is nothing more important for a venture than serving customers. The value creation process doesn't end with the delivery of a product or service to a customer. In fact, it usually doesn't even begin there. Expert entrepreneurs know that pre-sales customer service can be vital to making a sale. They also know that after-sale support and service can generate goodwill, referrals, and potential lifelong customers. In this section, we'll look at various things entrepreneurs can do to develop a complete and satisfying experience for customers.

Customer service plays a big role in customer loyalty, but probably not in the ways you might think. Conventional wisdom holds that companies should strive to "exceed customer expectations." And you probably have heard that phrase from a wide range of companies. The funny thing about it, however, is that exceeding customer expectations can be costly, difficult to measure, and, ironically, not very effective in generating loyalty. Research has indicated that customer loyalty is driven primarily by the quality of the products and services offered by the venture. The most important finding regarding customer service is not that it is a driver of customer loyalty, but it can be the primary driver of customer disloyalty.[24] That is to say, poor customer service will drive customers to seek alternatives, but service that exceeds their expectations does little to promote their loyalty. Customer loyalty programs should focus on providing customer service that is simple, straightforward, and honest. Customers don't want to struggle to get in touch with a company's customer service representatives, and they want any problems they encounter to be resolved quickly. For example, research has shown that customers experience the following common obstacles to resolving issues with customer service:

- 56 percent report having to re-explain an issue multiple times.
- 57 percent report having to switch from the web to the telephone.
- 59 percent report having to spend moderate to high effort to resolve an issue.
- 59 percent report begin transferred from one representative to another.
- 62 percent report having to repeatedly contact the company to resolve an issue.

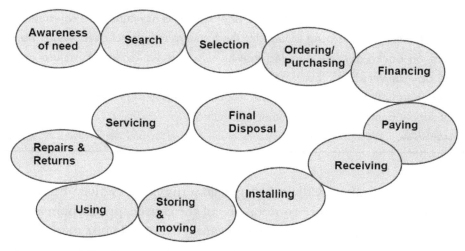

EXHIBIT 9.4   The Consumption Chain

Source: MacMillan & McGrath, 'Discover New Points of Differentiation' HBR, 1977

These kinds of problems can be addressed relatively easily for new ventures by using third-party services, including services that originate offshore. Many new ventures use call centers or help desk support firms that provide big-company style services at affordable rates—many charge only for the actual calls they take or problems they resolve. Despite some resistance to using offshore sources for this support, it can be a very productive and inexpensive alternative for startup ventures.

Too many ventures have failed because the entrepreneur assumed that a superior product or superior service was reason enough for customers to buy. But the performance of a product or service is usually not all that the customer experiences. Exhibit 9.4 illustrates the concept of the **consumption chain**. The consumption chain is the set of interactions that customers tend to have with businesses and their offerings.

Note that the consumption chain provides a relatively comprehensive set of transactions that customers traverse as they attempt to interact with a venture. The list includes everything from searching for your venture to disposal of the product/service after it has been used up. Each one of these components of the consumption chain needs to be attended to in order for your venture to provide customers with a complete and satisfying experience.

Expert entrepreneurs have learned that given industries may be underperforming on one or more of the components of the consumption chain. If that underperformance is a **point of pain** for customers, the entrepreneur may be able to address that and develop a sustainable competitive advantage. The following Mini-Case highlights one Houston, Texas–based entrepreneur who built a furniture empire by addressing a customer point of pain in the retail furniture business.

MINI CASE

Jim "Mattress Mack" MacIngvale and Gallery Furniture

Jim "Mattress Mack" MacIngvale calls his Gallery Furniture store in Houston, Texas "the world's furniture store." While that may be a typically oversized Texas boast, it's clear that Mack has developed a very unique furniture store. He launched his retail furniture venture in 1983 on a small piece of land next to a busy Houston freeway. Mack realized that to stand out in the crowded furniture retail industry he had to differentiate his store in a unique way. Recalling his brief stint as a furniture store salesman in Dallas, Mack recalled how his customers hated having to wait for the furniture they purchased. Many had to wait weeks for items that were on backorder. He decided that he would build Gallery Furniture around the simple promise of "same day delivery." In other words, customers would receive their furniture on the same day they bought it. Over nearly thirty years of business, Mack has kept that promise, and Gallery Furniture has flourished on that simple commitment to customer satisfaction.

Source: Adapted from MacIngvale, J., T.N. Duening, and J.M. Ivancevich, *Always Think Big* (Chicago: Dearborn Press, 2002).

There are countless examples, in addition to Jim MacIngvale's Gallery Furniture, of entrepreneurs who have addressed one or more components of the consumption chain as a means of better serving customers and developing competitive advantage. Part of your market exploration strategy should focus on which of these components of the consumption chain is the greatest point of pain for customers in your industry. Addressing these as part of your product/service offerings can become a major focus of your value proposition.

Some of the components of the consumption chain are clearly in the pre-sale category, and others concern after-sale service and support. Any one of these, if currently managed poorly within your industry can provide substantial opportunity for differentiation and customer capture. Many novice entrepreneurs think of customer service as a necessary evil. They reason that, since customer service is usually an **after-sale expense,** it constitutesnon-revenue-generating overhead. While customer service is often an after-sale business function, it impacts revenue in two ways. First, dissatisfied customers may elect to return their purchases—resulting in lost revenue. Research has amply demonstrated that poor service after the sale can injure the business by word of mouth spread by customers who are dissatisfied.[25] Second, satisfied customers may tell others about their positive customer-service experiences—resulting in new revenue for the venture. This type of revenue is particularly good since it is based on **word of mouth** or **referral** and is among the least expensive revenue the venture will enjoy.

Customer service strategies can become a source of competitive advantage for entrepreneurial ventures if they can determine a way to offer a service that competitors either don't offer or don't perform effectively. An example of this is product support. Many software providers have notoriously offered poor technical support to customers who attempt to install and use their product for home or business.[26] Others may then enter the market with a product that is comparable or maybe even slightly less advanced, but they win customers based on superior technical support.[27]

Many companies emphasize **pre-sale customer service** as a means of acquiring paying customers. Pre-sale customer service may include such things as call center services to prospective customers who may have questions about pricing, product/service features and benefits, and the after-sale support they'll receive from your company.[28] Although this information is normally included in the marketing collateral offered by the organization, some prospective customers don't take the time to read the material. Many entrepreneurial ventures are able to offer pre-sale customer service by outsourcing the activity to a vendor that specializes in the area. Pre-sale customer service is not intended to execute a sale, but rather to develop a relationship with the prospective customer. In that sense, the customer service agent needs to understand how to meet the prospective customers' needs and to know when to refer the prospective customer to a trained salesperson.[29]

In many businesses, customer service can also produce revenue through the sale of **warranties**. An example of this is home appliances. Most home appliances today are built with solid-state electronics, which rarely fail. Insuring these items against failure does not entail much risk to the retailer. Consequently, warranties sold to appliance customers have a high margin. In fact, some scholars regard the sale of extended warranties to consumers for solid-state electronics and durable goods as unethical.[30] Nonetheless, the practice is legal, and many consumers gladly pay the warranty fee to give them peace of mind that they will not have a large expense if the product should fail.

Almost all extended warranties offered to customers are limited warranties. A limited warranty has certain conditions and limitations on the parts covered, type of damage covered, and/or time period for which the agreement is valid. To avoid risk, many retailers establish their limited warranty to cover only items that rarely fail within the specified time limit. Therefore, a limited warranty provides a service to customers who prefer to warrant their purchases, but does not add much cost to the retailer.

Customer service strategy also includes the selection and implementation of appropriate technologies. Many firms today use **customer relationship management** (CRM) software. CRM software focuses on organizing and managing information about customers. CRM solutions record customer transactions and serve as a repository for customer information that has been collected by the venture. This information can then be analyzed and customer behavior patterns and preferences can be determined. Many firms have learned that CRM helps them identify customers that have a large impact on revenue and also those who may be more trouble than they are worth. Either finding can help a firm improve its revenue and gross margins.

Customer service is integrated with sales and marketing through the entrepreneur. The overall strategy of the firm sets the tone for the organization concerning how it will identify, acquire, and care for customers. Marketing identifies customers, sales acquires them, and customer service cares for them.

Measuring Your Customer Service

There are few things that are more valuable for entrepreneurs to measure and track than their performance with respect to customer service and satisfaction. Understanding your market includes understanding what things are important to consumers and keeping track of how well your venture is performing with respect to those key metrics.

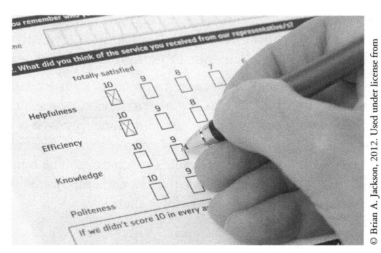

© Brian A. Jackson, 2012. Used under license from Shutterstock, Inc.

You've probably been exposed to various customer satisfaction surveys. Such instruments are commonplace in many types of modern business ventures. It is nearly impossible to visit a retailer where they don't tell you about the survey that you can take to win a prize. And, oh yeah, they normally tell you that they'd really appreciate if you gave them a perfect rating.

In Chapter 5 we introduced you to the concept of "thriving on bad news." You want to create customer service metrics that don't simply pat you on the back for all the good things you do, you want metrics that alert you when things are going wrong. You also want to create metrics that can tell you how well customers are responding to your offerings. Let's review a few key metrics that you may want to use to keep track of your venture's performance with respect to customer service.

NET PROMOTER SCORE: Net promoter score (NPS) is a relatively new metric is designed to provide feedback to the venture regarding whether customers would promote the venture to other potential customers. NPS is generated at the customer-facing points of the venture. That is, those employees who are the direct service providers to your customers are responsible for gathering NPS information. Ventures that use this approach design simple customer feedback forms, or they use a third-party customer survey firm, to gather data immediately after a customer service transaction. NPS categorizes all customers into one of three types: promoters, passives, or detractors. Promoters are those who will speak highly of the venture and recommend it to their friends and colleagues. Passives are those who are relatively indifferent to the venture but who intend to remain loyal. Detractors are those who will shop elsewhere and speak negatively about the venture to friends and colleagues.[31]

FIRST CONTACT RESOLUTION (FCR) SCORE: A common metric used by ventures to keep track of how well they are performing on problem resolution is referred to as the "first contact resolution (FCR) score." This score is intended to help the venture focus on resolving customer problems and reduce the need for customers to make repeated calls to resolve an issue. To generate this score the venture simply tracks repeat calls within a specified period (say, seven to fourteen days).

CUSTOMER EFFORT SCORE (CES): The Customer Effort Score is measured by asking customers the question: "How much effort did you personally have to expend to handle your request?" This is typically scored on a 1 to 5 scale with "1" being "low effort" and "5" being "very high effort." This metric can be coupled with the FCR score and others to gather detailed information on where the venture can improve. Research indicates that 94 percent of customers who report "low effort" expressed intentions to purchase more from the venture, while 88 percent said they would increase their spending. On the other hand, 81 percent who reported difficulty in resolving a problem indicated they intended to spread the word to others.

There are many other ways for entrepreneurs to track and measure their customer service programs. It's important to find the metrics and customer service programs that are right for your venture and your customers. At the same time, research is abundantly clear that customer loyalty is not affected by service that greatly exceeds their expectations, but they are affected negatively by service that does not meet their expectations. The best rule that we can offer here is to keep service simple, resolve problems quickly, and empower employees to own customer problems and find creative, effective ways to resolve them.

SUMMARY OF LEARNING OBJECTIVES

1. **Understand** the concept of a "value proposition." *A venture's value proposition is an articulation of what it is offering to customers. The value proposition should be clear, specific, and targeted to the market.*

2. **Construct** a compelling value proposition for your business concept. *Constructing a value proposition must begin with your target market. The value proposition must communicate with your target market in terms it can understand and that enables the target market to make a decision.*

3. **Understand** various strategies for setting prices for your venture. *We explored a number of pricing strategies in this chapter, including value pricing, freemium pricing, penetration pricing, and price skimming. The main thing for entrepreneurs to remember regarding pricing of products and services is that the market sets the price. That is, markets don't care about your costs. Entrepreneurs must find ways to generate profits at prices that the market will bear.*

4. **Use** various techniques to serve and support customers. *Customer service is an important, yet often overlooked, component of new venture success. Entrepreneurs tend to focus more on the venture's offering rather than the service transaction between the venture and its customers. While service that greatly exceeds customer expectations has been found to have little effect on loyalty, service that fails to meet customer expectations has a dramatic impact and tends to drive customers away.*

5. **Measure and track** a venture's customer service efforts. *New ventures should develop customer service metrics that enable them to measure and track important details about their customer service interactions. Several metrics discussed in this chapter included the Net Promoter Score (NPS), the First Call Resolution (FCR) score, and the Customer Effort Score (CES). These and many others can and should be used to ensure the venture is working constantly to improve its customer service.*

6. **Recognize** the value of customer service as part of a venture's offerings. *Customers will vote with their feet if they find a venture's customer service to be poor. It's important to understand what customers need and how much effort they are willing to spend to interact with a venture and to purchase its offerings. Entrepreneurs must recognize that customer service can be managed, tracked, measured, and improved on a continuous basis.*

STUDY QUESTIONS

1. What does the typical expert entrepreneur think about standard market research? Why?

2. What is the first step for the entrepreneur in developing a compelling value proposition? Explain how the entrepreneur should go about achieving the first step.

3. Why is it important to use the right language in forming your value proposition? What does it mean to say that creation of a value proposition is a "discovery process"?

4. What is a vertical market? How does an entrepreneur migrate his or her venture's offerings from one vertical market to another?

5. In formulating a value proposition many entrepreneurs make the error referred to as *benefit assertion*. What does that mean? Many also make the error of *value assumption*. What does that mean?

6. What is meant by the term *cost-plus pricing*? What does it mean to say "the market sets the price"?

7. Explain what is meant by the terms *customer acquisition cost* and *customer lifetime value*. How should the entrepreneur use these concepts to help in setting the price for the venture's offerings?

8. Describe and differentiate between the pricing strategies of *freemium pricing*, *penetration pricing*, *price skimming*, and *value pricing*.

9. Explain what is meant by the term *pricing power*. How can an entrepreneurial venture develop pricing power?

10. Explain the *consumption chain*. How can an entrepreneur use the consumption chain as a means of finding a business opportunity?

11. Explain the customer service metrics *net promoter score*, *first contact resolution score,* and *customer effort score*.

OUT-OF-CLASS EXERCISE

For this exercise students are requested to collect and analyze value propositions. Value propositions can be found in magazines, on the web, and in sales collateral material issued by companies. The point of this exercise is to compare and contrast various value propositions and to address the following questions about each of those that have been collected as part of an in-class discussion.

1. Which of the value propositions that have been collected seems to be the most compelling? In other words, which of the value propositions do you feel best motivates customers to buy? What makes this value proposition compelling?

2. Which of the value propositions that have been collected seems to be the weakest? Why do you judge that value proposition to be weak?

3. Do any of the collected value propositions suffer from benefit assertion? Do any of them suffer from value assumption?

4. Can you identify a resonating focus in any of the value propositions? Explain why that is true of the value proposition identified and not true of the others.

5. Select a value proposition that does not have a resonating focus. Can you suggest how to improve it so that it does?

KEY TERMS

After-sale expense: Customer service that occurs after a sale has been made, e.g., technical support, and thus constitutes an after-sale expense.

Benefit assertion: A common error in developing a value proposition whereby the entrepreneur claims advantages for benefits and features that offer no real benefit to customers.

Brand recognition: This term refers to consumers recognizing a brand and making purchase decisions in part based on the brand name.

Consumption chain: The set of interactions that customers tend to have with businesses and their offerings.

Core prices: Prices associated with a company's most important sources of revenue.

Core price protection: The practice of companies of holding core prices at a standard level to protect profit margins.

Cost of goods sold: These are the variable costs associated with your venture and identified in the income statement.

Cost-plus pricing: An approach to pricing that sets the price of products/services by adding up all of the costs involved in bringing the product or service to market, then adding a specific amount for profit.

Customer acquisition cost (CAC): The costs involved in acquiring each new customer.

Customer relationship management (CRM): CRM software enables a venture to track each customer and his or her interactions with the venture's representatives.

Discounting: Reducing the price of offerings to entice customers to make a purchase.

Early adopters: Those who are most likely to try your new offerings.

Elastic market: A market in which the overall demand in the market will expand if prices are lowered.

Gross margin: Gross margin is defined as gross profit divided by revenue. The ratio enables you to compare your venture to others despite differences in scale.

Inelastic market: A market in which demand will not respond to price changes.

Lifetime value (LTV): How much a customer will spend with you for his or her lifetime (i.e., the total number of products bought from you over time multiplied by the price of each product).

Point of pain: A link in the consumption chain that customers find to be inefficient, ineffective, or not working.

Points of parity: Those elements of your offerings that are on par with the competition.

Pre-sale customer service: Service that includes such things as call center services to prospective customers who may have questions about pricing, product/service features and benefits, and the after-sale support they'll receive from your company.

Price sensitive: The degree to which price influences consumer decisions regarding which of various competing products to purchase.

Price war: When companies offering similar products compete primarily based on price.

Pricing power: Businesses that are able to raise prices without cost increases and without sacrificing sales possess what is called pricing power.

Recurring revenue: Selling additional products and services to existing customers.

Resonating focus: Emphasizing a few elements that matter the most to customers, demonstrating and documenting the value of this superior performance, and communicating it in a way that indicates a deep understanding of the customer's business.

Value assumption: An error in creating a value proposition whereby the entrepreneur emphasizes points of difference in his or her venture's offerings that are not important to the customer.

Value proposition: An articulation of what the venture is offering to its customers.

Vertical market: A market that consists of customers in a particular and discrete industry.

Warranties: Warranties are representations to customers about what type of performance they should expect from your venture's offerings.

Word of mouth referral: Sales generated by satisfied customers who tell others about the venture and its offerings.

ENDNOTES

[1] Read, S., and S.D. Sarasvathy, "Knowing What to Do and Doing What You Know: Effectuation as a Form of Entrepreneurial Expertise," *Journal of Private Equity,* 9(1)(2005): 45–62.

[2] Wang, J., "Speed to Market," *Entrepreneur,* 39(8)(2011): 90.

[3] Dunn, P., C.A. Kogut, and L.E. Short, "Pricing Practices in Very Small Businesses," *Entrepreneurial Executive,* 16(2011): 35–48.

[4] Anderson, J.C. and J.A. Narus, "Business Marketing: Understand What Customers Value," *Harvard Business Review,* 76(6)(1998): 53–65.

[5] Anderson, J.C., J.A. Narus, and W. van Rossum, "Customer Value Propositions in Business Markets," *Harvard Business Review,* 84(3)(2006): 90–99.

[6] Lucas, Mike R., "Pricing Decisions and the Neoclassical Theory of the Firm," *Management Accounting Research* (September 2003): 201–217.

[7] Hanson, Ward A., and Kirthi Kalyanam, "A Cost-Plus Trap: Pricing Heuristics and Demand Identification," *Marketing Letters* (July 1994): 199–209.

[8] Boote, Alfred S., "Price Inelasticity: Not All that Meets the Eye," *Journal of Consumer Marketing* (Summer 1985): 61–66.

[9] Eilers, Bernard, and Joseph Schweiterman, "Strategies to Stimulate Discretionary Air Travel: An Internal Perspective," *Journal of Transportation Law, Logistics & Policy* (Fall 2003): 123–136.

[10] Desjardins, Doug, "Price Wars Bode Ill for Innovation," *DSN Retailing Today* (December 15, 2003): 28.

[11] Skok, D., "Startup Killer: The Cost of Customer Acquisition," *For Entrepreneurs,* accessed at http://www.forentrepreneurs.com/startup-killer/ on March 26, 2012.

[12] Owen, T.B., "Why Freemium Is a High Risk Charging Model," *Information World Review,* 267(2011): 10.

[13] Williams, G., "Name Your Price,." *Entrepreneur,* 33(9)(2005): 108–115.

[14] Holden, R.K. 2007. "Pricing Strategy." *Sales & Service Excellence,* 7(7): 10.

[15] Yan, R., and S. Bandyopodhyay, "The Profit Benefits of Bundle Pricing of Complementary Products," *Journal of Retailing & Consumer Services,* 18(4)(2011): 355–361.

[16] Baumgarten, J., O. Bushnell, and D. Vidal, "Pricing: The 'Value Meal' Approach," *ABA Bank Marketing,* 42(5)(2010): 16–21.

[17] Lynn, J., "Pricing Power," *Entrepreneur,* 25(2(1997): 36–37.

[18] "The Consumer Psychology of Rates," *Advances in Consumer Research,* 2003, pp. 106–108.

[19] Bill Merrilees and Kim Shyan Fam, "Effective Methods of Managing Retail 'Sales'," *International Review of Retail, Distribution, and Consumer Research* (January 1999): 81–92.

[20] Johnson, Lauren Keller, "Dueling Pricing Strategies," MIT *Sloan Management Review* (Spring 2003): 10–11.

[21] Lisante, Tony, "Wal-Mart: Benchmark for Global Retailing," *Drug Store News* (January 19, 2004): 14.

[22] Fulcher, Jim, "Plan for Demand," *Manufacturing Systems* (February 2003): 34–36.

[23] White, Gregory L., "GM's Deep Discounting Strategy Helps Auto Maker Regain Ground," *Wall Street Journal—Eastern Edition* (January 17, 2003): A1.

[24] Dixon, M., K. Freeman, and N. Toman, "Stop Trying to Delight Your Customers." *Harvard Business Review,* 88(7/8)(2010): 116–122.

[25] Zeelenberg, Marcel, and Rik Pieters, "Beyond Valence in Customer Dissatisfaction: A Review and New Findings on Behavioral Responses to Regret and Disappointment in Failed Services," *Journal of Business Research*(April 2004): 445–465.

[26] Lovelace, Herbert W., "Superior IT Service? Get Help-Desk Superstars," *InformationWeek* (July 12, 2004): 64.

[27] Raskin, Robin, and Rachel Derby Teitler, "Support & Satisfaction," *PC Magazine* (July 1, 1994): 273–277.

[28] "Ask Dr. Jon," *Customer Inter@action Solutions*(July 2003): 68.

[29] Huisken, Brad, "The Fine Art of Selling Right," *JCK* (May 2004): 88–89.

[30] "Extended Warranty Market Unfair to Consumers," *Business Law Review* (February 2004): 49–50.

[31] Markey, R, F. Reicheld, and A. Dullweber, "Closing the Customer Feedback Loop." *Harvard Business Review,* 87(12)(2009): 43–47.

ENTREPRENEURIAL MARKETING, PROMOTING, AND SELLING

Learning Objectives

As a result of studying this chapter, students will be able to:

* **Define** the term *product* and distinguish between consumer and industrial products.

* **Understand** the history of marketing and the "marketing concept."

* **Explain** product development and its various stages.

* **Describe** the stages of the product life cycle and explain how ventures can extend it.

* **Explain** the role of promotion in marketing and list five promotional objectives.

* **Explain** the purposes of branding, packaging, and labeling.

* **Outline** the personal selling process and describe each step.

* **Explain** what is meant by distribution and identify different modes of distribution.

INTRODUCTION

Now that you've learned how to create a compelling value proposition, set your prices, and serve your customers, you have to go out into the marketplace and get customers. The customer acquisition process for ventures includes a wide variety of decisions and activities. This chapter is organized into five sections: marketing, product, promotion, selling, and distribution.

Marketing is the overarching concept that involves all of the things your venture does to better understand your customers and ensure that their needs are being met. We introduced you to the process of exploring your market in Chapter 9. Entrepreneurs must understand their market and its needs and wants to be effective creators of value. As we have stated throughout this text, value is defined by the market. Entrepreneurs must manage the entire customer experience from the messages they receive about the venture, through the experience of buy-

ing, to after-sale support. This overall concern and management of it constitutes the full meaning of the term *marketing*. Marketing often is said to be comprised of the 4Ps: product, price, promotion, and placement. We have discussed price in the previous chapter. In this chapter we will be concerned with product, promotion, and placement (today, more commonly referred to as *distribution*). We also include a separate section on selling and the sales process, which is generally regarded to be a part of product promotion.

The term **product** refers to the offerings that your venture intends to bring to the marketplace—whether a physical product or a service. As we've discussed in other chapters, the expert entrepreneur focuses on creating value for a target market. In order to create value you have to be able to define what value means to that market. You were introduced to the concept of a value proposition in the last chapter. Your value proposition is what you communicate with your customers and potential customers about your venture's offerings. In this chapter, we'll highlight how products evolve over time and how the savvy entrepreneur manages products throughout the product life cycle.

Promotion refers to the means the venture uses to communicate about its offerings to potential customers. You are familiar with many types of promotion, including print advertising, radio and television advertising, advertising on the web and mobile devices, billboards, and many other ways that companies communicate their messages to potential customers. Depending on what type of venture you create, different promotion tactics and strategies will be more or less effective. In this chapter, you'll learn how to evaluate various promotion alternatives and how to determine which of them will work for your venture.

Promoting products to customers via various communication channels is just the beginning. You would not be in business for long if all you did was communicate with your market. Ultimately, any business has to find a way to sell its offerings to its customers. The selling process will vary widely by industry, just as the marketing process does. In this chapter we'll introduce you to some fundamental aspects of selling that will help you determine the approach that is best for your venture. For example, if your venture sells high-cost or high-complexity products or services, the selling process may be longer and more involved than if you sell lower-cost or less complex items. The process of selling industrial equipment to manufacturing companies, for example, may take longer for the venture to close a sale than selling potato chips in the company's vending machines.

Placement(distribution) refers to the distribution of products to wholesalers, retailers, or directly to customers. The entrepreneur has a number of decisions to make about distributing products to customers, perhaps even considering the potential to reach a worldwide customer base. Logistics and transportation have improved dramatically over the past several decades, and international trade is far easier today than it was a few decades ago. In this chapter, we'll discuss your distribution options and some of the key factors to consider when deciding what distribution channels are best for your venture.

Let's begin this chapter by exploring the concept of marketing.

MARKETING YOUR VENTURE

When people hear the term **marketing,** many think of advertising or selling. Although those are part of marketing, and the part we see most, marketing is much more. As the American Marketing Association defines it, marketing is the activity for "creating, communicating, delivering, and exchanging offerings that have value for customers."

This definition emphasizes the diverse activities marketers perform: deciding what products to offer, setting prices, developing sales promotions and advertising campaigns, and making products readily available to customers.

Ultimately the purpose of marketing activities is to bring about exchanges between buyers and sellers. **Exchange** consists of one party providing something of value to another party, who gives something in return. Just as the "something of value" is not always a physical good, the "something in return" is not always money. For example, the American Cancer Society markets the idea of quitting smoking to live a longer, healthier life. This is an intangible product, one that cannot be physically touched. For smokers who "buy" that idea, the price is the effort required to break a habit that they find pleasurable.

Consumers make buying decisions based on how well a product is perceived to meet their needs. Consumer choice has been extensively studied by market research specialists. They typically boil consumer choice down to two types of goods: **utilitarian** and **hedonic.**[1] Utilitarian goods are those that meet a consumer need, while hedonic goods appeal more to consumer emotions. As an example, the individual out to purchase a new car may be interested in the good gas mileage from the utilitarian perspective. The sporty design of the vehicle may be appealing from a hedonic perspective. Entrepreneurs must tailor their message to appeal appropriately to different markets at different times.

A Brief History of Marketing

When organizations and individuals conduct marketing activities today, they usually have consumers' needs and desires clearly in mind. But that has not always been true. Beginning with the Industrial Revolution in the nineteenth century and the capability for mass production that resulted, most businesses had a **production orientation.** Demand for new manufactured goods was so great that producers were concerned primarily with increased production and operating efficiency rather than with consumer preferences. As goods rolled off the production line, marketing consisted of taking orders and shipping products.

By the mid-1920s manufacturers discovered that supplies of basic consumer goods had caught up to demand. They were now producing an abundance and, in some cases, an overabundance, of goods. Needing to sell their products to markets that had increasing choices and decreasing demand, companies had to switch from a production orientation to a **sales orientation**. Companies began to emphasize advertising and sales. Companies started using sophisticated sales techniques to increase demand for existing products, but they still did not look to the marketplace to ensure that consumers' needs and desires were met.

Not until the early 1950s did companies begin to develop a **consumer orientation**. With soldiers returning from World War II, reentering the workplace, and starting families, demand for consumer goods and services surged. Competition among companies striving to meet that demand also surged. Somewhere during this postwar industrial boom, marketers realized that the way to sell products was to focus on satisfying customers. One of the first companies to state a policy of customer satisfaction was General Electric. GE said that a focus on customer satisfaction should be integrated into each phase of business. The policy of customer satisfaction has become known as the marketing concept.

The Marketing Concept

During the "customer satisfaction revolution," many adaptations in industrial practices were initiated. For example, at Whirlpool, the marketing department conducted a survey that showed that customers wanted a cooking range that was easy to clean. Engineers then designed a range with electronic touch pad controls, which could be cleaned with the sweep of a cloth or sponge. Industry wisdom suggested touch pads would fail, because earlier models with push buttons failed. Marketing, design, and engineering worked closely together to test consumer reactions every step of the way, and the new range succeeded where the old pushbutton design had failed.

The **marketing concept** is a management philosophy stating that an organization should strive to satisfy the needs of consumers through a coordinated set of activities that also allows the organization to achieve its objectives.[2] Thus, customer satisfaction is the major force underlying the marketing concept and driving the entire company. The marketing concept calls for everyone in the venture to be committed to pleasing customers.[3] The firm must determine consumer needs and wants, develop quality products that satisfy them, make products readily available at prices acceptable to buyers (and that allow a reasonable profit), and provide service and after-sales support. If a firm can answer yes to the following questions, it is customer oriented:

- Are we easy for customers to do business with?
- Do we keep our promises?
- Do we meet the standards we set?
- Are we responsive to customer needs?

New ventures benefit from executing under the marketing concept from the beginning. Ventures that do so tend not to waste money on developing and marketing products that don't meet customer wants or needs. Also, customers will pay more for products they believe will provide greater value and satisfaction, and if they are pleased with their purchase they come back and they refer business. Repeat business lowers sales costs and boosts profits; holding onto current customers is about one-fifth the cost of acquiring new ones.[4] Some marketers say the marketing concept helps set up a cycle of success: Customer satisfaction leads to loyal customers, which produces higher profits that make employees want to stay with the firm, which in turn makes for better customer service and satisfaction.

Focusing on the customer sounds like an obvious, commonsense way to run a successful business, but not all companies gear their marketing activities closely to the customer. The marketing concept is not always easy to put into practice. Entrepreneurs must be committed to it and must gain the commitment of other members of the team. A venture may need to restructure responsibilities from time to time to better coordinate customer relationship activities. Often a venture must be willing to forgo short-term profits for long-term customer satisfaction. And because consumer tastes and preferences constantly change, the venture must continually obtain information about customers and their needs and tailor its products to meet changing consumer preferences.

Beyond the Marketing Concept

Does giving consumers what they want and need serve the long-term interests of society? In addition to satisfying customers to meet company goals, many companies today also take into consideration how marketing affects society. The broader **societal orientation** means that companies are concerned with the welfare of society as well as their own interests and those of consumers. Examples of entrepreneurial ventures that have built a business on the societal orientation includes Tom's Shoes—where the company gives a pair of shoes to a needy child for each pair that is purchased—to Method—which makes eco-friendly home and personal care products and sells them in recyclable plastic packaging.[5]

Many companies and nonprofit organizations take active roles in dealing with issues such as scarce resources, environmental destruction, hunger, housing shortages, and illiteracy.[6] Forward-thinking companies and their employees are involved in programs to work on such problems, as well as to help their communities, improve education, support the arts, and provide job training and opportunities for disadvantaged children and adults.

The marketing activities we discuss throughout this chapter focus on satisfying consumer needs and wants. In the next section we'll look at the processes involved in developing products that meet customer needs and how those products evolve through a lifecycle.

PRODUCT DEVELOPMENT

The concept of product varies from one venture to another as well as from one consumer to another. In order to innovate and manage products successfully, the entrepreneur must define the product or "offering" in the context of the target market. It is important to understand the nature of the product—the total offering of the firm that satisfies the needs of the customer. This concept of product is broad and focuses on the most important aspect, the imperative to satisfy customer needs. This satisfaction can be derived from such things as the benefits of product use, pride of ownership, or dependable, reliable performance. In addition, the product encompasses all those ancillary items that make it what it is, such as the package, the brand, the service, the quality, the options, the guarantee, and the warranty.

Product Development

One of the most useful tools for growing a business is the product planning and development process (see Exhibit 10.1).[7] Although the actual process and the time and sales involved in each step vary greatly, not only from industry to industry but within a given industry, the overall process still provides a framework for evaluating and developing new products as well as formulating basic marketing strategies. In order to implement the product planning and development process, it is essential that an effective method for obtaining new product ideas be established.

Ideas for new products can emerge from a wide variety of sources—customers, competition, distribution channels, federal government, research and development, and company employees. Many ventures ask their customers to submit ideas either informally or through an established process. These ideas can even be in the form of complaints. New ideas often emerge from the company's attempt at solving the problem. The following Mini-Case highlights a venture that has always focused on learning from customer suggestions.

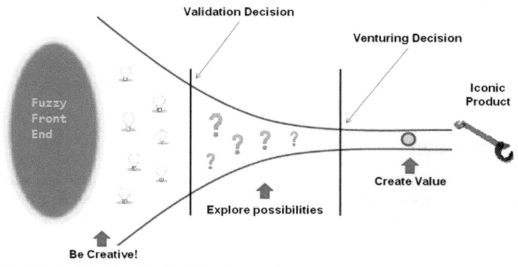

EXHIBIT 10.1 The New Product Development Process

Volusion Uses Customer Feedback to Generate New Products

Even at a young age, Kevin Sproles understood the importance of listening to customers. Sproles was 16 when he founded Volusion, an Austin-based maker of e-commerce software. In the early years, Sproles would spend hours a day on the phone with small-business owners who had signed up for his service, asking them how Volusion might improve, say, its customer checkout pages.

Now that Volusion has more than 20,000 clients, collecting customer feedback has become more difficult. In 2009, Sproles and his team, including Volusion's newly hired chief customer officer, David Mitzenmacher, began developing a formal process of soliciting and analyzing customer suggestions—as well as a system for quickly turning those ideas into new software features for customers.

Volusion started by sending out monthly surveys to customers. Volusion includes questions about which improvements customers would like to see. To encourage even more suggestions, Volusion built its own online forum that lets customers submit ideas and vote for suggestions they like. One customer used Volusion's forum to request a mobile version of the company's software. The suggestion received 36 votes from other Volusion customers. The company launched a mobile platform in March 2010.

In addition to the suggestions that come through the online voting system, Volusion also collects suggestions during customer service calls. Shana Bentivegna, a Volusion customer who runs Organic Pet Boutique, a Jersey City retailer of organic pet food and supplies, often calls with suggestions. During one conversation, Bentivegna complained that two fraudulent orders had been placed on her website.

Her feedback helped spur the development of Fraud Score, a feature that assigns a risk rating to incoming orders based on several factors, including the shopper's billing address, IP address, and recent credit card activity. Volusion charges an extra $13 to $50 a month for the Fraud Score service.

Source: Adapted from: Joyner, A.,"E-Commerce Company Volusion Designed a System for Collecting Customer Feedback—And Turning It Into New Products."*Inc. Magazine* (November 1, 2010).

Once a new product idea has evolved, it is very important for it to receive a very careful and thorough evaluation. Entrepreneurs should screen out as many new product ideas as possible in the early stages, allowing more time and money to be spent on products with a greater probability for market success. The early stage of new product development is often referred to as the **fuzzy front end** because of the many ideas that are generated and the few that actually make it to the marketplace.[8]

The new product ideas that successfully make it to the concept stage should be further evaluated, analyzed, and where appropriate, refined for market success. This often takes the form of determining consumer acceptance by presenting drawings or explanations of the new product to various consumers and members of the distribution channel. Even when there is no actual product prototype, this procedure will obtain valuable information from consumers. The product's advocates must be able to develop a so-called **business case** for the product to allow it to continue in the development process. That is, the product's advocates should develop sales forecasts and demonstrate how the product fits within the portfolio of other products offered by the venture.[9] A strong business case should also demonstrate how the venture is uniquely qualified to develop and bring the product to market.

Once the new product business case has received a positive evaluation, it is necessary to transform the concept into a physical product or **prototype**. A prototype is a working version of the product that can be tested with customers. It may not be the final design or be made of the final materials, but the prototype should be able to perform much like the final product that you intend to bring to the marketplace. Whenever possible prior to mass production, the technical and product feasibility of the item should be determined through the development of a prototype that has customer appeal.[10]

Test marketing is not used for all products prior to commercialization. It is a costly and time-consuming process that gives the competition time to react to your initiatives. It is frequently used for industrial products, regional products, and specialty goods where the information gained is worth the cost of the test. Some products absolutely require testing prior to commercialization. Medical devices, drugs, and consumer goods that present potential hazards should be thoroughly tested prior to commercialization. Entrepreneurs can limit their potential liability with products that may pose hazards by using independent testing agencies such as the **Underwriters Laboratories(UL)**. These organizations will test products and, if they pass the testing, provide their stamp of approval which can help limit potential liability.[11]

Only a few new products actually reach the market. The capital expenditures for launching the product into the market are extensive and should only take place for those new products that have a high probability of success. In addition to the costs of new equipment and facilities for production, the company has the marketing expenses of training salespeople, extensive introductory advertising, and sales promotion in the trade.

The Product Life Cycle

Like living things, products go through several stages, known as the **product life cycle**. New products enter the market during the introduction stage, they gain momentum and begin to bring a profit during the growth stage, they stabilize during the maturity stage, and finally they fade away in the decline stage. Exhibit 10.2 illustrates the four stages of the product life cycle.

Products pass through these five stages over time. For some products, the life cycle may be very short. Fad items such as basketball shoes last for only a few years. Nike combats the short lifecyle of its Michael Jordan shoes by coming out with a revised model every few years. Other products, such as washing machines and television sets, can have life cycles of a decade or more. Let's examine what generally occurs at each stage of the product life cycle.

INTRODUCTION STAGE: In the first stage of the product life cycle, a firm makes the new product available to customers, who gradually become aware of it. Profits for a newly introduced product are negative because initial sales are low during this stage and the firm must recover its research and development expenses while it is spending large sums for promotion and distribution. Notice in Exhibit 10.2 that sales move upward from zero. As we mentioned in Chapter 9 regarding penetration pricing, a portion of your target market may consist of what are called "early adopters." These are customers who are enthusiastic about obtaining your offerings and may help spread the word to others about what you are brining to the market. Apple knows this group well and caters to them around the world with each new product release.[12]

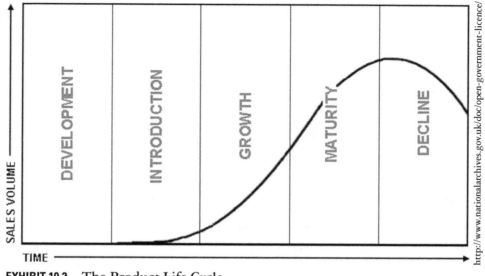

EXHIBIT 10.2   The Product Life Cycle

Source: Business Link: www.businesslink.gov.uk/bdotg/action/detail?itemId=1087240996&type=RESOURCES, accessed on April 9, 2012.

http://www.nationalarchives.gov.uk/doc/open-government-licence/

Entrepreneurs face several challenges during a product's introduction. They must develop and carry out promotional programs to inform potential customers about the product's availability and its features. Entrepreneurs must monitor sales, which may be slow, and make early adjustments in the product or in promotional efforts if needed. Many products don't survive the introduction stage.

GROWTH STAGE: Sales increase more rapidly during the growth stage, and the product begins to generate a profit. Competitors, seeing an opportunity, are likely to enter the market with similar products during this stage. The venture that originated the product may reduce its price as a result of new competition and decreased production costs.

A product in the growth stage usually faces intense competition from similar offerings. Ventures must rely heavily on repeat purchases for continued sales growth. Entrepreneurs therefore attempt to establish consumer loyalty to their products. They often create fresh promotional programs to emphasize the product's benefits and to encourage loyal customers to continue buying the same brand. Current growth stage products include products like InstaGram, Pandora, and the Apple TV.

MATURITY STAGE: During the maturity stage of the product life cycle, sales peak as profits continue to decline. As other products are introduced with new features and improvements, the product may become somewhat outdated. Examples of products in the maturity stage include LCD flat screen televisions, laptop computers (especially since the advent of the iPad), and sushi bars.

Intense competition from many different ventures forces some products out of the market. Ventures may cut prices further and increase their promotion budgets to compete for customers. They also may try product improvements, new package designs, and changes in style to encourage consumers to keep buying the product.

DECLINE STAGE: Sales fall rapidly during the decline stage of the product life cycle. Profits also continue to fall, and sometimes additional price-cutting leads to losses. Consumers often prefer new products in earlier stages of their lifecycles that provide greater satisfaction or meet different needs or wants. Entrepreneurs must decide at which point to eliminate a product nearing the end of its life cycle. Some products in the decline stage, such as DLP flat screen televisions are not immediately eliminated. Sometimes ventures generate a profit from decline-stage products by reducing promotional costs and selling to only the most profitable markets.

Extending the Product Life Cycle

Ideally, entrepreneurs would like their products to remain forever in the growth stage, when profits are highest. Although products eventually reach the decline stage, that some survive for decades is no accident. Entrepreneurs can extend the life cycle of a product in several ways.

INCREASING THE FREQUENCY OF USE: Entrepreneurs commonly try to keep their product sales growing by encouraging consumers to use their goods and services more. Energy drinks, for example, originally targeted helping people get through their afternoon slump in energy. More recently, energy drink makers have been emphasizing energy drinks as useful pick-me-ups any time of day.[13]

IDENTIFYING NEW USERS: Another way to extend a product's growth stage is to identify new target markets and promote the product to them. For example, computer game companies have moved away from serving only young, heavy computer using teens to focus on family activities and games.

FINDING NEW USES: Entrepreneurs sometimes maintain and increase sales by showing consumers alternative ways to use a product. For example, Weight Watchers had for years been a popular diet program appealing to women. In recent years, the company has targeted overweight males through celebrity spokesmen, such as basketball's Charles Barkley.[14]

PRODUCT MODIFICATION: As products encounter fierce competition and reach the maturity stage, ventures may need to modify products to compete more effectively. Product modification is a lifecycle extension strategy that involves changing a product's quality, features, or style to attract new users or increase usage. Quality modification means altering the materials used to make the product or changing the production process. Adding longer life to a battery is a quality modification. Functional modification is achieved by redesigning a product to provide additional features or benefits.

Deleting Products

Products in the decline stage of the product life cycle may become too costly for a firm to continue offering. A company may decide the money would be better spent on developing new products or modifying existing ones that are still profitable. For example, as consumers moved to buying music for digital devices like the iPod, reducing demand for musical DVDs, which had already displaced CDs, cassette tapes, and vinyl albums.

A firm can delete a product in one of several ways. A phaseout approach gradually eliminates the product without any change in the marketing strategy. When using a runout strategy, ventures may increase distribution and promotion and try to exploit any strengths left in the product. If a product is very unprofitable, a firm often makes an immediate-drop decision.

PROMOTION AND PUBLICITY

Promotion, an important element in the marketing mix, supports products, pricing, and distribution decisions. It is critical to the success of any venture. Before deciding what type of promotional program to conduct, a firm needs to establish its objectives. Ventures set promotional objectives that will help meet their broader marketing and organizational objectives. Promotional programs can be built around a single objective or multiple objectives.

© Sunny_baby, 2012. Used under license from Shutterstock, Inc.

Informing

The basic objective underlying all promotion is providing information. New ventures want to tell potential customers about themselves as well as what products are available, where they can be purchased, and for what price. A new restaurant, for example, may advertise in local newspapers or magazines and on radio and television stations, distribute coupons in the mail, invite the newspaper restaurant critic to review and publicize it, rent billboards, and buy a listing in the telephone directory.

Increasing Sales

Aside from providing information, encouraging prospective customers to purchase products is the most common promotional objective, since sales mean survival and success for entrepreneurial ventures. Using advertisements, coupons, and other promotional methods, ventures attempt to persuade customers to buy new products, remind them of the benefits of products that have been on the market awhile, and reinforce their choice of particular brands.

Stabilizing Sales

Entrepreneurial ventures also rely on promotional activities to reduce or eliminate substantial variations in demand throughout the year. Companies marketing seasonal products may step up promotional efforts during slow times of the year to use production facilities and distribution systems most effectively.

Positioning the Product

Often a firm uses promotion to position a product as different or superior to competing products. Positioning means emphasizing certain product features to create a specific image for the product and add to its appeal. Entrepreneurial ventures often rely on advertising to position products.

Building a Public Image

Sometimes a company wants to develop a certain image through promotion. Publicity and, to a lesser extent, advertising provide effective vehicles for image building. Mobil, for example, sponsors programs on public television stations to provide quality entertainment for viewers and to foster goodwill toward the corporation.

Developing Your Brand

A name, sign, symbol, design, or combination of these used to identify a product and distinguish it from competitors' offerings is called a **brand**. The part of the brand that can be spoken is the **brand name**.

Expert entrepreneurs are acutely aware of the importance of brand names.[15] Good names sell products. Entrepreneurs often search for short names that are easy to pronounce and easy to remember, such as Facebook, Hulu, and Zappos. Names can also suggest the product's function or its performance such as Diehard batteries. Brand names must also fit the image the company desires for its product, like Jaguar automobiles or Red Bull energy drinks.

TYPES OF BRANDS. Brands are classified as manufacturer, private, or generic. A **manufacturer (or producer) brand** is owned and used by the manufacturer or service provider. Some ventures use manufacturer brands to market products throughout the United States and abroad in many stores and outlets. Such brands identify who makes the products and provide the consumer with a nationally known, uniform, and widely available product such as Wrangler jeans or Chevrolet trucks.

A **private (or store) brand** (often also referred to as "private label")is owned by a wholesaler or retailer. Examples of private brands include Sears' Craftsman tools and Walmart's Sam's Cola. A venture offering private brands often can sell them at lower prices, achieve higher profits, and encourage customer loyalty. Most products sold under private brands are produced by companies that also market products under manufacturer brands. The number of private label brands is growing in response to value-conscious consumers who demand higher-level quality at a reasonable price.[16]

Some products have no brand name at all. These are **generic products**,usually sold in simple, no-frill packages that identify only the contents. Many grocery items such as canned vegetables, cereals, crackers, and paper goods are available as generics. Generic products offer consumers an alternative to manufacturer and private brands. By using plain packages and keeping advertising to a minimum, producers and stores can sell generics at reduced prices. Sometimes, but not always, products sold as generics are not uniform in size or appearance or are of lower quality than branded goods.[17]

It is also possible for the entrepreneur to revive a brand that had been abandoned. Entrepreneurs may be able to substantially increase chances of success by reviving brands, rather than spending the enormous amount of capital required to build new brand image. Research suggest that the revived brand must be repositioned to satisfy today's customer values. Evidence also suggests licensing a revived brand name to unrelated industries may prove very profitable for the entrepreneur.[18]

BRAND LOYALTY: Consumers frequently buy only their favorite brands of certain products. They will not switch brands even if an alternative is offered at a lower price. **Brand loyalty** is the extent to which a consumer prefers a particular brand.[19]

Entrepreneurs measure consumers' brand loyalty at three stages. The first, **brand recognition**, means consumers are familiar with a manufacturer's product. Buyers are more likely to choose a brand they recognize than an unfamiliar one. At the second stage of brand loyalty, **brand preference**, consumers will buy the product if it is available. At the third stage, **brand insistence**, buyers will not accept a substitute for their favorite brand.

The degree of brand loyalty varies from customer to customer and from product to product. For example, a study by J. D. Powers & Associates found that older car buyers are twice as loyal to a particular make as younger customers to be loyal to their car brand. Ventures can establish brand loyalty through the product's performance, packaging, price, and advertising and other promotional efforts. Loyalty keeps customers coming back for more.

Packaging: **Packaging** involves designing a product container that will identify the product, protect it, and attract the attention of buyers. It is important to both consumers and manufacturers. Packaging can make a product easier to use, safer, and more versatile. It can also affect consumers' attitudes toward a product, which in turn affects their purchase decisions.

Originally, packages were designed mostly for their functional value; they protected products from damage or spoilage. Today packaging also has significance as a marketing tool. To develop an appealing package that will catch the buyer's eye, marketers consider not only function but also shape, color, size, and graphic design. The following Mini-Case highlights how Red Bull used packaging as part of its marketing campaign designed to differentiate the energy drink from other carbonated beverages already in the marketplace.

Ventures work to create innovative packages to meet the needs of the consumers they want to reach. The impact of packaging on the environment has become another critical issue many entrepreneurs are facing. Packages from foods and consumer goods make up much of the tons of waste dumped into landfills each day in the United States. In response, some ventures make it a part of their marketing to let customers know they are using environmentally friendly packaging.

MINI-CASE

Red Bull Dominates Market via Branding and Marketing

The success of Red Bull energy drink is a testament to the power of effective brand building and marketing. The product was discovered by founder Dietrich Mateschitz on a trip to Thailand where locals enjoyed a drink called "Krateng Daeng" (which literally translated means "Red Water Buffalo"). Today, Red Bull commands nearly 70 percent of the energy drink market, with an estimated 3.9 billion cans sold in 2009.

Mateschitz and his team founded Red Bull in Austria in 1984. The founders conducted extensive market research while awaiting the product's approval in Europe. They tested over 200 packaging options prior to their Austrian launch in 1987. As well as differentiating their brand from other canned beverages (such as Pepsi and Coke), Red Bull's distinctive colors (blue and silver) and can's shape (taller and narrower than others on the market) helped to emphasize its difference from other soft drinks. Red Bull's founders also elected to stand out by charging higher prices than other carbonated beverages, emphasizing the company as a premium brand in the marketplace. Through these various efforts, Mateschitz and his team succeeded in positioning the product as something different, unique, and beneficial to consumers.

Source: Adapted from Gorse, S., S. Chadwick, and N. Burton, "Entrepreneurship Through Sports Marketing: A Case Analysis of Red Bull in Sport," *Journal of Sponsorship*, 3(4)(2010): 348–357.

LABELING: Manufacturers communicate with buyers through **labeling**. The label is the part of the package that identifies the brand and provides essential product information regarding contents, size, weight, quantity, ingredients, directions for use, shelf life, and any health hazards or dangers of improper use. Labels also provide the means for automatic checkout and inventory monitoring. The universal product code (UPC), an electronic bar code on labels that identifies manufacturers and products, enables supermarkets and other stores to use computerized scanners at the checkout counter. Most new ventures also use quick response or "QR" codes to enable customers to scan the code with their mobile devices, which then are automatically redirected to web pages that contain more information about the product.[20]

The Consumer Product Safety Commission and the U.S. Food and Drug Administration (FDA) require that labels indicate warnings, instructions, and manufacturer's identification. Federal laws mandate that labels include content information and potential hazards. Manufacturers are required to be truthful in listing product ingredients on labels. Ingredients must be listed in order, beginning with the ingredient that constitutes the largest percentage of the product down to the ingredient that makes up the smallest percentage. Snack chips that contain more vegetable oil than potatoes, for example, must be labeled to show oils as the first ingredient.

The Promotion Mix

To inform, influence, and remind customers in their target markets or the general public, new ventures often use personal selling (person-to-person approach) and advertising, sales promotion, and publicity (nonpersonal approaches). How these four elements are combined to promote specific products is called the **promotion mix**.

© bloomua, 2012. Used under license from Shutterstock, Inc.

A promotion mix may contain any or all of the four elements, depending on the firm's objectives, promotional strategy, product characteristics, and target market characteristics. The entrepreneur should carefully monitor the marketing mix to ensure that the various **marketing channels** being used are effective. A marketing channel is simply a mode of communicating with customers. For example, advertising could be conducted via television, radio, or the Internet. Each of thse is a different marketing channel that the entrepreneur may choose to use as part of the promotion mix. Of course, the expert entrepreneur never forgets that each dollar is precious to the new venture and he or she must be vigilant that the marketing dollars spent on any given channel are providing adequate returns.

ADVERTISING: Any paid form of nonpersonal communication to a target audience through a mass medium such as television, newspapers, or magazines is **advertising**. Of all promotional activities, consumers are most familiar with advertising. We see and hear many advertisements every day. Organizations and individuals spend over $412 billion on advertising in the United States each year.[21]

An advertiser can use any of several different types of advertising, depending on its promotional objectives. Companies advertise brands, industries advertise products, and companies or individuals advertise themselves, their activities, and their beliefs. We examine three major categories of advertising: primary-demand, selective (brand), and institutional.

- **Primary-Demand Advertising:** At times organizations want to create or increase demand for all products in a product group. This is referred to asprimary-demand advertising. The Florida Department of Citrus, for instance, sponsors advertisements to persuade consumers to buy and drink more orange juice. Their advertisements promote orange juice without mentioning any particular brand or producer.

- **Selective Advertising:** Most often a firm wants to create selective demand, or demand for a specific brand of product rather than for other, competing products. Selective advertisingmakes up the majority of advertising; marketers of virtually all goods and services use it in their promotion mixes.

- **Comparative Advertising:** Comparative advertising identifies competitors and claims the superiority of the sponsor's brand. Comparative advertising has grown in popularity during the last decade. Research indicates that comparative advertising is most effective when it involves indirect comparative claims made by new products.

- **Institutional Advertising:** When a venture desires primarily to build goodwill and create a favorable public image rather than promote a specific product, it employs institutional advertising. For example, British Petroleum in the wake of the major oil spill in the Gulf of Mexico in 2009 now advertises that it is engaged in cleaning up and protecting the environment.

- **Advertising Media:** The different outlets that present advertisements are called advertising media. The most commonly used are newspapers, television, direct mail, radio, magazines, and the yellow pages. Advertising on the Internet has exploded over the past decade, and now mobile devices are also a major channel of communication with customers and potential customers.

To obtain the greatest benefit from these media expenditures, entrepreneurs must develop an effective **media plan** that selects the specific media (particular television, social media, and/or mobile ads, etc.) to be used and the dates, times, and locations that advertisements will appear. The entrepreneur or skilled media planner developing the media plan tries to communicate with the largest number of persons in the target market per dollar spent on media.

New ventures go to considerable effort and expense to design, create, and evaluate advertisements that will accomplish their promotional goals. Developing an effective advertising campaign generally takes these steps:

- Identify the target audience of the advertisements.

- State the objectives to be accomplished (increase sales, build awareness, etc.).

- Determine how much money to spend.

- Develop an advertising platform consisting of the points to be emphasized to consumers.

- Outline a media plan, indicating specific media in which advertisements will be run and when they will be run to reach the target markets.

- Create the actual advertisement.

- Place the advertisements with the media.

- Through sales or research, evaluate the effectiveness of the ads (see if the objectives were met).

Some entrepreneurs handle their own advertising through in-house staff that plan, design, and create advertisements and place them with the media. Others use specialists outside the organization. An advertising agency is a business that specializes in planning, producing, and placing advertising and offers other promotional services for clients. Agencies, ranging from small firms handling local and regional advertising to large firms with national and international clients, can offer expertise and production facilities unavailable in many entrepreneurial ventures. Newspaper, radio, and television companies also offer advertising assistance, as do freelance writers, artists, and producers. Entrepreneurs often find that these sources can provide needed assistance at a reasonable cost.

SOCIAL MEDIA: Today many entrepreneurial ventures are finding marketing success through effective use of various social media technologies. Facebook, Twitter, LinkedIn, and many other platforms enable entrepreneurs to connect with and remain in contact with their customers on a continuous and ongoing basis.[22] Social media provides many opportunities for entrepreneurs to interact effectively with their customers. Some platforms, such as Facebook, are similar to websites in that they enable timely updating of company information and events. However, Facebook is preferrable to a website as a more informal way of keeping customers informed of the venture's ongoing activies. Formal websites are not good places for some types of information that would commonly be posted to Facebook. In addition, the venture's website will be visited by a wider cross-section of people—customers, investors, suppliers, vendors, and others—and should have more functional elements than a Facebook page would have.

LinkedIn, Twitter, blogs, and other forms of social media can also enable firms to keep in touch with customers. However, it's imperative if such social media platforms are used that they be regularly monitored and updated. Customers who visit a venture's blog and find that it has not been updated for a year or more might wonder about the viability of the venture. Virb, a web design firm based in New York, for example, has several employees who do nothing but manage the venture's social media activities. The Bullet Breakout provides tips on using social media effectively for your venture.

BULLET BREAKOUT

Tips for Leveraging Social Media as a Marketing Tool

- **Focus more on your web presence than your website:** Your website is what you say about you—your web presence is what others say about you.

- **Be consistent and current with social media:** You don't need to respond to every Twitter about your venture, but you do need to keep listening to your customers, competitors, and market influencers.

- **Build an editorial calendar:** Take a monthly calendar view and look at how you intend to create and share content of interest to your market.

- **Be visible:** To create the best value for your community keep a steady flow of interesting and useful information going.

- **Create social media guidelines:** Establish a set of criteria for using social media that everyone in the venture should follow. These should include things like build trust, be direct, give due credit, be honest, be responsible.

- **Monitor your blog for customer feedback:** Starting a blog and inviting customers to leave comments is a great way to keep an eye out for potential issues.

Source: Adapted from Brogan, C., "Cultivating Visibility," *Entrepreneur*, 40(1)(2012): 50; Burrus, D.,"Create Social Media Guidelines to Reach Your Customer," *Home Business Magazine*, 18(1)(2011): 32–35.

PUBLICITY. Like advertising and sales promotion, **publicity** is a nonpersonal form of communication. But it is transmitted by a mass medium in news story form and is not paid for directly by a sponsor. Publicity is actually part of **public relations**, a set of communications activities designed to create and maintain a favorable public image for a firm.

New ventures attempt to gain publicity for several purposes. They may want to increase awareness of their products, to build a positive image with the general public, to gain recognition for employees and their accomplishments, to encourage others to participate in community projects, or at times to counter negative events or news stories.

New ventures may use several vehicles to obtain publicity. The **news release** is a brief report—a page or two—that announces an organization's national, regional, or local events. New ventures distribute news releases widely and include the names of people within the firm for media representatives to contact for more information. A **feature article** is a longer, more detailed story about a firm, its products, or its people. It may run as long as 3,000 words and include photographs or illustrations. Some entrepreneurs do their own writing and submit feature articles to specific magazines or newspapers. To release important or timely news, a firm may invite media representatives to a **news conference** to make announcements, hand out supplemental materials, and answer questions.

Another approach gaining use is sponsorship of events, programs, people (such as Nike's sponsorship of golfer Tiger Woods), and sports stadiums. Besides publicity, sponsorship can involve advertising and sales promotion activities such as samples and contests. Each year thousands of entrepreneurial ventures sponsor sporting events, arts festivals, public radio and television programs, and public interest advertisements.[23]

© dorshock, 2012. Used under license from Shutterstock, Inc.

Publicity also poses several limitations. A venture exerts little or no control over a message—its content, placement, timing, or whether the media transmits it at all. News editors may have different ideas of what is news than do members of an organization seeking publicity. A news story may run on the late news show and reach only a fraction of potential viewers. Or it may be cut to a line or two in a newspaper column full of corporate news. Publicity does not always enhance a firm's image. At times the media people report negative events and criticize a firm's activities, policies, or products.

To foster positive and effective publicity, a venture must conduct well-planned, regular efforts. Many ventures employ advertising or public relations firms, or freelance writers or consultants to help them with their media planning and execution. Such companies can supply the media with newsworthy, well-written publicity releases, handle media requests, and build cooperative relationships with reporters, editor, news directors, and other media "gatekeepers."

SALES AND THE SELLING PROCESS

Now we get to the real test of your entrepreneurial intentions. Can you actually sell the products or services that your venture has created and marketed? There is no business if you cannot sell what you've created. For many novices this is the aspect of entrepreneurial success that provides the greatest anxiety. Many novices have not sold anything before, and they may even have a negative attitude about selling and the sales process.

The role of sales within the entrepreneurial venture is to adapt the marketing message to the individual customer's needs. Adaptive selling is a technique that is used by many ventures. This approach provides some flexibility for the salesperson to alter the marketing message within reasonable boundaries based upon the needs of a particular customer.[24] This technique has proven to be effective, but it must be kept within boundaries. Salespeople who are overly eager to adapt the venture's offerings to the customer's needs are prone to promise nearly anything. It is actually better for a venture to say NO to a customer than to say YES and not be able to deliver on the promise. Salespeople should be trained to be adaptive, but not so adaptive that they fail to recognize when the customer needs something that the venture cannot provide.

Advertising acquaints potential customers with a product or service and makes the personal selling experience more pleasant and possible. **Personal selling** is communicating person-to-person with one or more prospective customers to make a sale. At one time or another, all of us have encountered personal selling. Has a car salesperson ever taken you on a test drive? Or maybe a salesperson helped you during a recent clothing purchase. These activities are highly visible because they are aimed at consumers. Yet they represent only a fraction of the situations involving personal selling.

For many new ventures personal selling is a critical element in the promotion mix. Personal selling is also the most costly component of the promotion mix. Salespeople play an important role in the success of most ventures. The best are highly trained professionals who before and after the sale help buyers satisfy their wants and needs. They know the product and effectively communicate their knowledge to buyers face-to-face. They also keep track of new products and competitors' activities.

The processes involved in selling and the length of time it takes to close a sale is known as the **sales cycle**. Most industries have fairly standard sales cycles and you can determine whether your venture's approach to selling is in line with the industry standard or whether you have some work to do.[25] Of course, the startup will probably have a much longer sales cycle than the industry standard at first and will move closer to the standard over time as its products and brand become better known in the industry.

Sales Roles in the Venture

Entrepreneurial ventures employ different types of salespeople for various selling situations, depending on such factors as type of product, price, number of customers, and channels of distribution used. We examine three common types of salespeople: order getters, order takers, and support salespeople.

ORDER GETTERS: A salesperson responsible for selling products to new customers and increasing sales to current customers is an order getter. Order getters engage in creative selling. They size up a customer's needs and convey product information in a thorough and persuasive manner. Creative selling is especially important when customers are carefully weighing alternatives in making their purchase, when they are not aware of product features and benefits, or when the product is a new one. Many industries, including insurance, computers, appliances, and heavy machinery, employ order getters.

ORDER TAKERS: The person who receives and processes orders for repeat sales, with the objective of maintaining positive relationships with customers, is an order taker. The major function of order takers is to ensure that customers have the right amount of products they need when and where they need them. Order takers include salespeople who handle telephone and mail orders in a sales office and salespeople in retail stores. Other order takers handle routine sales of products such as milk, potato chips, bread, and beverages. They call on stores to check stock, inform managers of inventories, and make deliveries.

SUPPORT PERSONNEL: New ventures commonly employ support sales people to assist in selling, primarily to locate potential customers, educate them about products, build goodwill, and provide service after sales. Support people must often help sell industrial products.

The Selling Process

A salesperson's work is outlined in the steps that take place in the **selling process** (see Exhibit 10.3). Of course, not all salespeople perform their jobs in exactly the same way, and an individual salesperson may alter tactics for different situations. But the ultimate goal of the selling process is a long-term relationship with the customer. In the current highly competitive business environment, many entrepreneurs have discovered that retaining current customers is more economical than finding new ones.

PROSPECTING: Locating potential customers is called prospecting. Salespeople find prospects through many sources, including current customers, trade directories, business associates, telephone directories, newspaper or magazine articles, or public records. At this stage in the selling process, the salesperson tries to identify as possible customers those who have a need for a product and the financial ability and authority to purchase it.

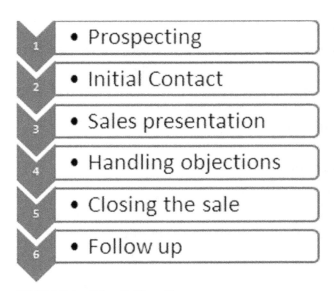

EXHIBIT 10.3 The Selling Process

CONTACTING: The second step involves making the initial contact with, or approaching, a prospect. A salesperson's approach makes the all-important first impression with a potential customer. Adequate preparation and knowledge increase a salesperson's chances of making a good first impression. In approaching the prospect, a salesperson may mention a referral from an acquaintance or business associate or remind the prospect of a previous meeting. Salespeople may make the call "cold"—without the prospect's prior knowledge or an appointment.

PRESENTING: The next step is actually presenting the promotional message to the potential customer. During the presentation, a salesperson points out the product's features and benefits and emphasizes any advantages the product offers over competitor's products. When possible, salespeople encourage potential customers to hold, touch, or use products to experience them personally and reinforce significant points of the presentation. A salesperson also needs to ask the client questions and listen carefully to determine the client's needs and focus the presentation on those needs.

HANDLING OBJECTIONS: After presenting, the salesperson gives a prospect sufficient opportunity to ask questions or raise objections. By responding to objections, the salesperson increases the likelihood of a sale. This step gives the salesperson a second chance to tell the major benefits of the product or service and point out additional features, guarantees, service, and so forth.

CLOSING: In closing the sale, the salesperson asks the prospect to buy the product. Some salespeople ask directly if the prospect is ready to make a purchase. Others use trial closing to imply that the customer will buy the product. A salesperson can ask questions such as Would you like us to finance the car for you? or When would you like delivery? to encourage customers to finalize the purchase. Sometimes salespeople offer prospects a chance to try the product for a period of time with no obligation to buy.

FOLLOWING UP: A salesperson would make a critical mistake to assume that the selling process ends after the sale. To follow up, a salesperson contacts the customer to make sure that the product was delivered and installed properly (if needed) and to ask if it is performing as expected. When a problem exists, an effective salesperson assists the customer in resolving it. Providing service after a purchase encourages future sales and helps build a long-term relationship.

Sales Promotion

Sales promotion is a paid form of nonpersonal communication that provides direct incentives to customers, salespeople, and marketing intermediaries for purchasing a product. Methods such as coupons, contests, and displays can get consumers excited about a product, motivate salespeople to be enthusiastic, and stimulate dealers to be interested and involved in distributing it. Sales promotion activities, generally short-term, offer the advantage of immediacy; new ventures can implement them and obtain results quickly. Entrepreneurs use sales promotions occasionally or year-round to support their personal selling, advertising, and publicity programs. Major types of sales promotion options are noted below:

CONSUMER SALES PROMOTION: New ventures that market consumer products frequently use consumer sales promotion,activities that encourage customers to buy certain brands or to shop at a particular store. Companies are shifting marketing dollars from advertising to consumer sales promotions. The most common consumer sales promotion methods are coupons, rebates, samples, gifts, premiums, trading stamps, contests, and sweepstakes. Entrepreneurs may use one or more of these methods in a promotional campaign.

COUPONS: Entrepreneurs can provide special price reductions for consumers through coupons. The reduction may be a specified amount ranging from a few cents to several dollars, or a certain percentage to be deducted from the price of a product. Entrepreneurs often use coupons to encourage consumers to try new products. Some try coupons to reverse a decline in sales of a product. Sometimes a venture will distribute coupons as a defensive tactic when a competitor introduces a new product or begins a new sales promotion program.

REBATES: Ventures may offer customers who buy a product and send in proof of their purchase an extra discount or refund in the form of a rebate. Rebates range from a small percentage of the purchase price to the full purchase price. Ventures typically use rebates both to motivate consumers to try new products and to provide incentives for purchasing established products. Manufacturers offer rebates for all types of products, from convenience items such as toothpaste to big-ticket goods such as cars.

FREE SAMPLES: An effective way to encourage consumers to get familiar with a product is to provide them with a free sample of the merchandise. New ventures may mail or deliver samples to homes, give them out in stores, or distribute coupons for free products. Although providing samples is the most expensive method of consumer sales promotion, it generally works the best to induce buyers to try new products.

© Eric Broder Van Dyke, 2012. Used under license from Shutterstock, Inc.

CONTESTS AND SWEEPSTAKES: Contests and sweepstakes probably generate more excitement than do other promotional methods. To stimulate sales, new ventures offer consumers the chance to win free trips, cash, and merchandise. In a contest,consumers compete for prizes based on some skill.

Food manufacturers, for example, often sponsor cooking contests in which contestants use certain products to create new recipes. In a sweepstakes,consumers send in their names to enter a drawing for prizes. Sweepstakes cost considerably less than contests and attract many more participants.

TRADE SALES PROMOTION: A manufacturer often uses trade sales promotion activities to encourage wholesalers and retailers to stock and promote its products or salespeople to increase sales. Common methods of trade sales promotion are point-of-purchase displays, trade shows, trade allowances, premium or push money, and sales contests.

POINT-OF-PURCHASE DISPLAYS: Manufacturers or wholesalers provide and set up signs, posters, freestanding shelves, and other specialized materials to use as point-of-purchase displaysi n retail stores. For example, a large, inflatable plastic Green Giant may stand atop the frozen vegetable case in a supermarket to grab attention and promote that brand. A display may contain the product being promoted.

TRADE SHOWS: Sellers in an industry gather at trade shows to exhibit their merchandise. Their manufacturers display and demonstrate products to potential customers and gather names of prospects. Industries representing food, fashion, furniture, computers, toys, and many other products hold trade shows each year, usually in large cities. Although manufacturers conduct most trade shows for retailers, some also are designed for a consumer audience, such as shows featuring home building and interior decorating products, or boats and recreational vehicles.

TRADE ALLOWANCES: A manufacturer may give retailers and wholesalers a trade allowance, a discount for performing certain functions or for making purchases during a specified time period. For instance, a firm could offer price reductions to retailers to encourage them to stock a product and pass the savings on to consumers. A retailer also may earn a discount for setting up a special display to promote a manufacturer's products.

Compensating Sales

Sales compensation tends to be the most complicated of compensation plans because it must be fully integrated with the revenue strategy. It's impossible to address all the complexities of sales compensation design in a single chapter. Sales compensation is the pay opportunity available to employees who are responsible for persuading the customer to act. This is important because who is eligible for sales incentives, including commissions, can become confusing when customer service people get involved with customers.

Most people enter a sales career because they are motivated by the opportunity for income that is not limited to a salary. That is, most salespeople prefer to earn a living through commissions rather than through a salary. Commissions are payments made to salespeople based on the number of units they are responsible for selling. Commissions are usually calculated as a percentage of the overall sale price. The commission structure established by the venture is an important source of motivation or demotivation to the sales force.

For example, a commission structure that pays a higher percentage of the sale price for larger sales can generate extremely high levels of motivation. On the other hand, a commission structure that doesn't allow a salesperson to earn above a certain dollar amount—say, the amount the entrepreneur pays himself or herself in salary—can be demotivating. The entrepreneur must establish a motivating commission structure to maximize revenue through the sales function.

DISTRIBUTION

Distribution—the movement or flow of the product from the firm to the consumer—primarily involves the transportation and storage of the product. Two components of distribution—transportation and storage—will be the main focus here. Getting the right goods to buyers at the right time and at the lowest possible cost is an important aspect of every good marketing program. The functions of physical distribution can be classified in four major areas:

- Location of distribution centers; these may be company-owned centers, public warehouses, or centralized distribution centers where products are stored for longer periods.

- Development and maintenance of an inventory control system.

- Development and maintenance of an order-processing system and a customer service department.

- Determination of the best transportation method.

Distribution involves the cost of moving goods to consumers from a variety of facilities such as factories, sub-assembly plants, company-owned warehouses, public warehouses, or trucker-owned warehouses, as well as the additional costs involved in storing and handling the inventory in each of these locations.

Distribution is also directly related to customer service, the lack of which can result in several costs. First, when the warehouse is out of a product, in-store shelves will not receive the needed stock, causing initial lost sales that can be permanent if the customer switches to a competitive product. Second, there may be a lack of inventory to handle periodic demand generated by such things as customer-initiated promotion. This out of stock will result in customer irritation. Third, goods damaged in transit or while stored in the warehouse can result in nonsalable merchandise or damaged merchandise that can also cause negative customer reaction.

Physical distribution is important due to several factors. Warehouse costs have increased significantly due to increases in labor and material costs. Transportation in a world of variable energy costs has become more expensive. Also, money for financing inventory is more costly and often difficult to obtain.

Modes of Transportation

Five basic modes of transportation are available to the technology entrepreneur to move the goods forward to the consumer: trucks, railroads, airlines, oceangoing vessels and vessels on inland waterways, and pipelines.

Trucks are considered the most flexible carrier and the most suitable for moving small quantities relatively short distances. Since trucks eliminate much of the in-transit unloading and loading, they provide a fast

© s_oleg, 2012. Used under license from Shutterstock, Inc.

service without the handling costs. While truck rates are usually reasonable for the service rendered, for some higher-valued commodities, truck rates are sometimes equal to or lower than rail rates.

Railroads are generally used to move products long distances. Their rates, where water is not accessible, are almost always lower than truck rates.

The airlines are, of course, the fastest, but also the most expensive means of transportation. Air freight requires little capital, inventory, and warehouses. In some cases, transporting products by air is comparable in cost due to other factors in physical distribution, such as the need to develop and manage a warehouse or maintain a significant amount of a wide variety of inventory to ensure no out of stocks occur.

Ships are usually the least expensive carriers. Their rates are often one third of those of rail, but they are slow and tie up money in "floating" inventory. In addition, the amount of product necessary to fill a ship is considerably more than the amount necessary to fill a rail car. Oceangoing vessels are of course used extensively in international marketing.

Pipelines traverse the world. They are located under land and below the surface of most of the world's major bodies of water. Pipelines are critical for the movement of a wide range of commodities, including water, gasoline, natural gas, oil, and many other things. Pipelines today also include the movement of information, as the vast network of fiber-optic cables, satellites, and other technical electronic devices have interconnected the world's data and information sources and users.

It is important to evaluate each possible type of transportation in terms of its cost, speed, absolute and percent delivery time variability, and the amount of loss or damaged products in order to make sure the product is always available at the lowest possible cost.

Transport Services

There are a variety of transport services available that the entrepreneur should know about. The two most important are freight forwarders and warehouses. Freight forwarders are brokers of air, ship, rail, and truck transportation who make their living on the differences between full car or truckload, which they obtain from the less than carload (LCL) or less than truckload (LTL) rate paid by each shipper. Occasionally they charge an additional small fee. Although paying the higher LCL or LTL rate, freight forwarders have the advantage for faster service and less handling than what occurs in full car and truckload lots. For a small firm, the freight forwarder actually becomes the firm's traffic manager, determining the best way to ship the product. For small manufacturers or retailers who are shipping numerous small quantities to many different places, freight forwarders are extremely valuable. Even in large companies, their services are often used in overseas shipments.

In most large cities, there is usually more than one trucker-owned warehouse. As the name implies, each of these warehouses is owned by a trucking company that usually specializes in local delivery within the metropolitan area. For many companies, these can be used to develop the most economical method of delivery—a combined trucking and warehousing service. The company can transport in either carload or truckload lots directly to the trucking company's warehouse, where the trucker's fleet of trucks distribute to local customers. This provides the company with cheaper rates for local delivery. Often, these warehouses can furnish full services such as billing and collection as well.

Public warehouses are warehouses providing almost any kind of space (refrigerated or non-refrigerated) or service needed by the manufacturer. Warehouse receipts can be obtained from public warehouses and used for financing inventories. Many companies prefer to own their own warehouses. These warehouses are operated by the firm's personnel.

Managing Distribution

There are several practices in physical distribution that you should understand in order to develop the best physical distribution system for your firm.

In terms of customer service, the major factors that are affected by physical distribution are the following:

- The length of time from the placement of an order to the delivery date.

- The percent of "out-of-stock" orders.

- The quantities of merchandise stocked to cover special promotions or emergency needs of the customer.

- The availability of parts and/or installation services of the manufacturer.

- The condition and care with which merchandise is delivered to the customer.

- The manufacturer's willingness and promptness in replacing defective merchandise.

Each of these factors should be evaluated to determine the cost of imperfect customer service. This figure can then be used to evaluate the many issues involved in speed and size of inventories.

While accurate forecasting is the key to managing a business efficiently and controlling all the marketing factors, it is also certainly the key to maintaining a minimum level of inventory and the established target level of customer service. There is probably no other factor more important for minimizing costs in physical distribution than accurate forecasting. Accurate forecasting can avoid excess rental of warehouse space as well as unnecessary inventory. A decrease in both factors helps increase money turnover.

While too much inventory can result in significantly higher holding costs, too little inventory can result in lost sales. Some factors that need to be considered in developing an inventory model include the repetitiveness of the inventory decision (are most orders being processed on time or are they repeat orders); whether the source of supply is inside or outside the company; the amount of knowledge available about future demand (variable or constant); knowledge of the amount of lead time needed (variable or constant); and the type of inventory system in use (perpetual or periodic).

SUMMARY OF LEARNING OBJECTIVES

1. **Define** the term *product* and distinguish between consumer and industrial products. *The term* product *refers to the offerings that a venture intends to bring to the marketplace—whether a physical product or a service. Consumer products are those intended for consumers and industrial products are those intended to be sold to large organizations such as businesses, educational institutions, or others.*

2. **Understand** the history of marketing and the "marketing concept." *During the early stages of mass production at the beginning of the 20th century companies focused on what is referred to as the "production orientation." This gave way to the "sales orientation" as demand was satisfied and companies had to work harder to win customers. The sales orientation gave way to the "consumer orientation" as demand for consumers goods exploded following WWII. Today, the "marketing concept" urges that companies satisfy customer demand through a reciprocal exchange of innovation and feedback.*

3. **Explain** product development and its various stages. *Product development proceeds through various stages. The so-called "fuzzy front end" is where product ideas are entertained from a wide range of sources. Eventually, the number of potential ideas must be filtered and only those for which a business case can be devised should move forward to the prototype stage. Next, prototypes should be exposed to potential market participants and adapted, changed, or eliminated based on the feedback of those market participants.*

4. **Describe** the stages of the product life cycle and explain how ventures can extend it. *The product life cycle highlights the various stages that most products inevitably go through in the marketplace. From product development, to introduction, growth, maturity, and, finally decline. Each stage of the life cycle requires different marketing tactics to maximize returns. The product life cycle can be extended by identifying new users or by modifying the product.*

5. **Explain** the role of promotion in marketing and list five promotional objectives. *Promotional activities are critical to the success of any venture. The basic objective underlying promotion is to inform potential customers about the venture's products. Other objectives of promotion are increasing sales, stabilizing sales, positioning the product, and building a public image.*

6. **Explain** the purposes of branding, packaging, and labeling. *Branding helps identify and distinguish the ventures products in the marketplace. A good brand name can help the venture sell products and build customer loyalty. Good packaging can make a product easier to use, safer, and more versatile. It can also affect consumers' attitudes toward a product, which in turn affect their purchase decisions. The label is the part of the package that identifies the brand and provides essential product information regarding contents, size, weight, quantity, ingredients, directions for use, shelf life, and any health hazards or dangers of improper use. Labels also provide the means for automatic checkout and inventory monitoring.*

7. **Outline** the personal selling process and describe each step. *Personal selling is communicating person-to-person with one or more prospective customers to make a sale. At one time or another, all of us have encountered personal selling. The steps in the personal selling process include prospecting, initial contact, sales presentation, handling objections, closing the sale, and followup.*

8. **Explain** what is meant by distribution and identify different modes of distribution. *Distribution—the movement or flow of the product from the firm to the consumer—primarily involves the transportation and storage of the product. Distribution involves the cost of moving goods to consumers from a variety of facilities such as factories, sub-assembly plants, company-owned*

warehouses, public warehouses, or trucker-owned warehouses, as well as the additional costs involved in storing and handling the inventory in each of these locations. There are five basic modes of transportation: trucks, railroads, airlines, ships, and pipelines.

QUESTIONS FOR DISCUSSION

1. Explain what is meant by the "marketing concept." Explain in turn each of the various orientations to the marketplace: production orientation, sales orientation, consumer orientation, societal orientation.

2. Identify the stages of product development. Why do they call the concept stage the "fuzzy front end"? When should a venture move from concept to the prototype stage? What are some of the components of a strong business case?

3. What are the various stages of the product life cycle? How should a venture deal with these various stages? What are some of the tactics an entrepreneur can use to extend the product life cycle?

4. Why is a brand important to a new venture? Identify the various stages of brand loyalty and discuss some of the things a new venture can do to increase brand loyalty among its customers.

5. In what ways do packaging and labeling affect a new venture's marketing efforts? Discuss some innovative packaging that you've encountered in the last few years. How do the now ubiquitous QR codes affect consumer decisions to purchase a product?

6. Discuss how the entrepreneur can determine the best promotion mix for a new venture. What are some strategies the entrepreneur can use to determine whether the promotion mix is working?

7. Describe the various types of advertising that the new venture can use to promote its products. What is meant by the term *marketing channel*? What should the entrepreneur do to determine that the marketing channels selected are providing adequate returns?

8. What various forms of publicity are available to the entrepreneur? Describe how the entrepreneur might use a news release to generate publicity. A feature article. A news conference.

9. What does the term *sales cycle* refer to? Why do you think that an entrepreneur should be concerned about the sales cycle in his or her industry?

10. Describe the selling process. Which of these stages of the process do you think will be the most difficult for you personally? Explain how you would overcome those difficulties.

EXERCISE

Social Media and Entrepreneurial Ventures

This exercise is designed to examine the social media activities of emerging entrepreneurial ventures. The purpose is to get an idea of the types of activities new ventures are using in the social media space to connect with customers. This exercise can be conducted live, in class, or by assigning students to investigate several new ventures and provide a brief analysis of the types of social media activities they are using.

To get the exercise started, it is helpful to identify some emerging new ventures in a variety of industry categories. There is a large number of ways to identify such startups, but a good starting point will be to visit the following websites for some hot new ventures:

- www.techcrunch.com
- www.killerstartups.com
- www.entrepreneur.com
- www.inc.com

Identify several interesting new ventures in at least three different industry categories. For example, choose new ventures in technology, restaurant, and retail, or some other combination of different industries. This will provide the opportunity to examine how different industries utilize social media differently.

As part of the analysis for this exercise, consider addressing the following questions. Add additional questions depending on the discussions you have been having in the classroom.

1. What types of social media does each venture use? Twitter? LinkedIn? Facebook? Blogs? Other?

2. Are the uses of social media aligned with the Bullet Breakout tips that were discussed in this chapter?

3. What problems do you see with each venture's use of social media?

4. Do you see differences across the various industries in how they are using social media?

5. Are you able to determine whether customers are interacting with the social media used by the various ventures?

6. What recommendations would you give to the various ventures to help them better communicate with and respond to their customers?

KEY TERMS

Advertising: Any paid form of nonpersonal communication to a target audience through a mass medium such as television, newspapers, or magazines.

Brand: A name, sign, symbol, design, or combination of these used to identify a product and distinguish it from competitors' offerings.

Brand insistence: The third stage of brand loyalty; customers will only purchase products bearing the brand they prefer.

Brand loyalty: The extent to which a consumer prefers a particular brand.

Brand name: That part of a venture's brand that can be spoken.

Brand preference: The second stage of brand loyalty; consumers will more likely choose a brand they recognize over an unfamiliar one.

Brand recognition: The first stage of brand loyalty; consumers are familiar with a venture's products.

Business case: A good business case is needed to move a product idea along in the product development process. Product advocates should develop sales forecasts and identify how the product fits within the portfolio of other products offered by the venture.

Consumer orientation: Philosophy that became more prevalent in the early 1950s, where marketers realized that the way to sell products was to focus on satisfying customers.

Distribution: The movement and storage of products as they make their way from the producer to the consumer.

Exchange: One party providing something of value to another party, who gives something in return.

Feature article: A detailed story about a firm, its products, or its people. It may run as long as 3,000 words and include photographs or illustrations.

Fuzzy front end: The early stage of new product development, where many ideas are generated and few actually make it to the marketplace.

Generic products: An alternative to manufacturer and private brands, using plain packages and keeping advertising to a minimum, allowing producers and stores to sell these products at reduced prices.

Hedonic goods: Goods that appeal more to consumer emotions than to their needs.

Labeling: The part of the package that identifies the brand and provides essential product information regarding contents, size, weight, quantity, ingredients, directions for use, shelf life, and any health hazards or dangers of improper use.

Manufacturer (or producer) brand: A brand owned and used by the manufacturer or service provider. Such brands identify who makes the products and provide the consumer with a nationally known, uniform, and widely available product such as Wrangler jeans or Chevrolet trucks.

Marketing: The activity, set of institutions, and processes for creating, communicating, delivering, and exchanging offerings that have value for customers, clients, partners, and society at large.

Marketing channel: A mode of communicating with customers. For example, advertising could be conducted via television, radio, or the Internet. Each of these is a different marketing channel that the entrepreneur may choose to use as part of the promotion mix.

Marketing concept: A management philosophy stating that an organization should strive to satisfy the needs of consumers through a coordinated set of activities that also allows the organization to achieve its objectives.

Media plan: A plan that selects the specific media to be used and the dates, times, and locations that advertisements will appear. To obtain the greatest benefit from these media expenditures, entrepreneurs must develop an effective media plan.

News conference: To release important or timely news, a firm may invite media representatives to a news conference to make announcements, hand out supplemental materials, and answer questions.

News release: A brief report that announces an organization's national, regional, or local events. New ventures distribute news releases widely and include the names of people within the firm for media representatives to contact for more information.

Packaging: The designing of a product container that will identify the product, protect it, and attract the attention of buyers.

Personal selling: Communicating person-to-person with one or more prospective customers to make a sale.

Placement This term refers to the distribution of products to wholesalers, retailers, or directly to customers.

Private (or store) brand: A brand owned by a wholesaler or retailer. A venture offering private brands often sells them at lower prices, achieving higher profits, and encouraging customer loyalty.

Product: The offerings that your venture intends to bring to the marketplace—whether a physical product or a service.

Product life cycle: New products enter the market during the introduction stage, they gain momentum and begin to bring a profit during the growth stage, they stabilize during the maturity stage, and finally they fade away in the decline stage.

Production orientation: Demand for new manufactured goods was so great during the Industrial Revolution that producers were concerned primarily with increased production and operating efficiency rather than with consumer preferences.

Promotion: The means the venture uses to communicate about its offerings to potential customers.

Promotion mix: To inform, influence, and remind customers in their target markets or the general public using personal selling and advertising, sales promotion, and publicity. How these four elements are combined to promote specific products is called the promotion mix.

Prototype: A working version of the product that can be tested with customers.

Publicity: A nonpersonal form of communication transmitted by a mass medium in news story form and not paid for directly by a sponsor.

Public relations: A set of communications activities designed to create and maintain a favorable public image for a firm.

Sales cycle: The processes involved in selling and the length of time it takes to close a sale.

Sales orientation: By the mid-1920s manufacturers discovered that supplies of basic consumer goods had caught up to demand. Needing to sell their products to markets that had increasing choices and decreasing demand, companies had to switch from a production orientation to a sales orientation.

Sales promotion: A paid form of nonpersonal communication that provides direct incentives to customers, salespeople, and marketing intermediaries for purchasing a product.

Selling process: The process used to sell products to customers and consisting of prospecting, initial contact, sales presentation, handling objections, closing the sale, and followup.

Societal orientation: Companies are concerned with the welfare of society as well as their own interests and those of consumers.

Underwriter's Laboratories (UL): An example of a third party (independent) firm that will test a venture's products and provide an opinion as to the product's safety.

Utilitarian goods: Those that meet a consumer need, while hedonic goods appeal more to consumer emotions.

ENDNOTES

[1] Dhar, R., and K. Wertenbroch, "Consumer Choice Between Hedonic and Utilitarian Goods," *Journal of Marketing Research,* 37(1)(2000): 60–71.

[2] Gamble, J., A. Gilmore, D. McCartan-Quinn, and P. Durkan, "The Marketing Concept in the 21st Century: A Review of How Marketing Has Been Defined Since the 1960s," *Marketing Review,* 11(3)(2011): 227–248.

[3] Tadajewski, M., and D.G.B. Jones, "Scientific Marketing Management and the Emergence of the Ethical Marketing Concept," *Journal of Marketing Management,* 28(1/2)(2012): 37–61.

[4] Lawler, J., "Rewarding the Repeaters." *Entrepreneur,* 38(2)(2010): 63.

[5] Filser, M., and E. Vernette, "Charity Business Marketing 3.0: Version Tom's Shoes," *Decisions Marketing,* 55(2009): 5–6.

[6] Marshall, R., "Conceptualizing the International For-Profit Social Entrepreneur." *Business Ethics,* 98(2)(2011): 183–198.

[7] Stam, E., and K. Wennberg, "The Roles of R&D in New Firm Growth," *Small Business Economics,* 33(1)(2009): 77–89.

[8] Naimi, L.L., and B.S. Glassman, "Managing the Fuzzy Front End of Innovation," *Global Conference on Business & Finance Proceedings,* 7(1)(2012): 543.

[9] Cooper, R.G., "Perspective: How to Innovate When the Market Is Mature," *Journal of Product Innovation Management,* s1(2011): 2–27.

[10] Wang, J., "The Solution to the Innovator's Dilemma," *Entrepreneur,* 39(8)(2011): 24–32.

[11] Parker, P.M., *The 2009 Report on Testing Laboratories: World Market Segmentation by City.* City Segmentation Reports (January 19, 2010).

[12] Chappuis, B., B. Gaffey, and P. Parvizi, "Are Your Customers Digital Junkies?" *McKinsey Quarterly,* 3(2011): 20–23.

[13] Jacobsen, J., "A Drink for Every Waking Moment," *Beverage Industry,* 102(4)(2011): 36.

[14] "Charles Barkley Dons Halter Dress, Heels for Weight Watchers' 'Lose Like A Man' Campaign," *Huffington Post,* retrieved on April 12, 2012.

[15] Andruss, P., "Branding, Inc." *Entrepreneur,* 40(4)(2012): 59–60.

[16] Goldsmith, R.E., L.R. Flynn, E. Goldsmith, and E.C. Stacey, "Consumer Attitudes and Loyalty Towards

Private Brands," *International Journal of Consumer Studies,* 34(3)(2010): 339–348.

[17] Steenkamp, J-B.E.M., and N. Kumar, "Don't Be Undersold!" *Harvard Business Review,* 87(12)(2010): 90–95.

[18] Bellman, L.M., "Entrepreneurs: Invent a New Brand Name or Revive an Old One?" *Business Horizons,* 48(3)(2005): 215–222.

[19] Lindner, S.J., "The Perfect Formula to Build Your Brand," *Entrepreneur,* 37(7)(2009): 70.

[20] Handley, A., "Cracking the Mobile Code," *Entrepreneur,* 40(4)(2012): 74.

[21] Retrieved from www.intenseinfluence.com/blog/how-much-money-is-spent-on-advertising-per-year, April 12, 2012.

[22] Pullen, J.P., "Dollars, Sense, and Social Media Marketing," *Entrepreneur,* 39(6)(2011): 59–61.

[23] Crush, P., and J. Anderson, "How Small Businesses Can Win the Sponsoring Game," *Management Today* (May 2001): 82–84.

[24] Weitz, Barton A., Harish Sujan, and Mita Sujan, "Knowledge, Motivation, and Adaptive Behavior: A Framework for Improving Selling Effectiveness," *Journal of Marketing* (October 1986).

[25] Farber, B., "Wrap it Up," *Entrepreneur,* 32(8)(2008): 84.

COMPETITIVE POSITIONING AND ENTREPRENEURIAL STRATEGY

Learning Objectives

As a result of studying this chapter, students will be able to:

- **Develop** a mission statement for your venture and understand why a mission statement can be important.

- **Understand** what sustainable competitive advantage is and how to attain it.

- **Undertake** a competitor analysis and differentiate a venture from competitors.

- **Develop** an entrepreneurial strategy that increases venture competitiveness.

- **Implement** an entrepreneurial strategy based on real-options reasoning or resource-based reasoning.

- **Integrate** a venture's various stakeholders into the venture's overall strategy.

INTRODUCTION

Customers have choices. They have choices about which products or services to buy, and they have choices to decide where to buy these products and services. What makes a customer decide to buy a particular product from one company and not another? Does this choice depend only on the characteristics of the product (price and quality for example), or are there other factors? Understanding and influencing how customers perceive your venture's offerings compared to those of your competitors is a critical element of building and managing an entrepreneurial venture.

© Tyler Olson, 2012. Used under license from Shutterstock, Inc.

The term *position* connotes a relative location. **Competitive positioning** determines where your venture's products and services are located relative to those of competing firms. However, the location is not physical or geographical. It is a location defined by customer perceptions of the relative value of the products and services of the firms in an industry. This location is determined by a number of factors, including price, quality, marketing, and a firm's resources, among others. Positioning is establishing how your firm and its offering differ from the competition and then communicating that message to the market. An entrepreneurial venture should position its offerings in a narrow niche, or beachhead, in the market, one that is too small for large competitors but big enough that your venture can grow and be profitable.[1]

In this chapter, we will explore several topics relevant for competitive positioning in a startup firm. In particular, in this chapter, we will

1. Introduce you to the role of a venture **mission statement** in guiding strategic decision making and communicating the venture's intentions to customers and potential customers.

2. Define the concept of sustainable competitive advantage and explain how firms build and maintain a sustainable competitive advantage.

3. Describe the basic concepts of competitive positioning and explain how some relatively straightforward tools and techniques can be used to develop a competitive positioning for your venture.

4. Explain and explore various approaches to entrepreneurial strategy.

5. Identify how the venture's various stakeholders should be enlisted into the venture's strategy and competitive positioning.

Let's begin by examining the role of the mission statement in the competitive positioning of the entrepreneurial venture.

ESTABLISHING YOUR MISSION STATEMENT

A venture's mission statement defines it raison d'être (French for "reason for being"), the fundamental purpose it's designed to serve. The organizational mission statement answers the question "What is this organization's purpose?" for employees, customers, and other constituents. Whereas a strategy addresses ongoing goals and procedures, the firm's mission statement describes an even more fundamental rationale for its existence.

Some organizational theorists assert that organizational missions should be based on something even more abstract, an organizational vision. In other words, a mission statement should flow out of the vision. A true vision is a snapshot of the future that allows an organization the flexibility of means to build toward it. A vision is important because it helps the firm model strategic plans and provides a kind of touchstone for goal setting. It can be critical in a shifting industry by offering a hedge to reactive decision making. A vision keeps a firm focused on its superordinate, or long-term, goals.

To establish a mission statement, a venture must take into consideration its history, distinctive competence(s), and environment.

History

For established firms, the mission should be consistent with what is known about the firm's history. This history includes accomplishments and failures, objectives and policies, decisions, employees, and more. An organization must assess its history to determine its current resource base, its image, and its various capacities. Startups need a mission statement too, but have no history upon which to base a long-term vision. Instead, startups can look to the history of the industry they are part of, or to the history of the human needs and expectations they hope to satisfy through organized activity.

Distinctive Competence

Although a firm is likely to be capable of doing many things, strategic success stems from the firm identifying and capitalizing on what it does best and also what customers' desire. A **distinctive competence** is a capacity that's unique to the firm and that's valued in the market.

Environment

The business environment contains opportunities, constraints, and threats to the firm. Before a mission is articulated, these conditions must be analyzed and evaluated, as discussed in the preceding. The mission should be responsive to the organization's environment.

Characteristics of a Mission Statement

For effective organizations, the mission statement that results from the analysis of history, distinctive competence, and the environment must be (1) customer-focused, (2) achievable, (3) motivational, and (4) specific.

CUSTOMER-FOCUSED. Mission statements in high-performance ventures emphasize a customer focus. Many entrepreneurial ventures have faltered or failed because they defined themselves in terms of what they produced rather than in terms of whom they served. High-performance ventures formulate strategy based on the premise that customer satisfaction and, better yet, customer delight and loyalty are necessary for enduring success. The reasons are many and fundamental. Finding new customers is far more expensive than keeping current customers. Dissatisfied customers not only fail to return to buy again, they are also likely (1) to decline to express the reasons for their dissatisfaction (which could be a source of learning and growth for the firm) and (2) to share their dissatisfaction with other potential customers. As quality expert W. Edwards Deming noted, "no one can guess the future loss of business from a dissatisfied customer."[2] Customers, not employees, are a firm's best salespeople.

ACHIEVABLE. While a mission statement should be challenging, it must also be achievable. Unrealistic ambitions can exceed a firm's capabilities. Although it's important to ensure that goals are achievable, it's equally important to guard against setting your sights too low. Organizational missions should provide future targets that can both be measured and attained and still provide motivation for even greater achievements. For example, to be a leader in a particular market segment is both measurable and provides a constant challenge to attain and/or retain that vaunted position.

MOTIVATIONAL. The mission must serve as a source of motivation at all levels. Effective mission statements have meaning to every employee, allowing each of them to translate the mission's words into their own motivation, and serving as a guide for decisions and actions.

© Rehan Qureshi, 2012. Used under license from Shutterstock, Inc.

SPECIFIC. A mission statement must be clear enough to allow employees and customers to know in what business the firm competes as well as in what business it doesn't compete. Being specific in the mission allows employees to focus their energy and to be more productive, making the entire firm more profitable. Broad statements of value or goodness (e.g., "the highest quality at the lowest price") do not make a good mission statement. By attempting to be all things to all people, a firm's energy is scattered, making the firm less able to develop distinctive competence and making it nearly impossible to please anyone.

Most mission statements are directed both inside and outside their respective organizations, providing a message to management, staff, clients, and customers. When writing a mission statement, an organization should step back and reflect on what it's trying to do. It needs to focus on the fundamental elements that both define the organization and make the difference between its success and failure.[3]

Mission Statement Examples

To get an idea of what a mission statement is and the kind of language that is used to in effective mission statements we have selected a few to highlight here. The first example is the mission statement for the Angel Capital Association. On its website the ACA indicates that its mission is to "fuel the success of angel groups and private investors that invest in high growth, early-stage ventures". This simple statement has enabled the ACA to grow dramatically during its brief history. Today, the ACA is a predominate organization for angel investor groups around the world. It offers services to these groups including conferences, training, research and publications, and other things.

Some experts in mission statements argue for pithy and to-the-point statements. Their reasoning is that such statements are easier for employees and others to recall and act upon. On the other hand, some experts argue for a more comprehensive mission statement. They reason that such statements provide all constituents with a clear idea of how they fit into the organization's strategy and business plan. The following Bullet Breakout provides some tips on creating your venture's mission statement.

BULLET BREAKOUT

Tips for Creating a Mission Statement

- **Include the Four Key Elements:** There are four key elements found in effective statements: value, inspiration, plausibility, and specificity.

- **Keep It Short and Sweet:** Try to sum up your entire company's mission in one or two sentences. Concise mission statements are memorable and effective.

- **Consider Long-Term vs. Short-Term:** The idea here is to choose whether you want your company's statement to reflect its short-term goals or its long-term aspirations. Be sure to choose only one; specificity is key to an influential mission.

- **Test It:** Distribute drafts of the mission statement to every employee and ask them what, if anything, should be added or changed.

- **Revisit It Often:** Evolution is inevitable. Incorporate the ideas and themes of the statement in how you run your business, and be sure to revisit it regularly to make any necessary changes.

Source: Adapted from "5 Tips for a Successful Mission Statement," Inc.com, www.inc.com/ss/5-tips-on-developing-an-effective-mission-statement#5

COMPETITIVE POSITIONING

In any business, to be successful, you must convince customers to buy your products or services instead of the products or services offered by other companies. The concept of competitive advantage addresses that key to success. **Competitive advantage** is defined as a factor or action that gives a firm an advantage in the marketplace and leads customers to buy its products or services instead of those of other firms. It is also a strategy that is not currently being used by a firm's current or potential competitors.[4] A firm's competitive advantage can come from many sources. For example, price decreases or promotions will likely lead to an increase in revenue. However, simply reducing prices will probably also yield only a temporary advantage over competitors. The reduction in price might reduce profits, and competitors will probably reduce their prices as well. An ice cream shop might introduce a new and different jalapeño-flavored ice cream that sells very well and entices customers from other ice cream shops. However, there is nothing to prevent rival ice cream shops from offering the same flavor. Any advantage from this new flavor is likely to be temporary. In both cases, the competitive advantage is easily copied by competitors. In the first example, competitors may simply drop their prices; in the second, competitors may easily offer the same flavor of ice cream.

Therefore, for a startup firm, or any firm for that matter, what is more important to success is to gain a sustainable competitive advantage (SCA). A **sustainable competitive advantage** is an advantage over a firm's competitors and potential competitors that cannot be duplicated, will last a reasonably long time, and is the source of a firm's sustained superior performance.[5] In general, it is the firm's collection of resources that can provide a sustainable competitive advantage.

A sustainable competitive advantage means that your venture can offer something to customers that its competitors cannot offer. The unique set of valuable, rare, inimitable, and non-substitutable resources can provide lower cost, better quality, more convenience, faster response, or some other set of product or service attributes that a customer will value. To decide how to use your firm's bundle of resource most effectively, it is important to understand how your firm compares to its competitors.

Competitor Analysis

As a startup firm, you must be able to identify the companies against which you will compete for your customer's hard-earned money. In earlier chapters, we explained how to identify your target industry and target customer segments. You should have also identified companies in this industry that offer the same or similar products and services to the same groups of customers. These companies are your direct competitors. An important task in competitor analysis is to identify the relevant characteristics that distinguish companies in this industry. For example, characteristics such as size, profitability, market share, productivity, and sales growth are likely to be important dimensions to consider in most industries. However, if you are in a high-tech industry, another firm characteristic that might be particularly important would be spending on research and development as a percentage of sales. Similarly, in a consumer products industry, marketing expense as a percentage of sales might be an important comparison point. Identifying the important dimensions for comparison and then using them to compare your venture against your competitors can provide a picture of your firm's competitive position in the industry—that is, your firm's strengths and weaknesses compared to the competition. A simple matrix comparing competitors on these relevant dimensions can be very helpful in a competitor analysis. An example is provided in Table 11.1 below.

Company B in this analysis is the biggest of the three and has the greatest market share. However, this company spends the most on marketing but the least on R&D, and its profitability is lower than the other two competitors.

TABLE 11.1 Competitor Analysis Matrix

Competitive Factor	Company A	Company B	Company C
Sales	$30 million	$150 million	$50 million
Operating Profit %	10%	8%	15%
Gross Profit %	60%	50%	65%
R&D spending as % of Sales	15%	10%	20%
Marketing spending as % of Sales	5%	8%	6%
Market Share	6%	30%	10%

Along with completing a matrix similar to Table 11.1 for your venture's likely competitors, it is important to perform an honest assessment of your firm's strengths and weaknesses to understand how you will compare to these competitors. In what areas do you think you will have an advantage? Where will you be at a disadvantage?

Product and Service Positioning

After performing an initial analysis of likely competitors, you will have an idea of how your company compares to its rivals along some organizational and performance characteristics. However, what is probably more important is to understand how your venture's products or services will compare to those of your competitors. For this analysis, you need to go back to thinking about your customers. What do they think creates value in a product or service? Price is obviously one attribute that influences a customer's perceptions of value. However, there are many others as well. Having a deep understanding of your customers' wants and needs is critical to being able to perform this part of competitive positioning. Ultimately, your goal is to differentiate your venture's products and services from those of your competitors. **Differentiation** means that firm's offerings are recognizably different from what your competitors are offering on some set of relevant attributes.[6] Positioning comes down to offering a product or service that is unique and provides a high level of value in the perceptions of customers.[7] For a startup, an effective position in the market will accomplish the following:

- Accurately reflect your actual distinctive competencies and differential advantage
- Focus on unserved or underserved market segments
- Be achievable given current resources
- Be sustainable over the longer term
- Be defensible in the face of competitive response.

It is critical to understand that a true competitive position is defined by customers and how they perceive products and services in the market, not by the entrepreneur.[8] Differentiation begins with identifying what customers value in a product or service. The entrepreneur must offer a product or service that provides a unique set of features, benefits, or other attributes valued in its target market segment. The key terms here are unique and value. The combination of attributes must provide unique value in the minds of customers compared to what is offered by competitors. Some product and service attributes to consider might include:

- Price
- Quality
- Performance
- Convenience
- Perceived quality
- Features
- Ease of use
- Benefits

- Status

- Value (a combination of performance and price)

Once you have determined the set of product and service attributes relevant to your positioning, there are various techniques that can be used to help you assess and then refine your position relative to competitors. A simple matrix that shows relative ratings of your firm's products are important characteristics can be a powerful tool. These ratings should be based on the perceptions of your customers, not just your own. An example of such as matrix is shown in Table 11.2. In this example, Burger Barn is a fast food restaurant serving a menu limited to burgers and fries; Healthy Eats is a quick-service restaurant serving a wide range of healthier food but at a higher price; Fast and Fun Food is a fast food restaurant serving a wide range of burgers, sandwiches, tacos, and other fast food. The four characteristics on which these restaurant meals will be compared will be price, taste, nutrition, and variety. Ratings can range from 0 to 10, where 10 is the best and 0 is the worst. Therefore, for price, a 10 would mean that the restaurant has the least expensive meals possible, and 0 would be extremely expensive. A rating of 10 on taste would be a rating for the best tasting food imaginable; 0 would be the rating for food that is virtually inedible. Based on the ratings from customers in this market, a competitive position comparison matrix might look like Table 11.2.

When comparing these restaurants, one can see three distinct positions. Burger Barn is inexpensive with very limited choice in food; Healthy Eats serves a wide variety of nutritious food; Fast & Fun Food serves a wide variety of fast food at a lower price than Healthy Eats but at a higher price than Burger Barn.

Another commonly used tool is the perceptual map. The perceptual map provides a graphical depiction of the competitive positions of products or services in a market segment. It shows the location of a product or service in relation to two dimensions along which products or services in the market might be differentiated. The location is based on the perceptions of customers in the target segment. Because price is typically thought of as a tradeoff with other product characteristics, price is commonly used as one dimension in a perceptual map. Features or some measure of performance is often used as a second dimension. A dot or an "X" or some other marker is placed in the two-dimensional space at "coordinates" corresponding to product's values for each of the dimensions. The products for all competitors are placed on the map in the same manner. A perceptual map may also be used to show the relative positions of firms by aggregating the firms' offerings in each dimension. Exhibit 11.1 shows the general form of a perceptual map. Firm A's products are rated medium on both characteristics; Firm B's products are rated low on both characteristics; and Firm's C's products are rated high on Characteristic 1 but low on Characteristic 2.

TABLE 11.2 Example Competitive Positioning Comparison Matrix

Restaurant	Price	Taste	Nutrition	Variety
Burger Barn	9	5	1	1
Healthy Eats	4	7	9	7
Fast & Fun Food	5	6	3	6

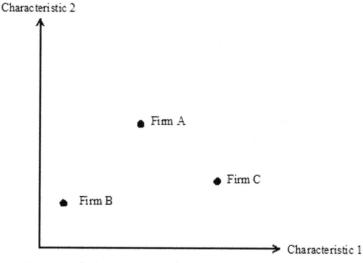

EXHIBIT 11.1   General Form of a Perceptual Map

A perceptual map shows where there might be an opportunity to position your product in a market niche that has not been addressed. For example, there may be an opportunity for a new firm that offers products that are high on Characteristic 2 but low on Characteristic 1.

Exhibit 11.2 shows an example of a perceptual map for the three restaurants from the competitive position comparison matrix example in Exhibit 11.2. Note that only two characteristics can be compared in a perceptual map; for this example, we will compare price and nutrition.

Based on perceptual map shown by Exhibit 11.2, there may be an opportunity for a competitor to provide medium variety and low price.

Note that the characteristics used in competitive positioning comparison matrices or perceptual maps might be much more qualitative and subjective than price or performance, and it is important to use attributes that are meaningful to customers and specific to the products or services being compared in a particular market segment. For example, in the video game industry, players might evaluate a game on how "fun" it is to play, and how long they are likely to play a game (which might be termed "engagement"). A more commonly used dimension such as price might also be important to some extent, but price is unlikely to be the determining factor for a customer deciding which game to buy.

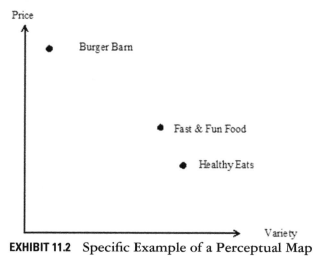

EXHIBIT 11.2   Specific Example of a Perceptual Map

ENTREPRENEURIAL STRATEGY

After all of your hard work in identifying competitors, analyzing their strengths and weaknesses developing a competitive positioning, and then communicating that position to the market, all you need to do is to sit back and wait for the profits to roll in, correct? Well, not exactly. Even if all of these positioning activities were done perfectly, you have a great product serving an unexploited niche market, and you have delivered the message to your customers, that's not all there is to the story. Existing firms who are your competitors are unlikely to sit idly by and watch you take market share away from them. Expect a competitive response, think about what that response might be, and what you will do next. In some cases, you will have a sustainable competitive advantage, and you will be able to withstand the actions of your competitors; in other cases, you may not.

Harvard Business School management researcher Michael Porter has developed several useful frameworks for developing an organization's strategy. One of the most popular among managers making strategic decisions is the **value chain**. The value chain is all the activities an organization undertakes to create value for a customer.

According to Porter, competitive advantage grows out of the way firms organize and perform the various activities of their value chain. To gain competitive advantage over rivals, a firm must either provide comparable buyer value but perform the activities of the value chain more efficiently (reducing costs) or perform the activities in a unique way that creates higher value and commands a premium price.

Strategy guides the way a venture organizes its value chain and performs the individual activities. Competitive organizations understand their value chain not as a set of isolated functions or organizational silos, but as linked activities. Entrepreneurs building high-performing ventures view the value chain as a system. Improvements to the system are usually made by teams of individuals representing the various activities.

Value-chain strategy encompasses various elements. In addition to cultivating partnerships and building trust with immediate customers and suppliers, it also includes initiatives that create ripple effects across multiple tiers of a given chain. Among them:

- Inventory strategies such as JIT delivery, real-time inventory tracking, synchronizing supply/demand planning, and cross-docking of materials at warehouse locations.

- Sharing critical information with suppliers, customers, and other value-chain partners. Providing access to real-time information on production plans, sales orders, and inventory levels can smooth the flow of materials and reduce inventory costs throughout the chain.

- Collaborative product development, specifically, initiatives that involve suppliers and customers in the early stages of the development process.

- Adoption of web technologies, including various e-business solutions that improve the flow of information throughout a value chain, improve logistics management, and reduce cash-to-cash cycle times.

Entrepreneurs use the value chain perspective and other frameworks to engage in strategic thinking. Such frameworks are useful to narrow the range of issues considered, focusing on the forces and sources of competitive advantage. Another phase of strategic development in a firm is the strategic planning process.

The Strategic Planning Process

Strategic planning is the process of examining the organization's environment, establishing a mission, setting desired goals and objectives, and developing an operating plan. During the strategic planning process, firms will typically ask themselves, "What do we want the future to be?" or "What must we do now to better ensure that the desired future is achieved?"

In high-performance ventures strategic planning never ends. Either the venture is formulating a new strategy or it's implementing an existing one, assessing progress, and revising processes as needed. In well-managed ventures a direct relationship exists between strategic planning and the planning employees do throughout the venture.

Strategic planning is best conceived as a cyclical process that is fueled by strategic thinking. The strategic planning process outlined in this chapter consists of four steps: (1) assessing the organization's internal and external environments; (2) establishing a mission statement; (3) establishing goals and objectives; and (4) establishing an operating plan. Exhibit 11.3 shows the four major components of strategic planning, each informed by strategic thinking. The cyclical representation is best because it connotes that strategic planning never ends. Competitive organizations are always thinking strategically and are frequently involved in one or more of the components of strategic planning. For example, many firms have five-year strategic plans. If they are competitive, they probably continuously revise and modify the plan. Static, one-year or five-year plans do not reflect reality. Thus, continuous reviewing, modifying, and evaluating the strategic plan is becoming the preferred approach in most organizations.

Assessing the Organization's Environment

A strategy, plan, or mission for the future begins with an assessment of the current situation in which the company finds itself. A systematic, thorough analysis requires attention to four things: internal strengths and weaknesses, and external opportunities and threats. Such an analysis is often referred to as a **SWOT analysis** (Strengths, Weaknesses, Opportunities, Threats). Historically, the SWOT analysis has provided managers with useful signals for strategic change. Many organizations, profit and nonprofit, use this technique as a starting point for data gathering in their strategic planning process.

A company's strengths are usually derived from its financial, human, and other resources. The firm's financial assets include cash, securities, receivables, and other tangible resources usually

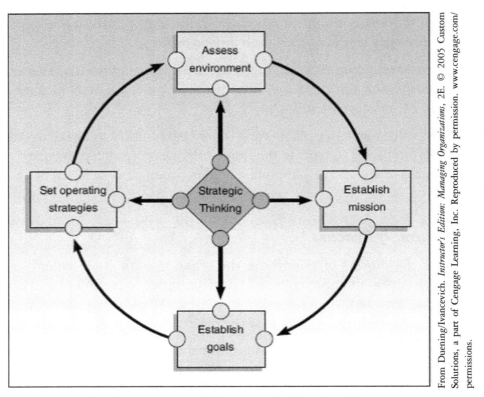

Source: Duening/Ivancevich. *Instructor's Edition: Managing Organizations*, 2E. © 2005 Custom Solutions, a part of Cengage Learning, Inc. Reproduced by permission. www.cengage.com/permissions.

EXHIBIT 11.3 The Components of the Strategic Planning Process

Source: Duening, T.N. and J.M. Ivancevich, *Managing Organizations* (Cincinnati, OH: Atomic Dog Publishing, 2006).

presented on its balance sheet and other accounts. Human resources are less easy to evaluate, yet that is a primary component of modern organizations. Human resources include the ideas, ingenuity, patents, and other intangible yet essential bases for competitiveness that only human beings can provide to an organization.

Externally, the company's business environment presents both threats and opportunities. An opportunity is anything that has the potential to increase the firm's strengths. For example, a pending reduction of trade barriers may allow a firm to increase its business in another country. A threat is anything that has the potential to hurt or even destroy a firm. For instance, a change in tax laws may portend ruin for a firm that specializes in using tax breaks that are to be eliminated by the change.

Key components of an organization's environment include the sociocultural milieu, technological developments, economic conditions, and political climate. Each of these is explained in more detail in the following text.

Sociocultural Milieu

Change is constant in modern societies. Entrepreneurs, therefore, must be able to identify the changing cultural and social conditions that will influence the venture. Unfortunately, many ventures still don't consider the impact such changes will have, or they underestimate their impact. Entrepreneurs need to be aware of developments in the sociocultural milieu. The following Bullet Breakout box highlights how preparing for the next generation's needs and tastes can be organized within a strategic planning process.

As we stated in earlier chapters, successful ventures routinely use measurements of customer-perceived value to develop new products and services and improve existing offerings. Today, an increasing number of innovative ventures are relying on customer feedback to redesign key parts of their organizations. First, they obtain precise information on the needs and values of their internal and external customers. Then, they use this information to, among other things, tailor products and services to meet distinct market segment requirements. As a result, they not only see performance improve, but they have also given their customers the opportunity to define what customer satisfaction means. This allows firms to reduce costs and improve customer service, while increasing profitability.

Technological Developments

Changes in technology can influence a venture's destiny. Technological innovations can create new industries or vastly alter existing ones. The Internet didn't exist twenty years ago, and now any venture that doesn't make the Internet a central part of its overall strategy is likely to fail. Even more important, the mobile computing revolution of the past decade is proceeding rapidly and will potentially threaten the long-term health of many high-flying Internet companies. For example, Facebook's IPO in May 2012 turned into a fiasco as the stock dropped rapidly from its initial offering price. Many analysts speculate that the reason for the drop was Facebook's inability to adapt its technology to mobile platforms. A company that boasts nearly a billion users could be threatened by changing technologies.

BULLET BREAKOUT

Strategy is the Heart of Innovation and Competitiveness

Successful competitive strategy should address the following five critical elements that provide the framework for creating and sustaining competitive advantage:

- Choosing the future. A strategic vision is the guiding theme that articulates an organization's intentions for the future.

- Redefining competition. Successful market leaders pursue innovation in products, strategy, and operations as a means to deliver customer expectations and continually redefine the basis for competition in their markets.

- Turning ideas into action. The strategic plan is the managerial game plan for how the business intends to fulfill its mission, realize its vision, and achieve its objectives—how to move from ideas to action.

- Accelerating competitive performance. A company's strategy is realized through its leadership structure, operating model, organizational culture, strategic relationships, and competitive capabilities.

- Sustaining competitive advantage. Strategic leadership is the capability to build and strengthen the company's long-term position in the face of emerging market developments, technology advancements, and organizational challenges.

Source: Adapted from Corrigan, Karen, "Steps to Competitive Advantage," *Marketing Health Services* (Winter 2004): 48.

Another industry that is threatened by new technologies is the textbook industry. Textbooks like the one you are holding in your hand are fated to be transformed by hand-held devices such as Apple's iPad. Many of the major publishers are scrambling to provide e-reader textbooks that provide the same learning and teaching features of the standard, paper-based textbook. Time will tell which of the major publishers will survive this technology-based industry shakeout.

Economic Conditions

The world economy in the first decade of the twenty-first century is increasingly integrated and increasingly competitive. New players enter the global economic game every day. New alliances form, new trading blocs come into existence, and new rules of fair competition are constantly being drafted and debated. The global economy will create a more complex economic playing field than ever before. Stock markets operate all night around the world. Major investment banks monitor and issue buy and sell orders overnight on the international stock markets. Everywhere, CEOs wake up on some mornings to find a dramatically different economic climate than when they went to sleep the night before. Terrorism shakes investor confidence. Major and respected companies—such as MF Global—collapse overnight. The world of business never sleeps, and managers need to stay connected to be competitive.

Entrepreneurs will need to make a wide variety of adjustments on a continuous basis if they want their ventures to remain competitive. New companies will come into being, and old ones that don't adapt will die. This is an era of instant communication and fast-changing technologies. It's also an era of employee empowerment and changing global relationships and structures. Traditional ways of doing business are gone, along with comfortable relationships. If companies are going to achieve success, they must stay abreast of and adapt to changing economic conditions.

Political Climate

The political climate that propelled the United States into a world superpower no longer exists. Nations of the world no longer need to align themselves with one of two opposing economic giants. The collapse of the Soviet Union did bring an end to the Cold War that had kept the world on the edge of its nuclear seat since World War II. Business must be prepared for volatile, even revolutionary changes in geographic boundaries, contract and licensure regulations, and limitations on direct investment.

Perhaps the greatest change in the world's political climate is being created in the world's most populous countries: China and India. India's politicians have taken deliberate actions to orient the nation's economy toward the West. India has become a prime destination for outsourcing a wide range of business processes, including technical support, call centers, and software development. This opening of the country to business opportunities linked to exporting services has dramatically altered the country's internal politics, as a rising and prosperous middle class begins to gather influence.

China will present even greater political challenges in the coming years as it continues its path of reform away from strictly communist policies and toward more free-market policies. China's transformation to an economic superpower in the coming years will not only bring a wide range of new products to the United States—including the first line of Chinese automobiles expected to arrive in 2005[34]—but also opens up new market opportunities for U.S. firms. The coming decades will surely see dramatic transformations in strategy as firms adjust to the inroads being made by companies located in these two large and highly competitive nations.

Approaches to Strategic Planning

Entrepreneurial strategy is the process of determining how best to deploy the assets of the venture to create value. Early on, when the company is very small and may consist of the founding entrepreneur and one or two other founding partners, the only strategy may be to survive until tomorrow. As the business grows, however, and employees and additional investors are brought into the venture, strategy setting is far more complex and challenging. Responsibility for setting and executing strategy falls squarely on the shoulders of the entrepreneur, who is increasingly recognized as the venture's chief executive officer (CEO). To reduce some of the pressure and uncertainty surrounding strategy setting, the entrepreneur should rely on trusted advisors that he or she has been able to attract to the venture for input and advice. The complexities associated with entering markets, setting prices, defining customer value, and spending scarce cash can be daunting, especially for novice entrepreneurs. Establishing a board of advisors or leveraging the venture's board of directors for strategic advice and consultation can help reduce the unknowns in the venture's environment.

Entrepreneurial strategy has been studied by scholars and invented by practicing entrepreneurs. While the final word will never be written about entrepreneurial strategy, scholars have been able to identify several recurring themes that entrepreneurs tend to use and return to as they invent venture after venture. In this final section of this chapter we will explore and discuss several approaches to entrepreneurial strategy. However, it must be noted that all discussions of entrepreneurial strategy necessarily will be incomplete and pertinent to a particular time and set of circumstances. In this light, the discussion below focuses on early 21st century technology ventures and the challenges they face in an increasingly global and fast paced economy. There are several main lines of thinking regarding entrepreneurial strategy that we will explore:

- Real-Options Approach
- Resource-Based Approach

THE REAL-OPTIONS APPROACH. The **real-options approach** to entrepreneurial strategy is derived from the world of financial management. Financial managers must have some rationale for the choices they make in allocating the scarce financial resources of a corporate venture. To manage that, they often make reasonable guesses about the probability of certain outcomes, and the financial implications they would have. Simple multiplication of the financial outcomes by the probability of a particular event enables decision makers to quantify and justify the decisions they make. A real option is defined as the right, but not the obligation, to undertake a certain business decision. In the world of corporate finance, this is normally the decision to make or abandon a capital investment.

The real-options approach to entrepreneurial strategy assumes that strategic decision making occurs amidst a great deal of uncertainty. Entrepreneurs must make choices daily about which markets to pursue, which capital expenditures to make, who to hire, and what features and benefits to include and exclude from an offering. The real-options approach also assumes that entrepreneurs are action oriented, opportunistic, and capable of coping with ambiguity. The progenitors of this approach to entrepreneurial strategy are Wharton School of Business professors Rita Gunther McGrath and Ian MacMillan.[9]

The foundation of the real-options approach to strategy setting is what McGrath and MacMillan call the "entrepreneurial mindset." There are several characteristics they highlight as essential to this mindset, including:

1. A passion for seeking new opportunities.
2. Opportunities are pursued with enormous discipline.
3. Only the very best opportunities are pursued.
4. An intense focus on execution—especially what is referred to as "adaptive execution."
5. An ability to engage the energies of others in pursuit of opportunity.

Real-options reasoning advocates that aspiring entrepreneurs and practicing entrepreneurs alike maintain what is referred to as an **opportunity register**. The opportunity register is a record of business opportunity insights that may or may not become the basis of new revenue opportunities. Under the real-options approach, there are five categories of economic opportunity:

* Redesign products and services
* Redifferentiate products or services
* Resegment the market
* Completely reconfigure the market
* Develop break through competencies, or areas of competitive strength, that create new competitive advantages

Through a process referred to as **directed discovery** the entrepreneur constantly examines the environment for these types of opportunities. Directed discovery is a process of plotting a direction into an uncertain future, then making adjustments as reality unfolds. The requisite elements of directed discovery are speed, capacity for rapid response, and insight. Speed is necessary as many economic opportunities are fleeting. The capacity for rapid response suggests the entrepreneur has organized the resources necessary to seize an opportunity for economic gain. Finally, insight is required to create a value proposition for the opportunity that differentiates it from existing offerings.

RESOURCE-BASED APPROACH. Another approach to understanding entrepreneurial strategy is the so-called **resource-based approach** to sustainable competitive advantage.[10] It has been applied to entrepreneurial ventures, but it has its origins in understanding large corporations. In the latter context, the theory holds that large organizations form to create and sustain some type of competitive advantage over rivals based on the resources they control. The resources that provide advantage are those that have the following four characteristics:

- They are rare.
- They are valuable.
- They are difficult to copy.
- They have no ready substitutes.

When applied to entrepreneurial ventures, these various attributes of resources are exploited to develop a startup with a sustainable competitive advantage from the beginning.[11] The entrepreneur uses insight into these various characteristics of resources to gather those necessary to exploit an opportunity.

Resources are rare if they are not widely available to potential competitors. Examples of rare resources for technology ventures include things like patents on key technologies, access to inexpensive technical labor pools, and knowledge possessed by only a few individuals.

Valuable resources help the venture implement its strategy effectively and efficiently. In other words, valuable resources help a venture exploit opportunities and minimize threats. Examples of valuable resources to a startup technology venture may include real property, capital equipment, key people with unique talents and skills, and cash.

Ventures that possess rare and valuable resources will have an advantage over other ventures if those resources are difficult to replicate or copy. Several factors may conspire to make it difficult for ventures to copy each other's key resources, including unique historical conditions, complex social relationships (such as exclusive contracts), and ambiguous cause and effect so that the key resources are difficult to identify amidst a variety of factors.

Finally, non-substitutable resources are strategic resources that cannot be replaced by commonplace resources. For example, an expert system may replace a manager's knowledge about running an efficient operation. However, it may be far more difficult for a venture to find a commonplace substitute for the charismatic leadership that may be provided by a founding entrepreneur. There are many instances of the latter. Perhaps no better example exists than computer companies that have attempted to use commonplace resources to substitute for the charismatic leadership of a Steve Jobs, Bill Gates, or Michael Dell. For the most part, these iconic leaders of the computer age are impossible to replace with substitute leaders.

STAKEHOLDERS AND STRATEGY

The renewed emphasis on quality, competitiveness, innovation, and speed that has occurred among new ventures has strong implications for overall strategy. For instance, the drive to grow and expand must be tempered by an ability to maintain contact with customers. Many entrepreneurs learn the hard way that bigger is not better if all contact with customers is lost. At the same time, companies have learned that customers, or *stakeholders,* come in a variety of forms. There are internal and external stakeholders. One important internal stakeholder that has gone through cycles of neglect in American business is the employee. Today, high-performance ventures are focusing on employees as their most vital resource.

Employees

Whereas the traditional view of strategy suggests that managers and shareholders are a company's most important asset, a modern view directs attention to the customers and non-management employees. These stakeholders are highlighted in modern ventures because they are critical in defining and adding value to the product or service. Increasingly, organizations are relying on their own people as the source of new ideas, energy, and creativity.

A view of employees as a resource has replaced the traditional view of labor as a cost of production. The only sustainable competitive advantage for a firm in the global marketplace is its human resources. Although cash, equipment, facilities, and infrastructure can be quickly transferred, built, or acquired, human resources are not so easily or quickly developed. Strategic management of employees requires managers to dedicate time, money, and attention to their training and development. This not only increases workers' value; it also enhances their capacity for continuous improvement. In a global market, allowing a workforce to grow stagnant without ongoing training is to invite failure.[12] Research has shown that training and development offer significant contributions to any organization in enhancing the abilities of employees.[13]

The prudent approach is to adopt a long-term strategy, then build a sensible training program that helps employees develop skills that can be applied to problems throughout the organization. Employees want training that will help them make progress in their careers, but managers have to recognize that progress in modern organizations has been redefined. Career paths in the modern organization often don't follow the traditional "corporate ladder." In the customer-focused organization, employees spend more time moving along a horizontal ladder, doing projects with people from different departments in their organization, than climbing the vertical ladder.[14]

Much of the work in organizations involves collecting, organizing, and analyzing information. In short, professional work is knowledge work. To help employees succeed requires not only training, but also an organizational structure conducive to continuous learning. The main difference between training and learning is that training is often a group activity; learning is often more effective as an individual activity. Managers who provide both training and a learning environment for employees will create more innovation, better service, and more efficient operations than competitors.

Customers

Defining organizational strategy in terms of customer expectations is fundamental to the modern approach to strategic management. Customers are defined as the end users of the organization's products and/or services. For some companies, a variety of customers or groups may use its products and services. For example, a hotel may rent single rooms to walk-up business customers, to tourists in small groups, or to a business manager of a professional organization who secures rooms for thousands of convention goers. Similarly, a household goods moving firm may sell its full range of services to corporate clients at a discount for large volume and at regular rates to single households that use only some of the firm's services (e.g., shipping but not packing of household goods). Careful identification of the firm's customers is essential.

How does a company find and develop loyal customers? There is no simple answer to this critical question. Happy customers return and refer other customers. Unhappy customers not only fail to return; they are likely to turn away other potential customers. One estimate is that one dissatisfied customer can produce 250 non-customers (people who are indifferent, perhaps even hostile to a firm's product or service).[15] In a free market economy, where customer choice and freedom are paramount, satisfied customers are the fundamental focus of any strategy.

Customers use the goods and services produced by a firm. Many firms, in turn, are customers of suppliers. Working with suppliers to ensure a steady flow of high-quality raw materials is vital to a firm's overall success.

Suppliers

Suppliers provide essential raw materials for the firm. The traditional view of suppliers is that a single supplier of any one raw material can threaten a firm's flexibility, especially its capacity to force price concessions by playing off two or more suppliers against one another. This is compounded by a traditional view of purchasing as a low-cost function where the business is awarded to the supplier offering the lowest cost per

© nikkyrok, 2012. Used under license from Shutterstock, Inc.

unit. A more effective strategy focuses on developing long-term relationships with key suppliers, focusing on building partnerships, continuously improving product quality, and driving down costs. Special attention is devoted to eliminating defective parts and to involving the supplier in the design process for the firm's product(s). This type of relationship is the basis of such process innovations as just-in-time manufacturing.

Stockholders

Publicly traded firms have another set of constituents interested in the firm's performance: stockholders. While many stockholders are interested only in maximizing returns on their investment, most also realize that this is best accomplished through an effective quality strategy.[16] Stockholders are those who own a firm's stock.

The traditional view of business in the United States has placed highest priority on satisfying stockholder expectations, which, because of their exclusively financial interest, usually meant paying close attention to the quarterly report. This focus results in a heavy emphasis on short-term profit improvements, often realized at the expense of long-term investment.

In Japan, by way of contrast, stockholders and senior management are the first to suffer in bad business times. The traditional U.S. approach to a downturn in the business cycle has been to lay off workers first while the firm waits for customer demand to return. A 1980 NBC News White Paper, "If Japan Can, Why Can't We?" showed how Mazda of Japan, during an energy-cost-induced sales crisis, assigned engineers to selling jobs, to learn more about the customer, without layoffs.

A major responsibility of managers is communication with stockholders. Perhaps the most effective communicator is Warren Buffett, chairman of the investment firm Berkshire Hathaway and one of the world's wealthiest people. Buffett is well known for his annual reports to shareholders. In fact, many people purchase Berkshire Hathaway stock just to have an opportunity to read Buffett's message.

Community

Another stakeholder of most organizations is the community. The community is an important stakeholder in that it defines the rules for legal business activity and is the source of many important resources for the organization's continued success.

The community consists of private citizens plus government and other public or regulatory agencies. Traditionally, the community is dependent on the firm and is grateful for the salaries and taxes it pays and for its use of community suppliers and contractors. Many communities and states offer companies special inducements to bring their production to the community.

Not only must a firm act in a legal, ethical fashion with each stakeholder, the community also expects a strong sense of social responsibility from the firm. Further, most communities view the firm as needing to make a positive contribution to the community, beyond the firm's payroll, purchases, and taxes. The strategic view of the community as a stakeholder must also be long term.

SUMMARY OF LEARNING OBJECTIVES

1. **Develop** a mission statement for your venture, and understand why a mission statement can be important. *A venture's mission statement should take into account the venture's history (or, for a startup, the industry's history), distinctive competence, and the environment. A good mission statement should be customer-focused, achievable, motivational, and specific. A mission statement is important because it guides the strategic decision making of the venture.*

2. **Understand** what sustainable competitive advantage is and how to attain it. *Sustainable competitive advantage is an advantage in the marketplace that cannot be duplicated by competitors and is the source of sustained superior performance. It is conferred by having resources that are valuable, rare, not easily imitated, and not easily substituted.*

3. **Undertake** a competitor analysis and differentiate a venture from competitors. *Some of the basic tools of competitive positioning are the competitor analysis matrix (used to compare your firm with its competitors), the competitive positioning comparison matrix (used to compare your firm's offerings with those of its competitors along several dimensions), and the perceptual map (a graphical method to compare firms or products along two dimensions). Used together, these tools can help a startup firm develop its competitive positioning.*

4. **Develop** an entrepreneurial strategy that increases venture competitiveness. *Entrepreneurial strategy is the process of determining how best to deploy the assets of the venture to create value. Strategy setting should be undertaken with input from employees, advisors, investors, and other stakeholders.*

5. **Implement** an entrepreneurial strategy based on real-options reasoning or resource-based reasoning. *The two approaches to strategy discussed in this chapter include the real-options approach and the resourcebased approach. The real-options approach utilizes probabilities to determine rational action in the present. The resource-based approach asserts the venture can develop sustainable advantage around resources that are rare, valuable, difficult to imitate, and difficult to substitute.*

6. **Integrate** a venture's various stakeholders into the venture's overall strategy. *In order for a venture successfully to execute strategy over the long run, it must pay attention to various stakeholders and integrate them into the overall strategy. The stakeholders mentioned in this chapter include employees, customers, suppliers, stockholders, and the community. Each of these stakeholders has the potential to positively or negatively impact the venture's strategy. Experienced entrepreneurs know that these stakeholders must be actively integrated into the venture's overall strategy on an ongoing basis. Too many firms fail because they lose track of customers, employees, or some other important stakeholder.*

QUESTIONS FOR DISCUSSION

1. What is the difference between competitive advantage and sustainable competitive advantage? What do you need to develop a sustainable competitive advantage?

2. What are some of the dimensions on which product and service positioning can be based?

3. What is the purpose of a venture's mission statement? What are some things to keep in mind when developing your venture's mission statement?

4. What is meant by the term *entrepreneurial strategy*? How should the entrepreneur go about establishing a strategy for the venture?

5. Define what the real-options approach to strategy entails. How does the real-options approach provide guidance in the strategy-setting process?

6. Identify the four basic components of strategy setting that are highlighted by the resource-based approach to strategy. How do these four components result in competitive advantage for a venture?

7. Porter's value chain identifies the essential functions that most ventures perform to serve customers. What are these? How can a venture develop competitive advantage based on an analysis of its value chain?

8. Explain what is meant by the term *SWOT analysis*. How can an entrepreneur use a SWOT analysis to develop competitive advantage?

9. In this chapter we identified some important stakeholders that must be integrated into the venture's overall strategy. Identify each stakeholder and explain why they are important to venture strategy. Provide some suggestions about how the venture can ensure it stays connected to each stakeholder type.

10. Explain the concept of *differentiation*. Why do you think it is important for an entrepreneur to be able to differentiate the venture? How can an entrepreneur develop a sustainable competitive advantage?

IN-CLASS EXERCISE

For this exercise, students will create a perceptual map for an existing industry. They should work in groups of two or three on this exercise. Each group will be assigned an industry with well-known companies (e.g., automobiles, computers, airlines, electronics firms). The industry to be used should offer products or services to consumers, because these firms and their products or services are likely to be better understood than business-to-business industries. Each group should follow these steps and then answer the questions in steps 6 and 7:

1. Identify at least eight companies in this industry.

2. For each company identify at least two distinct products.

3. Determine three important product characteristics for these products.

4. Assign a score of 0 to 10 for each of these characteristics for each product, where 0 is worst and 10 is best. Then average the scores for all of the products for each company.

5. Create three perceptual maps for this industry using all combinations of pairs of the product combinations as the X and Y axes on the perceptual maps. Use the average product scores as coordinates on these maps.

6. Compare the perceptual maps for different combinations of product characteristics. Are there differences, or do they look similar?

7. If you had a startup firm, where would you choose to be located on each of the perceptual maps? Why?

KEY TERMS

Competitive advantage: A factor or action that gives a firm an advantage in in the marketplace and leads customers to buy its products or services instead of those of other firms.

Competitive positioning: Competitive positioning determines where your venture's products and services are located relative to those of competing firms.

Differentiation: The firm's offerings are recognizably different from what competitors are offering on some set of relevant attributes.

Differentiation strategy: One of the three options in the Porter competitive strategy approach where a venture offers a higher-priced product equipped with more product-enhancing features than its competitors' products.

Directed discovery: A process of plotting a direction into an uncertain future, then making adjustments as reality unfolds.

Distinctive competence: A capacity that's unique to the firm and that's valued in the market.

Entrepreneurial strategy: The process of determining how best to deploy the assets of the venture to create value.

Mission statement: A venture's mission statement defines it raison d'être (French for "reason for being"), the fundamental purpose it's designed to serve.

Opportunity register: A record of business opportunity insights that may or may not become the basis of new revenue opportunities.

Real-options approach: An approach derived from the world of financial management; managers must make reasonable guesses about the probability of some outcome. They can use these probabilities to develop a justification for a present action.

Resource-based approach: This approach to setting strategy asserts that a venture can develop sustainable advantage around resources that are rare, valuable, difficult to imitate, and difficult to substitute.

Sustainable competitive advantage: An advantage over a firm's competitors and potential competitors that cannot be duplicated, will last a reasonably long time, and is the source of a firm's sustained superior performance.

SWOT analysis: A strategic planning tool that involves assessing a venture's strengths, weaknesses, opportunities, and threats.

Value chain: All the activities an organization undertakes to create value for a customer.

ENDNOTES

[1] Kawasaki, G., *The Art of the Start* (New York: Portfolio, 2004).

[2] Deming, W.E., *Out of the Crisis* (Cambridge, MA: MIT Press, 1986).

[3] Anonymous, "This Month's Focus: The Mission Statement," *Manager's Magazine* (February, 1995): 30–31.

[4] Barney, J., Sergio Olavarrieta, and Alexander E. Ellinger, "Resource-Based Theory and Strategic Logistics Research," *International Journal of Physical Distribution & Logistics Management*, 27(9)(1997): 559–587.

[5] Ibid.

[6] Czinkota, M. and M. Kotabe, "America's New World Trade Order," *Marketing Management*, 1(3) (1992): 46–54.

[7] Kawasaki, op. cit.

[8] Everett, R.F., *The Entrepreneur's Guide to Marketing* (New York: Praeger Publishing, 2008).

[9] McGrath, R.G., and I. MacMillan, *The Entrepreneurial Mindset: Strategies for Continuously Creating Opportunity in an Age of Uncertainty* (Boston: Harvard Business School Press, 2000).

[10] Barney, J., "Firm Resources and Sustained Competitive Advantage," *Journal of Management*, 17(1991): 99–120.

[11] Dollinger, M.J.,*Entrepreneurship: Strategies and Resources* (Upper Saddle River, NJ: Prentice-Hall Publishing, 1999).

[12] Porter, M.E., "What Is Strategy?" *Harvard Business Review*, 74(6)(1996): 61–78.

[13] Stewart, T., *Intellectual Capital* (New York: Currency, 1997).

[14] Buick, I., and M. Ganesan, "An Investigation of the Current Practices of In-House Employee Training and Development Within Hotels in Scotland," *Services Industries Journal*, 17(4)(1997): 652–668.

[15] Penzias, A., "New Paths to Success," *Fortune*, (June 1995): 90–93.

[16] Morgan, A., *Strategic Leadership: Managing the Firm in a Turbulent World* (Dubuque, IA: Kendall Hunt, 2001).

OPERATING SYSTEMS AND SCALABILITY

Learning Objectives

As a result of studying this chapter, students will be able to:

- **Understand** the elements of an operating system and how they relate to one another.

- **Understand** the principles of operations strategy and how it relates to business strategy.

- **Understand** how to make structural and infrastructural decisions for your venture's operating system.

- **Learn** the advantages and disadvantages of outsourcing.

- **Apply** the principles of process management so that your venture will be scalable.

- **Understand** different types of processes and the principles to use in choosing processes for a new venture.

- **Understand** common approaches to defining and managing quality.

- **Understand** different types of performance measures and be able to use them in a new venture.

- **Link** the principles of managing operating systems to the entrepreneurial method.

INTRODUCTION

In earlier chapters, you learned how to develop a venture idea and specify the products and services the venture will offer to customers. You also have determined how to position your venture and its offerings against your competitors on price, quality, convenience, or some other factors. You have decided on your business model and your value proposition. It is now time to determine how you will provide your products or services to your customers. The **operating system** is the combination of internal processes and supply chain collaborations that provide products and services to a venture's customers. Managing the set of activities included in the operating system that are required to produce a product or service and get it to your customers is referred to as **operations management**.[1] The operations function is fundamental to any organization, but it often does not receive a great deal of attention from entrepreneurs because they are focused on the other demands of getting a venture off the ground.

© wavebreakmedia, 2012. Used under license from Shutterstock, Inc.

Designing a product or service, coming up with a marketing plan, and raising money often seem to be of more immediate importance. For any new venture, there are different approaches to delivering a product or service to its customers. The objective in managing the operations is to accomplish this task in such a way to support the venture's strategy, business model, and competitive positioning.

Figuring out how to produce the product or delivering the service may appear to be something that will be easy to do once the important design and technical details of a new product are worked out. This view is understandable—after all, if a product has not been designed yet, one doesn't need to worry about understanding how it will be produced. All too often, however, an entrepreneur will not realize that the pricing strategy or product features that are a critical part of a business plan are not compatible with the realities of actually producing the product. Operations can also be a very costly function for a new venture, so a thorough understanding is very important when determining the financing requirements of a startup. A second fundamental reason for devoting attention to the operations function early in the life of a startup is that the operating system will be directly related to the **scalability** of an enterprise. Scalability is defined to be the ability to meet increasing demand with decreasing marginal costs. The operating margin for a scalable business increases as volume increases.[2] Entrepreneurial ventures are defined in this textbook to have the potential for rapid growth. Achieving high growth has two requirements. One is creating high growth in demand; the other is being able to satisfy that demand by producing products or services at the rate demanded by customers. Developing an operating system that is scalable and can therefore meet rapidly growing demand without increasing costs proportionally can be critical to the success of an entrepreneurial venture. Companies such as Facebook and Monster.com are examples of businesses that exhibit scalability.

There are several dimensions of operations management that must be considered in a startup firm. One is **operations strategy**, which for a startup is the determination of how the competitive positioning, value proposition, and business model of the venture will translate to requirements of the operating system.[3] For example, the core product of a new venture may be positioned as a higher-quality alternative to what is currently offered in the market. The operating system must therefore be capable of providing the level of quality that will be expected by customers. Similarly, a food-service venture that envisions providing a meal with the taste of a four-star restaurant at the price of a quick-service restaurant must design an operating system that has some very special capabilities. The operations strategy for a new venture must specify the performance dimensions in which the operating system must excel. These dimensions typically include cost, quality, reliability, speed, and flexibility.[4] It is important to note that there are usually tradeoffs associated with these different dimensions. For example, it is very difficult, although not impossible, to have high degrees of flexibility and low cost at the same time.

A second key dimension of operations management is the choice of whether to produce the product or service in-house or to outsource its production to some external firm. **Outsourcing** has many advantages for a new venture, particularly for a firm that is offering a tangible product. Outsourcing can result in lower costs and more flexibility, but there are potential drawbacks as well. Related to outsourcing is the design and management of the firm's **supply chain**, which is "the network of organizations that work together to convert and move goods from raw materials stage to the end customer."[5] Both outsourcing and supply chain management will be covered in more detail below.

A third key area of operations management is the selection and design of the **process** that will be used to produce the product or service your firm will offer. A process is simply the series of steps that are used to transform a set of inputs (labor, information, materials) into a valuable output (product or service).[6] The choice and design of a process depends on many factors. Some of these factors include, but are not limited to, the type of venture (recall the four types from Chapter 3), the firm's strategy, the value proposition, and the business model. The choices made with respect to a venture's processes are critical, because they can play a significant role in determining your product's cost and quality. Those attributes in turn influence pricing strategy and overall profitability.

Quality can be critical to a startup's success, as quality is an important consideration in how customers assess the value of the firm's products and services. Firms whose products or services are perceived to have higher quality tend to be more profitable and have a competitive advantage in the marketplace.[7] Therefore, the management of quality is a critical part of operations management. Quality management has several different elements, including deciding how quality will be defined, measuring quality, controlling quality, and improving quality.

One concept is particularly relevant for operations management in new ventures is **lean thinking**. Lean thinking is an approach to management that can be characterized as "doing more with less."[8] A new venture usually doesn't have a lot of resources and therefore must use what resources it does have as effectively and efficiently as possible. Lean thinking provides a managerial mindset whose main goals are to minimize waste and maximize customer value.

It should be noted that these three dimensions are interrelated and depend on one another. Operations strategy is driven by the overall strategy, business model, and competitive positioning of the venture. In turn, the decisions made with respect to outsourcing, supply chain management, and process selection and design are driven by the operations strategy. In established firms, there are often different operations approaches that will lead to successful business outcomes. The same holds true with new ventures, with one important distinction. Successful new ventures typically have a high degree of flexibility in their operations. Flexibility in this case refers to the general ability to respond to uncertainty.[9] Because very little in the startup world is certain, being able to deal with uncertainty provides a greater chance of survival and eventual prosperity for an entrepreneurial firm.

Finally, an important element of managing operations in any firm, but particularly in a startup firm, is **performance measurement**. Measuring and tracking performance is important for a new venture, as these activities enable the entrepreneur to understand where the firm is doing well and where it needs improvement. Performance can and should be measured along different dimensions and using different methods. Monitoring the performance of a venture in different areas will enable the entrepreneur to understand where to best to devote his or her managerial efforts, both to maintain good performance and to improve performance where it is lacking.

OPERATIONS STRATEGY

In any organization, there is an overall business strategy that specifies in a broad way how the business intends to compete and gain an advantage over its competitors. One approach to characterizing business strategy is the idea of a generic strategy, where the firm competes on the basis of cost or differentiation. In a cost leadership strategy, the firm will attempt to provide its products or services at a lower cost than its rivals. For a differentiation strategy, the firm will attempt to provide products or services that are different (and better) than those of its competitors on one or more dimensions, such as quality or convenience.[10] There is also a functional strategy for each of the major functions of the organization that supports the overall business strategy. The operations strategy is one of these functional strategies, along with the marketing strategy, finance strategy, or human resource strategy. Operations strategy can be thought of as the set of plans and decisions to use the resources of the operations function to best support the long-term competitive strategy of the firm.[11]

Competitive Priorities

As noted above, generic business strategies can be classified into cost and differentiation. However, a venture will need to be more precise about how it will compete and the characteristics of the firm's offerings that will be required to win customers over its competitors. One of the key elements of the operations strategy is to specify these characteristics as they relate specifically to the operations function, which in turn will help determine the decisions with respect to how the operating system will be designed and managed. These characteristics, or **competitive priorities**, are the dimensions along which the firm intends to excel and gain an advantage in the marketplace. Competitive priorities include cost, quality, time, innovation, and flexibility. How should a firm choose its competitive priorities? They should follow directly from the choices made for the firm's business strategy. Cost as a competitive priority of the operations strategy supports a low-cost generic business strategy. Quality, time, innovation, or flexibility would support a generic differentiation business strategy.

Cost as a competitive priority generally requires that the firm be the lowest cost provider in its market, which generally is passed on to customers in the form of low prices. Firms that use cost as a competitive priority include Walmart and Southwest Airlines. **Quality** can be defined many different ways. One approach is to distinguish between consistent quality and performance quality. **Consistent quality** means that the product or service meets specifications and performs as expected in a consistent manner, even if it is not the best in the market. McDonald's is an example of a company that competes on consistent quality. **Performance quality** refers to a product or service that is superior to most or all of the offerings of a firm's competitors. Firms such as Mercedes-Benz and Ritz-Carlton Hotels are examples of firms that compete on performance quality. **Time** can refer to speed in delivery, reliability in delivery, or speed in product development. FedEx is a company that competes on both speed and reliability. Almost all successful high-technology firms must compete on product development speed. **Innovation** refers to the ability to develop and introduce new, useful, and distinctive products and services. Apple is an example of a company that competes on innovation. **Flexibility** in general refers to the ability to respond to uncertainty and changes in demand. Several different types of flexibility are relevant competitive priorities. **Customization** allows a firm to produce a product or service that fits the needs of the customer. Dell Computers is an example of a firm that competes on customization. **Variety** means that a firm is able to produce a wide range of products or services. A general hospital is able to treat a large range of diseases and is an example of an organization that competes on variety. Volume flexibility is the ability to adjust the volume of a product or service easily to meet variations in demand. A grocery store that can add cashiers to meet higher demand during busy periods is an example of a firm that competes on volume flexibility.[12]

Operating System Decisions

Decisions about the operating system must be consistent with the competitive priorities chosen as the strategic objectives of the operations strategy. These decisions fall into two broad categories: **structural decisions** and **infrastructural decisions**. Structural decisions are long-term decisions that generally require relatively large investments. These decisions include choices about capacity, facilities, technology, facility location, and sourcing. They are made relatively infrequently and are difficult to change. Infrastructural decisions, on the other hand, are made more frequently, require less investment, and are easier to change. They generally involve people and systems, specifically those decisions related to the workforce, quality systems, planning and scheduling systems, and organizational structure.[13] Taken together, the set of structural and infrastructural decisions determine how the operations strategy is implemented and whether the competitive priorities intended by the firm are likely to be achieved. In many firms, particularly startups, these decisions may not be consciously made in a purposeful way; instead, they are often made in a piecemeal fashion in reaction to events as they occur over time.

Two important principles should guide the formulation of these decisions. One is called internal fit, or internal consistency. The individual structural and infrastructural decisions should be consistent with one another, should mutually reinforce one other, and should be intended to support the same competitive priorities. Southwest Airlines' operations system decisions provide an excellent example of internal fit. Southwest Airlines' primary competitive priority is low cost, and its operating system decisions all work together to achieve that objective. For example, they use only one type of airplane, which reduces training and maintenance cost; they limit their flights to routes that are most cost efficient; they do not serve full meals, which reduces in-flight costs; they do not have first class service, which allows additional seats to provide greater capacity on each flight; and their open-seating system allows faster boarding, which means that each plane can be used for more flights each day. All of these operating system decisions work together to reduce the cost of providing airline service to its passengers. This set of operating system decisions also illustrates the second principle, external fit with the needs of the company's chosen market segment. This set of decisions supports a low-cost strategy that Southwest customers value. Contrast these decisions with those of a traditional airline such as United or American. A traditional airline uses several different types of airplanes of different size and manufacturers, provides first class service, serves meals, offers flights to almost all locations, and offers reserved seating. These decisions increase cost but may offer some elements of higher quality service. Some customers of these airlines may value comfort and convenience over low cost, but they are unlikely to attract any customers who value the low cost service Southwest provides.

Focus, Tradeoffs, and Operations Strategy in a New Venture

The concepts of **tradeoffs** and **focus** are critical in developing an effective operations strategy. The concept of tradeoffs refers to the idea that some goals are incompatible with one another. For example, it is very difficult to have high flexibility and low cost. Similarly, low cost and high performance quality do not generally go together. Therefore, it is important for a firm to focus on a relatively narrow set of goals and activities that are particularly important to its success and devote its resources to achieving that set of goals. Being focused allows a firm to save money, time, and other resources. Moreover, a firm that concentrates on a smaller set of activities generally becomes better and more efficient at those activities, which results in better quality and lower costs. In a startup firm, resources are usually at premium, so achieving focus can be even more critical to success than in a larger, more established firm.

SUPPLY CHAIN MANAGEMENT AND OUTSOURCING

An important area of management in a new venture is the management of the supply chain and sourcing of materials and services. A supply chain is a network of organizations that work together to convert raw materials to finished goods, and supply chain management is the planning and coordination of the activities in a supply chain. A simplified supply chain for a sandwich shop is shown graphically in Exhibit 12.1. Sourcing refers more narrowly to the activities involved in choosing and managing relationships with suppliers.[14] As noted above, sourcing is a key decision area in a firm's operations strategy. In a manufacturing firm, the purchased parts and materials might contribute as much as 75 to 80 percent of the total cost of a product.[15] Sourcing decisions and management can also affect other competitive priorities as well, including quality, flexibility, speed, and innovation. However, sourcing decisions can be even more important than

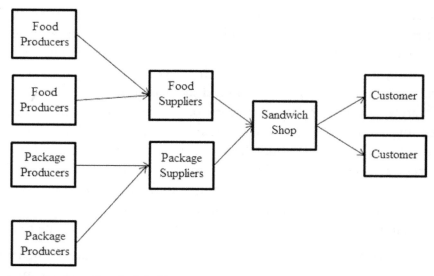

EXHIBIT 12.1 Supply Chain for a Sandwich Shop

their direct effect on competitive priorities. Startup firms, in particular, usually have limited resources and must focus on a narrow range of activities. Sourcing decisions can extend beyond the procurement of materials and components to the purchase of support services and even the manufacture of final products. Deciding which activities to perform internally and which to outsource to external firms can be critical to achieving focus.

Just as there is an operations strategy for a single firm, there is also a supply chain strategy for the collection of firms in a supply chain. As in an operations strategy, a supply chain strategy consists of decisions about the supply chain that will support the firm's overall competitive strategy and its operations strategy. These decisions depend on the uncertainty associated with demand and supply in the supply chain. When demand and supply are stable, the supply chain should be designed to provide efficiency. When the demand and supply are uncertain, the supply chain should be designed to provide agility and responsiveness to deal with that uncertainty. The specifics of designing and managing these types of supply chains are beyond this scope of this book, but what is important to know is that the notions of tradeoffs and focus also apply to supply chain strategy. The choices made to handle increasing levels of uncertainty come with increasing costs.[16]

Most startup firms lack resources in some area, such as time, capital, or expertise, which dictates that the firm will need to procure products and services from external organizations. This process is called outsourcing.[17] The decision to outsource an activity can be made on the basis of several different criteria. One criterion is cost, and that is often the reason for an activity to be outsourced. It is often much less costly to outsource the production of a product to a contract manufacturer. However, in general, the decision of whether to

outsource an activity (either a product or a service) is usually much more complex. There are many different potential reasons for outsourcing and there many different potential benefits. Some of the benefits include lower costs, lower capital investment, and better quality.[18] There are potential drawbacks as well. For example, outsourcing results in the loss of control over the activity, which may result in lower quality. A more serious concern would the potential loss of proprietary technology or information. Ultimately, however, for a new venture, outsourcing can be an effective way to achieve focus. By concentrating on only the most critical activities, such as product development and marketing, a startup can focus its resources and efforts on those activities that will be most important to its ultimate success. However, an effective outsourcing relationship is not simply a transaction. After the decision to outsource is made, the firm must carefully choose a partner and manage that relationship over time to obtain the optimal benefits of outsourcing. Continually reviewing performance of the outsourcing partner is important for the long-term success of the relationship.[19]

Finally, an important part of supply chain management is logistics management. Logistics management "includes management of inbound and outbound transportation, material handling, warehousing, inventory, order fulfillment and distribution, third-party logistics, and reverse logistics (the return of goods from customers)"[20] Most new ventures that provide a physical product will primarily be concerned with outbound logistics, which is the delivery of products to customers. For most startup firms, particularly those marketing their products on the Internet, the best logistics decision is usually to outsource this activity to a package carrier such as Federal Express, United Parcel Service, or the United States Postal Service.

PROCESS MANAGEMENT

At the heart of the operating system for a firm is a process or set of processes. A process is a series of steps that transform a set of inputs into a set of outputs.[21] The product or service your venture provides to its customers is produced using a process. Inputs into the process can include labor, materials, equipment, or facilities. Outputs of the process include products and services sold to customers. Processes exist in all parts of an organization, although here the focus is on processes used to create products and services to be offered by the firm. Some processes operate only within the firm, and some extend across the supply chain to suppliers and customers. An understanding of how processes are managed is important in the success of your firm because understanding how processes work allows an entrepreneur to have a better idea about what the firm is capable or not capable of providing to its customers. For example, a thorough knowledge of the process used to provide the service it will offer to customers enables a better projection of costs, financial requirements, and the volume of customers the venture will be able to serve. Moreover, a good understanding of processes and how to manage them will lead to a better chance of rapid growth when provided the opportunity.

Process management refers to the choice of the type of process to be used, the design of that process, and the analysis and improvement of that process. The choice and design of a process should be driven by the operations strategy and its competitive priorities, as well as other characteristics of the firm's offerings. Note that even if you have chosen to outsource the production of your firm's products, an understanding of process management is important. It is unlikely that you will outsource all activities. Support processes for order receipt, order fulfillment, or customer service may not be directly involved in the production of the product or service to be offered to customers, but they may be as important, or possibly even more important, to the success of your venture.

Process Choice

For a manufacturing process, two product characteristics to consider in the choice of a process are volume and variety. Typically, products that have high variety (or customization) have relatively low demand for any one individual product. In contrast, products that have high demand tend to have low variety (highly standardized). As in the examination of competitive priorities in operations strategy, the notion of tradeoffs comes into play in process choice. Different combinations of product and volume and variety lead to the selection of different manufacturing process types. Processes that are able to produce high volumes tend to be most effective in producing a low variety of products. For example, think of the assembly line process used to produce automobiles. On the other hand, processes that provide high levels of variety (or customization) tend to be most effective in producing at low volumes. At this extreme would be a commercial printer, where every printing run is different.[22] There are also process types that provide better performance with medium levels of both volume and variety.

Volume and variety can also be used in some cases to select service processes, but in many cases two other dimensions, labor intensity and customization, are more useful in process selection. In using this approach for service process selection, these two dimensions lead to four types of processes. One is the **service factory** (low labor intensity and low customization). Examples of service factories would be airlines and hotels. The second process type would be the **service shop** (low labor intensity and high customization). Examples of service shops would be automobile repair shops and hospitals. The third type would be the **mass service** (high labor intensity and low customization). Examples of mass services include retail banks and grocery stores. Finally, the fourth type of service process is the **professional service** (high labor intensity and high customization). Examples include lawyers, physicians, and accountants.[23]

A detailed examination of each of these process types is beyond the scope of this book, but it is important to understand the basic idea that not all products or services should be produced using the same type of process. The choice of a process type is linked to the operations strategy in that each type of process has a relatively consistent set of operating system decisions and supports a similar set of competitive priorities. The type of process selected affects costs, quality, technology and equipment requirements, labor requirements, the capacity of customers that can be served, and ultimately financing requirements.

Process Analysis and Improvement

Process choice is a strategic decision in process management. A more tactical element of process management is process analysis and improvement. Existing processes can almost always be improved along some dimension (e.g., time, cost, or quality), but the first step in improvement is to understand them. Process analysis refers to a set of

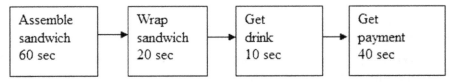

EXHIBIT 12.2   Process Map for a Sandwich Shop

techniques that lead to a better understanding of how a process functions. One category of process analysis techniques can be classified into the broad umbrella of process mapping. There are various forms of process mapping (flowcharting, time-function mapping, service blueprinting, value stream mapping, process charts), but the general idea is to develop a schematic drawing of the movement of materials, products, people, and information through the process.

Various forms of process maps can also show different resources, such as equipment or labor, which are used in the process, as well as the times taken to complete various steps in a process. Constructing a process map requires that the analyst understand the various elements in the process and therefore is one of the first steps in analyzing a process. After a process map has been constructed, other steps in process analysis might include the identification of bottlenecks (parts of the process where the process is slowest). Process analysis can also help to identify where resources might be wasted or where it might be helpful to add resources. Process improvement then is the logical successor to process analysis, where the results of the analysis are used to reduce cost, reduce time through the process, or improve the quality of the outputs of the process.[24] A detailed guide to process analysis and improvement is beyond the scope of this chapter, but it is important to understand the potential of this technique in the management of the venture. Exhibit 12.2 shows an example of a simplified process map for a sandwich shop process. Each process step is shown in a box, along with the time taken to complete that step. The arrows show the direction of the flow of materials and customers through the process. This process map could be used to calculate the overall time taken to complete the process, calculate the maximum capacity of sandwiches that could be produced in a given time period, and identify where best to add resources such as additional workers.

Process Management over Time

In this textbook, an entrepreneurial venture must have the potential for rapid growth, which is generally necessary to be an attractive opportunity for investors. Rapid growth in a new venture requires two things. One is rapidly growing demand for the venture's offerings. The other is the capacity for the venture to provide those offerings to customers effectively and efficiently. Many promising ventures have failed in the process of attempting to make the transition from a small to a medium to a large company. Even if the venture's founders plan to exit before the company has grown to be large, investors must be able to see how that transition will be made. It is not likely that the process used to produce a product or service at the start of a venture's life will be the same one that will be used when demand increases. Therefore, the entrepreneur must be able to plan for this transition and understand the capabilities of different process types will enable growth over time.

This discussion leads to the idea of **scalability**, which is derived from the concept of economies of scale. A firm that exhibits economies of scale has lower per unit costs with higher production volumes. Another way to characterize scale economies, as the term is sometimes known, is that per unit costs do not grow in proportion to production volume. Scalability, then, is the capability of a venture to increase its revenues without a proportional increase in per-unit costs.[25] A business such as iTunes is an example of a scalable process. The incremental cost to provide a song to a customer over the Internet is negligible, but the customer pays an additional $0.99 or more to Apple for that song. The selection of a process that is scalable, or the understanding of how to move from a process that is not scalable to one that is scalable, is necessary for the long-term success of the venture. One way that many ventures manage growth and achieve scalability is to outsource production. Outsourcing provides the flexibility to choose partners that can produce efficiently at low, medium, and high volumes as demand grows. The Research Link below discusses the relationship between operating system decisions and scalability in E-commerce businesses.

QUALITY

Quality is an important driver of overall business performance. Companies whose products and services have higher quality tend to be more profitable. Quality is one way customers assess the value of a firm's offerings, and customers will generally pay a premium for a product they perceive to have higher quality.[26] In some cases, better quality can also reduce costs. Achieving high quality is not easy, however. There is not even a generally agreed upon definition of quality, as "quality" has different meanings to different people. One author identified eight dimensions of quality: performance, features, reliability, conformance, durability, serviceability, aesthetics, and perceived quality.[27] Another set of ten dimensions has been identified to characterize the quality of a service: reliability, responsiveness, competence, access, courtesy, communication, credibility, security, understanding and knowing the customer, and tangibles.

RESEARCH LINK

"Scalability": The Paradox of Human Resources in E-commerce

In this study, Roger Hallowell examines the factors that affect scalability in an Internet business. Several E-commerce businesses that provide different types of services to customers were analyzed in this study. Differences in the characteristics of these services lead to different combinations of operating system decisions, which in turn lead to different levels of scalability. The key dimension differentiating high- and low-scalability businesses is the extent to which a service is "virtual" (pure information or completely automated) or "physical" (some degree of human intervention is required). At one end are businesses that provide only information. These businesses can be considered to be "infinitely scalable." Moving down the scalability continuum are services that provide commodities that require only standardized physical handling. Books would be an example. At the other end of the spectrum are businesses that are not scalable at all. These businesses sell unique products that require unique physical handling. Therefore, the degree to which these businesses require physical service, or the use of human resources, decreases the scalability of the venture. However, there is more to this study. Customers may prefer and be willing to pay a premium for the better service provided by human resources. It may be that an E-business would be better off using some human resources, even at the cost of being less than infinitely scalable.

Source: Hallowell, R., "Scalability": The Paradox of Human Resources in E-commerce," *International Journal of Service Industries Management*, 12(1) (2001): 34–43.

From a more general perspective, other authors have distinguished between consistent quality (the product or service meets expectations and is free of defects) and performance quality (the product is superior to other products on features or performance). Consistent quality is defined primarily from a production perspective, while performance quality is defined primarily from a user perspective. Another definition is simply "The ability of a product or service to meet customer needs." This definition is particularly useful, because it focuses on the characteristics of the company's offerings that are important to customers.

One approach to managing quality is **total quality management (TQM)**, which dates from the 1980s. Although it is regarded by some as a management fad whose time has passed by the 1990s, many of its principles have become *de facto* best practices for managing quality. The elements of TQM include top management commitment, employee participation, customer focus, management decision making using objective data, and continuous improvement. One of the fundamental goals of modern quality management is the attempt to reduce unnecessary and unplanned variation in a process. Other systems for quality improvement and management are **ISO 9000** and **Six Sigma**. ISO 9000 refers to a certification that an organization has met a set of standards issued by the International Organization for Standardization (ISO) that describe guidelines and requirements for quality improvement. The ISO is an international, nongovernmental organization that sets worldwide standards in many areas, including quality management. The term *Six Sigma* originates from a quality standard where the defect rate is about three out of one million. It refers more broadly to a system of management that is designed to improve quality, reduce costs, and increase customer satisfaction through a formal process improvement model.[28] These systems are not mutually exclusive, nor will they necessarily guarantee high levels of quality in the venture's products or services. However, following these general principles is a good general approach to managing quality.

In a new venture, outsourcing the production of goods or services is commonly used. When outsourcing is used, the quality of products and services is not under the direct control of the venture. In this case, the entrepreneur must monitor the quality of the goods or services obtained from the outsourcing partner. A thorough understanding of the principles of quality management discussed above is useful to accomplish this monitoring activity. In addition, there are quality control statistical techniques used for the inspection of goods purchased from suppliers.[29] From a more general perspective, working with suppliers or outsourcing partners in a cooperative relationship often is the best way to identify and solve quality problems with purchased goods or services.[30]

PERFORMANCE MEASUREMENT AND CONTROL

In any new venture, the entrepreneur will need a system for controlling its operations. The type of venture will determine in large part the specific nature of the control system, but any control system will have the following elements:

- Performance measures
- Performance standards
- Feedback and control techniques

Performance measures can be classified in different ways. One is to consider operational performance in areas such as productivity, cost, time, capacity, and quality. A second category of performance measurement would be the use of financial measures, such as financial ratios or discounted cash flow methods. Another approach focuses specifically on customer-related assessments of performance, although these measures are often grouped with quality measures. For most of these measurement categories, there are both quantitative measures (e.g., waiting time) and qualitative measures (e.g., customer reviews of service quality). A broader perspective on assessing performance on an organization-wide basis is the Balanced Scorecard approach.[31]

© michaeljung, 2012. Used under license from Shutterstock, Inc.

Whatever the measure, the entrepreneur will need to establish standards for acceptable performance. The actual performance for a particular measure can then be compared to assess whether improvement is needed. There also needs to be some sort of feedback and control technique to ensure that those areas of the venture that fall short of the standard will be identified so that action may be taken to correct the problem causing the substandard performance.

Productivity

Productivity is a fundamental measure of how well a firm is using its resources (e.g., labor, equipment, materials, or capital) to produce products or services. It is therefore a fundamental measure of performance, particularly from an operations perspective. A firm's productivity has a direct relationship to the costs incurred in providing products and services to its customers. The formula to calculate productivity is very simple:

$$\text{Productivity} = \text{Outputs} / \text{Inputs}$$

Productivity is a measure where higher values indicate better performance, so to improve productivity, we would like to increase outputs while holding inputs the same, reducing inputs while holding outputs the same, or increase outputs while reduce inputs (the best case). Productivity is best used as a comparative measure, where its value is compared against productivity of other firms in the same industry or compared over time within the venture.

Productivity can be expressed as partial productivity, multifactor productivity, or total productivity. A partial productivity measure would be the ratio of output to a single input, such as labor, capital, or materials. A multifactor productivity measure would be the ratio of output to the sum of two or more inputs, such as labor and capital or energy and materials. Total productivity would be the ratio of output to all resources. Examples of productivity measures are shown in Exhibit 12.3.

EXHIBIT 12.3 Productivity Measure Examples

Productivity Type	Examples
Partial Productivity	Output / Labor or Output / Materials or Output / Capital
Multifactor Productivity	Output / (Labor + Materials) or Output / (Materials + Energy)
Total Productivity	Output / (All Inputs)

Venture Type	Partial Productivity Measure
Manufacturing Plant	Units of output per labor hour
Airline	Seat-miles per plane
Retail Store	Sales per square foot
University	Students taught per instructor

In calculating multifactor or total productivity, it is necessary to convert the input levels into the same unit of measure, which is usually dollars.[32] Another measure that is used sometimes to provide a rough measure of overall organizational productivity is sales per employee, which can be particularly enlightening in comparing companies within the same industry.[33]

Operational Performance Measures

Other measures of operational performance include costs, time, and capacity. These measures are particularly useful when measuring the performance of a process. Costs that are most important in an operational sense are direct costs of producing a good or service. These direct costs can include costs for labor, equipment, energy, and materials and are most useful for operational control when they are calculated on a per-unit basis.

Time is a very important category of performance measures. There are several time-based measures that are useful. One example is **lead time**, which is the total time taken to complete a process (or sub-process) from start to finish. For example, for a pizza delivery business, lead time would be the time elapsed from when an order it taken to when it is delivered to the customer and payment is received. For an automobile assembly line, a measure that is important is the **cycle time**, which is the time interval between the completion of successive finished automobiles. In a business where customer service is important, the waiting time to be served would be an important measure of performance.

The **capacity** of a business can be an extremely important performance measure. Capacity is typically expressed as the maximum of output an operating system can reasonably produce in a given length of time. For example, the capacity of an automobile plant might be expressed as the number of cars produced per year, or the capacity of a hospital might be expressed as the number of patients treated per year. In some types of businesses, particularly those businesses where the time taken to produce a unit of output varies greatly, capacity is expressed in terms of the quantity of a key input. For example, the capacity of an airline could be expressed as the number of available seat miles, where one available seat mile refers to one airplane seat flying for one mile.[34] A related measure is capacity utilization, which is the percentage of available capacity that is actually used. Higher levels of utilization usually are associated with lower per unit costs because the resources used to provide that capacity are being used more productively. However, utilization levels that are too high can have a harmful effect, as they can restrict a venture's ability to deal with fluctuations in demand and supply, and can lead to burnout among workers. What is judged to be a reasonable utilization level varies with the type of venture and industry.[35] For example, demand in service ventures usually has more variability, so utilization levels are typically lower.

Quality Measures

Quality, its importance, and approaches to managing quality were addressed above. An important element of managing quality is measuring quality. There are several different ways to measure quality performance. Some measures are internal to the venture and are directly linked to the production of the good or service. Examples of these types of measures are defect rates in a factory or the percentage of orders delivered on time by a delivery service. Another type of quality measure is related to the performance of the product or service. An example here would be the horsepower of an automobile or the qualitative review of the taste of the food in a restaurant meal.[36] There are also specific approaches to measuring quality in services. One is the SERVQUAL tool, where customers provide their perceptions of the gaps between their expectations of service performance and the service they actually received.[37] Some firms use customer satisfaction surveys or feedback forms to assess how customers view the firm's products and services. However, these tools, while useful in some ways, have some potential disadvantages as well and should be used with caution.[38]

The **costs of quality** comprise another set of quality performance measures. These costs include

- **Internal failure costs.** Internal failure costs are the costs of defects, scrap, repair, or rework that occur during the production of the product or service and are discovered before the product or service is provided to the customer.

- **External failure costs.** External failure costs are costs that occur because of quality problems and are discovered after the product or service has been provided to the customer. Examples include product return costs, warranty costs, and product liability costs.

- **Appraisal costs.** Appraisal costs include the costs of discovering quality problems or the costs to ensure that quality standards are met. Examples include inspection and testing costs.

- **Prevention costs.** These costs are the costs incurred to prevent quality problems from occurring. Examples include costs of training workers, identification of the causes of quality problems, and actions taken to correct quality problems.

Typically, increases in prevention costs result in better quality and fewer problems, so failure costs are reduced. Better quality usually also reduces the need for inspection and testing, so appraisal costs are reduced as well.[39]

Financial Performance Measures

There are several different financial measures of performance. Three common measures that are used to assess the outcomes of investments are **payback method**, **return on investment**, and **net present value**. Any basic finance textbook provides the details of how to calculate these measures.

There are also measures calculated as ratios from information in the venture's financial statements. There are several different categories of commonly used ratios. Profitability ratios show the income performance of a firm. Liquidity ratios provide measures of the venture's ability to meet short-term obligations; solvency ratios show the firm's ability to meet long-term obligations. Exhibit 12.4 below lists commonly used ratios in each category.

© Jirsak, 2012. Used under license from Shutterstock, Inc.

Financial ratio measures can be particularly useful because they can be used to compare performance of different firms within an industry regardless of the size of the firm.[40]

Regardless of the performance measures are calculated and tracked, whether financial or operational, they are useful only if they are employed as a basis for improvement over time. Standards should be set along each dimension of performance and actual performance compared to these standards. A good performance measurement system provides the entrepreneur with the information to show where managerial attention should be directed. An entrepreneur's time is limited, so it is imperative to know the area of the venture where his or her efforts are best used.

EXHIBIT 12.4 Commonly Used Financial Ratios

Profitability Ratios	
Return on sales	Net income / Total revenue
Gross margin	Gross profit / Total revenue
Return on assets	Net income / Total assets
Liquidity Ratios	
Current ratio	Current assets / Current liabilities
Acid-test ratio	(Cash and near cash assets) / Current liabilities
Accounts receivable turnover	Credit sales / Average accounts receivable
Inventory turnover	Cost of goods sold / Average inventory
Solvency Ratios	
Solvency	Net income before interest and taxes / Interest expense
Debt to equity ratio	Assets financed by debt / Assets financed by equity
Debt to assets ratio	Total debts / Total assets

LINKING OPERATING SYSTEMS TO THE ENTREPRENEURIAL METHOD

In this chapter, we have provided a general, relatively brief, overview of many of the key principles and concepts important in managing operating systems. There are entire courses and college majors devoted to this topic, so we have necessarily touched on only the basics. There are many more references and resources available for you as you need them during the growth and development of your venture. Before ending this chapter, however, we want to focus on some considerations in managing operating systems that are particularly relevant to new ventures and the entrepreneurial method.

Lean Thinking

One of the principles of the entrepreneurial method is to consider the question, "What resources do I control?" In most startups, the answer to this question is "not much." Therefore, in a new venture, the production or delivery of the firm's products or services must usually be accomplished in an efficient, but effective manner. The principles of lean thinking can be very powerful in accomplishing this objective. At its most fundamental level, lean can be described as "doing more with less"—less equipment, less technology, less labor, less space, and less capital—in short, less of all types of resources compared to what a typical organization would need to use to accomplish the same outcome.[41] Any entrepreneur can relate to the need to do more with less, so lean management is an approach that can be used to manage the entire enterprise, not just its operations. The underlying philosophy of lean, and the mechanism through which "doing more with less" is achieved, is the reduction of waste in an organization. Waste is defined to be anything or any activity that does not add value.[42] If you don't expend resources (e.g., money or time) on materials or activities that produce no value, those resources can be directed toward the activities that are valuable.

How can lean thinking be implemented in a new venture? There are several basic principles of lean systems, but for a startup, there are three are probably the most important. One is to understand value from the customer's point of view. A second is to evaluate which parts of the value stream add value and which do not; the steps that do not should be eliminated. The third is to pursue perfection through continuous improvement.[43] In a startup, getting an innovative product or service to market that customers are willing to pay for is probably the most important goal. In the *Lean Startup*, Eric Ries has transformed these basic lean principles into an approach to managing an entrepreneurial firm. The key principle of the *Lean Startup* is that a new venture must be managed in a structured way to quickly learn how to build a sustainable business that will provide customers with products and services they will value. The Lean Startup translates the general philosophy of more traditional lean thinking to enable continuous innovation and business success.[44] The following Bullet Breakout highlights some of the key principles of the Lean Startup.

Flexibility

The entrepreneurial method stresses the importance of creating opportunities using who you are, what you know, and the resources you control. In the previous section, we discussed how you can use the principles of lean thinking to most efficiently employ your resources to create value. However,

Principles of the Lean Startup

- **Eliminate Uncertainty:** The lack of a tailored management process has led many a startup to abandon all process. They take a "just do it" approach that avoids all forms of management. Using the Lean Startup approach, companies can create order not chaos by providing tools to test a vision continuously. Lean isn't simply about spending less money. Lean isn't just about failing fast, failing cheap. It is about putting a process, a methodology around the development of a product.

- **Work Smarter not Harder:** The Lean Startup methodology has as a premise that every startup is a grand experiment that attempts to answer the questions: "Should this product be built?" and "Can we build a sustainable business around this set of products and services?"

- **Develop an MVP:** A core component of Lean Startup methodology is the build-measure-learn feedback loop. The first step is figuring out the problem that needs to be solved and then developing a minimum viable product (MVP) to begin the process of learning as quickly as possible. When this process of measuring and learning is done correctly, it will be clear that a company is either moving the drivers of the business model or not.

- **Validated Learning:** Progress in manufacturing is measured by the production of high quality goods. The unit of progress for Lean Startups is validated learning—a rigorous method for demonstrating progress when one is embedded in the soil of extreme uncertainty. Once entrepreneurs embrace validated learning, the development process can shrink substantially. When you focus on figuring the right thing to build—the thing customers want and will pay for—you need not spend months waiting for a product beta launch to change the company's direction. Instead, entrepreneurs can adapt their plans incrementally, inch by inch, minute by minute.

what happens when things change? Technology can change; customer preferences can change; new competitors can emerge. How will your venture handle these kinds of changes? The answer is flexibility. Flexibility has been defined from a general perspective as the ability to respond to uncertainty. It can be more precisely defined in many different ways, which are outlined in the Introduction to this chapter. Although these forms of flexibility would certainly be likely to help the success of your venture, we would like to consider another form of flexibility: resource flexibility. Resource flexibility is defined here to be the commitment of minimum level of resources that are absolutely necessary to accomplish a specific goal. Resources can include capital, labor, equipment, facilities, or anything else that is necessary to develop and operate your venture. Resource flexibility of this sort will provide your venture with the ability to acquire new resources more easily and apply them to a wider range of possible opportunities, which should provide a better chance of survival and eventual success. Note that this view of flexibility fits well with the notion of lean thinking. The two concepts reinforce and support one another. Ultimately, your goal is to produce a product or service that provides value to your customers while enabling your venture to survive, grow, and profit over time.

SUMMARY OF LEARNING OBJECTIVES

1. **Understand** the elements of an operating system and how they relate to one another. *The operating system is the set of internal processes and supply chain relationships that work together to provide products and services to the venture's customers. The choice and design of internal processes will determine in part the price and quality of your venture's offerings.*

2. **Understand** the principles of operations strategy and how it relates to business strategy. *Operations strategy is long-term planning for how the operating system will support the venture's business strategy. Business strategy goals of cost leadership or differentiation are directly related to operations strategy competitive priorities, such as cost, quality, flexibility, innovation, and time. Structural and infrastructural decisions will be one determinant of which competitive priorities will be achievable for the operating system.*

3. **Understand** how to make structural and infrastructural decisions for your venture's operating system. *Structural decisions are strategic decisions relating to capacity, technology, processes, location, and sourcing. Infrastructural decisions are strategic decisions relating to the workforce, quality, planning and scheduling, and organizational structure. They should exhibit consistency with one another and should fit with the operations strategic competitive priorities.*

4. **Learn** the advantages and disadvantages of outsourcing. *Outsourcing is the procurement of products and services from external organizations. The can be advantages to outsourcing, such as lower cost and more flexibility. However, there can be disadvantages as well, such as the potential loss of control of proprietary technology.*

5. **Apply** the principles of process management so that your venture will be scalable. *It is important that your venture be scalable. Your venture will be scalable if the marginal costs decrease with increasing volume. It is important to choose a process that can easily meet increasing demand without proportional increases in marginal costs. The use of outsourcing can also be an important means to achieve scalability.*

6. **Understand** different types of processes and the principles to use in choosing processes for a new venture. *Operating system processes can be categorized in different ways. Different types of processes have different capabilities and drawbacks and can therefore support different strategic objectives more effectively than others. The choice and design of a process is therefore a critical strategic decision.*

7. **Understand** common approaches to defining and managing quality. *Quality is a term that can be defined in different ways. Two approaches to defining quality are consistent quality, which is the extent to which the product or service meets expectations, and performance quality, which is the extent to which the product or service is superior to other products on features or performance. Quality management systems include total quality management, ISO 9000, and Six Sigma.*

8. **Understand** different types of performance measures and be able to use them in a new venture. *Performance measures can be into two categories: operational measures, such as productivity, quality, capacity utilization, and time; and financial measures, such as net present value, profitability, and liquidity. Performance measures are used to monitor how the venture is operating and to identify areas for improvement.*

9. **Link** the principles of managing operating systems to the entrepreneurial method. *Two key aspects of managing operating systems are particularly relevant to the entrepreneurial method: lean thinking and flexibility. Lean thinking in managing operations enables the entrepreneur to use*

his or her resources effectively and efficiently. Flexibility helps the new venture to survive uncertain times and to take advantage of unexpected opportunities when they present themselves.

QUESTIONS FOR DISCUSSION

1. What is an operating system and what is operations management? Why is operations management important in a startup firm?
2. Discuss how process management is related to operations strategy.
3. Discuss the four types of quality costs and explain how they are related to one another.
4. How would you make a decision about whether to outsource the production of your venture's next new product?
5. How does a venture's operating system relate to its degree of scalability?
6. How is productivity related to a venture's cost to provide its service?
7. Why is it important for a startup firm to have flexibility?

IN-CLASS EXERCISE
Formulating the Operations Strategy for a New Venture

For this exercise, students will formulate an operations strategy for a new venture. They should work in groups of two or three on this exercise. The written part should be done as a take-home assignment. Each group should write a short description of the venture, the products and services it will offer to its customers, and specify the type of venture it is (B2B/product, B2B/service, B2C/product, or B2C/service). The strategy formulation process should follow these steps:

1. Describe the overall business strategy (cost or differentiation) and the business model.
2. Describe the value proposition.
3. Identify the competitive priorities.
4. Identify tradeoffs in competitive priorities that must be made.
5. Make structural decisions about the operating system for the venture:
   a. Capacity
   b. Process(es)
   c. Technology
   d. Location(s)
   e. Supply chain/outsourcing
6. Make infrastructural decisions about the operating system:
   a. Workforce
   b. Quality systems
   c. Planning and scheduling systems
   d. Organizational structure

KEY TERMS

Appraisal costs: The costs of discovering quality problems or the costs to ensure that quality standards are met.

Capacity: The maximum of output an operating system can reasonably produce in a given length of time.

Competitive priorities: The performance dimensions along which the firm intends to excel and gain an advantage in the marketplace. Competitive priorities include cost, quality, time, innovation, and flexibility.

Consistent quality: The product or service meets specifications and performs as expected in a consistent manner, even if it is not the best in the market.

Costs of quality: The costs incurred as a result of quality problems, efforts to assess quality performance, or efforts to improve quality. Costs of quality include internal failure costs, external failure costs, appraisal costs, and prevention costs.

Customization: A form of flexibility that allows a firm to produce a product or service that fits the needs of the customer.

Cycle time: The time interval between the completion of successive finished units in a process.

External failure costs: Costs that occur because of quality problems and are discovered after the product or service has been provided to the customer.

Flexibility: In general, the ability to respond to uncertainty.

Focus: The narrowing of the range of activities over which a venture chooses to engage.

Infrastructural decisions: Strategic decisions that generally involve people and systems, specifically those decisions related to the workforce, quality systems, planning and scheduling systems, and organizational structure.

Innovation: The ability to develop and introduce new, useful, and distinctive products and services. Apple is an example of a company that competes on innovation.

Internal failure costs: The costs of defects, scrap, repair, or rework that occur during the production of the product or service and are discovered before the product or service is provided to the customer.

ISO 9000: A certification that an organization has met a set of standards issued by the International Organization for Standardization (ISO) that describe guidelines and requirements for quality improvement.

Lead time: The total time taken to complete a process (or sub-process) from start to finish.

Lean thinking: A managerial mindset whose main goals are to minimize waste and maximize customer value.

Mass service: A process type that has high labor intensity and low customization such as retail banks and grocery stores.

Net present value: The total of all future cash flows from an investment (taking into the time value of money), less its original cost.

Operating system: The combination of internal processes and supply chain collaborations that provide products and services to a venture's customers.

Operations management: Managing the set of activities included in the operating system that are required to produce a product or service and deliver it to customers.

Operations strategy: The determination of how the competitive positioning, value proposition and business model of the venture will translate to requirements of the operating system.

Outsourcing: The process of procuring products and services from external organizations.

Payback method: An approach to measuring financial performance that calculates the length of time the profits from an investment will take to recover the investment's cost.

Performance measurement: The management activity concerned with assessing performance of specific areas of a business for the purposes of improvement and control.

Performance quality: A characteristic of a product or service that is superior to most or all of the offerings of a firm's competitors.

Prevention costs: The costs incurred to prevent quality problems from occurring.

Process: The series of steps that are used to transform a set of inputs (labor, information, materials) into a valuable output (product or service).

Process management: The choice of the type of process to be used, the design of that process, and the analysis and improvement of that process.

Productivity: A performance measure where Productivity = Outputs / Inputs.

Professional service: A process type that has high labor intensity and high customization, such as lawyers, physicians, and accountants.

Quality: The ability of a product or service to meet customer needs (there are other definitions in the chapter).

Return on investment: A measure of profitability calculated by dividing profit by the amount invested.

Scalability: The ability to meet increasing demand with decreasing marginal costs.

Service factory: A process type that has low labor intensity and low customization, such as airlines and hotels.

Service shop: A process type that has low labor intensity and high customization, such as an automobile repair shop.

Six Sigma: A system of management that is designed to improve quality, reduce costs, and increase customer satisfaction through a formal process improvement model.

Structural decisions: Long-term strategic decisions that generally require relatively large investments. These decisions include choices about capacity, facilities, technology, and sourcing.

Supply chain: A network of organizations that work together to convert raw materials to finished goods.

Time: Time can refer to speed in delivery, reliability in delivery, or speed in product development.

Total quality management (TQM): An approach to managing quality whose elements include top management commitment, employee participation, customer focus, management decision making using objective data, and continuous improvement.

Tradeoffs: The principle of operations strategy that holds that decisions must be made between incompatible goals. It is related to the idea of focus.

Variety: A form of venture flexibility whereby the venture is able to produce a wide range of products or services.

ENDNOTES

[1] Heizer, J., and B. Render, *Operations Management* (Upper Saddle River, NJ: Prentice-Hall, 2011).

[2] Hallowell, R.,"'Scalability': The Paradox of Human Resources in e-commerce," *International Journal of Service Industry Management,* 12(1)(2001): 34–43.

[3] Anderson, J.C., G. Cleveland, and R.G. Schroeder, "Operations Strategy: A Literature Review," *Journal of Operations Management,* 8(2)(1989): 133–158.

[4] Jacobs, R.F., R.B. Chase, and N.J. Acquilano, Operations & Supply Management (New York: McGraw-Hill, 2009).

[5] Boyer, K.K., and R.Verma, *Operations & Supply Chain Management for the 21st Century* (Mason, OH: South-Western, 2010).

[6] Swink, M., S.A Melnyk, M.B. Cooper, and J.L. Hartley, *Managing Operations Across the Supply Chain.* (New York: McGraw-Hill, 2011).

[7] Zeithaml, V.A., L.L. Berry, and A. Parasuraman, "The Behavioral Consequences of Service Quality," *Journal of Marketing,* 60(2)(1996): 31–46.

[8] Simons, D., and R. Mason, "Lean and Green: 'Doing More with Less'," *ECR Journal,* 3(1): 84–91.

[9] Gerwin, D., "Manufacturing Flexibility: A Strategic Perspective," *Management Science,* 39(4): 395–410.

[10] Porter, M., *Competitive Strategy: Techniques for Analyzing Industries and Competitors* (New York: Free Press, 1998).

[11] Jacobs, Chase, and Acquilano, op. cit.

[12] Boyer and Verma, op. cit.; Jacobs, Chase, and Acquilano, op. cit; Stevenson, W.J., Operations *Management* (New York: McGraw-Hill, 2009).

[13] Boyer and Verma, op. cit.

[14] Ibid.

[15] Swink, Melnyk, Cooper, and Hartley, op. cit., p. 284.

[16] Fisher, M.L., "What is the Right Supply Chain for Your Product?" *Harvard Business Review,* 75(2)(1997): 105–116; Lee, H.L., "Aligning Supply Chain Strategies with Product Uncertainties," *California Management Review,* 44(3)(2002): 105–119.

[17] Lankford, W.M., and F. Parsa, "Outsourcing: A Primer," *Management Decision,* 37(4): 310–316.

[18] Jacobs, Chase, and Acquilano, op. cit.

[19] Swink, Melnyk, Cooper, and Hartley, op. cit.

[20] Stevenson, op cit., p. 512.

[21] Shuiabi, E., V. Thomson, and N. Bhuiyan, "Entropy as a Measure of Operational Flexibility," *European Journal of Operational Research,* 165(3)(2005): 696–707.

[22] Hayes, R.H., and S.C. Wheelwright, *Restoring our Competitive Advantage* (New York: John Wiley and Sons, 1984).

[23] Schmenner, R.W., "How Can Service Businesses Survive and Prosper?" *Sloan Management Review,* 27(3)(1986): 21–32.

[24] Cachon, G., and C. Terwiesch, *Matching Supply with Demand: An Introduction to Operations Management* (New York: McGraw-Hill/Irwin, 2009).

[25] Hallowell, op. cit.

[26] Zeithaml, V.A., L.L. Berry, and A. Parasuraman, "The Behavioral Consequences of Service Quality," Journal of Marketing, 60(2)(1996): 31–46.

[27] Garvin, D.A., "Competing on the Eight Dimensions of Quality," Harvard Business Review, 65(6) (1987): 101–109.

[28] Heizer and Render, op. cit.; Boyer and Verma, op. cit.

[29] Stevenson, op. cit.

[30] Trent, R.J., and R. Monczka, "Achieving World-Class Supplier Quality," *Total Quality Management,.* 10(6): 927–938.

[31] Kaplan, R.S., and D.P. Norton, "The Balanced Scorecard—Measures that Drive Performance," *Harvard Business Review*, 70(1): 71–79.

[32] Jacobs, Chase, and Acquilano, op. cit.

[33] Griffith, R., E. Huergo, J. Mairesse, and B. Peters, "Innovation and Productivity across Four European Countries," *Oxford Review of Economic Policy*, 22(4)(2006): 483–498.

[34] Cachon and Terwiesch, op. cit.

[35] Kimes, S.E., "Yield Management: A Tool for Capacity-Constrained Service Firms," *Journal of Operations Management*, 8(4)(1989): 348–363.

[36] Fynes, B., C. Voss, and S. de Burca, "The Impact of Supply Chain Relationship Quality on Quality Performance," *International Journal of Production Research*, 96(3): 339–354.

[37] Parasuraman, A., V.A. Zeithaml, and L.L. Berry, "SERVQUAL: A Multiple-Item Scale for Measuring Consumer Perceptions of Service Quality," *Journal of Retailing,* 64(1)(1988): 12–40.

[38] Duening, T.N., and W.W. Sherrill, *Entrepreneurism* (Cincinnati, OH: Atomic Dog Publishing, 2006).

[39] Jacobs, Chase, and Acquilano, op. cit.

[40] Duening and Sherrill, op. cit.

[41] Womack, J.P., and D.T. Jones, *Lean Thinking: Banish Waste and Create Wealth in Your Corporation* (New York: Simon & Schuster, 1996).

[42] Womack and Jones, op. cit.

[43] Boyer and Verma, op. cit.

[44] Ries, E., *The Lean Startup* (New York: Crown Business, 2011).

ENTREPRENEURIAL LEADERSHIP

Learning Objectives

As a result of studying this chapter, students will be able to:

- **Understand** various theories of leadership and how they affect leadership behaviors.

- **Apply** the situational approach to leadership.

- **Understand and develop** personality traits that are important to leadership.

- **Develop** the traits and skills of charismatic leadership.

- **Apply** both task-oriented and person-oriented leadership styles.

- **Craft** a "Big Hairy Audacious Goal" (BHAG) for a venture.

- **Understand** how entrepreneurial leadership is important to the entrepreneurial method.

- **Develop** your leadership skills, values, and attitudes.

- **Act** according to basic principles of entrepreneurial ethics.

INTRODUCTION

Leadership is a topic that has been discussed, debated, and researched for thousands of years. Ancient civilizations, primitive tribes, and modern people all express fascination for leadership and for those who are chosen to be leaders. If you think hard about leadership, you probably will agree that there is an air of mystery surrounding the term. For example, we probably can all agree on people that we'd classify as leaders. The following list comes to mind:

- Abraham Lincoln
- Martin Luther King, Jr.
- Mahatma Gandhi
- Margaret Thatcher
- Steve Jobs
- Bill Gates
- Oprah Winfrey

What we would have a more difficult time agreeing upon is what *makes* each of these people leaders. Some might say that all leaders have charisma. Others might say that all leaders are outgoing, intelligent, tall, articulate, or possibly hundreds of other things. As it turns out, however, scholarly research into the traits or characteristics that are *necessary* for leadership has come up empty. It seems clear from the research that leaders are highly diverse. What all leaders do have in common is the ability to influence other people, and to inspire them to high levels of performance. How that is achieved, however, varies greatly from leader to leader.

We can probably all agree that leadership is relatively easy to observe, but very difficult to define. **Entrepreneurial leadership** is our topic in this chapter. Fortunately, since we are not trying to describe leadership in a general sense, our task of defining our topic and finding ways to help you develop your own entrepreneurial leadership skills is a bit easier. We define entrepreneurial leadership as:

> *Leadership that creates visionary scenarios that are used to assemble and mobilize a 'supporting cast' of participants who become committed by the vision to the discovery and exploitation of strategic value creation.*[1]

This definition includes several key components that you've already learned about in this text. For example, the notion of "visionary scenarios" was discussed in Chapter 1 when we introduced you to the entrepreneurial method. There, you learned that expert entrepreneurs tend to envision multiple potential outcomes based on the resources they currently control. These visionary outcomes are inconceivable to someone who sets a single goal and then goes out and tries to acquire the resources necessary to achieve that goal. The expert entrepreneur, in contrast, is not entirely sure where his or her journey will end, but there are multiple possible outcomes that would constitute success.

The "supporting cast" referred to in the definition above is simply the "Crazy Quilt Principle." You learned that expert entrepreneurs rarely achieve their success without a cadre of strong and talented people around them. The expert entrepreneur is adept at attracting people to his or her venture and mobilizing them for directed action to pursue market opportunities.

We have also been discussing throughout this text the notion of entrepreneurship as a discovery process. You've learned that expert entrepreneurs aren't interested in attempting to remove every bit of uncertainty before they proceed to explore their markets. They use price, feature sets, and various strategic initiatives to learn more about their customers and their true wants and needs rather than settling for their stated wants and needs.

In this chapter we are going to introduce you to various ways of understanding entrepreneurial leadership and discover how you can develop your own leadership capacity. First, we'll discuss several different conceptions of leadership. These conceptions apply to business leaders in a wide range of settings. Each of these conceptions has some utility to entrepreneurial leaders, but none of them are complete or comprehensive in isolation. That is to say, scholars are largely in agreement that leadership depends in large part on the context, circumstances, and situations in which it is exercised. Some contexts call for quick action and authoritarian style—imagine a fire chief on the scene of a raging house fire and, before taking action, organizing a brainstorming session with the firefighters on the scene to determine the best action to take to quench the fire. Such an "open leadership" style in that circumstance would not be a sound choice. Other contexts call for more participation, deliberation, and collaboration. Consider the entrepreneur who wants the venture to explore new foreign markets with the existing product set. Clearly such an adventure will require a collaborative effort that may include some people in the foreign countries. Entrepreneurs who rush into new foreign markets may find themselves completely unprepared for the conditions there and may place the entire venture in jeopardy.

Fortunately, entrepreneurship presents a relatively stable context of value creation, market discovery, and profit seeking. In this relatively stable context it is possible to identify leadership tactics that, generally, are more effective than others. We will explore the leadership tactics of expert entrepreneurs and provide you with some clear guidelines that have proven effective in a wide range of entrepreneurial settings.

Finally, entrepreneurial leadership is not necessarily something that you were born with. Rather, leadership is a personal characteristic that you can develop. In Chapter 2 we discussed the concept of "deliberate practice." There, we recommended using this technique of expertise development to enhance your cognitive skills in the areas of opportunity recognition, risk minimization, resilience, design thinking, and effectual reasoning. Deliberate practice can also be used to develop and enhance your entrepreneurial leadership skills. We will provide you with some clear objectives and character traits that you can work on via deliberate practice and deliberate performance to improve your entrepreneurial leadership capacities.

Let's begin with a brief overview of some of the leading concepts of leadership that have been developed over the past several decades.

OVERVIEW OF LEADERSHIP

The exercise of influence is often said to be the essence of leadership behavior. Seven influence strategies have been proposed as vital for practicing leadership roles:[2]

- Reason—Using facts and data to develop a logically sound argument

- Friendliness—Using supportiveness, praise, and the creation of goodwill

- Coalition—Mobilizing others in the organization

- Bargaining—Negotiating through the use of benefits or favors

- Assertiveness—Using a direct and forceful approach

- Higher Authority—Gaining the support of your board, investors, and other stakeholders

- Sanctions—Using rewards and incentives to motivate the venture team

Leaders need to learn a variety of influence strategies; they cannot rely solely on the traditional strategy of exercising the power they possess by virtue of their position in the formal hierarchy. In addition, in entrepreneurial settings it's recognized that employees should be allowed to influence the way the organization works. Organizational psychologist Noel M. Tichy said, "The ultimate test for a leader is not whether he or she makes smart decisions and takes decisive action, but whether he or she teaches others to be leaders and builds and organization that can sustain success even when he or she is not around."[3]

Leadership has been one of the most studied topics in management, yet the conclusions reached have been contradictory, exaggerated, and controversial. Part of the problem lies in the definitions, measurements, and theories used to study leadership. The three main approaches at the center of the debate surrounding leadership are as follows:

- **Trait Theory of Leadership**: Attributes performance differences among employees to the individual characteristics (traits) of leaders.

- **Behavioral Theory of Leadership**: Attributes performance differences to the behaviors and style of leaders.

- **Contingency Theory of Leadership**: The leader's behavior and style in combination with situational factors are the key reason for performance differences.

Over the years each of these main approaches has been refined and various dimensions have been added, but they still remain the primary basis for leadership theory, research, and application discussions.

Trait Theory of Leadership

We observe strong leaders such as Mark Zuckerberg of Facebook, Indra Nooyi of Pepsi, and Ursula Burns of Xerox. So it's natural to ask whether the secret of leadership is to be found in the individual characteristics of leaders. Are there differences between leaders and non-leaders in terms of personality traits, physical characteristics, motives, needs? Many people believe that effective leadership has roots in a particular personality trait. Some even assume that unless one possesses that trait, he or she is doomed to fail as a leader.

The trait theory of leadership constitutes an important but somewhat controversial approach to understanding leadership. Boiling leadership down to specific human traits or characteristics seems simplistic. What trait or combination of traits could be consistently linked with leadership? None have been found. For example, not all effective leaders are tall or exceptionally smart. Not all effective leaders are charismatic or glib. In addition, there are cultural differences in the traits that are necessary for effective leadership. A good entrepreneurial leader in an American venture may not have the traits needed to be successful in, say, a Chinese venture.

© Gemenacom, 2012. Used under license from Shutterstock, Inc.

Although the trait theory has its problems, it can't be denied that leaders exhibit traits that followers admire. The systematic study of the personal characteristics and traits of leaders began as a consequence of the need for military officers during World War I. Many business and governmental organizations also began researching the characteristics that distinguished their most effective from the less effective managers.

Even today, some scholars believe that the trait theory is valid. They believe that leaders are defined by their various physical, personality, and intelligence traits.[4] Let's examine these in more detail.

PHYSICAL TRAITS: Some advocates of the trait theory contend that the physical characteristics of a person affect their ability to influence followers. For example, an extensive review of twelve leadership investigations showed that nine of the studies found leaders to be taller than followers; two found them to be shorter; and one concluded that height was not the most important factor.[5] Other physical traits that have been studied with no conclusive results include weight, physique, and personal appearance. One physical characteristic that consistently has been associated with leadership is "energy level." Sustained high achievement requires physical stamina and research has shown that good leaders typically have high energy levels and an ability to tolerate stress.[6]

PERSONALITY TRAITS: A number of studies have found several personality factors to be related in some, but not all, cases of effective leadership.[7] These studies have found that leaders with the drive to act independently and with self-assurance (e.g., with confidence in their leadership skills) are successful in achieving task and group performance. Research suggests that leadership in entrepreneurship requires intelligence, common sense, high energy levels, a willingness to work hard, and good timing.[8] Further, leadership writer Max Depree lists twelve attributes of successful leadership as identified in the following Bullet Breakout:[9]

In fact, there may be as many personality attributes of leaders as there are scholars of the topic. Nonetheless, you can probably find some similarity across the different lists. Common themes that seem to emerge include: intelligence, curiosity, empathy, and high energy. Another leadership factor that has been the subject of much study over the recent past is ethics.

INTELLIGENCE TRAITS: After surveying the literature, one scholar concluded that leadership ability is associated with the judgment and verbal facility of the person.[10] Another researcher concluded

Max Depree's List of Necessary Attributes for Leadership

- Integrity

- Vulnerability

- Discernment

- Awareness of the human spirit

- Courage in relationships

- Sense of humor

- Intellectual energy and curiosity

- Respect for the future, regard for the present, understanding of the past

- Predictability

- Breadth

- Comfort with ambiguity

- Presence

that within a certain range, one's intelligence is an accurate predictor of managerial success.[11] Above and below this range, the chances of successful leadership decrease significantly. However, the leader's intelligence should be close to that of the followers. The leader who is too smart or not smart enough may lose the followers' respect.

Warren Bennis, a scholar of leadership, has argued that leaders of the future will need very high IQs to deal with increasingly complex organizations. He said, "The basis for effective leadership in the future will be the cognitive capacity to deal with complex issues. I think that by 2020 we will see chairs of neuroscience in business schools to deal with these issues." Bennis still believes that leaders are made rather than born. However, "We must make people brainier and we really need to rethink how we educate people to go into business."[12]

New research has identified another kind of intelligence—emotional intelligence—as also important to leadership. Research has suggested that a person's emotional quotient, or EQ, underpins many of the decisions that business leaders make. There are a number of characteristics that make up a person's EQ: trusting relationships; effectiveness under pressure; authenticity, emotional honesty, integrity, and accountability; constructive discontent; unique potential and purpose; initiative; and creativity and innovation.

Charismatic Leadership

Another trait that is often associated with leadership is **charisma**. Warren Buffett at Berkshire Hathaway, Richard Branson of Virgin Group, and Elon Musk of Tesla Motors are examples of leaders with charisma. A charismatic leader is a person who by force of personal abilities and style is capable of having a profound and extraordinary effect on followers.[13] The charismatic leadership view combines both traits and behaviors to describe this type of leader.

What Buffett, Branson, and Musk are able to do because of their energy, self-confidence, and dominating personalities is to project a conviction in the moral rightness of their beliefs.[14] Charismatic leaders generate excitement and increase the expectations of followers through their visions of the future. Research suggests that charismatic leadership is a function of what followers perceive. Some fortunate individuals are born with this gift, but most charismatic leaders apparently learn it and use it with great success.[15] Through interviews with ninety reputedly charismatic leaders, researchers identified a set of behavior strategies used by these individuals as follows:

- **Focusing attention** on specific issues of concern, concentrating on analysis, problem solving, and action.

- **Communicating** with empathy and sensitivity.

- **Demonstrating consistency** and trustworthiness by one's behavior, being honest, sticking with a decision, and following through on decisions.

- **Expressing active concern for people** including one's self, thus modeling self-regard, and reinforcing feelings of self-worth in others.[16]

Others have developed a matrix of five characteristics of charismatic leaders:

- Strategic vision and articulation

- Sensitivity to the environment

- Unconventional behavior

- Personal risk

- Sensitivity to other's needs

These five characteristics are good predictors of whether people consider a leader charismatic or non-charismatic. Their presence in a leader is significantly associated with the perception that that leader is charismatic.[17] The findings also indicate that charismatic leaders may be trained to use charismatic leadership behaviors. The following Research Link describes a 2011 study that indicated people can learn to be more charismatic.

RESEARCH LINK

Can You Learn to be Charismatic?

An interesting study was reported in the scholarly literature on leadership in 2011 that addresses whether charisma can be taught. The investigators created a training program that was designed to test whether they could teach individuals to behave more charismatically. The study group consisted of forty-one MBA students who were videotaped in the laboratory giving a speech. Next, the investigators taught the students how to behave more charismatically in the delivery of their speech and they redelivered the same speech six weeks later. Results from the study indicated that the charisma training had significant effects on the independent ratings of each speaker's charisma. The investigators concluded, "The results of our laboratory study indicate that charisma can be taught."

Source: Antonakis, J., M. Fenley, and S. Liechtl, "Can Charisma be Taught? Tests of Two Interventions," *Academy of Management Learning & Education*, 10(3)(2011): 374–396.

Behavioral Theory of Leadership

The disappointing results of the search for leadership traits have led to a somewhat different line of thought. Rather than focusing on the characteristics of effective leaders, an alternative is to focus on their behavior. The question of behavioral leadership theories then becomes: What do effective leaders do that ineffective ones do not do? For example, are effective leaders democratic rather than autocratic, permissive rather than directive, person-oriented rather than task-oriented? Generally, these behaviors refer to whether the leader's style reflects primary concern for the work or for the people who are doing the work. We noted earlier that the essence of leadership is getting work done through others. One point of view holds that the best way to lead is to be task-oriented.

TASK-ORIENTED LEADERSHIP: Task-oriented leaders emphasize the need to plan each worker's job tasks and job outcomes. The leader is assumed to be the most competent individual in planning and organizing the work of subordinates. To ensure that each task is performed according to the plan, the worker is paid on an incentive basis. The performance standards are stated in terms of quantity and quality of output, and the worker is paid for each unit of acceptable quality.

Although the origins of task-oriented leadership can be found in literature first published some seventy years ago, some modern leaders still believe that task-oriented behavior is the most effective for obtaining performance. At the same time, an emerging perspective that has gained wide influence is person-oriented leadership.

PERSON-ORIENTED LEADERSHIP: Rensis Likert is a pioneer in the development of the idea that the behaviors of the most effective leaders are person oriented. Likert and his associates at the University of Michigan have conducted studies in various organizational settings such as industrial, governmental, educational, and healthcare. These studies have led Likert to conclude that the most effective leaders focus on the human aspects of their groups. They attempt to build effective teamwork through supportive, considerate, and non-punitive employee-centered behavior. Such leaders were found to be more effective than those who emphasized task-centered behavior; that is, leaders who specifically detailed the work of subordinates, closely supervised them, and rewarded them only with financial incentives.[18]

Thus, it would seem that we are left with the choice that the effective leader is *either* task oriented or person oriented, but not both. And if this is the case, then aspiring leaders need only a narrow range of skills. If the most effective leaders are task oriented, then leaders need only be skilled in the technical aspects of planning and organizing the work of others. But if the most effective leaders are person oriented, then human relations and interpersonal skills are required. But what if both points of view are correct? Some believe that effective leaders are equally task and person oriented in their behavior toward subordinates.

Contingency Theory of Leadership

An increasing number of researchers are prone to believe that the practice of leadership is too complex to be represented by unique traits *or* behaviors. Rather, a current idea is that effective leadership behavior is contingent upon the situation. One variation of the idea assumes that leaders must change behaviors to meet situational needs. A second variation assumes that leaders' behaviors are difficult to alter and that the situation itself must be changed to make it compatible with the leaders' behavior.

The contingency theory of leadership is considerably more complex than either the trait or the behavioral approach. As indicated in Exhibit 13.1, effective leadership depends on the interaction of

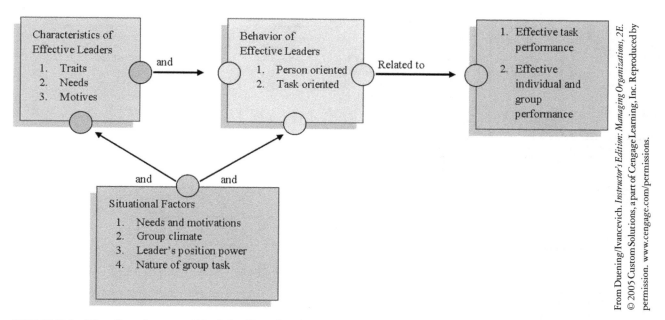

EXHIBIT 13.1 The Contingency Model of Leadership

Source: Duening, T.N. and J.M. Ivancevich, *Managing Organizations* (Cincinnati, OH: Atomic Dog Publishing, 2006).

the leader's personal characteristics, the leader's behavior, and factors in the leadership situation. In a sense, the situational approach is based on the idea that effective leadership cannot be defined by any one factor. This approach does not deny the importance of the leader's characteristics or behavior. Rather, it states that both must be taken into account and considered in the context of the situation.

LEADERSHIP FLEXIBILITY FIT THE LEADERSHIP STYLE TO THE SITUATION: A recurring theme in leadership theory and practice is the concept of "participation" by subordinates in decision making. This theme originated in the writings of the behavioral approach to management, and it has held a prominent place in the thinking of managers for the last forty years. The fundamental idea is shown in Exhibit 13.2.[19]

At the extremes of this continuum are boss-centered leadership and subordinate-centered leadership. Between these extremes are five points representing various combinations of managerial authority and subordinate autonomy. One of the extreme positions, boss-centered leadership, represents a leader who simply makes a decision and announces it. The subordinate-centered leader permits subordinates to participate fully in decision making. Within prescribed limits, the subordinates act as partners with the leader.

The proponents of participative leadership believe that the difficulty is not so much in convincing people that they must change their behavior as the situation changes, but in teaching leaders how to recognize the need for the change. Whether a leader should make the decision and announce it (boss-centered) or share the problem with subordinates and seek group consensus (subordinate-centered) depends on the interaction of factors related to the problem and to the subordinates. Factors related to the problem are:[20]

- The likelihood that one solution to the problem is more effective than another.

- The extent to which the leader has sufficient information to make a high-quality decision.

- The extent to which alternative solutions are known with some certainty.

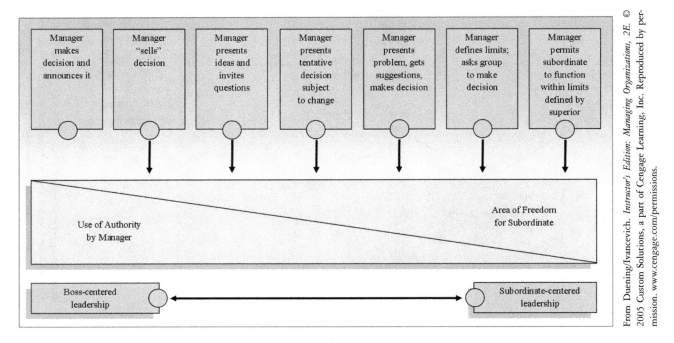

| Manager makes decision and announces it | Manager "sells" decision | Manager presents ideas and invites questions | Manager presents tentative decision subject to change | Manager presents problem, gets suggestions, makes decision | Manager defines limits; asks group to make decision | Manager permits subordinate to function within limits defined by superior |

Use of Authority by Manager

Area of Freedom for Subordinate

Boss-centered leadership ⟷ Subordinate-centered leadership

EXHIBIT 13.2 Flexibility Model of Leadership

Source: Duening, T.N,. and J.M. Ivancevich, *Managing Organizations* (Cincinnati, OH: Atomic Dog Publishing, 2006).

Factors related to subordinates are:

- The likelihood that effective implementation of the solution depends on subordinates accepting it as appropriate.

- The likelihood that if the leader makes the decision, the subordinates will accept it.

- The extent to which subordinates recognize and accept the organizational objectives to be attained by the solution.

- The likelihood that conflict among subordinates will result if the preferred solution is adopted.

In a practical sense, combining these seven factors creates different situations. At one extreme are situations for which a number of solutions exist, none of which require acceptance by subordinates for effective implementation. The leader should make the decision and announce it. On the other hand, participation is warranted to the extent that only one solution is likely and its consequences are not known with certainty and subordinates have relevant information and their acceptance is necessary for implementation. The effective leader changes style whenever the situation demands it. That is, the leader is flexible enough to be relatively task-centered or employee-centered as situations change.

Contingency theory also suggests that leadership style should be matched to the strategic choices available in the firm's competitive environment. Research has indicated that entrepreneurs who align their strategic choices to the competitive environment are more successful than those who cling to a single strategic direction.[21]

LEADERSHIP FLEXIBILITY: FIT THE LEADERSHIP STYLE TO FOLLOWERS: Paul Hersey and Kenneth H. Blanchard have developed the **situational theory of leadership**.[22] This explanation is based on the belief that the most effective leadership style varies with the readiness level of followers. Readiness level is viewed as consisting of two components—job-related and psychological. Job-related readiness refers to the ability to perform a task. Psychological readiness refers to a person's willingness to perform a job. Four distinct levels of maturity exist:

R1: Person is unwilling and unable to perform the job.

R2: Person is unable but willing to perform the job.

R3: Person is able but unwilling to perform the job.

R4: Person is able and willing to perform the job.

The situational theory suggests that as the individual matures from R1 to R4, the leadership style must change to fit that changing maturity level. Hersey and Blanchard identified four leadership styles:

S1: Telling—the leader has to tell the employee what to do in great detail;

S2: Selling—the leader has to sell the employee on the value of the task;

S3: Participating—the leader participates in the task with the employee;

S4: Delegating—the leader fully delegates the task to the employee.

There are some exceptions to the situational theory. For example, when faced with a crisis situation involving filling an important order, a leader may find it necessary to be very task oriented (e.g., use telling style (S1) even when the followers are very mature (R4)). However, using the high-task, low-relationship leadership style over an extended period of time likely will result in a backlash from followers. A mature follower wants to be treated in a particular way.

The situational theory has intuitive appeal. However, the theory assumes that leaders are perceptive enough to accurately pinpoint maturity levels. The theory also assumes that followers will agree with a leader's assessment of their maturity level.

Also, the situational theory assumes that a leader is flexible enough to move through four phases or back and forth. Is this amount of flexibility possible? Hersey and Blanchard think so, but research evidence to support their views is quite limited. In fact, the validity of measurement instruments and the relationship of the model to performance has not been carefully investigated by independent researchers.

Despite some shortcomings, the situational theory has generated interest among practicing managers. It calls attention to the need to be flexible. Leadership is, after all, a dynamic process that requires flexibility. Also, the situational theory illustrates the interactive nature of leadership. That is, a leader can influence followers, but followers, because of their maturity level, can also influence leadership behavior.

ENTREPRENEURIAL LEADERSHIP

Most advocates of organizational effectiveness will argue that leadership should pervade the organization. The same thing is true of entrepreneurial ventures. Leadership is something that expert entrepreneurs want to encourage and cultivate among everyone in the venture. Yet, there must be a **lead entrepreneur** who creates the vision and structure that others will practice their leadership within. When we refer to entrepreneurial leadership, then, keep in mind that we are talking primarily about the role of the so-called lead entrepreneur. Typically, this is the founder of the venture, but it may be an individual who has replaced the founder during later stages of a venture's growth and life.

A hallmark of the entrepreneurial leader is the ability to attract other key people to the venture team, and then building the team for success. The quality of the team that the entrepreneurial leader is able to attract and motivate is strongly connected with the growth and success potential of the venture.[23] An effective entrepreneurial team is able to devise creative strategies to aggregate and gain control of vital resources. It is also adept at identifying entrepreneurial opportunities to enable firm growth.[24]

Another key skill of the entrepreneurial leader is the ability to frame challenges so that members of the team can understand them and act autonomously to overcome challenges and achieve venture goals. The entrepreneurial leader frames the overall challenge facing the venture via creation of a **vision** that captivates the attention of the venture team and motivates them to strive for common goals.

In their book *Built to Last* Jim Collins and Jerry Porras advocated that entrepreneurial leaders should develop what they call "Big Hairy Audacious Goals" or **BHAGs**. In their book the authors elaborate that "a true BHAG is clear and compelling, serves as a unifying focal point of effort, and acts as a catalyst for team spirit. It has a clear finish line, so the organization can know when it has achieved the goal; people like to shoot for finish lines. A BHAG engages people—it reaches out and grabs them. It is tangible, energizing, highly focused. People get it right away; it takes little or no explanation."[25] Exhibit 13.3 provides an illustration of how a BHAG combines passion, expertise, and economic reality.

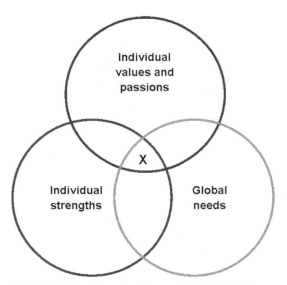

EXHIBIT 13.3   Creating Your BHAG: "X" Marks the Spot

Another key skill the entrepreneurial leader needs to develop is tolerance of ambiguity and uncertainty. In fact, the lead entrepreneur should develop the ability to absorb ambiguity, enabling the rest of the team to focus on the BHAG. The uncertainty that all new ventures experience can only be relieved over time via market exploration and discovery. The entrepreneurial leader must decide on which experiments the venture will run and how to interpret the results to enable forward progress. Entrepreneurial leaders must also be effective communicators and skillful networkers. Expert entrepreneurs know that the ability to develop and maintain relationships can be vital to overcoming challenges.

The entrepreneurial leader must demonstrate resolve in the face of competition and other obstacles to growth. Expert entrepreneurs understand that there are no pat answers regarding how obstacles to growth are to be overcome. This is where innovation and creativity come into play. The entrepreneurial leader must be the driving force that propels the team toward success through constant innovation and a fierce determination to overcome all obstacles to growth. Interestingly, expert entrepreneurs know that determination to succeed must be tempered by flexibility in strategies and tactics.

Finally, the entrepreneurial leader must be the venture's primary **change agent**. A change agent is someone who is comfortable with instigating and managing change. All ventures experience unexpected opportunities and/or setbacks for which it is currently unprepared. For example, the venture's primary product may experience far greater demand than had been forecast. This can be disastrous if the venture team is unable to adjust and find creative ways to increase production to meet the greater-than-forecast customer demand. The entrepreneurial leader must recognize the pressures that affect the venture's ability to deliver value to customers and to encourage and motivate the team to creatively adjust the venture to meet the unexpected challenges.

Entrepreneurial Leadership and the Entrepreneurial Method

Let's now examine how entrepreneurial leadership meshes with the entrepreneurial method. In Chapter 1 we described the principles of the entrepreneurial method. Entrepreneurial leadership cuts across all of these principles. For example, the "Crazy Quilt" principle speaks to the entrepreneurial leader's need to develop networks and relationships that can be leveraged in time of need. The "Bird in the Hand" principle speaks to the need to recognize the resources that are currently controlled and for the need to continue to gather new resources as the venture grows and learns. The entrepreneur must exhibit leadership in managing the venture's limited resources, and drive that cost consciousness throughout the organization. The "Pilot in the Plane" principle defines the expert entrepreneur's propensity toward self-determination. The entrepreneur must exhibit the determination that we described as necessary to earn buy-in from others to achieve the BHAG vision. The "Affordable Loss" principle addresses the need for the venture to manage risk effectively. The entrepreneur, as we stated, must be willing to absorb the ambiguity and risk the venture faces so that others can focus on what they do best. And, finally, the "Lemonade Principle" speaks to the ability to respond to obstacles and surprises with resilience and determination. The entrepreneur needs inspire the team to develop innovative responses to the challenges the venture inevitably will face.

Entrepreneurial leadership also cuts across all of the cognitive skills that we discussed in Chapter 2. To refresh your memory, the five cognitive skills that we identified with expert entrepreneurs include:

- Opportunity recognition
- Design thinking
- Risk management

- Resilience
- Effectual logic

It's clear from our discussion above that the entrepreneurial leader must be adept at opportunity recognition. In addition, the entrepreneurial leader should also encourage and promote opportunity recognition among the venture team. As we identified in our discussions on customer service, it is often the customer-facing employees of a venture who are most likely to receive feedback that can be converted into new venture opportunities. The entrepreneurial leader is often not involved in day-to-day customer interactions. As such, it is imperative that the leader encourage opportunity recognition among all of the venture's employees and stakeholders. The entrepreneurial leader should also be open to gathering and sharing customer information broadly with the venture team to promote innovative approaches to solving customer problems and meeting customer needs.

Design thinking is a mindset used by entrepreneurial leaders to create the type of organization and organizational culture where everyone on the venture team is aligned with the venture's goals. Entrepreneurial leaders design workspaces that promote interaction and fluid workflow. They also design jobs and responsibilities that align well with the skills and talents of the individuals recruited to the venture. Entrepreneurial leaders must develop the capacity to assess the talents of the individuals that comprise the venture team and then put them into positions where they can effectively use those talents to benefit the venture. It is wasteful to recruit, train, and place someone into the venture's structure if they are not put in a position where they can be successful.

Design thinking also affects the offerings that a venture brings to the marketplace. Obviously, offerings must be designed according to what is desirable to customers, what is possible to create with current technologies, and what is the minimally viable offering that the marketplace will accept. These principles are illustrated in Exhibit 13.4.

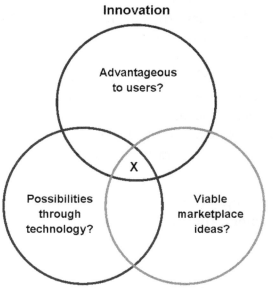

EXHIBIT 13.4 Design Thinking Applied to the Venture's Offerings

Resilience is one of the more central characteristics that is required of the entrepreneurial leader. The turbulence that most startups endure is often difficult to manage emotionally, financially, and physically. The entrepreneurial leader must be the one who maintains the equilibrium of the venture through the turbulence. Everyone possesses some ability to remain strong in the face of ambiguity, uncertainty, and stress. The entrepreneurial leader should be exceedingly aware of his or her personal capacities in this area, and strive to improve through experience, reflection, and personal growth. Increased resilience will happen naturally through experience for most entrepreneurs as they struggle, fail, and recover. But there are things the entrepreneurial leader can and must do to enhance personal resilience. For example, we discussed in Chapter 3 the need for emotional intelligence. This means that the entrepreneurial leader is aware of personal emotions and uses proven and tested strategies to manage them. For example, if the venture is experiencing difficult times financially, the entrepreneurial leader must control personal feelings about those difficulties to prevent those feelings from affecting the performance of the venture team. If the leader walks around with a "woe is me" look or grumbles aloud about the state of the venture's finances, it is likely to have a negative effect on team performance. At a time when performance is needed more than ever, the entrepreneurial leader's lack of emotional control could subvert that performance. The following Mini-Case highlights one young entrepreneur who preserved through several failed ventures to achieve eventual success.

MINI-CASE

Resilience Proves Vital for One Entrepreneur

Jesse Schwarz was always trying new things to make money. In college, he ran a small used car lot with his friend. Later, he opened a chicken restaurant that lasted a total of thirty days before going under. Dusting himself off from that failure, Jesse launched a new business providing high-end coffee makers to professional offices. This lasted until his foreign suppliers proved too unreliable to build a scalable business around. With a dwindling savings account, a wife, and two kids, Jesse knew his next venture had to be a hit. So, rather than investing in some new product, restaurant, or other scheme, he decided to invest in himself. Even though he had no technical background, Jesse decided to teach himself how to succeed in e-commerce. He learned everything he could from free resources on the Internet. Eventually, he decided to launch a service that would provide consumers with an easy-to-understand comparison shopping site for high-speed Internet service providers. Using Commission Junction as his primary service for managing click-through transactions, Jesse built a thriving business. Within months he was making more than $3,000/month, and within a couple of years his venture was cash flowing more than $50,000/month. Jesse's resilience through several failed ventures led to his ultimate success.

Source: Duening, T.N., *Experience Starting an Internet Marketing Company* (Colorado Springs, CO: Businesses2Learn Publishing, 2011).

Risk management is definitely the job of the entrepreneurial leader. Risk management can only be effective when the organization is aware of the risks that it faces. Entrepreneurial leaders who don't allow the venture team to share data and information with each other are likely to be ineffective risk managers. As we stated earlier, many new venture leaders are averse to bad news and may even react negatively when bad news is brought to their attention. Venture team members will notice this behavior pattern and may develop the propensity to hide bad news, or at least shield the entrepreneurial leader from the bad news. And yet, it is the bad news that must be communicated so that the venture can respond and manage it. The risk of venture failure grows in proportion to its inability to absorb and respond to the bad news related to its performance in the marketplace. Entrepreneurial leaders must encourage a venture culture where bad news is seen as a necessary evil in order to develop the venture's capacity to manage the various risks that it faces.

Finally, effectual logic is the province of the entrepreneurial leader, but also that of others—and maybe everyone—on the venture team. Recall that effectual logic begins with the means, rather than the ends, firmly in mind. The entrepreneurial leader is the one who establishes the vision of how the venture's resources are to be deployed to explore and exploit the business opportunities before it. While it would not be appropriate for everyone on the venture team to conjure their own unique visions, they can use effectual logic to imagine new ways to use resource under their own control to meet the objectives of the venture. Very few new venture jobs will be as routine as jobs that may be found, for example, on a factory production line. Rather, jobs within a new venture will be characterized by variety, uncertainty, and goal ambiguity. As such, the entrepreneurial leader should encourage venture team members to think autonomously, make good decisions, and use their own creative and innovative ideas to achieve venture goals. Exhibit 13.5 illustrates how effectual logic differs from other logics commonly used in larger organizations that no longer rely on the non-predictive control that expert entrepreneurs use to build their ventures.

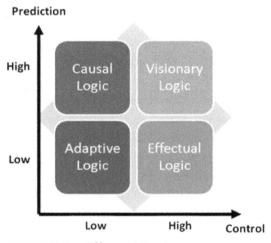

EXHIBIT 13.5   Effectual Logic

As you can see, you cannot escape the role of entrepreneurial leader, or of becoming the lead entrepreneur, in your own venture. In order to realize the principles and mindsets of the expert entrepreneur, you must adapt, accept, and develop your leadership capabilities. Perhaps this is obvious, as it seems to follow that one cannot succeed as an entrepreneur unless one is also a good leader. But in reality, many entrepreneurs become their own worst enemies and are unable to grow their ventures because they fail to develop their leadership capabilities. The annals of entrepreneurial ventures are awash with tales of entrepreneurs who were terrific founders, but poor leaders. Some of these ventures are rescued by kicking the founding entrepreneur out of the venture to enable someone with superior leadership skills to take over. In order to prevent that from happening to you, you need to be aware of your own current leadership skills and abilities, and of the need for you to develop them as you grow your venture.

DEVELOPING YOUR LEADERSHIP SKILLS

Developing your abilities as an entrepreneurial leader requires paying attention to the principles of the entrepreneurial method and the mindsets that are important to develop as an aspiring entrepreneur. We've already described the processes of deliberate practice and deliberate performance in Chapter 2. Certainly, these techniques of expertise development should be used in your journey to become a more effective leader.

In this section we want to offer some suggestions about leadership skills and abilities that you can work on to improve your personal leadership capabilities. Let's begin with an ability that you will use every day and that is often cited as the skill set that is the most deficient: communication.

Communication Skills

Developing your abilities to communicate with your venture team is critical to your long-term success as an entrepreneur. One type of communication travels from individual to individual in face-to-face and group settings. Such flows are termed **interpersonal communication**, and the forms vary from direct verbal orders to casual, nonverbal expression. Interpersonal communication is the primary means of managerial communication; on a typical day, over 75 percent of an entrepreneurial leader's communication occurs via face-to-face interactions.[26]

The problems that can arise when leaders attempt to communicate with other people can be traced to perceptual and interpersonal style differences. Each person perceives the world in terms of his or her background, experiences, personality, frame of reference, and attitude. The primary manner in which people relate to and learn from the environment (including people in that environment) is through information received and transmitted. The way leaders receive and transmit information depends partly on how they relate to themselves and others. The way a leader commonly relates to others is known as interpersonal style.

INTERPERSONAL STYLE: Interpersonal communication style differs among individuals, and understanding these differences is important for managerial and organizational performance. **Interpersonal style** refers to the way in which an individual prefers to relate to others. The fact that much of the interaction among people involves communication indicates the importance of interpersonal style.[27]

Some communication style differences among people are unintentional or unconscious. For example, research into differences between male and female voice tones has indicated that they differ acoustically, and sex-stereotyped attributions are formed based on gender of voice. This research reported that men's voices are less nasal than women's voices, and that nasality of voice is inversely related to perceptions of persuasiveness. In other words, the less nasal the voice, the more persuasive it was perceived to be by listeners.

Good communicators learn to recognize their interpersonal style and the styles of others. They also learn to modify their style to enhance the likelihood of effective communications. For example, look at the following groups of words, and identify which group you are most like, and which you are least like.

- Group 1: direct, bold, daring, self-starter, challenge-oriented, competitive
- Group 2: enthusiastic, persuasive, sociable, inspiring, talkative, optimistic

- Group 3: amiable, relaxed, patient, good listener, steady, logical
- Group 4: perfectionist, analytical, precise, diplomatic, accurate, restrained

Let's say that you are most like Group 2, and least like Group 4. You work with a colleague who is quiet, cautious, analytical, and somewhat pessimistic, a behavioral style clearly quite different from yours. If you communicate with your usual enthusiastic, optimistic verve, it is likely to be less effective when dealing with this person. Learning to adapt your style, however, diminishes communication tension. In this situation, by simply moderating some of your enthusiasm and slowing down your pace of speech, you will inevitably establish better rapport.[28]

Individuals striving to become better communicators must accomplish two separate tasks. First, they must improve their messages—the information they wish to transmit. Second, they must improve their own understanding of what other people are trying to communicate to them; they must become better listeners.

© Orna Ydur, 2012. Used under license from Shutterstock, Inc.

ACTIVE LISTENING: Effective interpersonal communication requires that each participant not only hear the words that are said but also understand their meaning. This task requires the ability to listen—to focus on the speaker, block out distractions, and carefully comprehend the communicator's message. Although listening is a key requirement for effective communication, most individuals listen at only a 25 percent level of efficiency.[29]

Several factors hinder effective listening. Perhaps the primary obstacle is in an individual's free time while listening. On average, an individual speaks about 125 words a minute but listens at a rate that is more than three times as fast (from 400 to 600 words a minute). As a result, 75 percent of listening time is free time-that is, time to become mentally sidetracked by any number of distractions.[30] The physical surroundings, the speaker's appearance, his mention of a controversial concept or idea, or a problem nagging at the listener—can all compete for a listener's attention.[31]

Time, money, and opportunities are frequently lost because of poor listening skills. A poor listener is not only rude, but is not prepared to take advantage of a situation, to seize an opportunity, or to properly be in position to help others. Too many people take active listening skills for granted. They believe that hearing and listening are synonymous terms. They do not realize that listening is much more than hearing sound vibrations. Active listening is hard work because a person not only hears what is said, but also attempts to understand the facts and feelings of the speaker and tries to convey to the speaker that, "I understand what you are saying."

Decision-Making Skills

All entrepreneurs must make decisions, and the quality of these decisions determines their degree of effectiveness. An entrepreneur's decision-making skill in selecting a course of action is greatly influenced by his or her ability to deal with ambiguity. One of the hallmarks of startup ventures is their ambiguity.[32] They are often ambiguous with respect to their market, their value proposition, their competition, and even their ability to persist. Entrepreneurs must learn to resist pressures for a quick fix when problems and issues arise. They must learn to live with uncertainty and ambiguity and to recognize subtleties in what works and what does not.[33]

Decision making in startup ventures is almost always done in the face of irresolvable ambiguity. This is something that the entrepreneur must learn to accept. Yet, the ambiguous nature of many of the issues the entrepreneur faces must not lead to inaction or paralysis. The entrepreneur must have a predilection toward action and must be able to make decisions in the face of incomplete information. The term that is often used to describe this situation is **satisficing**. This means that the entrepreneur must choose the best solution to a problem despite incomplete information about both the problem and the likely outcome of the decision that is taken.[34] Choosing the best alternative is a vastly different decision than choosing the *correct* alternative. Making a decision among alternatives in running a startup venture is different than selecting among alternatives on a multiple-choice exam or in crafting a solution to a problem posed in a textbook. In the world of the startup, there usually is no *correct* course of action, but there often is a best one.

Team-Building Skills

Rare is the lone-wolf entrepreneur. Most ventures are too complicated for a single person to operate without help from others. Successful entrepreneurs are usually talented team builders. They are able to attract other people to their vision, and then build them into a coherent team, all focused on pursuing the same goals. Team building is based on identifying gaps in talent and skills that are required for the venture to succeed, then finding people with these necessary traits. Successful entrepreneurs are able to attract employees, advisors, and investors who provide them with missing talent that is required to achieve venture goals.

Building successful teams requires each of the skills mentioned above, and also a strong helping of humility. Successful entrepreneurs attest to the importance of hiring and motivating people more talented than themselves. In fact, the strongest performing entrepreneurial leaders are not afraid to hire people who are more talented than they are. This statement may seem obvious, but it is not uncommon for entrepreneurs to feel intimidated by people who are more talented than they are. Entrepreneurs must replace their feelings of competitiveness among their peers with competitiveness as a venture leader. That means swallowing one's ego and hiring talented people who will help the venture compete in its market and achieve its goals. Analytical skills in evaluating, selecting, and motivating talented people are immensely important in venture performance.

The foundation of successful teams is simple: clarity of goals and responsibilities. Highly talented people are usually self-motivated to a high degree. They want to do a good job and enjoy working on goals that are clearly defined and are measurable. Expert entrepreneurs have learned that they can expect a high degree of commitment from talented people without a lot of managerial intervention. That is, talented people usually perform at their peak when leaders provide them with their goals, then get out of their way. Teams organized around specific projects and goals will often self-organize. Google, for example, allows its engineers to choose the projects that they work on, with very little day-to-day oversight on their work. This relaxed approach to managing can only work in an environment where the vision and goals are clear and understood by all and where rewards and incentives are directly linked to performance that helps the venture achieve its objectives.

Self-Awareness Skills

Improving yourself in any role you are in, such as being a student, a parent, a friend, or a leader, requires taking control of determining who you are by conducting your own personal analysis. You need to think about situations in which you succeeded. What were the factors that led to that success? Hard work? Good planning? Problem-solving skill? Patience? Examining previous experiences involves self-talk, reflection, and analysis.

Unfortunately, memories often leave out data, information, and critical incidents. Creating a daily journal or diary is a good method to keep track of vital components of your successes. Keeping a journal for 10 to 20 days about your interactions with other people—friends, colleagues, teachers, bosses, vendors—requires discipline. The journal can be simply structured by using a date and summary comments about:

1. What I did today
2. Whom I interacted with today
3. What kind of thoughts I had today
4. What I used to solve any problems or new situations I was faced with

Simple, concise journal entries will help you conduct a review and analysis. About ten days of entries will provide, at a minimum, a picture of how you typically behave and think.

A second method of data gathering for self-awareness is to complete self-assessment surveys. They can be a confidential source of information that only you control. To improve any skill, there is a need for feedback. Online assessments about your personality, skills, abilities, and attitudes can provide eye-opening feedback for you.

Friends and colleagues are another source of feedback. Some colleagues and friends will be reluctant to provide honest, accurate, and revealing feedback. You may have to create a framework and presentation that explains clearly why you need their feedback. Asking for their help to improve your understanding and knowledge of "who you are" can be convincing when presented as a request for assistance.

Matching the feedback of others with your own self-awareness analysis is educational and can be invaluable. You learn firsthand how others see you and it enables you to match this information with your self-concept. Discrepancies can occur and need to be evaluated carefully. The evaluation should consider the information—your own and that of others. Once a thorough evaluation is completed and analyzed it is then time to consider what skills you need to work on to improve. What skills do I need to be successful in my life, career, and job? The feedback process will definitely provide you with insight into areas that need to be sharpened and refined. Overall, you self assessment should focus on three major areas that you can focus on as a means of improving your personal leadership skills: personality, values, and attitudes.

PERSONALITY: Personality is a set of physical and psychological variables that create individual uniqueness. A key personality factor is self-concept; the view you hold of yourself as a physical, social, and spiritual person. Two related aspects of self-concept are self-esteem and self-efficacy. **Self-esteem** is a belief about one's own worth. People with high self-esteem see themselves as worthwhile, vital, and important. **Self-efficacy** is a person's belief that he or she can successfully accomplish a job, a task, or an activity.

VALUES: **Values** are a person's preferences concerning appropriate courses of action. Values provide a picture of a person's sense of what is correct, fair, or right. Parents, mentors, friends, teachers, and role models in general impact a person's values. Since learning and experiences differ from one person to another, values are also differences.

The noted psychologist Milton Rokeach developed two broad value categories. **Terminal values** reflect a person's preferences concerning the "ends" to be achieved. **Instrumental values** reflect a person's preferences for the means to be used in achieving end states.[35] Exhibit 13.6 presents Rokeach's classification of values system.

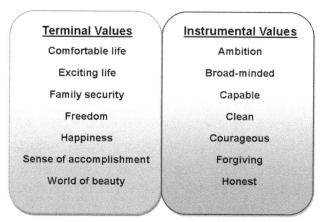

Terminal Values

Comfortable life

Exciting life

Family security

Freedom

Happiness

Sense of accomplishment

World of beauty

Instrumental Values

Ambition

Broad-minded

Capable

Clean

Courageous

Forgiving

Honest

EXHIBIT 13.6   Rokeach's Value Classification

Empirical research has determined that both terminal and instrumental values differ across groups (e.g., leaders, union members) and individuals.

ATTITUDES: Attitudes can be characterized in various ways. First, they tend to persist unless something is done to change them. Second, attitudes can be favorable or unfavorable. Third, attitudes are directed toward some object about a person's feelings and beliefs. Thus, **attitudes** are a persistent tendency to feel and behave in a particular way toward some object.

Attitudes can be depicted as consisting of three components: emotion, information, and behavior. The emotional component consists of a person's feelings or affect. The informational component consists of the beliefs and information you have about an object. It doesn't matter whether the information is correct or incorrect. The behavioral component consists of your tendencies to behave in a certain way. Only the behavioral component can be observed by others. One cannot see emotions unfold or the beliefs a person has about something. These two components must be inferred.

Attitudes serve a number of functions. First, attitudes help people adjust to their work environment.[36] When employees are treated well, fairly, and honestly they tend to develop positive attitudes. When employees are embarrassed, intimidated, and threatened by leaders, they are likely to adopt negative attitudes toward others, the job, and the employer. Second, attitudes help you defend your self-images. By changing and altering attitudes, a person is able to keep a balanced self-concept and ego. Keeping one's self-image positive and in balance are important for being motivated to perform well. Third, attitudes provide the basis for expressing your values. For example, a person who has a strong work ethic will tend to voice attitudes about the importance of providing "a good day's work for a good day's pay." The person's core values are articulated to others and this provides a view of what the person represents.

ENTREPRENEURIAL ETHICS

Ethics is often a difficult topic to address in a business-oriented textbook. For the most part, people who excel in business are not also deeply familiar with the terminology and concepts that comprise a standard course in ethics. Many business people also regard the topic as "fuzzy" and difficult to comprehend because there are so many differing perspectives on the topic. In fact, many business people live daily by the adage "if you can't measure it, it doesn't exist."

Ethics can be simple or hard. It is simple when individuals decide on a few basic principles that will guide them in their lives and stick with these principles, come what may. It is hard when people believe that ethics can be nuanced and that situations must be judged independently to know what the right course of action may be. This textbook does not have enough space to take the nuanced approach to understanding entrepreneurial ethics. As such, it takes a more straightforward, principles-based approach to understanding this important topic.

Fortunately, it does not require that you have a master's degree in philosophy to understand some basic principles of entrepreneurial ethics. One very successful media entrepreneur, Karl Eller, summed up entrepreneurial ethics in the title of a book he wrote about his own successful ventures: *Integrity Is all You've Got*.[37] **Integrity** is defined, basically, as doing what you say and saying what you do.

© Alike You, 2012. Used under license from Shutterstock, Inc.

Integrity is a good starting point for a set of ethical principles. It would be difficult to argue the opposing perspective that integrity is not important, or that a lack of integrity is important to business success. In fact, most successful business people will attest to the role that integrity plays in their ability to make things happen. Most business is transacted within a framework of trust. Business people trust that those with whom they are associated will follow through on commitments and contracts to which they are counter-parties. Although contracts and commitments are normally also governed by legal rules, business people don't want to have to resort to lawyers, lawsuits, and the court system every time they want to achieve a business goal. Rather, they want to work with people who will deliver on promises. A single failure to fulfill a contractual obligation, or to honor one's word, or to deliver on a promise can ruin a reputation.

Another principle that should be closely aligned to integrity is honesty. In business, the virtue of honesty is also sometimes referred to as "transparency." This simply means that the venture is operating each day in a manner that would pass a formal financial audit, and it is operating generally according to what is referred to as "good faith." This term means that counterparties to a contract or business relationship are using their best efforts to deliver their end of the contract.

Clearly, not all business transactions or arrangements live up to their expectations. However, parties that act in good faith and in a transparent manner generally will not suffer any negative legal consequences as a result of a failure. The free-market system is often described as a profit and loss system. That is, business transactions occasionally fulfill and even exceed profit expectations. On the other hand, often times they do not, and parties to the transaction suffer financial loss. This is normal, and parties can recover to work together again in the future if they believe each has operated honestly and in good faith and will likely act similarly in the future.

A final ethical principle that we will discuss in this chapter and that seems essential for business success is humility. Humility has often been described as a character trait, but it can also be expressed as an ethical principle. An individual who expresses humility is one who recognizes that many of the good and bad things that happen in life and in business are often a function of chance events. Consider the founders of Google, Sergey Brin and Larry Page. Certainly these are two shining stars among the entrepreneurs of our time. They not only have created a singularly impressive company, but they have achieved incredible levels of personal wealth. Their success, no doubt, can be attributed to their respective talents in computer programming and website design. These talents are clearly relevant to the technology age in which we live. But, what if Page and Brin had come of age in 1890 rather than 1990? Would their unique talents have been as applicable in that long-ago time period? Clearly, they would not have founded Google. Not only was there no Internet in 1890, there were no computers, databases, or even electric power. The point is, despite the great success of Google, Page and Brin have to admit they were lucky to have been born during an age when their unique talents are highly prized and rewarded. That would not have been the case had they come into the world 100 years earlier.

Most success is attributable to a complex mix of personal talent, fortunate circumstance, and chance events. Entrepreneurs who recognize that will be able to maintain an authentic humility during times of success and will also be more balanced personally during difficult times. In fact, several authors have coined the term "egonomics" to refer to the importance of keeping one's ego in check and developing humility.[38] These authors list four warning signs that indicate when an individual's ego has taken over:

1. **Being Comparative:** When we're comparative, we tend to either pit our strengths against another's weaknesses, which may lead us to an exaggerated sense of confidence, or we compare our weaknesses to their strengths, which can cause negative self-pressure.

2. **Being Defensive:** When we can't "lose," we defend our positions as if we're defending who we are, and the debate shifts from a we-centered battle of ideas to a me-centered war of wills.

3. **Showcasing Brilliance:** The more we want or expect people to recognize, appreciate, or be dazzled by how smart we are, the less they listen, even if we do have better ideas.

4. **Seeking Acceptance:** When we equate acceptance or rejection of our ideas with acceptance or rejection of who we are, we "play it safe." We tend to swim with the current and find a slightly different way of saying what's already been said as long as acceptance is the outcome. That not only makes us a bland follower, but an uninspiring leader.

It is important to recognize how humility fits within the spectrum of possible character orientations, from a completely empty ego to egotism. Exhibit 13.7 provides a useful illustration that humility is in the middle of these two ends of the spectrum. According to this illustration, humility represents a healthy and intelligent understanding of one's unique talent and skills, but avoids the destructive potential of overconfidence and egotism.

EXHIBIT 13.7   The Humility Continuum

SUMMARY OF LEARNING OBJECTIVES

1. **Understand** various theories of leadership and how they affect leadership behaviors. *In this chapter, we discussed the trait, behavior, and contingency theories of leadership. There is consensus that leaders possess a diversity of traits, but none are necessary for leadership. Leadership behaviors center on task or person orientation, each of which has different contexts where they are appropriate. Contingency theories, such as the situationalist theory of leadership, require the leader to be flexible and adapt behaviors to followers.*

2. **Apply** the situational approach to leadership. *The situational approach to leadership requires that the leader adjust his or her behavior to the maturity or readiness level of the follower.*

3. **Understand and develop** personality traits that are important to leadership. *Scholars have identified a range of personality traits that are important to leadership, including things like integrity, vulnerability, discernment, courage, sense of humor, and others.*

4. **Develop** the traits and skills of charismatic leadership. *Charismatic leaders have well-developed skills in focusing the attention of followers, communicating with empathy and sensitivity, demonstrating consistency and trustworthiness, and expressing active concern for others.*

5. **Apply** both task-oriented and person-oriented leadership styles. *Task-oriented leaders tend to focus on getting things done at the expense of interpersonal relationships. Person-oriented leaders tend to focus on keeping people satisfied. Strong entrepreneurial leaders learn when each style is appropriate and how to develop a blend of each orientation.*

6. **Craft** a "Big Hairy Audacious Goal" (BHAG) for a venture. *A BHAG is a compelling vision that is communicated throughout the venture and motivates people to perform at high levels.*

7. **Understand** how entrepreneurial leadership is important to the entrepreneurial method. *Each of the principles and mindsets of the entrepreneurial method is a component of and vital to effective entrepreneurial leadership.*

8. **Develop** your leadership skills, values, and attitudes. *Leadership skills highlighted in this chapter include communication skills, decision-making skills, team-building skills, and self-awareness skills.*

9. **Act** according to basic principles of entrepreneurial ethics. *Entrepreneurial ethics can be consolidated into three primary characteristics that the entrepreneurial leader should strive to develop: integrity, honesty, and humility.*

QUESTIONS FOR DISCUSSION

1. Identify several people that you regard as leaders. What do these people have in common? How are they different? Do you think they were born to be leaders or did they develop their own capabilities?

2. How do you think entrepreneurial leadership differs from leadership in other walks of life? Explain your response.

3. Explain the various theories of leadership: trait theory, behavioral theory, contingency theory. What can the aspiring entrepreneurial leader take away from these various understandings of leadership?

4. Explain the situationalist theory of leadership. How can the entrepreneurial leader use this approach to deal with members of the new venture team?

5. How do you identify a leader who is charismatic? How would you use personal charisma to lead an entrepreneurial venture?

6. How does "task-oriented" leadership differ from "person-oriented" leadership? How should the entrepreneurial leader use each of these approaches in leading a new venture?

7. What does the term "Big Hairy Audacious Goal" (BHAG) mean? How does the entrepreneurial leader develop a BHAG? How does the entrepreneurial leader use the BHAG to motivate others?

8. Explain how entrepreneurial leadership is a major part of the entrepreneurial method. Explain this in terms of the five principles of the entrepreneurial method. Explain this in terms of the mindsets of the entrepreneurial method.

9. What is meant by the term "entrepreneurial ethics"? What are the key characteristics the entrepreneurial leader should develop to be regarded as an ethical leader?

IN-CLASS EXERCISE

This is a short test of a person's entrepreneurial personality. As mentioned in this chapter, self-knowledge is an important part of entrepreneurial success. While this short quiz will not definitively determine whether one can be or is an entrepreneur, it is the beginning of self-knowledge.

Yes   No   Maybe

1. I am persistent.
2. When I'm interested in a project, I needless sleep.
3. When there's something I want, I keep my goal clearly in mind.
4. I examine mistakes and learn from them.
5. I keep New Year's resolutions.
6. I have a strong personal need to succeed.
7. I have new and different ideas.
8. I am adaptable.
9. I am curious.
10. I am intuitive.
11. If something can't be done, I find a way.
12. I see problems as challenges.
13. I take chances.
14. I'll gamble on a good idea even if it isn't a sure thing.
15. To learn something new, I explore unfamiliar subjects.
16. I can recover from emotional setbacks.
17. I feel sure of myself.
18. I'm a positive person.
19. I experiment with new ways to do things.
20. I'm willing to undergo sacrifices to gain possible long-term rewards.
21. I usually do things my own way.

22.   I tend to rebel against authority.

23.   I often enjoy being alone.

24.   I like to be in control.

25.   I have a reputation for being stubborn.

Scoring:

For each "Yes" response give yourself 3 points. For each "Maybe" response give yourself 2 points. For each "No" response give yourself 0 points.

If you scored between 60 and 75, you can start that business plan. You have the earmarks of an entrepreneur.

If you scored between 48 and 59, you have potential but need to push yourself. You may want to improve your skills in your weaker areas. This can be accomplished by either improving yourself in these areas or by hiring someone with these skills.

If you scored between 37 and 47, you may not want to start a business alone. Look for a business partner who can complement you in the areas where you are weak.

If you scored below 37, self-employment may not be for you. You will probably be happier and more successful working for someone else. However, only you can make that decision.

Source: Adapted from the U.S. Small Business Administration, www.sba.gov/starting_ business/startup/entrepreneurialtest.html

KEY TERMS

Attitudes: A persistent tendency to feel and behave in a particular way toward some object.

Big hairy audacious goal (BHAG): A goal that is clear and compelling, serves as a unifying focal point of effort, and acts as a catalyst for team spirit.

Change agent: Someone who is comfortable with instigating and managing change.

Charisma: A person who by force of personal abilities and style is capable of having a profound and extraordinary effect on followers.

Entrepreneurial leadership: Leadership that creates visionary scenarios that are used to assemble and mobilize a "supporting cast" of participants who become committed by the vision to the discovery and exploitation of strategic value creation.

Instrumental values: Values that reflect a person's preferences for how ends are to be achieved.

Integrity: Doing what you say and saying what you do.

Interpersonal communication: Communication between people that involves oral, written, and nonverbal modes of expression.

Interpersonal style: The way in which an individual prefers to relate to others.

Lead entrepreneur: New ventures are characterized by many team members being entrepreneurs. Yet, someone must be the lead entrepreneur and establish the vision for the venture.

Satisficing: The decision-making skill where the entrepreneur doesn't look for the perfect solution, but looks for the best one under the circumstances.

Self-efficacy: A person's belief about his or her own ability to successfully accomplish a task, job, or activity.

Self-esteem: A belief about one's own worth.

Situational theory: A contingency theory of leadership that says the effective leader must adapt his or her leadership style to the readiness or maturity level of the follower.

Terminal values: Values that reflect a person's preferences for the ends to be achieved.

Values: A person's preferences concerning appropriate courses of action.

Vision: A future state articulated by the lead entrepreneur and that captivates and motivates the new venture team.

ENDNOTES

[1] Gupta, V., I.C. MacMillan, and "Synopsis of Entrepreneurial Leadership: Developing and Measuring a Cross-Cultural Construct," *Journal of Business Venturing*, 19(2004): 241–260.

[2] Kipnis, D., S.M. Schmidt, C. Swaffin-Smith, and I. Wilkinson, "Patterns of Managerial Influence: Shotgun Managers, Tacticians, and Bystanders," *Organizational Dynamics*, 12(3)(1984): 58–67.

[3] Cited in V. Pospisil, "Nurturing Leaders" *Industry Week* (November 17, 1997): 35.

[4] Baker, R.A., "How Can We Train Leaders If We Do Not Know What Leadership Is?" *Human Relations*, 4(1997): 343–362.

[5] Stogdill, R., "Personal Factors Associated with Leadership," *Journal of Applied Psychology,* 1(1948): 35–71.

[6] Loehr, J., "The Making of a Corporate Athlete," *Harvard Business Review*, 79(1)(2001): 120–128.

[7] Ghiselli, E.J., "Managerial Talent," *American Psychologist*, 10(1963): 631–641.

[8] Warren, E.K., "Dealing with Change," *The CPA Journal*, 67(8)(1997): 68–69.

[9] DePree, M., "Attributes of Leaders," *Executive Excellence*, 4(1997): 8.

[10] Stogdill, op cit., 40–42.

[11] Ghiselli, op cit., 633–635.

[12] Pickard, J., "Future Organizations Will Need Higher IQs," *People Management,* 3(24)(1997): 15.

[13] House, R.J.,"Research Contrasting the Behavior and the Effect of Reputed Charismatic Visions Reported by Non-Charismatic Leaders," Paper presented at the annual meeting of the Administrative Science Association of Canada, Montreal.

[14] Boal, K.B., and J.M. Bryson,"Charismatic Leadership: A Phenomenological and Structural Approach," in *Energy Leadership Vistas,* ed. J.G. Hunt, B.R. Billiga, H.P. Dachler, and C.A. Schriesheim (Lexington, MA: Lexington Books, 1998), pp. 11–28.

[15] Howell, J.M.,"A Laboratory Study of Charismatic Leadership," Paper presented at the annual meeting of The Academy of Management, San Diego.

[16] Bennis, W.G., and B. Nannus, *Leaders* (New York: Harper & Row, 1985); and M. Sashkin, *Trainer Guide: Leader Behavior Questionnaire* (Bryn Mawr, PA: Organizational Design and Development, 1985).

[17] Conger, J.A., R.N. Kanugo, et al., "Measuring Charisma: Dimensionality and Validity of the Conger-Kanugo Scale of Charismatic Leadership," *Canadian Journal of Administrative Sciences,* 9(1997): 290–302.

[18] Likert, R., "Management Styles and the Human Component," *Management Review,* 66(10)(1977): 23–28; 43–45.

[19] Tannenbaum, R., and W.H. Schmidt, "How to Choose a Leadership Pattern," *Harvard Business Review,* 51(3)(1973): 162–180.

[20] Vroom, V., and A. Jago, "Decision Making as a Social Process: Normative and Descriptive Models of Leader Behavior," *Decision Sciences,* 5(4)(1974): 743–770.

[21] Priem, R.L., "Executive Judgment, Organizational Congruence, and Firm Performance," *Organizational Science,* 5(3)(1994): 421–437.

[22] Hersey, P., and K.H. Blanchard, *Management of Organizational Behavior* (Englewood Cliffs, NJ: Prentice-Hall, 1979).

[23] Watson, W.E., L.D. Ponthieu, and J.W. Critelli, "Team Interpersonal Effectiveness in Venture Partnerships and Its Connection to Perceived Success," *Journal of Business Venturing,* 10(1995): 393–411.

[24] Timmons, J.A., New Venture Creation: *Entrepreneurship in the 1990s* (Homewood, IL: Irwin Publishing, 1999).

[25] Collins, J.C., and J.I. Porras, Built to Last: *Successful Habits of Visionary Companies* (New York: HarperBusiness, 1994).

[26] Luthans, F., and J.R. Larsen, "How Managers Really Communicate," *HumanRelations,* 39(2)(1986): 161–178.

[27] Hill, J., "Communications Revisited," *California Management Review* (1973): 56–67.

[28] Aldisert, L., "What Is Your Communication Style?" *Bank Marketing,* 32(10)(2000): 46.

[29] Walker, S., "Listening Skills for Managers," In J.L. DeGaetani (ed.), *The Handbook of Executive Communication* (Homewood, IL: Dow Jones-Irwin, 1986), p. 651.

[30] Hamilton, C., and B.H. Kleiner, "Steps to Better Listening," *Personnel Journal,* 2(1987): 20–21.

[31] Kiechell, W., III., "Learn How to Listen," *Fortune,* 8(1987): 107–108.

[32] Companys, Y.E., and J.S. McMullen, "Strategic Entrepreneurs at Work: The Nature, Discovery, and Exploitation of Entrepreneurial Opportunities," *Small Business Economics,* 28(4)(2007): 301–322.

[33] Ucbasaran, D., "The Fine 'Science' of Entrepreneurial Decision Making," *Journal of Management Studies,* 45(1)(2008): 221–237.

[34] Winter, S.G., "The Satisficing Principle in Capability Learning," *Strategic Management Journal,* 21(10/11)(2000): 981–996.

[35] Rokeach, M., *The Nature of Human Values* (New York: Free Press, 1973).

[36] Katz, R.L., "Skills of an Effective Administrator," *Harvard Business Review,* 33(1)(1974): 90–102.

[37] Eller, K., *Integrity Is All You've Got* (New York: McGraw-Hill, 2004).

[38] Marcum, D., and S. Smith, Egonomics: *What Makes Ego our Greatest Asset (or Most Expensive Liability).* Fireside Publishing, 2007)

VALUING AND EXITING YOUR VENTURE

Learning Objectives

After studying this chapter, students should be able to:

- **Prepare** the venture for due diligence.

- **Conduct** a valuation of the venture using several techniques.

- **Build** a venture in a manner that maximizes enterprise value.

- **Select** an exit strategy that best fits the wishes of the owners.

- **Execute** the various exit strategies options available.

- **Recognize** the various factors that may influence a decision to use merger as an exit strategy.

- **Understand** the various advantages and disadvantages of each exit strategy.

INTRODUCTION

Perhaps the most ironic part of the entrepreneurial method is the need to build your venture everyday with some idea of how you will exit. The reason this is important is that there are different options for exiting your venture and each option requires that you build your venture in different ways. For example, if you intend to pass on your venture to your heirs, there are things that you should do to prepare them for a smooth succession. On the other hand, if you are planning on exiting your venture via a sale of stock on a public stock exchange, you will be focusing on different types of things than if you were handing the keys to your heirs.

A good bit of advice that expert entrepreneurs learn to follow is to "manage your business every day as if you are going to sell it tomorrow." The reason this is good advice is because you never really know when the right offer may come along that enables you to sell the business that you've diligently been building. If you've been practicing good business techniques along the way, the path to completing the sale will be far smoother. For example, no one wants to purchase a business at top dollar if it has been doing a terrible job with its accounts or if it is dealing with multiple ongoing lawsuits. Expert entrepreneurs know that it is important to pay attention to the details of the business. And this needs to be done whether it is the entrepreneur or someone else who actually keeps track of the details. Ultimately, of course, the entrepreneur is responsible for creating the business culture that leads to a well-run business venture.

In the case that you intend to sell your venture to another party, whether it is another entrepreneur, another venture, or to a venture capital firm, the other party is going to perform what is called **due diligence** on your venture. The due diligence process usually includes a thorough on-site visit to your venture's headquarters, review of the accounts, and many other things. In this chapter, we'll introduce you to the due diligence process and discuss how you can be prepared for that in the event that you will one day desire to sell a venture you've created.

The due diligence process is generally undertaken for two purposes. One is to evaluate the long-term viability of the venture, as we've mentioned. The other reason to conduct due diligence is to help establish a value for the venture. **Valuation** is the term used to refer to the process and calculations used to establish a dollar value for your venture. You will need to establish a value for your venture when you exit. You'll also need to establish a value for your venture any time you sell equity to others. We discussed valuation very briefly in Chapter 8 when we explored the venture fundraising process. The same techniques that you use to value your venture for an exit are used to value your venture for a fundraising transaction. We will provide you with some simple techniques that can be used to establish a reasonable value for your venture.

The primary purpose of a venture's **exit strategy** is to develop a roadmap by which early-stage investors can realize a tangible return on the capital they invested. The entrepreneur spells out a reasonable scenario—the exit strategy—by which Shareholders will be able to realize the cost value of their ownership interest in the venture.[1] Second, the intent of an exit strategy is to suggest a proposed window in time that investors can tentatively target as their **investment horizon,** placing a limit on their involvement in the early-stage funding deal. The founding team wants to assure investors that the venture will grow to a point whereby the initial investors will receive all of their original investment back, plus a sizable return for the risks they took by investing in a startup venture. To investors and other shareholders of a private venture the exit is a **liquidity event.** It is the event that enables them to convert their shares into cash.

The problem in projecting an exit strategy is that it's based on several major assumptions. The speed of market penetration, the ability to sell at expected price levels, the costs of doing business, the margins on sales, the management team's ability to arrange consistent deals, and the impact of competition and other economic factors collectively affect the new venture's projected market share and bottom line. Certainly, when these factors are all aligned in the most favorable way, the firm will experience significant market share, consistent high-growth sales rates, strong profit margins, and positive earnings. And such a scenario in the first two to three years is typically the story told by firms that eventually go public.

In this chapter, we provide an overview of the various ways that you may elect to exit your venture. The options that we will review include passing on the venture to heirs (succession), selling the venture to another party (acquisition), merging the venture with another firm, or taking the venture public through an initial public offering (IPO). Each of these exit strategies provides you with different challenges and opportunities as the entrepreneur/owner. We will examine each exit strategy, discuss how the venture should be positioned during its growth stages to best pursue each of the various exit strategies, and review the advantages and disadvantages of each.

Let's begin by examining the due diligence process that precedes most exit strategies.

DUE DILIGENCE

The exit process normally involves deep analysis of the venture, its operating history, future prospects, and any other things. This analysis is referred to as *due diligence* and is normally conducted by the parties that are interested in acquiring or investing in the venture.[2] Due diligence involves examining a number of key elements of the target venture, including its financial health, the status of the target firm's product line, the potential for synergy, the market position and future potential of the venture, the research and development history and roadmap for the venture, legal considerations, and plans for managing the acquired entity.[3] Let's examine each of these factors in turn with an eye toward common analyses used in the due diligence process and how the entrepreneur can prepare.

Finances

The due diligence process begins with a financial analysis—analyzing the profit and loss figures, operating statements, and balance sheets for the years of the company's operation, concentrating on the more recent years. Past operating results, particularly those occurring in the preceding three years, indicate the potential for future performance of the company. Key ratios

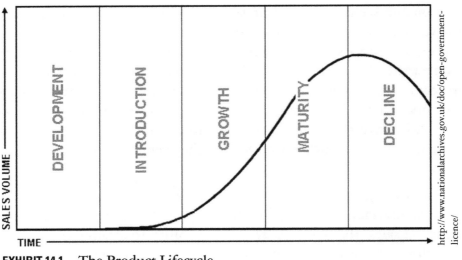

EXHIBIT 14.1 The Product Lifecycle

and operating figures, concepts discussed in detail in Chapters 6 and 12, indicate whether the company is financially healthy and has been well managed. Areas of weakness, such as too much debt, too little financial control, dated and slow-turning inventory, poor credit ratings, and bad debts are also carefully evaluated. The entrepreneur can prepare the venture for this portion of the due diligence process by ensuring accurate, timely, and regular accounting reports have been prepared and filed. Here's where the entrepreneur can take advantage of having invested in hiring an accountant to ensure all the books have been well managed and stand up to auditing review.

Product/Service Line

The past, present, and future of a firm's product lines will also be examined. The strengths and weaknesses of the firm's products are evaluated in terms of design features, quality, reliability, unique differential advantage, and proprietary position. The life cycle and present market share of each of the firm's products are verified. One method for evaluating the product line is to plot sales and margins for each product over time.[4] Known as S- or lifecycle curves, these indicate the life expectancy of the product and any developing gaps. The S-curve analysis could reveal that all products of this firm are at or near their period of peak profitability. We discussed the product lifecycle in Chapter 10. Exhibit 14.1 is a representation of the product lifecycle. It's important to know the lifecycle status of the venture's product lines to understand whether there is a fit with the acquiring party's product portfolio and operating expertise. For example, a venture that is good at introducing new products would not be a good fit with a company whose primary product line is mature and stable.

Synergy

The phrase, "the whole is greater than the sum of its parts" is a good definition of the concept of **synergy.** Entrepreneurs who seek to exit their companies via acquisition should consider whether the company provides any synergies to potential acquirers.[5] The synergy should occur in both the business concept—the acquisition functioning as a vehicle to move toward overall goals—and the financial performance. Acquisitions should positively impact the bottom line of the acquiring firm, affecting long-term gains and future growth. Lack of synergy with the existing business is one of the most frequent causes of an acquisition failing to meet its objectives.

Markets and Customers

The due diligence process includes evaluation of the entire marketing program and capabilities of the venture. Although all areas of marketing are assessed, particular care is normally taken in evaluating the quality and capability of the established distribution system, sales force, and manufacturers' representatives. For example, one company may acquire a venture primarily because of the quality of its sales force. Another may acquire a venture to obtain its established distribution system, which allows access to new markets. Entrepreneurs should be aware of which of these elements of enterprise value will be of interest to potential acquirers.

Acquiring companies can gain insight into the market orientation and sensitivity of target ventures by looking at their marketing research efforts. Does the venture have facts about customer satisfaction, trends in the market, and the state of the art of the technology of the industry? Ventures that are setting up for an exit by acquisition should be collecting, storing, and actively mining their customer data.

Research and Development

The future of the venture's products and market position is affected by its research and development. The due diligence process normally probes the nature and depth of the venture's research and development, and its ability to adjust to changing market conditions. The due diligence process will assess the strengths and weaknesses of the venture's innovation capabilities. Although the total amount of dollars spent on research and development is usually examined, it is more important to determine if these expenditures and programs are directed by the venture's long-range plans and whether the venture has been successful in introducing new offerings to customers.

Operations

The nature of the venture's business processes—the facilities and skills available, its efficiency and workflow, its productivity and many other things—are also examined as part of the due diligence process. Are the facilities obsolete? Are they flexible and can they produce output at a quality and a price that will compete over the coming years? Acquiring firms do not want to build this infrastructure themselves. Typically, an acquiring company focuses on the growth prospects of the target venture, and looks carefully at its overall operation to determine if it is poised to deliver on its growth potential.[6]

Management and Key Personnel

Finally, the due diligence process evaluates the management and key personnel of the venture. The individuals who have contributed positively to past success in sales and profits of the firm should be identified. If a company is conducting due diligence as part of a potential acquisition, it wants to know if the key personnel will stay once acquisition occurs. Have they established sound objectives and then implemented plans to successfully reach those objectives?

Additionally, acquiring companies examine whether any of the venture's personnel are indispensable. Generally, it is not good for the acquiring company if there are such individuals. There is too much risk associated with those key people leaving, becoming disabled, or worse. As such, technology ventures strive to ensure that knowledge and other key assets are not dependent on any single individual or groups of individuals.

VALUATION

Investors expect entrepreneurs in whom they invest to use their money wisely and carefully to build **enterprise value**. Enterprise value refers to the value of the enterprise as a whole. Enterprise value is easy to determine for companies that trade on the many public stock markets worldwide. The value of an enterprise whose shares trade on public markets is simply the price per share times the number of outstanding shares. This is also referred to as the firm's **market capitalization** or **market cap**. In the case of private ventures, the efficiency and effectiveness of operations are the essence of its enterprise value. Efficiency refers to the cost effectiveness of the venture's systems. Effectiveness refers to how well the systems produce value that customers demand.

Operating a venture consists of many things, but primarily it involves establishing repeatable systems that can deliver consistent value to customers. No matter if the venture is product based, service based, or some combination of both, growing a company requires setting up a variety of interlinked systems, including:

- Production systems
- Customer relationship management systems
- Sales and marketing systems
- Logistics systems
- Information technology systems
- Policy systems
- Human resource systems

Each of these systems becomes increasingly difficult to manage as the business grows. Experienced entrepreneurs develop systems early in the life of the venture and begin to establish work rules and routines that provide structure to the growing enterprise. Each of these various systems is essential to an operating venture. Enterprise value is measured to a large extent by how efficiently these systems interact to create market value. One medical device entrepreneur said: "Run your company every day as if you intend to sell it tomorrow."[7] What this means is that putting operating systems in place early in the venture's life, with due attention to their efficiency and effectiveness, can lead to enhanced enterprise value at the time of exit.

As we noted in Chapter 8, only accredited investors are allowed to invest in private equity offerings. This is because the Securities and Exchange Commission (SEC) assumes such investors are aware of and willing to accept the risks associated with investing in new ventures. Although investors in technology startups are willing to accept risk—including the risk of total loss of invested capital—they also expect to be rewarded, eventually, for the risks they take.

Valuation Techniques

There are a number of techniques that can be used to determine the value of a venture.[8] Some of these techniques employ sophisticated mathematical formulas and statistics; others use primarily qualitative judgments and educated hunches. We'll look at a subset of these techniques, including the multiples technique and the discounted cash flow method.

MULTIPLES TECHNIQUE: The multiples technique is the least mathematical of the methods for determining venture valuation and perhaps the one most often used. It is a straightforward technique that relies on identifying a key metric within an industry and on identifying industry comparables that have had a definitive valuation because of being acquired or having executed a recent equity sale. For example, in the Internet industry a common key metric is "registered users." Instagram was acquired by Facebook in 2012 for $1 billion. At the time of the acquisition, Instagram had only a dozen or so employees, no revenue, and no real business model. However, it did have something that Facebook valued highly: registered users. At the time of the acquisition, Instagram boasted 33 million registered users, and it had only launched eighteen months prior. In essence, Facebook calculated that the value of each registered user was approximately $33. To arrive at the $1 billion valuation, then, is simple arithmetic:

$$30,000,000 \text{ users} \times \$33/\text{user} = \$1,000,000,000$$

Companies in similar industries can now use the same multiple (i.e., $33 per registered user) to develop a reasonable valuation. Note that the valuations vary depending on which variable a venture chooses to use in generating a reasonable valuation. In general, the owners of a venture will want to choose the variable that gives them the greatest value, while potential investors will argue for the variable that gives the venture the least current value. There is no such thing as an "absolute" or "true" venture value. It all depends on the argument that can be made for one or another metric and comparable company to serve as the baseline for calculating valuation.

Discounted Cash Flow Technique:

For most startup ventures the old mantra clearly applies: "Cash is king." What that simple phrase means is that startup ventures must organize their growth and operations to ensure an ample supply of cash on hand to meet current obligations, including operating expenses and debt liabilities. One of the primary ways that entrepreneurs track and manage cash in the venture is via the cash flow statement. Unlike the income statement, the cash flow statement does not track operating performance according to rules of accounting. The cash flow statement tracks the actual movement of cash into and out of the firm. The technical term "discounted cash flow" is a refined measure of cash, which subtracts one-time capital expenses and dividend obligations from the projected cash position at some future date.

To determine valuation using the discounted cash flow method requires understanding the concept of **present value**. Present value is defined as the value in the present of some future cash flow. A simple technique has been developed to determine the present value of a future cash flow. Let's say that you are promised some cash right now or $100 dollars one year from now. How much cash would you need to receive right now to decide to forego the $100 future cash flow? Important to this consideration is how much a person could have earned by investing cash in hand over the one-year period. If the investment would return more than the $100, then you should take the cash in the present and invest it. If it would return less than the $100, then you should take the money in the future. The interest rate used to determine the return on current cash is called the **discount rate**. Here's how the calculation works:

$$PV = FV/(1+r)$$

In this equation, PV is the present value of the future value (FV) divided by the discount rate, r. If the discount rate was 8 percent (.08) with a FV of $100, someone would need to give you at least $92.59 in the present to make it worth your while to forego the future cash. Applying this logic to a venture requires identifying a future cash flow that will be put into the calculation above. As we've noted previously, your business plan should include a financial forecast that provides interested investors with cash projections for at least three years into the future. A simple way to generate the FV variable in this equation is by using the projected cash position of the venture at the end of the three year period. This would be the last line of the cash flow statement in month 36 (if you need a refresher on the cash flow statement, see Chapter 6).

Investor expectations of future returns are based on their estimate of risk. One element of that risk is the alternative investments they could have made. One alternative investment would be to purchase fixed-income securities, such as U.S. Treasury Bills. Such notes are backed by the United States government and are assumed to be risk free. Thus, the prevailing interest rate paid on U.S. Treasuries is known as the risk-free rate of return. At minimum, investors in startup ventures would expect to meet and exceed this risk-free rate. If the entrepreneur cannot demonstrate how that is possible, then investors would purchase the bonds instead.

In addition to the alternative investments that comprise one element of the risk associated with investing in any particular venture is the risk of the venture itself. The risk-free rate of return is relatively straightforward and can be known with a high degree of accuracy. However, the risks that are associated with any particular venture are more difficult to quantify. One technique that is used to arrive at a discount rate that includes both the alternative investment risk and the venture risk is known as the **risk-adjusted discount rate** method or RADR. This approach is summarized in the equation below.

$$r_{vt} = r_{ft} + RP_{vt}$$

This equation states that, for a particular venture, v, that yields an uncertain cash flow at some future time, t, the discount rate is expressed as rvt. In the equation above, rft is the so-called risk free rate of return, and RPvt is the risk premium that is associated with the venture. The discount rate that is used to determine the present value of future cash flows, then, is a combination of the risk-free rate and the risk premium. This is the minimum rate of return that investors would expect to receive on their exit from the venture.[9]

The important point to remember is that, using this method, valuation is based on the likely future cash flows that will be generated by the venture. The various assets of the organization, such as intellectual property, products and services, customer lists, brand value, and many other things are not considered. Many entrepreneurs don't have a lot of experience in predicting future cash flows, and they are at a disadvantage when the time comes to place a value on the venture. This lack of experience can be offset by consulting with independent firms that specialize in placing a value on ventures. Paying for such a service prior to seeking capital, especially from experienced venture capital firms who are usually very good at determining the value of a venture, can be a worthwhile expense. Arming oneself with rational and defensible arguments about the future value of a venture can help when the time comes to negotiate with others about the value of a venture.

EXIT VIA SUCCESSION

Succession is a common exit strategy used in family-owned businesses. Such ventures often are handed down from generation to generation. Some of the largest private companies in America, such as Koch Industries and Milliken & Company, are family owned and continue to be run primarily by members of the Koch and Milliken families, respectively. These companies have developed detailed succession planning guides

that help them groom and prepare the next generation to take over the company. Exhibit 14.2 indicates the primary industry categories for family businesses in the United States.

Many family-owned businesses aspire to keep the business in the family via succession, but they don't plan very well for it. As a result, many family-owned businesses suffer setbacks and occasionally bankruptcy because of poorly designed succession. For example, many fail to help the next generation come to terms with the difficulties of running a company, assuming instead that a college degree or MBA will prepare them for leadership. By way of contrast, family-owned ventures that manage the succession process effectively realize that there's no better way for the next

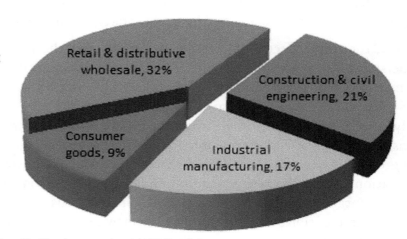

- Retail & distributive wholesale
- Construction & civil engineering
- Industrial manufacturing
- Consumer goods

Retail & distributive wholesale, 32%

Construction & civil engineering, 21%

Consumer goods, 9%

Industrial manufacturing, 17%

EXHIBIT 14.2 Industry Types for Family Businesses in the United States

generation to learn the business than the way the first generation did. Effective succession planning generally exposes the upcoming generation to all facets of the business. Family members who aspire to lead the venture someday will spend time "in the trenches" with other employees learning about the business from the ground up. Such lessons can be invaluable as the older generation steps aside and the next generation takes over.

There has been extensive research into the processes that can be used to better manage the succession process. One of the first things that should be considered in succession planning is to ensure that the transfer process doesn't incur burdensome taxation. A good accountant will be essential to help ease the tax burden associated with transferring ownership of a major asset (the business) to heirs.[10] Many family businesses have had to be liquidated on succession because the heirs could not afford the taxes associated with ownership transference. An estate planning accountant and attorney can be valuable in avoiding that problem.[11]

Of course, in order to use a succession strategy, there must be someone in the family willing and able to take over the business. If no one has a passion for that, it would be wiser to exit the venture via acquisition—selling to someone outside the family. If there is someone in the family who passionately wants to run the business and is prepared to take over, you have no problem. But what if multiple family members are interested in the business? If that circumstance arises, there are several things that can be done to avoid hard feelings. The most common strategy in such a situation is to bring everyone together and determine who is best suited for which role in the venture. This is best handled after the family members have each had an opportunity to work in various roles within the venture to determine the best fit for their own talents and experience. Allocating roles within the venture is part of the challenge when multiple family members are interested in running the venture; the other challenge is ownership percentages. A good way to manage that is to transfer ownership based in part on performance goals. In that way, no one can claim a large ownership stake without having demonstrated the ability to manage and lead the venture effectively.

Ultimately, the decision must be made concerning who will be in charge of running the company on succession of the current CEO. A firm decision must be made on this important part of the succession plan. Some family businesses opt for leadership by committee, where a committee of family members makes most of the major decisions for the venture. This can work but it can also be unwieldy and political as the venture grows and/or experiences challenging times. Not many large companies are run by committee, and it is not recommended that family businesses operate under that style. Most management and leadership scholars will point to the value of having a single individual who ultimately is responsible for the strategic and operational effectiveness of the venture.

Finally, the most effective succession planning eases the new generation into their respective leadership roles rather than all-at-once immersion. We mentioned before that it is useful for family members aspiring to leadership to work in various roles within the venture prior to assuming day-to-day leadership. It is also very useful to have the previous generation stay on during the early days of succession to help the new generation of leaders understand the context of their decisions. While it is not advisable for the senior generation to intervene too soon, as some of the greatest lessons for the new generation will come via mistakes, it is advisable for the senior generation to help the new generation understand the lessons being learned.[12] This is not to say that the outgoing leaders should sit idly by if disastrous decisions are being made. The point of the non-intervention strategy is to allow the new generation to make mistakes that don't threaten the health of the business. Gradually stepping aside and allowing the incoming generation to assume larger and larger responsibilities is the preferred succession management technique. In fact, succession planning can often be a ten-year process.[13] The gradual approach to succession is highlighted in the following Mini-Case.

MINI-CASE

Succession in a Family-Owned Franchise

As he describes himself, McDonald's franchisee Brent Upchurch was raised, "with ketchup in his veins." Upchurch watched his father run several McDonald's outlets in South Florida. After college and a stint in the Marine Corps, he decided he wanted in on the family business. His father, Roger, agreed, but warned that it wouldn't he an automatic handoff. "My dad said, 'There's no easy way to do this. You have to learn from the ground up,'" said Upchurch, who did start at the bottom, working all the positions at his father's restaurants for four years and eventually working for two more years as a manager. Only then did his father submit his name to McDonald's for ownership approval. After that, there were two more years of training and evaluations.

In 2008, Upchurch was finally given the thumbs-up to own a franchise, but he didn't get majority ownership in his first store until August 2011. Upchurch's eleven-year apprenticeship may seem extreme, but successful succession planning is often a ten- to fifteen- year process, according to Dana Telford, a consultant with Chicago-based Family Business Consulting Group. In fact, succession planning has become the cause du jour for franchisors, who have figured out that smooth transitions can allow them to focus on new units, instead of backtracking to fix or sell existing units where the handover process went awry.

Source: Daley, J., "Family Affair," *Entrepreneur*, 39(12)(2011): 97–105.

Glenn and Martha Dodd opened their Fastsigns franchise in 1994, fully expecting their children to pursue other paths in life. For the Dodds the succession process proved to be relatively painless.

Advantages of Exit via Succession

There are a few advantages to exit via succession. Perhaps a primary advantage is that the current business owner can decide when, where, and how he or she will exit. Family successions can be managed over a long period of time, as the incoming generation is brought up to speed on managing the venture. In addition, for business owners who have a difficult time "letting go" of the venture, the exit via succession option can allow them to ease out over a longer time. Family members are generally going to be more tolerant of a former owner having some responsibility than is a total stranger.

Another advantage of exit via succession is the opportunity to pass on a healthy and viable business to one's family members. Many entrepreneurs work long and hard hours in large part for the benefit of their family. This motivation is strong for many entrepreneurs and small business owners and is rewarded when the next generation is groomed effectively to take over the business.

Disadvantages of Exit via Succession

There are some disadvantages as well to the exit via succession strategy. Obviously, one of the disadvantages is the potential for family squabbles to arise. For example, if one family member is passed over to lead a business in favor of another family member, hard feelings could arise. In that sense, it is important for a succession plan to be put in place early so that people are allowed to "grow into" their future roles in the business.

Another disadvantage of exit via succession is that the current owner may not receive full compensation for the hard work he or she has put into the venture. An outright sale of the venture to a non-family member would be negotiated more strenuously than would the transition to next-generation ownership. As such, the current owner must take as part of his or her reward for years of hard work the satisfaction of passing on the venture to family members.

As we mentioned, the first thing that is required for the succession strategy to be used to exit the venture is to have a willing and able family member who is ready to take over. If that is not present, the business owner may be better positioned to exit the venture via selling to another party. This is known as "acquisition." Let's explore exit via acquisition next.

EXIT VIA ACQUISITION

Before the entrepreneur can build value attractive to a potential acquirer, he or she must understand the buyer's perspective.[14] Most **acquisitions** are undertaken because the acquiring company sees one or more strategic advantages that can be obtained by buying another business. These advantages or **value drivers** vary from industry to industry. They also change over time in specific industries

because of evolving product life cycles and external developments that affect the industry. Generic categories of strategic value drivers include:

- **Broader product lines:** The buyer adds complementary products to increase revenues. This is a common strategy for both product and service companies.

- **Expanding the technology base:** The buyer adds technology skills or intellectual property that enhances or complements the company's current base.[15]

- **Adding markets and distribution channels:** The acquirer obtains channels it doesn't currently serve. Companies that start out with a *vertical strategy* can add new industry expertise by widening its distribution capabilities. A vertical strategy is one where a venture develops expertise in a given industry that can be expanded to other industries with only slight modifications.

- **Increasing the customer base:** The buyer adds a company that is similar in product offerings or in its business model yet focuses on a different customer segment. This strategy is enhanced if the target company has a good reputation or strong brand. It also can expand the acquirer's geographic coverage.

- **Creating economies of scale:** The combined company can offer a more efficient use of physical assets or overhead—a critical need in consolidating industries.

- **Extending internal skills:** The buyer can add new capabilities such as consulting or service offerings, international management skills, or various types of management and business skills. These skills can be offered as independent revenue producers or enhance a company's competitive edge.[16]

Many acquirers hope to leverage several value drivers in a single deal. Google, for example, has regularly used acquisitions as a strategic tool to bring in new skills, new technology, and, sometimes, new customers. Google has developed expertise for integrating these newly acquired technologies into its complete product offerings.

When the perspective of potential buyers is factored into the development of a new venture's strategy, the strategic planning process becomes very important. Internal characteristics of the company will influence the acquirer's final valuation.[17] These factors are related to fundamental business management, strong cash flow, and accurate books and records. While they obviously are necessary to closing a deal, they must be augmented by significant value drivers to motivate the buyer to pay a premium price.[18] The following Research Link box highlights some things entrepreneurs can do to prepare their venture for an eventual acquisition.

RESEARCH LINK

Preparing Your Venture for Acquisition

As you begin to study your industry, you will need to look at both industry trends and the strategies of competing companies in handling those trends. Some of the questions that need answers include:

- Why are your customers presently buying from you?

- What are the customers' sourcing alternatives, including direct competitors, internal competition within the customer company, inaction or not buying at all, and innovative alternate solutions?

- How will customers' needs change?

- What alternatives will customers have tomorrow?

- What is happening in related markets to influence buying patterns?

- What will the market look like tomorrow?

- What will other players be looking for in executing acquisitions?

The critical conclusion to this process is in the last two questions about the future. Doing your homework through the earlier points should help you develop a vision of future trends and value drivers in the industry.

Source: Adams, M., "Exit Pay-Offs for the Entrepreneur," *Mergers & Acquisitions: The Dealmaker's Journal,* 39(3)(2004): 24–28.

The Acquisition Deal

Once the venture has been identified as a good candidate for acquisition, an appropriate deal must be structured. Many techniques are available for acquiring a firm, each having a distinct set of advantages to both the buyer and seller. The deal structure involves the parties, the assets, the payment form, and the timing of the payment. For example, all or part of the assets of one firm can be acquired by another for some combination of cash, notes, stock, and/or employment contracts. This payment can be made at the time of acquisition, throughout the first year, or extended over several years.

The two most common means of acquisition are the **direct purchase** of the target venture's entire stock or assets, or the **bootstrap purchase** of these assets. In the direct purchase of the firm, the acquiring company often obtains funds from an outside lender or the seller of the company being purchased. The money is repaid over time from the cash flow generated from the operations. Although this is a relatively simple and clear transaction, it usually results in a long-term capital gain to the seller and double taxation on the funds used to repay the money borrowed to acquire the company.

In order to avoid these problems, the acquiring company can make a bootstrap purchase, acquiring a small amount of the firm, such as 20 to 30 percent, for cash. The acquiring company then purchases the remainder of the target venture by a long-term note that is paid off over time out of the acquired company's earnings. This type of deal often results in more favorable tax advantages to both the buyer and seller.

Advantages of Exit via Acquisition

There are numerous potential advantages of the acquisition strategy. The most obvious is that the entrepreneur and any other owners of the venture's equity have the opportunity to convert their interest into cash. This is the ultimate goal of a lot of entrepreneurs and certainly is the goal of every one of the investors. The amount of cash that will be involved in the acquisition transaction depends upon the valuation of the venture. The more enterprise value the entrepreneur has created, the greater will be the cash required to purchase the venture. The cash that is used to purchase the venture is then distributed to each of the investors according to their percentage of ownership interest.

Another advantage of acquisition is that the entrepreneur now has the cash needed to launch a new venture. Many so-called **serial entrepreneurs** continue to build new ventures with the cash they have obtained through past deals. You may have heard of the boom-and-bust nature of entrepreneurship. Many entrepreneurs obtain a lot of cash early in their careers and erroneously conclude that entrepreneurship is easy, or that they are uniquely talented. Some end up bankrupt because they used all of their cash to try to achieve the thrill of success once again. Expert entrepreneurs follow the affordable loss principle throughout their entrepreneurial careers. That is, even though they may have had a big payday from a successful exit via acquisition, they don't risk all of their gains on their next ventures. Instead, they put away enough money to live on, if they can, and continue to leverage other investors to help them reduce their personal financial risk.

Other advantages of the acquisition strategy include the opportunity to exit a venture that has grown too large for the entrepreneur. By getting out of a growing venture that exceeds the entrepreneur's leadership and management skills, the entrepreneur can avoid the problems associated with decline and, potentially, failure. Handing over the reins of the venture to better qualified leaders is common for expert entrepreneurs who prefer starting ventures over managing large and growing ones. Finally, the entrepreneur gains more respect and credibility among investors and other potential stakeholders if he or she can demonstrate a track record of building and selling companies. It will be far easier in future ventures for the entrepreneur to raise capital and acquire needed resources with such a track record of success.

Disadvantages of Exit via Acquisition

One of the major disadvantages of exit via acquisition is that the entrepreneur loses control of the venture that he or she has been nurturing. In the succession exit, as we've seen, it is very useful for the previous generation to stick around and help the incoming generation manage the venture for awhile. This not only provides the incoming generation with valuable mentoring as it comes up to speed on leading the venture, but it also lets the outgoing generation ease slowly into retirement. Many entrepreneurs who sell their companies are not prepared for the idleness that comes with the sales transaction. Most acquiring ventures are not interested in keeping the founder around and will simply take over the operation as soon as the sales transaction is closed. For some entrepreneurs, the lack of a place to go, challenges to meet, and people to interact with can be upsetting. In fact, many entrepreneurs quickly leap into a new venture because they simply are not ready to be idle.

Another disadvantage of exit by acquisition is that the parties to the deal must come to agreement on the valuation of the venture. This can be a lengthy and potentially expensive process that may take the entrepreneur's attention away from running the business. The due diligence that needs to be conducted can also be disruptive to an operating venture. Employees who are aware of the potential for the acquisition may be concerned about their jobs and perform less well while the veil of uncertainty exists.

The final disadvantage of the acquisition exit strategy that we'll mention here is the challenge of finding a qualified buyer. This can be a major challenge, depending upon the type of venture. Ventures that are primarily based on local customers and local sales will most likely need to find a local buyer, or someone willing to relocate. If the economy is good there may be many potential buyers around. If the economy is not so good, there may be fewer potential buyers. The entrepreneur who wishes to exit via acquisition does not always have control over exactly when that may occur. It can take years to find a qualified buyer, in which case the value of the business may also change between the initiation of a search for a buyer and finally closing a deal. There are **business brokers** who can help entrepreneurs sell their companies, but they are fee-based agents who may also require an upfront retainer. In addition to business brokers, there are a number of websites that entrepreneurs can use to list their business for sale. Some websites that offer such as service include:

- www.bizbuysell.com
- www.businessesforsale.com
- www.businessmart.com
- www.businessbroker.net

In the event that a qualified buyer cannot be found in a reasonable time, the entrepreneur can consider exit via merger. A merger will result in a change of ownership, but does not always include cash as part of the transaction. An entrepreneur who can no longer wait for a buyer can exit the venture by merging with another entity, and then holding onto the stock of the merged enterprise. Of course, that is not the only time a merger strategy makes sense. Often two or more companies may be able to pursue significant new opportunities under a single venture than they could alone. Let's turn next to the exit via merger strategy.

EXIT VIA MERGER

Another method for exiting a venture is via a **merger**—a transaction involving two (or more) companies in which only one company survives. Acquisitions are similar to mergers and, sometimes, the two terms are used interchangeably. In reality, they are quite different, with the primary differences between mergers and acquisitions centering on the relative size of the entities involved, and on who is in control of the combined

© mangostock, 2012. Used under license from Shutterstock, Inc.

entity. Mergers generally occur when the relative size of the ventures involved is equal—or at least they are perceived to bring equal value to the merged entity.

When an entrepreneur decides to merge with another company, it's usually the case that the two entities are similar in size and offer similar value to the merged entity. For example, it would be quite unexpected for Google to merge with a five-person technology startup. More likely, Google, with its tremendous assets and global reach, would be in control and simply acquire the smaller venture.

When two entrepreneurial ventures merge, the question about who will control the merged companies is part of the merger negotiations. An entrepreneur who wants to exit a venture may elect to merge with another company, but it may take some time for the entrepreneur to wriggle free of the new company. Often, when a merger occurs the merged company requires that the top executives from each venture stay with the merged entity to ensure its success. Depending on the size of the new company, the entrepreneur may be able to negotiate a deal whereby he or she earns out of the company over a period of time.

An **earn-out strategy** is used for ventures that have begun to generate consistently strong positive cash flow.[19] The management team initiates a monthly or quarterly buyback of common stock from the owners of one of the merged entities. Typically, an earn-out can be accomplished over an agreed-upon period of time and can provide the entrepreneur seeking to exit with a strong return as company sales expand and costs decline because of increased operating efficiencies.

Why should an entrepreneur merge his or her venture with another firm? There are both defensive and offensive strategies for a merger. Merger motivations range from survival to protection to diversification to growth. When some technical obsolescence (loss of market or raw material) or deterioration of the capital structure has occurred in the entrepreneur's venture, a merger may be the only means for survival and exit. The merger can also protect against market encroachment, product innovation, or an unwarranted takeover. It can also provide a great deal of diversification as well as growth in market, technology, and financial and managerial strength.

A successful merger requires sound planning by the entrepreneur. The merger objectives, particularly those dealing with earnings, must be spelled out with the resulting gains for the owners of both companies delineated. Also, the entrepreneur must carefully evaluate the other company's management to ensure that it would be competent in developing the growth of the combined entity. The value and appropriateness of the existing resources should also be determined. In essence, this involves a careful analysis of both companies to ensure that the weaknesses of one do not compound those of the other. Finally, the entrepreneur should work toward establishing a climate of mutual trust to help minimize any possible management threat or turbulence.

Advantages of Exit via Merger

One major advantage for many entrepreneurs to the exit via merger option is that they can exit their venture more slowly and methodically than exit via acquisition. Usually, in exit via acquisition the entrepreneur is out on the close of the deal. In a merger, the entrepreneur (from either of the merging parties) may elect to stay with the new company after the merger deal. Of course, the entrepreneur may need to take on a lesser role in the merged entity. It is simply untenable for both of the former CEOs to retain that title, for example. The entrepreneur may elect to exit the merged entity over time via what is termed an earn-out strategy. That is, the entrepreneur will be retained by the new company through a period of time in which the entrepreneur's stock in the merged entity fully vests. At that point the entrepreneur may leave and start another venture.

Another major advantage to exit via merger is that the entrepreneur may realize greater value in his or her stock holdings in the new company than would have been realized in the former venture. The entrepreneur may have been at the limits of his or her capabilities to lead and manage, and an exit via acquisition would have valued the venture at its current value. In contrast, by accepting ownership of the new, merged company the entrepreneur may realize significantly greater value due to the greater capabilities of the combined leadership team.

Disadvantages of Exit via Merger

The primary disadvantage of exit via merger is the need for the merging companies to integrate their businesses into a single business. This can be very difficult for a variety of reasons. For example, if the two companies have vastly different information systems, it can be expensive converting the merged entity to a single system. Another factor that is often cited as an impediment to a successful merger is if the merging businesses have different cultures. A venture's "culture" consists primarily of the unspoken understandings that people share about how work is done, customers are handled, and many other things. If these are not aligned, the merged entity may have a difficult time bringing the two workforces into a cohesive unit.

Another disadvantage of exit via merger is that it can be more time consuming and expensive than other exit options. For example, a merger will require that both of the merging parties undergo due diligence and valuation. The reason this is necessary is that shareholders in the separate entities need to be compensated proportionately based on the combined value of the newly merged entity. In order to determine one's share of the merged entity, it is necessary to have agreement on how much of the merged entity's value was contributed by each of the merging companies. That proportion will then be used to allocate new company shares to the combined ownership pool. This process of valuation, new stock creation and distribution, and other things associated with merging can be expensive and time consuming. Both parties need to be highly motivated to complete the deal.

EXIT VIA INITIAL PUBLIC OFFERING (IPO)

Going public via what is called an **initial public offering (IPO)** occurs when the entrepreneur and other owners of the venture offer and sell some part of the company to the public through a registration statement filed with the Securities and Exchange Commission (SEC) pursuant to the Securities Act of 1933. The resulting capital infusion to the company from the increased number of stockholders and outstanding shares of stock provide the company with financial resources and a relatively liquid investment vehicle. Consequently, the company will have greater access to capital markets in the future and a more objective picture of the public's perception of the value of the business. However, given the reporting requirements, the increased number of stockholders, and the costs involved, the technology entrepreneur must carefully evaluate the advantages and disadvantages of going public before initiating the process. Here, we'll review some of the major factors and documents associated with IPO transactions. We'll begin by examining the timing of the transaction.

Timing

Is this a good time for the venture to initiate an IPO? This is the critical question that entrepreneurs must ask themselves before launching this effort.[20] Some critical questions in making this decision follow.

© justrasc, 2012. Used under license from Shutterstock, Inc.

First, is the company large enough? While it is not possible to establish rigid minimum-size standards that must be met before a venture can go public, New York investment banking firms prefer at least a 500,000-share offering at a minimum of $10 per share. This means that the company would have to have a past offering value of at least $12.5 million in order to support this $5 million offering, given that the company is willing to sell shares representing not more than 40 percent of the total number of shares outstanding after the offering is completed. This size offering will only occur with past significant sales and earnings performance or a solid prospect for future growth and earnings.

Second, what is the amount of the company's earnings, and how strong is its financial performance? Not only is this performance the basis of the company valuation, but it also determines if a company can successfully go public and the type of firm willing to underwrite the offering.

Third, are the market conditions favorable for an initial public offering? Underlying the sales and earnings, as well as the size of the offering, is the prevailing general market condition.[21] Market conditions affect both the initial price that the entrepreneur will receive for the stock and the aftermarket—the price performance of the stock after its initial sale. Some market conditions are more favorable for IPOs than others.

Fourth, how urgently is the money needed? The entrepreneur must carefully appraise both the urgency of the need for new money and the availability of outside capital from other sources. Since the sale of common stock decreases the ownership position of the technology entrepreneur and other equity owners, the longer the time before going public, given that profits and sales growth occur, the less percentage of equity the technology entrepreneur will have to give up per dollar invested.

Finally, what are the needs and desires of the present owners? Sometimes the present owners lack confidence in the future viability and growth prospects of the business, or they have a need for liquidity. Going public is frequently the only method for present stockholders to obtain the cash needed. The following Mini-Case discusses the 2012 Facebook IPO and what it meant to shareholders.

MINI-CASE

Facebook IPO Raises $18B

Oh, to be 28 and a multibillionaire. That's the outcome of Facebook's IPO for founder and 50 percent shareholder Mark Zuckerberg. Facebook went public on the NASDAQ exchange on May 18, 2012 amidst much fanfare and hype. The stock was priced at $38/share but opened at over $42/share. More than 82 million shares of the Internet giant were traded in the first 30 seconds after it began trading. On opening day, the stock reached a high of $45/share before settling down and closing just above the IPO price of $38/share. Final trading volume for the day was more than 573 million shares. Zuckerberg's stake in Facebook is estimated to be more than $19 billion. The IPO raised $16 billion for the company to use to grow and hunt for ways to monetize its more than 800 million active users. That is roughly one-eighth of the entire world's population.

Source: Adapted from Koba, M. 2012. "Facebook's IPO: What we Know," *CNBC.com*, www.cnbc.com/id/47043815/Facebook_s_IPO_What_We_Know_Now, accessed on May 20, 2012; Deluca, M. 2012. "Facebook IPO by the Numbers: Zuckerberg's Loot and More," *The Daily Beast*, www.thedailybeast.com/articles/2012/05/18/facebook-ipo-by-the-numbers-zuckerberg-s-loot-more.html, accessed on May 20, 2012.

Selecting an Investment Bank

Once the entrepreneur has determined that the timing for going public is favorable, he or she must carefully select a managing **underwriter**, an investment bank that will take the lead in forming an **underwriting syndicate**.[22] For example, Goldman Sachs is an investment bank with broad and deep experience as an IPO underwriter. The firm selected to perform as the lead investment bank is of critical importance in establishing the initial price for the stock of the company, supporting the stock in the aftermarket, and creating a strong following among security analysts. A syndicate is a group of investment banks and other, usually institutional, investors who subscribe to the IPO. That means that they designate in advance how many shares they will purchase at the IPO. This is important because it could be disastrous for a venture to have an IPO where no one purchased the stock.

Since selecting the investment banker is a major factor in the success of the public offering, the entrepreneur should approach one through a mutual contact. Commercial banks, attorneys specializing in securities work, major accounting firms, providers of the initial financing, or prominent members of the company's board of directors can usually provide the needed suggestions and introductions. Since the relationship will be ongoing, not ending with the completion of the offering, the entrepreneur should employ several criteria in the selection process, such as reputation, distribution capability, advisory services, experience, and cost.

The success of the offering also depends on the underwriter's distribution capability. An entrepreneur wants the stock of his or her company distributed to as wide and varied a base as possible. Since each investment banking firm has a different client base, the entrepreneur should compare client bases of possible managing underwriters. Is the client base made up predominately of institutional investors, individual investors, or balanced between the two? Is the base more internationally or domestically oriented? Are the investors long-term or speculators? What is the geographic distribution—local, regional, or nationwide? A strong managing underwriter and syndicate with a quality client base will help the stock sell well and perform well in the **aftermarket**. The aftermarket is the term used to refer to the performance of a stock in the public markets after the excitement of the IPO has subsided. How a stock performs in the long run is often dependent on the ability of the underwriters to gain interest from *their* investors.[23]

The final factor to be considered in the choice of a managing underwriter is cost. Going public is a very costly proposition, and costs *do* vary greatly among underwriters. The average gross spread as a percentage of the offering between underwriters can be as high as 10 percent. Costs associated with various possible managing underwriters must be carefully weighed against the other four factors. The key is to obtain the best possible underwriter and not try to cut corners, given the stakes involved in a successful initial public offering.

Registration Statement and Timetable

Once the managing underwriter has been selected, a planning meeting should be held of company officials responsible for preparing the **registration statement**, the company's independent accountants and lawyers, and the underwriters and their counsel. At this important meeting, frequently called the "all hands" meeting, a timetable is prepared, indicating dates for each step in the registration process. This timetable establishes the effective date of the registration, which determines the date of the final financial statements to be included. The company's end of the year, when regular audited financial statements are routinely prepared, is taken into account to avoid any possible extra accounting and legal work. The timetable should indicate the individual responsible for preparing the various parts of the registration and offering statement. Problems often arise in an initial public offering due to the timetable not being carefully developed and agreed to by all parties involved.

After the completion of the preliminary preparation, the first public offering normally requires six to eight weeks to prepare, print, and file the registration statement with the SEC. Once the registration statement has been filed, the SEC generally takes four to eight weeks to declare the registration effective. Delays frequently occur in this process, such as (1) during heavy periods of market activity, (2) during peak seasons, such as March, when the SEC is reviewing a large number of proxy statements, (3) when the company's attorney is not familiar with federal or state regulations, (4) when a complete and full disclosure is resisted by the company, or (5) when the managing underwriter is inexperienced.

In reviewing the registration statement, the SEC attempts to ensure that the document makes a full and fair disclosure of the material reported. The SEC has no authority to withhold approval of or require any changes in the terms of an offering that it deems unfair or inequitable, so long as all material information concerning the company and the offering are fully disclosed. The National Association of Securities Dealers (NASD) will review each offering, principally to determine the fairness of the underwriting compensation and its compliance with NASD bylaw requirements.

The Prospectus

The prospectus portion of the registration statement is almost always written in a highly stylized narrative form, as it is the selling document of the company. While the exact format is decided by the company, the information must be presented in an organized, logical sequence and in an easy-to-read, understandable manner in order to obtain SEC approval. Some of the most common sections of a prospectus include the cover page, prospectus summary, the company, risk factors, use of proceeds, dividend policy, capitalization, dilution, selected financial data, the business, management and owners, type of stock, underwriter information, and the actual financial statements.

© gezzeg, 2012. Used under license from Shutterstock, Inc.

The cover page includes such information as company name, type and number of shares to be sold, a distribution table, date of prospectus, managing underwriter(s), and syndicate of underwriters involved. There is a preliminary prospectus and then a final prospectus once approved by the SEC.

The preliminary prospectus is used by the underwriters to solicit investor interest in the offering while the registration is pending. The final prospectus contains all of the changes and additions required by the SEC and blue sky examiners and the information concerning the price at which the securities will be sold. The final prospectus must be delivered with or prior to the written confirmation of purchase orders from investors participating in the offering.

PART II: This section of Form S-1 contains specific documentation of the issue in an answer format and exhibits such things as the articles of incorporation, the underwriting agreements, company bylaws, stock option and pension plans, and contracts. Other items presented include indemnification of directors and officers, any sale of unregistered securities within the past three years, and expenses related to going public.

FORM S-18: In April 1979, the SEC adopted a simplified form of the registration statement—Form S-18—for companies planning to register no more than $7.5 million of securities. This form was designed to make going public easier and less expensive by having less reporting requirements. Form S-18 requires less detailed description of the business, officers, directors, and legal proceedings; requires no industry segment information; allows financial statements to be prepared in accordance with generally accepted accounting practices rather than under the guidelines of Regulation S-X; and requires an audited balance sheet at the end of the last fiscal year (rather than the last two years) and audited change in financial positions and stockholders equity for the last two years (rather than the last three years). Although Form S-18 can be filed for review with the SEC's Division of Corporation Finance in Washington, DC, as are all S-1 forms, it can also be filed with the SEC's regional office.

The Red Herring

Once the preliminary prospectus is filed, it can be distributed to the underwriting group. This preliminary prospectus is called a **red herring**, because a statement printed in red ink appears on the front cover that states that the issuing company is not attempting to sell its shares. The registration statements are then reviewed by the SEC to determine if adequate disclosures have been made. Some deficiencies are almost always found and are communicated to the company either by telephone or a *deficiency letter.* This preliminary prospectus contains all the information contained in the final prospectus except that which is not known until shortly before the effective date: offering price, underwriters' commission, and amount of proceeds.

Reporting Requirements

Going public requires a complex set of reporting requirements. The first requirement is the filing of a Form SR sales report, which the company must do within ten0 days after the end of the first three-month period following the effective date of the registration. This report includes information on the amount of securities sold and still to be sold and the proceeds obtained by the company and their use. A final Form SR sales report must be filed within ten0 days of the completion or termination of the offering.

The company must file annual reports on Form 10-K, quarterly reports on Form 10-Q, and specific transaction reports on Form 8-K. The information in Form 10-K on the business, management, and company assets is similar to that in Form S-1 of the registration statement. Of course, audited financial statements are required.

The quarterly report on Form 10-Q contains primarily the unaudited financial information for the most recently completed fiscal quarter. No 10-Q is required for the fourth fiscal quarter.

A Form 8-K report must be filed within fifteen days of such events as the acquisition or disposition of significant assets by the company outside the ordinary course of the business, the resignation or dismissal of the company's independent public accountants, or a change in control of the company.

The company must follow the proxy solicitation requirements regarding holding a meeting or obtain the written consent of security holders. The timing and type of materials involved are detailed in the Securities and Exchange Act of 1933.

These are but a few of the reporting requirements of public companies. All the requirements must be carefully observed, as even inadvertent mistakes can have negative consequences on the company. The reports required must be filed on time.

Advantages of Exit via IPO

There are three primary advantages of going public: obtaining new equity capital, obtaining value and transferability of the organization's assets, and enhancing the company's ability to obtain future funds. Whether it is first-stage, second-stage, or third-stage financing, a venture is in constant need of capital. The new capital provides the needed working capital, plant and equipment, or inventories and supplies necessary for the venture's growth and survival. Going public is often the best way to obtain this needed capital on the best possible terms.

Going public also provides a mechanism for valuing the company and allowing this value to be easily transferred among parties. Many family-owned or other privately held companies may need to go public so that the value of the company can be disseminated among the second and third generations. Venture capitalists view going public as the most beneficial way to attain the liquidity necessary to exit a company with the best possible return on their earlier-stage funding. Other investors, as well, can more easily liquidate their investment when the company's stock takes on value and transferability. Because of this liquidity, the value of a publicly traded security sometimes is higher than shares of one that is not publicly traded. In addition, publicly traded companies often find it easier to acquire other companies by using their securities in the transactions.

The third primary advantage is that publicly traded companies usually find it easier to raise additional capital, particularly debt. Money can be borrowed more easily and on more favorable terms when there is value attached to a company and that value is more easily transferred. Not only debt financing but future equity capital is more easily obtained when a company establishes a track record of increasing stock value.

Disadvantages of Exit via IPO

Although going public present significant advantages for a new venture, entrepreneurs must also carefully weigh the numerous disadvantages. Some entrepreneurs want to keep their companies private, even in times of a hot stock market. Why do entrepreneurs avoid the supposed gold rush of an initial public offering (IPO)?

One of the major reasons is the public exposure and potential loss of control that can occur in a publicly traded company. To stay on the cutting edge of technology, companies frequently need to sacrifice short-term profits for long-term innovation. This can require reinvesting in technology, which in itself may not produce any bottom-line results, particularly in the short run.

Some of the most troublesome aspects of being public are the resulting loss of flexibility and increased administrative burdens. The company must make decisions in light of the fiduciary duties owed to the public shareholder, and it is obliged to disclose to the public all material information regarding the company, its operations, and its management. One publicly traded company had to retain a more expensive investment banker than would have been required by a privately held company in order to obtain an "appropriate" fairness opinion in a desired acquisition. The investment banker increased the expenses of the merger by $150,000, in addition to causing a three-month delay in the acquisition proceedings. Management of a publicly traded company also spends a significant amount of additional time addressing queries from shareholders, press, and financial analysts.

If all these disadvantages have not caused the entrepreneur to look for alternative financing other than an IPO, the expenses involved may. The major expenses of going public include accounting fees, legal fees, underwriter's fees, registration and blue sky filing fees, and printing costs. The accounting fees involved in going public vary greatly, depending in part on the size of the company, the availability of previously audited financial statements, and the complexity of the company's operations. Generally, the costs of going public are around $300,000 to $600,000, although they can be much greater when significant complexities are involved. Additional reporting, accounting, legal, and printing expenses can run anywhere from $50,000 to $250,000 per year, depending on the company's past practices in the areas of accounting and shareholder communications.

The underwriters' fees include a cash discount (on commission), which usually ranges from 7 to 10 percent of the public offering price of the new issue. In some IPOs, the underwriters can also require some compensation, such as warrants to purchase stock, reimbursement for some expenses—most typically legal fees—and the right of first refusal on any future offerings. The NASD regulates the maximum amount of the underwriter's compensation and reviews the actual amount for fairness before the offering can take place. Similarly, any underwriter's compensation is also reviewed in blue sky filings.

There are also other expenses in the form of SEC, NASD, and state blue sky registration fees. The final major expense—printing costs—typically ranges from $50,000 to $200,000. The registration statement and prospectus discussed later in this chapter account for the largest portion of these expenses. The exact amount of expenses varies, depending on the length of the prospectus, the use of color or black-and-white photographs, the number of proofs and corrections, and the number printed. It is important for the company to use a good printer because accuracy and speed are required in the printing of the prospectus and other offering documents.

Regardless of how much preparation occurs, almost every entrepreneur is unprepared and wants to halt it at some time during the makeover process. Yet for a successful IPO, each entrepreneur must listen to the advice being given to make the recommended changes swiftly.

SUMMARY OF LEARNING OBJECTIVES

1. **Prepare** the venture for due diligence. *Due diligence is the process that investors use to determine whether a venture is a viable opportunity. Typically, due diligence will involve review of a venture's finances, products, markets and customers, research and development, operations, and management team. To prepare for due diligence an entrepreneur should run his or her company every day as if he or she intends to sell it tomorrow.*

2. **Conduct** a valuation of the venture using several techniques. *Valuing a venture is a challenge for private companies whose stock does not trade in public markets. We reviewed a variety of valuation techniques in this chapter, and the techniques may produce varying results. The entrepreneur can take charge of the valuation of his or her venture by using the technique that is most common in the industry and that provides the greatest valuation of the venture.*

3. **Build** a venture in a manner that maximizes enterprise value. *Enterprise value was defined as the value that is created in the enterprise itself. This differs from the market value of a venture's assets, and includes estimates of growth potential and future value. The entrepreneur should build the venture from startup with the intention of building lasting enterprise value by paying attention to efficiencies, productivity, and the effectiveness of the systems that create value for customers.*

4. **Select** an exit strategy that best fits the wishes of the owners. *Entrepreneurs should have some idea of their preferred exit strategy from the startup of the venture. Strategies reviewed in this chapter include succession, acquisition, merger, and initial public offering. Each strategy has advantages and disadvantages and requires the entrepreneur to structure the venture in differing ways. Thus, it is important to have an idea of preferred exit strategy as that will affect decision making as the venture is growing.*

5. **Execute** the various exit strategies options available. *Each of the exit strategies reviewed in this chapter requires different tactics as the business grows. For example, if succession is the chosen strategy—passing the venture to an heir—steps should be taken to ensure that the individual who is to inherit the venture is prepared to lead when the founder elects to exit.*

6. **Recognize** the various factors that may influence a decision to use merger as an exit strategy. *Ventures merge with other ventures for a variety of reasons. Entrepreneurs seeking to exit via a merger strategy should look for potential merger parties that create synergies. Synergies can be developed from an enhanced product portfolio, access to new markets and customers, ability to leverage a superior supply chain, and many other things.*

7. **Understand** the processes and documents that are required for a venture to execute an initial public offering. *The initial public offering (IPO) is the most complex exit strategy that we examined. It usually requires that the entrepreneur work with experienced professionals, including investment bankers, who are experienced in the various filings that are required and will also help organize a syndicate of investment banks to distribute the IPO stock to investors.*

STUDY QUESTIONS

1. What is the difference between an acquisition and a merger?
2. How does a technology entrepreneur estimate the value of the venture using multiples? Give some examples.
3. What is the most important element in valuing a technology venture? Explain.

4. What is meant by the term *due diligence*?

5. Explain why the selection of an investment bank to be the lead underwriter is an important decision for a technology entrepreneur.

6. What are some of the costs associated with a company going public?

7. What are the various sections of a registration statement and what purpose does each of them serve?

8. Why does an acquiring firm want to understand the position in the product lifecycle of the products and services in the target venture's portfolio? Explain

9. What are some of the disadvantages of an IPO? Advantages?

10. Explain how an exit strategy can influence the day-to-day decision making of a technology entrepreneur.

KEY TERMS

Acquisition: A transaction involving two companies in which one company purchases the other. The company that is purchased no longer exists, but is incorporated into the other company.

Aftermarket: The performance of a stock after the excitement of the IPO has subsided. How a stock performs in the long run is often dependent on the ability of the underwriters to gain interest from their investors.

Bootstrap purchase: The acquiring company can acquire a small amount of a firm, such as 20 to 30 percent, for cash. The acquiring company then purchases the remainder of the target venture by a long-term note that is paid off over time out of the acquired company's earnings.

Business broker: A business broker is a professional service provider specializing in helping entrepreneurs in the buying and/or selling of businesses.

Direct purchase: A purchase where the acquiring company often obtains funds from an outside lender or the seller of the company being purchased.

Discount rate: In conducting a present value analysis, a future cash flow must be discounted by the rate of interest that otherwise could be earned by present dollars.

Due diligence: A process of examining a number of key elements of a target venture, including its financial health, the potential for synergy, the market position and future potential of the venture, the research and development history and roadmap for the venture, legal considerations, and plans for managing the acquired entity.

Earn-out strategy: An earn-out strategy is used for ventures that have begun to generate consistently strong positive cash flow. The management team initiates a monthly or quarterly buyback of common stock from the owners of one of the merged entities.

Enterprise value: The value of the enterprise as a whole.

Exit strategy: The entrepreneur's strategic withdrawal from ownership or operation of his or her venture.

Initial public offering (IPO): A process whereby a private company qualifies to sell its shares on a public stock exchange.

Investment horizon: The time an investor's money will be tied up in a technology venture until the time of exit.

Liquidity event: The exit from a private venture for shareholders representing their opportunity to covert shares to cash.

Market capitalization (market cap): The value of public companies calculated as a function of the number of outstanding shares times the price per share.

Merger: A transaction involving two or more companies in which the companies join to form a new bigger company.

Present value: The value in today's dollars of some future cash flow. Because money today can earn interest, future cash flows must be discounted by at least as much as that interest amount to convert to its present value.

Red herring: The preliminary prospectus document, given this name due to the red ink used in the printing of the front cover.

Registration statement: Document filed with the SEC before a company can go public. It consists of two parts: the prospectus and the registration statement.

Risk-adjusted discount rate: A discount rate used in the discounted cash flow valuation technique that includes both the alternative investment risk and the venture risk.

Serial entrepreneurs: Entrepreneurs who start and exit multiple ventures sequentially in their careers are referred to as "serial entrepreneurs".

Synergy: The phrase, "the whole is greater than the sum of its parts" is a good definition of the concept of synergy. Entrepreneurs who seek to exit their companies via acquisition should consider whether the company provides any synergies to potential acquirers.

Underwriter: A company that administers the public issuance and distribution of securities. A company will utilize one when filing an IPO.

Underwriting syndicate: A group of investment banks and other, usually institutional, investors who subscribe to an IPO.

Valuation: The term that refers to the process and calculations used to establish a dollar value for a venture.

Value drivers: Strategic advantages that lead to value creation in an industry and that are attractive elements of an acquisition candidate in an industry.

OUT-OF-CLASS EXERCISE

Since it was launched late in 1996, BizBuySell has become the Internet's largest business-for-sale site. Of the more than 10,000 listings in its databases, some 15 percent are listed by personal owners, and the remainder comprise about 700 business brokers. Manufacturing businesses account for 15 percent of the businesses listed; wholesale and retail for 40 percent; and services make up roughly 30 percent. Of the thousands of people who visit the site, most are looking for a business to buy. Not only may buyers search the database at no charge, they may also register to be notified about new business listings that match their interests.

Students should visit the BizBuySell website at www.bizbuysell.com and explore the variety of businesses listed there for sale. Each student should select a category (e.g., Pet Shops & Supplies) to explore and pick at least five small businesses that are listed for sale on the site. For each business selected, take note of the following information:

- Asking price
- Gross sales
- Cash flow
- Inventory
- Financing options

Compare the five businesses selected and consider the following questions:

Which one seems to offer the best deal?

Which one seems to have the highest valuation? Why?

Among the various industries, which ones seem to have the highest multiples of gross sales? Why?

ENDNOTES

[1] Capon, A., "Exit Strategies for Entrepreneurs," *Global Investor*, 107(1997): 16–19.

[2] Quinlan, R., "Ideal Acquisitions Need Effective Evaluation," *Financial Executive*, 24(5)(2008): 17.

[3] Watson, D.G., "Acquisitions: How to Avoid Implementation Pitfalls and Improve the Odds of Success," *Global Business & Organizational Excellence*, 27(1)(2007): 7–19.

[4] Kvesic, D.Z., "Product Lifecycle Management: Marketing Strategies for the Pharmaceutical Industry," *Journal of Medical Marketing*, 8(4)(2008): 293–301.

[5] Wang, C., and F. Xie, "Corporate Governance Transfer and Synergistic Gains from Mergers and Acquisitions," *Review of Financial Studies*, 22(2)(2009): 829–858.

[6] Morrison, N.J., G. Kinley, and K.L. Ficery, "Merger Deal Breakers: When Operational Due Diligence Exposes Risks," *Journal of Business Strategy*, 29(3)(2008): 23–28.

[7] Bill Colone, personal conversation with Thomas Duening. Mr. Colone launched, operated, and successfully sold his medical device company Endomed.

[8] Hering, T., and M. Olbrich, "Valuation of Startup Internet Companies," *International Journal of Technology Management*, 33(4)(2006): 409–419.

[9] Smith, J.K., and R.L. Smith, *Entrepreneurial Finance*, 2nd ed. (Hoboken, NJ: John S. Wiley and Sons, 2004).

[10] Fitts, J.A., and M.G. Rowe, "Family Business Transition Planning," *Journal of Accountancy*, 212(5) (2012): 22.

[11] Giamarco, J., "The Three Levels of Family Business Succession Planning," *Journal of Financial Services Professionals*, 66(2)(2012): 59–69.

[12] Scharfstein, A.J., "Making a Graceful Exit," *Family Business,* 22(3)(2011): 20–22.

[13] Daley, J., "Family Affair," *Entrepreneur,* 39(12)(2011): 97–105.

[14] Nolop, B., "Rules to Acquire By," *Harvard Business Review,* 85(9)(2007): 129–139.

[15] Andriole, S.J., "Mining for Digital Gold: Technology Due Diligence for CIOs," *Communications of AIS,* 20(2007): 371–381.

[16] Mero, J., "People Are His Bottom Line," *Fortune,* 155(7)(2005): 30.

[17] Dalziel, M., "The Seller's Perspective on Acquisition Success: Empirical Evidence from the Communications Equipment Industry," *Journal of Engineering & Technology Management,* 25(3)(2008): 168–183.

[18] Adams, M., "Exit Pay-Offs for the Entrepreneur," *Mergers & Acquisitions: The Dealmaker's Journal* (March 2004): 24–28.

[19] Vaughan, B., "Earn Outs Come Back into Fashion," *Buyouts,* 21(17)(2008): 24.

[20] Yoon-Jun, L., "Strategy of Startups for IPO Timing Across High Technology Industries," *Applied Economics Letters,* 15(11)(2008): 869–877.

[21] Beales, R., R. Cox, and L. Silva, "Master of Market Timing," *The Wall Street Journal, Eastern Edition,* 251(55)(2008): C12.

[22] Kulkarni, K., and T. Sabarwal, "To What Extent Are Investment Bank Differentiating Factors Relevant for Firms Floating Moderate Sized IPOs?" *Annals of Finance,* 3(3)(2007): 297–327.

[23] Gleason, K., J. Johnston, and J. Madura, "What Factors Drive IPO Aftermarket Risk?" *Applied Financial Economics,* 18(13)(2008): 1099–1110.

Lemonade principle

PLAN

CHAPTER 15

Scientific Method

pilot in the plane principle

O2

effectuation

Value

YOUR ENTREPRENEURIAL CAREER

Learning Objectives

After studying this chapter, students should be able to:

- **Recognize and refute** some of the myths of entrepreneurship and set your expectations accordingly.

- **Distinguish** among the various entrepreneurial career types and determine which is right for you.

- **Explore and understand** the various challenges that you'll likely face in your first startup venture and how to handle them.

- **Understand** the issues that are involved in setting up the office for your first venture.

- **Recognize** the various risks that are associated with entrepreneurial ventures and understand how to manage them.

- **Develop** resilience and manage stress to maximize your chances for succeeding with your first venture.

INTRODUCTION

Now that you've learned a bit about what we call the "entrepreneurial method," your next challenge will be a great one: becoming an expert entrepreneur. Of course, reading and learning from a single textbook will not prepare you for instant success as an entrepreneur. That was never our intent in writing this text. Instead, we prepared this text to provide you with a method that you can use throughout your life to discover and

© Monkey Business Images, 2012. Used under license from Shutterstock, Inc.

take advantage of entrepreneurial opportunities. You can never know when an opportunity will present itself, but those who learn to master the entrepreneurial method stand the greatest chance of seizing the opportunities that do arise.

As we stated in Chapter 1, it may take you up to ten years or more of deliberate practice and deliberate performance to master the entrepreneurial method. Your challenge as an aspiring entrepreneur is to learn from mistakes, failures, and setbacks to reach your eventual success. Some of you may find success in your first venture. Good for you. Be careful, however, not to get overconfident because of an early success.[1] Each venture that you start during your career will be different, and the decisions and strategies that worked in one venture may not work as well in another. As many entrepreneurs will attest, early success can be followed by a mid-life failure.[2] It is imperative to pursue each venture with the principles of the entrepreneurial method in mind, especially paying attention to the affordable loss principle to ensure that a mid-life venture failure doesn't jeopardize other financial obligations you may have.

You can also focus your entrepreneurial career on developing the five mindsets of the expert entrepreneur that we discussed in Chapter 2. As you begin your journey, it may not be clear why each of these mindsets is important to your eventual success. You should endeavor to pay attention to your development of the mindsets and accept challenges that will help you become more adept over time. For example, you may want to begin your entrepreneurial career in small steps, perhaps through turning a hobby into a small business that you can operate out of your home. The designing mind will be necessary to develop a system that can operate without a lot of expense or time commitment so that you can continue to work at your day job. Look for ways to streamline your processes, manage a website, fulfill customer orders, and manage your accounts. This is a great way to practice the skills of the entrepreneurial method and hone those skills without great risk.

This chapter is designed to help you understand more about what it means to fashion an entrepreneurial career. We will first tackle some of the myths that surround entrepreneurship so that you can get started with proper expectations. It is important to set your expectations appropriately so that you don't take your successes or your failures too personally. Young people who study entrepreneurship in college may be under the mistaken impression that entrepreneurship is now going to be easy or that they MUST become an entrepreneur. We have been carefully avoiding leading you into those traps. Entrepreneurship is almost always difficult, and no text or courses in entrepreneurship can enable you to avoid the need to try things out, practice, and learn entrepreneurial lessons in the real world.

Next, we will introduce you to some of the common entrepreneurial career types. For example, there are some entrepreneurs who definitely want to be the **lead dog**. That is, they want to be the Chief Executive Officer of the venture, and they want to be recognized as the leader and primary decision maker. Others are not interested in being the leader, but rather want to have a less visible role within the venture. We call this type of entrepreneur the **perennial partner**. The perennial partner wants the excitement of ownership and working in a small venture without the responsibilities of leadership. Each of these different career types, and others that we talk about, require application of the entrepreneurial method. We discuss the various different entrepreneurial career types and how they are different.

We will also discuss what it's like to start your first venture. The entrepreneurial method can be applied in any type of business, but each type will have some nuances and idiosyncrasies that we can't possibly cover in a single text. However, we can provide you with some tips on finding a mentor for your first venture and how to use mentors to your entrepreneurial advantage.

Finally, we will send you on your way with some parting advice and thoughts about entrepreneurship as a career.

MYTHS OF ENTREPRENEURSHIP

Much of this section is based on a book written by Case Western Reserve University's Scott Shane titled *The Illusions of Entrepreneurship*.[3] Shane is a well-regarded entrepreneurship scholar. His book was controversial in that it pointed out some common misperceptions of entrepreneurship that scholars, policymakers, and program managers have believed. These misperceptions can lead to false expectations among entrepreneurs, wasted money in programs that don't work, and other harmful consequences. We are only interested in communicating these myths to you, the aspiring entrepreneur, so that your expectations about your own entrepreneurial potential are appropriately set.

Myth 1: It takes a lot of money to finance a new business

The typical startup requires only about $25,000 to get started. Expert entrepreneurs, as you've learned, attempt to launch their ventures by preserving their resources, especially cash—the most precious resource. Expert entrepreneurs tend to use leasing instead of buying. And they turn fixed costs into variable costs by, say, paying people commissions instead of salaries. Later in this chapter we'll provide you with some insights into managing the costs associated with setting up the office of your first venture.

Myth 2: Venture capitalists are a good place to go for startup money

You learned the art and science of entrepreneurial fundraising in Chapter 8. There, you learned that the early financing for most ventures comes from the proverbial FFF—friends, family, and fools. Capital from other sources, such as angels and venture capital funds, only becomes available to ventures that have demonstrated market acceptance and the potential for high growth.

Myth 3: Most business angels are rich

Business angels are not necessarily wealthy individuals. Most startup ventures are able to attract capital from friends and family members who are not in the "rich" category. Research indicates that almost three-quarters of the people who provide capital to fund the startups of other people who are not friends, neighbors, co-workers, or family don't meet SEC accreditation requirements.

In fact, 32 percent have a household income of $40,000 per year or less and 17 percent have a negative net worth.

Myth 4: Startups can't be financed with debt

In Chapter 8 you learned about the various sources of debt financing for new ventures. Research indicates that debt funding for startup ventures is more common than equity financing. According to the Federal Reserve's Survey of Small Business Finances, 53 percent of the financing of companies that are two years old or younger comes from debt, and only 47 percent comes from equity. You learned about the various debt financing options, including Small Business Administration (SBA) loans that are available to entrepreneurs. In your quest adequately to finance your startup, don't forget to give full consideration to the debt financing options that are available to you.

Myth 5: Banks don't lend money to startups

Federal Reserve data shows that banks account for 16 percent of all the financing provided to companies that are two years old or younger. While 16 percent doesn't seem like a significant amount, consider that the next closest percentage lender to startups is trade creditors at 13 percent. In Chapter 8 you also learned that many entrepreneurs are able to secure loans from family members. Accepting loans from family members, you learned, should be treated as formally as accepting a loan from an institution.

Myth 6: Most entrepreneurs start businesses in attractive industries

© Blaj Gabriel, 2012. Used under license from Shutterstock, Inc.

Unfortunately, most first-time entrepreneurs do not start businesses in attractive industries. Many first-time entrepreneurs are what we describe below as "reluctant entrepreneurs." They have been laid off or downsized from a job and have not been preparing an innovative new venture. Most simply stay within the industry in which they were laid off and try to offer their skills and talents as a private consultant. In your quest to start your first venture, you should look for ways to leverage your talents, experience, and skills in high-growth industries. Of course, we have recommended throughout that you have to be the type of entrepreneur that suits you best.

Myth 7: The growth of a startup depends more on an entrepreneur's talent than on the business he or she chooses

Research indicates that the industry in which the entrepreneur chooses to start a company has a huge effect on the odds that it will grow. Over the past twenty-five years, about 4.2 percent of all startups in the computer and office equipment industry made the Inc. 500 list of the fastest growing private companies in the United States. By way of contrast, just 0.005 percent of startups in the hotel and motel industry and 0.007 percent of startups in the restaurant and bar industries made the Inc. 500. That means the odds that you will make the Inc. 500 are 840 times greater if you start a computer company than if you start a hotel or motel.

Myth 8: Most entrepreneurs are successful financially

We have been working hard throughout this text to remove the motivation of "getting rich" from your thinking about entrepreneurship. If that is your *primary* motivation, you may want to consider a different career. You should note that the typical profit of an owner-managed business is just $39,000 per year. In fact, only the top 10 percent of entrepreneurs will earn more money than comparable employees. What's worse is that the typical entrepreneur earns less money than he or she otherwise would have earned working for someone else. Research has indicated that the primary motivation of expert entrepreneurs is freedom rather than getting rich. If you crave above all the feeling of running your own venture and living by your own wits, then you probably have the right motivation to be a successful entrepreneur—and you might even get rich along the way.

Myth 9: Many startups achieve the sales growth projections that equity investors are looking for

Each year in the United States entrepreneurs launch 590,000 new businesses with at least one employee. Of this number, U.S. Census Bureau data indicate that only 200 reach sales of $100M in six years. This is the type of sales figure that most venture capital funds are looking for. About 500 additional firms reach the $50M in sales plateau. To help set your own expectations realize as well that of the 590,000 new businesses started each year, only 1.6 percent reach $5M in sales.

Myth 10: Starting a business is easy

You shouldn't be guilty of believing this myth. We have repeatedly articulated the difficulties of starting a venture that is able to grow and prosper. Anyone can register an LLC or other corporate legal form with his or her respective secretary of state. But that is not the same thing as starting a venture, building a customer base, and generating positive cash flow. That is difficult regardless of what industry you choose or how many times you've done it. Any expert entrepreneur will attest to the challenges that each new venture poses. Having the appropriate expectation that starting a venture is difficult will shield you from potential disappointment and the potential to give up too soon because you expected things to be easier.

ENTREPRENEURIAL CAREER TYPES

Just as there is no single way to be an accountant, chef, taxi driver, or engineer (and every other type of career), there is no single way to be a successful entrepreneur. If you think about famous entrepreneurs like Bill Gates, Mary Kay, and Richard Branson, you can get an idea that they all have different personalities and different styles. Some entrepreneurs, like Bill Gates, start a single company and build it over their lifetimes. Others, like Richard Branson, start multiple companies. Exhibit 15.1 on the next page provides a recent list of the companies Branson owns:

Acute vs. Serial Entrepreneurship

The **acute entrepreneur** is the Bill Gates in our example above, generally starting a single venture and growing it until retirement. By way of contrast, **serial entrepreneurs** aren't satisfied with a single venture and tend to start multiple ventures throughout their lifetimes. Richard Branson is, obviously, the serial entrepreneur in our example.

Exhibit 15.1 Companies Owned by Richard Branson

Name of Company	Description of Company
AirAsia X	Malaysian airline company (which is 16% owned by Virgin Group LLC)
V Festival	UK company which puts on two day music festivals (like Woodstock)
Virgin Active	A multi-national health club
Virgin America	American airline based in San Francisco Int Airport
Virgin Atlantic Airways	UK airline
Virgin Balloon Flights	Hot air balloon outfitter
Virgin Blue Holdings LLC	Pony conglomerate with 5 shell companies
Virgin Books	Book publisher
Virgin Brides	Wedding fashion shop
Virgin Cars	International car sales company
Virgin Charter	Private jets
Virgin Comics	Comic book publisher
Virgin Drinks	Drink manufacturer (Soda, Vodka, and Spirit Mixers)
Virgin Experience Days	Experience-based event coordinators
Virgin Flowers	International flower delivery and provider
Virgin Galactic	Interspace travel R&D corporations
Virgin Games	Electronic gaming producer and manufacturer
Virgin Green Fund	Venture capital firm dedicated to fund raising for alternative fuel R&D
Virgin Health Bank	Stem cell bank
Virgin Healthcare	Healthcare benefit provider
Virgin HealthMiles	Employee health productivity firm
Virgin Holidays	Conglomerated travel agency with 3 shell companies
Virgin Limited Edition	Hotel conglomerate with 7 hotels under its umbrella
Virgin Limobike	London-based passenger bike service
Virgin Limousines	Northern California-based limo service
Virgin Media	UK-based home cable company
Virgin MegaStores	Electronic media store
Virgin Mobile	Mobile phone services organization
Virgin Money	Fiscal services firm
Virgin Money Giving	Online fundraising website
Virgin Oceanic	Ocean exploration organization
Virgin Nigeria	Airline
Virgin Play	Spanish video game producer
Virgin Produced	Film and TV production firm
Virgin Racing	Formula One racing team
Virgin Radio	Broadcasting radio stations
Virgin Spa	Spa and cosmetics retailer
Virgin Trains	UK Railway
Virgin Unite	Charitable organization
Virgin Vacations	US travel agency
Virgin Vie at Home	Retailer
Virgin Wines	Internet wine retailer
Virgin Voucher	Gift voucher ghost company
Virgin Ware	Clothing retailer
Virgin Management	Custodial management and outsourcing team

Source: Answers.com, http://wiki.answers.com/Q/How_many_companies_does_Richard_Branson_own, accessed on May 27, 2012.

The difference between acute and serial entrepreneurship is likely a highly personal thing. Some entrepreneurs are very satisfied with the venture they have created. The venture provides them with unique new challenges that motivate them and keep them coming back for more. Jim McIngvale (Mattress Mac) of Houston's Gallery Furniture launched the venture in 1983. Over the years, McIngvale grew the single-site furniture store into one of the largest selling stores in the world. Yet, despite that success, customers could find McIngvale positioned at the front desk greeting customers as they entered. He enjoys building a company, greeting customers, and solving problems every day more than he enjoys starting companies. Mac was approached many times to open additional stores in Houston and elsewhere in the country, but has steadfastly refused.[5]

The serial entrepreneur enjoys the challenges and rigors of the startup process, and often becomes bored when the company begins to grow.[6] Growing companies present a different set of challenges and require different competencies than the new venture startup. Entrepreneurs like Richard Branson not only enjoy the startup phase of the new venture, they are adept at managing and leading during this phase. Serial entrepreneurs are motivated by bringing a new company to life, creating jobs, and generating positive cash flow more than they are motivated by solving human resource problems, organizational system problems, and other large company issues.

How do you know if you are an acute versus a serial entrepreneur? Probably the most potent indicator is whether you prefer the startup phase of venture development more than the growth phase. If you prefer the startup phase, you are perhaps better off conducting your entrepreneurial career as a serial entrepreneur. Of course, you don't have to start as many companies as Richard Branson to be successful. Serial entrepreneurs generally become wealthy by virtue of their collecting equity in the ventures they start, then selecting good people to run those ventures and enjoying the dividends and equity appreciation of those companies over time.

Acute entrepreneurs generate their wealth by growing their companies and paying themselves handsome salaries and dividends over the years. As the owner of the growing company, acute entrepreneurs don't answer to anyone (except other shareholders) and can take cash out of their ventures as they see fit.

Lead Dog vs. Perennial Partner Entrepreneurship

As we mentioned in the introduction to this chapter, some entrepreneurs prefer to be the Chief Executive Officer (CEO) of the ventures they create. This is a lofty title that often includes lofty expectations and responsibilities. Entrepreneurs who choose this career path prefer the challenges, heartaches, joys, and stresses of leadership.[7] We call such entrepreneurs *lead dog entrepreneurs.* They want to be responsible for the direction of the venture and the primary decision maker. Other entrepreneurs don't necessarily want to be the CEO of the ventures in which they participate. They prefer to use their talents in a startup environment, but they don't want the responsibilities of leadership. Such entrepreneurs we refer to as *perennial partners.*

Perennial partners are not necessarily weak or lacking in leadership skills. They are simply unwilling to assume the role of the CEO of the venture—which can be incredibly challenging even to expert entrepreneurs. Perennial partners may simply be the type of individual who knows himself or herself very well, including an accurate assessment of personal strengths and weaknesses. Such individuals may prefer to focus on working within a venture in a manner that best leverages their strengths. For example, highly skilled software engineers may prefer to stay within the software programming function of a new venture and avoid the extraneous challenges inherent to the CEO position. Such an individual would still be an entrepreneur. After all, he or she elected to practice their software engineering skills in a risky new venture rather than take a highly paid position with a major firm.

You may see yourself as a perennial partner. The important point to remember is that you don't have to be the CEO to be an entrepreneur. You can apply the entrepreneurial method as a principal in a new venture, or even in a series of new ventures, without ever assuming the mantle of ultimate leadership that is the CEO position.

The lead dog entrepreneur, in contrast, not only prefers to be in charge but has developed and seeks to continue to develop the skills necessary for the CEO role. These include mastery of the principles of the entrepreneurial method and of the mindsets of the expert entrepreneur. Lead dog entrepreneurs cannot escape the necessity of deliberate practice and deliberate performance to develop mastery. Being the lead dog entails the visibility that goes with the CEO position, and the acceptance of ultimate responsibility for the performance of the venture as a whole. Perennial partners do not have this visibility and they are held responsible only for their limited area of concern.

Pure vs. Cause Entrepreneurship

This distinction is based on the individual personality of the entrepreneur. **Pure entrepreneurs** are those who are agnostic about the type of industry and/or venture they create. They are only interested in economic opportunity, without regard to where or how they might find and exploit the opportunity (of course, we are talking about opportunities that lie within the framework of the legal system). Pure entrepreneurs are sort of like Richard Branson, with the multiple industries that he's entered. They may have successful ventures in the restaurant industry, auto racing, consumer products, and other things either simultaneously or throughout their careers.

© Goodluz, 2012. Used under license from Shutterstock, Inc.

Cause entrepreneurs, by way of contrast, are by nature unable to perform effectively except in the industries for which they have a true passion or "calling." Many cause entrepreneurs are drawn to what is referred to as **social entrepreneurship.** Social entrepreneurship is defined as venture creation that is focused on addressing a social challenge.[8] For example, Scott Harrison was a successful nightclub promoter living in New York City. When he was just 28 years old, he decided that his life wasn't fulfilling and he founded a nonprofit called "charity: water" (www.charitywater.org). His venture now provides clean drinking water to people in seventeen countries.[9]

Whether you are by nature better suited to be a pure or cause entrepreneur is something that you'll discover for yourself, if you don't already know it. If you find that there are some industries and/or causes about which you have an overriding passion and desire to commit your life to, you are undoubtedly a cause entrepreneur. For most of us, however, the passion may not be strong until we discover how, where, and when we can be most effective. Scott Harrison was living the life he had always dreamed of and discovered it to be less than he had hoped. He's now thriving and living passionately by pursuing the cause of providing drinking water to millions of underserved people.

Opportunistic vs. Accidental Entrepreneurship

The distinction between the opportunistic and the accidental entrepreneur is a common one. **Opportunistic entrepreneurs** are people who are constantly seeking an opportunity to launch a new venture. Notice that we are not talking about serial entrepreneurs here, necessarily. An opportunistic entrepreneur may very well launch only a single venture in his or her lifetime, but he or she was actively seeking the right opportunity to start.

Accidental entrepreneurs, in contrast, are people who are not looking for an economic opportunity, but have the entrepreneurial spirit to seize the ones that do arise. Accidental entrepreneurs are often also what we call **latent entrepreneurs.** Because they aren't opportunistic, they generally start their entrepreneurial careers in the latter part of their working lives.[10]

You have learned in this text that one of the mindsets of the expert entrepreneur is "opportunity recognition." Thus, the expert entrepreneur is by definition an opportunistic entrepreneur. You can't become an expert if you are not seeking economic opportunities and exploiting them through application of the entrepreneurial method.

On the other hand, accidental entrepreneurs are sometimes also reluctant entrepreneurs. They may be forced into entrepreneurship as a result of a layoff, business closing, or some other life event. Accidental entrepreneurs will be at a decided disadvantage over opportunistic entrepreneurs in that the accidental entrepreneur is not actively seeking to develop entrepreneurial skills—and may in fact be thrust into entrepreneurship with no prior experience with or knowledge of the entrepreneurial method. Still, the accidental entrepreneur can be successful and may even reach the level of an expert if he or she grasps the challenge and endeavors to grow, learn, and transform. Unfortunately, many accidental entrepreneurs don't do that; rather, they launch a business as a means of tiding themselves over until their life situation changes and they can once again become employed. That is likely a recipe for failure since, as we've stated throughout, success in entrepreneurship is difficult and requires complete commitment by the venture founder to have any chance of success.

Project vs. Venture Entrepreneurship

The entrepreneurial method can be applied to many things in life. Think about all of the challenges that you have faced, and will face in the future, where the outcomes are uncertain and success is not predetermined. You'll have to rely on your wits, rally others to your cause, aggregate and deploy resources, and be resilient in the face of challenges and setbacks. Sometimes you'll have to use the entrepreneurial method even though you are not interested in starting a venture around the outcomes that you're trying to achieve.

Project entrepreneurs are those who need to get something done and who use the entrepreneurial method to achieve the outcomes they desire. For example, if you notice that the street corner in your neighborhood is dangerous and needs to have traffic lights installed, what would you do? You'd have to rally your neighbors, meet with city leaders and their traffic engineers, develop an "elevator pitch" that convinces them to "invest" in your project, and see the project through to completion. Notice, however, that once the traffic light is installed, your job is done. You are not likely now to form a company that is dedicate to installing traffic lights on every street corner.

Venture entrepreneurs, on the other hand, are the entrepreneurs that we've been discussing throughout this text. They are the entrepreneurs who seek economic opportunity. That is, they seek to create a going concern that systematically creates value for customers. They don't see an end to their venture, although they may envision their personal exit from it as we explained in Chapter 14.

It is likely the case that most expert entrepreneurs are both project and venture entrepreneurs. That is, most expert entrepreneurs apply their mastery of the entrepreneurial method both to get projects completed and to start and grow new ventures. Bill and Melinda Gates represent a great example of people who have taken their entrepreneurial expertise into new domains, working on such long-intractable problems like malaria, hunger, and poverty in remote places of the world. Thus, your Master-1 of the entrepreneurial method enables you to apply it in both the venture creation domain as well as in the project domain. In fact, you will find your mastery of the entrepreneurial method predisposes you to leadership roles in many areas of your life—whether in school, in your community, or in the world.

YOUR FIRST VENTURE

Perhaps the most challenging period for any entrepreneur are those uncertain, ambiguous, and exciting days of launching the first venture. All of the lessons of this text, all of the personal fears and insecurities, and all of the tests of one's personal resolve will come into stark reality—and quickly—once the new venture has been launched. By virtue of studying this text, working the exercises, and beginning your deliberate practice of the entrepreneurial method, you cannot say that you were surprised by the challenges that await you in your first venture (and, likely, each subsequent venture that you launch).

In this section, we intend to focus on the kinds of problems and challenges entrepreneurs are likely to face as they launch their first venture. These are by no means exhaustive of the challenges you'll face, but they are common and often serve to trip up the unprepared first-time entrepreneur. The challenges we'll address are:

- Setting up the office
- Managing risk
- Coping with stress
- Developing Resilience

Setting up the Office

No entrepreneurship text could consider itself complete if it didn't address some of the mundane, yet necessary, items for setting up the venture's office and other startup fundamentals. While setting up an office is a vital piece of the startup puzzle, it is easy to neglect until the very last moment while everyone is preoccupied with planning, fundraising, acquiring customers, and other important things. Still, this part of your very first startup can't be left to chance and needs to be considered before you are truly open for business.

If your venture is of the traditional sort, where most of the people employed are working in the same physical space, you'll need to consider what works best for you. If you are not going to meet with customers or potential customers in your office space, that opens the range of possible settings for the office. For example, there are many famous stories of entrepreneurs that have launched ventures out of their homes, garages, or apartments. Your venture may not have employees in the early stages, and thus working out of the home may be a very good option. Don't think you need a fancy office to be able effectively to build a viable venture. Too many startups squander precious cash on fancy office space when something far more austere would have been sufficient.

If you do launch out of your home, there may come a time when the business grows beyond the limited space available. You always should be thinking about how your venture is going to expand. If you don't, then you are a small business owner instead of an entrepreneur. Office space is available in nearly every metropolitan area. Of course, there is a difference between office buildings, some are very high end and expensive, and some are nearly falling down and much less expensive. What type of space do you need? Some things to consider when searching for suitable office space include:

- The amount of square footage you will need
- The number of offices you need
- The amount of conference space you need
- The type of quality of technology infrastructure
- Whether you need a reception area
- Whether you need kitchen or break room space
- The number of parking spaces you need to accommodate your growing team
- The quality of the foyer and other public spaces in the building
- The amount that you are willing to pay per month
- The length of lease you are able to commit to

This is not an exhaustive list of considerations, but gives you an idea of how to begin thinking about the type of office space you need. The trick is to think not only of what you need now, but what you are going to need in the future. You will need to balance the expense of future needs with the current reality of your financial situation. One technique many entrepreneurs use is to lease more space than they currently need, and then sublease some of the space to another firm until they are able to grow into that space. It is easy enough to lease a large space and erect some walls that can later be removed. Another technique is to lease space in a building that is sparsely occupied, with an eye toward leasing additional space as needed.

Most office buildings will attempt to lock you into a three-year lease and also require that you pay a security deposit equal to one month's rent. Some startups find the three-year lease option daunting, given that the entrepreneur must often personally guarantee the lease payments in the event the business is unsuccessful. To avoid that trap, one can always attempt to negotiate better terms. Another technique for avoiding the three-year lease is to obtain office space in what are called **executive suites.** Executive suites are usually housed in an office building, and they provide quite a bit of lease flexibility. An executive suite space is owned by a separate company that will usually provide amenities such as a receptionist, office equipment, conference space, and other things. Startups can lease as many suites as they need, and the leases can be variable from monthly to annually. You may pay a bit more for the same square footage in an executive suite compared to leasing an office, but it may be worth the extra money to avoid begin locked into the three-year lease.

Many entrepreneurs also find that they can setup an office relatively inexpensively in local and regional incubators. A **business incubator** is a type of organization that exists to help startup entrepreneurs launch their ventures successfully. Many incubators are associated with universities or local governmental organizations. They generally provide counseling services, office space, conference rooms, and other amenities. You should check your local community to find an incubator that may be able to provide your venture with startup support.[11]

You will also need to think about the office equipment you'll need to operate your venture. This may include everything from computers and printers to telephones, cell phones, copiers, and other things. Many entrepreneurs avoid the expense of purchasing all of this equipment through leasing. Just about anything you need for your office, including desks, cubicles, tables, and the equipment just mentioned, can be obtained via leasing. The reason leasing makes sense for a startup is that it allows you to preserve cash. Paying a monthly lease on the equipment you need will involve less cash outflow in the short run than would outright purchase. You will have more cash to invest in acquiring those first customers and getting the cash flowing through sales activities.

Managing Risk

Every business runs the risk of exposure to liability simply by offering products and/or services that may not live up to expectations, or even fail. Medical devices, electronics, engineering design, and every type of product or service could fail to meet customer expectations, or fail—sometimes dramatically. On August 1, 2007, the I-35W Bridge that spans the Mississippi River in Minneapolis collapsed during rush hour. Tragically, thirteen people were killed and more than 140 injured. After an exhaustive review of the accident, the National Transportation Safety Board identified a fundamental design flaw as the likely cause of the collapse. Lawsuits filed by victims' families have identified an engineering consulting firm as one of the defendants.[12] The firm had inspected the bridge prior to its collapse and deemed it to be in need of repairs and upgrades, but otherwise stated that it was structurally sound. Although the consulting firm was not involved in the construction of the bridge or its original design, it nevertheless provides a service that makes it possible to be the defendant in a lawsuit.

Liability risk also includes other potential disruptions to business, including theft, natural disasters, and impairment of key personnel. Fortunately, different types of insurance can be purchased to cover most if not all of these potential risks.

Most businesses should insure against basic theft and liability. This is simply common sense and ensures that the business will not be disrupted in the case of an accident or loss of property. It is important to work with an insurance company that understands the needs of a growing business, and has scalable plans to meet the particular needs of the venture. **Product liability** involves the responsibility of business firms for negligence in design, manufacture, sale, and operation of their products. For example, workers sued keyboard makers for selling products that cause wrist injuries and not warning users of the potential risks.[13] Public interest groups constantly seek to broaden the liability of business and manufacturers of such products as breast implants, automobiles, cigarettes, and guns.[14]

In certain instances, product liability laws have been expanded to include cases in which the producer or marketer of the product is not proved negligent. Under **strict product liability,** the business is responsible for any damages that may result regardless of the care it observes to guard against such damages. Strict liability is commonly applied to "ultra-hazardous" business activities such as crop dusting, pile driving, and storing flammable liquids. No amount of care can prevent companies in ultra-hazardous industries from liability if their businesses should cause harm to a third party.

Liability insurance covers accidents that may occur on the venture's premises, as well as accidents that may occur through use of the venture's products and services. Business liability insurance protects a venture in the event of a lawsuit for personal injury or property damages. It will usually cover the damages from a lawsuit along with the legal costs. Depending on business needs, liability insurance can be purchased in three forms:

© elwynn, 2012. Used under license from Shutterstock, Inc.

- **General Liability Insurance:** This form of business liability insurance is the main coverage to protect a venture from injury claims, property damages, and advertising claims. General liability includes D&O liability and employer liability. **D&O liability** stands for "directors and officers"liability and is intended to cover the acts or omissions of those in the director or officer position. **Employer liability** is also known as "worker's comp," and it is a mandatory form of liability insurance coverage that all businesses must carry.

- **Professional Liability Insurance:** Ventures providing services may need professional liability insurance. This coverage protects a business against malpractice, errors, negligence, and omissions. For some professions, it is a legal requirement to carry such a policy. Doctors require coverage to practice in certain states. Technology consultants often need coverage in independent contractor work arrangements.

- **Product Liability Insurance:** Technology ventures selling or manufacturing products should be protected in the event of a person becoming injured as a result of using the product. The amount of coverage and the level of risk depend on the nature of the products and their potential for misuse.

The most likely person to ask about your insurance needs as a startup venture is your accountant. Accountants are not only trained in helping the ventures manage their financial tracking and reporting, but they also generally are connected to other financial experts, such as insurance providers. As with the venture's accountant, it is advisable to work with an insurance provider who has experience in the venture's industry. It is also advisable to work with a firm that has scalable policies and premium schedules that are a match with the needs of the venture.

Coping with Stress

Stress can be an important factor in your ability to perform as an entrepreneur.[15] You can be certain that your entrepreneurial career will include a certain amount of stress. The critical factor is how you deal with the stress you will inevitably face time and again throughout your entrepreneurial career.

There are numerous definitions and interpretations of stress available. Stimulus definitions talk about a force or stimulus upon a person that provokes a response. Response definitions focus on the psychological, physiological, and emotional responses a person makes to stressors. Stimulus-response definitions emphasize the consequence of the interaction between stimuli and a person's response. By reviewing each of these perspectives it is possible to use parts of each to create a working definition of stress:

> It is an adaptive response mediated by individual characteristics and/or psychological processes that are a consequence of any external action, situation, or event that places special physical and/or psychological demands upon a person.[16]

The individual characteristics may include age, sex, race, and health status. The psychological processes might include attitudinal components, beliefs, values, and other personality dimension such as tolerance or ambiguity.

Most discussions and presentations state or imply that stress is negative or bad. Dr. Hans Selye suggested that stressors can also produce eustress or positive stress that produces a positive outcome.[17] Making a superior presentation that is acclaimed by respected colleagues can be stressful but it can be **eustress**. Instead of anxiety, tension, and feeling pressure there could be a sense of fulfillment, challenge, and exhilaration. Eustress is necessary in life. Although this chapter focuses on managing and coping with negative stress it is important to note positive stress and the role it plays.

The relationship between stress and performance is intriguing. Finding the optimal amount of stress to achieve the best performance is difficult. Research studies suggest that performance reaches an optimal level when stress is at a moderate level. What is moderate tone individual is likely to be different to other individuals.[18]

A "moderate stress" inverted-U description is presented in Exhibit 15.2. When there is too little stress there is likely to be boredom and apathy. On the other hand, too much stress results in panic and indecisiveness. At the moderate level there is high energy, alertness, and high motivation.

Guessing, estimates, and subjective opinions suggest that stress is costly. Thus, it is important for entrepreneurs to attempt to cope with negative, excessive stress. Every job has its unique stressors—a big three, big ten or some number. There is also the issue of what is negative stress. What might be negative stress to one person on a job may be eustress to a colleague working on the same job. Determining with perfect accuracy what stress costs a company or an individual is not possible. Certainly there are costs, and it is in the best interest of the organization and entrepreneur to understand stress, understand individual reactions and the costs of stress, and develop and execute stress management and stress reduction techniques.

DEVELOPING RESILIENCE: Although there are no guarantees for success in entrepreneurship, there are some well known techniques for dealing with failure that can enhance its likelihood in the long run. For example, one of the hallmarks of successful entrepreneurs is a trait that is referred to as **resilience.**[19] Resilience is a term that has been used to refer to the ability to survive and even thrive under conditions of turbulence, change, or trauma. In general, it refers to an ability to absorb defeat and/or bad news without losing one's focus on goals and objectives.[20] This characteristic is especially useful for entrepreneurs since it has become common knowledge that entrepreneurship as a lifestyle will occasion failure.[21] The ability to rebound from entrepreneurial failure and continue the entrepreneurial lifestyle is a textbook example of what is referred to as resilience.

The ability to continue in the wake of entrepreneurial failure includes confronting a range of obstacles. Among these are personal and internal obstacles, including emotional state, financial condition, family matters, and others. Resilience means being able to manage these various

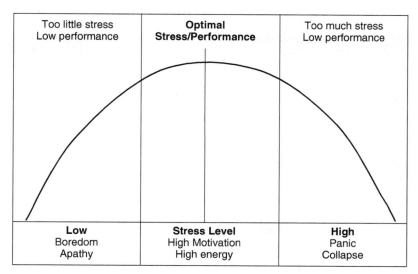

Too little stress Low performance	Optimal Stress/Performance	Too much stress Low performance
Low Boredom Apathy	**Stress Level** High Motivation High energy	**High** Panic Collapse

EXHIBIT 15.2   Inverted-U Relationship Between Stress and Job Performance

pressures in a manner that enables the continuance of the entrepreneurial lifestyle, regardless of whether a particular venture continues.[22] Entrepreneurial failure also brings a number of external pressures to bear, including the entrepreneur's reputation among peers, investors, and others with potential influence. This reputation may influence the entrepreneur's future ability to launch a new venture, raise necessary funds, or acquire needed resources.

As a personality trait, resilience requires emotional intelligence as well as social awareness. Emotional intelligence includes the ability for one to recognize disappointment, frustration, and even depression as legitimate emotions associated with loss. When the entrepreneur loses his or her business, it should be expected that some negative emotional state will arise. The ability to accept a negative emotion, deal with it effectively, and move on to new challenges is a major component of resilience. So is the ability to move about in the social world during periods of challenge and difficulty. Withdrawing into some neutral corner or lashing out at forces beyond one's control as responses to entrepreneurial failure can damage the entrepreneur's social reputation. Resilience also includes the ability to maintain one's equilibrium in social settings in the event of a venture failure.

Resilience can be developed through a variety of techniques. One of these has been termed *learned optimism*.[23] According to this perspective, optimism can be learned and practiced by entrepreneurs and others. Everyone has a tendency either toward optimism or pessimism. In fact, most ventures benefit by having both optimists and pessimists on hand. The optimists are the ones who focus on what's possible and the future. Pessimists tend to focus on the realities of the present and the constraint present reality places on visions of the future.

Resilience as a character trait, however, is aligned with optimism. Technology entrepreneurs can develop a tendency toward optimism by using some very straightforward techniques. For example, optimists tend to view the negative things that occur in business as within their power to influence. Pessimists tend to believe that forces beyond their ability to influence affect the outcome of business activities. This perspective can be changed, but the pessimist would need to recognize the thoughts behind the attitude and work to change them. The Bullet Breakout below offers some final suggestions for developing and maintaining resiliency as an entrepreneur.

BULLET BREAKOUT

Developing Resiliency

- **Make connections.** Networking doesn't just make good business sense, it makes good psychological sense. Form a network of professional and personal resources who can step in with advice or even just a sympathetic ear when times get tough.

- **Avoid seeing crises as insurmountable problems.** Whether your business has had to downsize or just changed markets to accommodate the economy, you should focus on the big picture and realize that these setbacks do not necessarily threaten the life of your business.

- **Accept that change is a part of living.** While change can be painful, accept that your business will change to meet new circumstances—whether it is an updated business plan or a new niche of customers served.

- **Move toward your goals.** Entrepreneurs tend to be very goal-oriented, but sometimes the inactivity forced by a stagnant market can stall an entrepreneur. Develop some realistic goals and do something regularly—even if it seems like a small accomplishment—that enables you to move toward those goals.

- **Take decisive actions.** Take decisive actions, rather than detaching completely from problems and stresses and wishing they would just go away. Problem-solving is an active and ongoing process that can increase resilience considerably.

- **Look for opportunities for self-discovery.** Entrepreneurs can focus so heavily on changes in the market that they forget that they also are evolving as entrepreneurs with each challenge they meet. People often learn something about themselves and may find that they have grown in some respect as a result of their struggles.

- **Nurture a positive view of yourself and your company.** Entrepreneurs may have been hit hard by the economy, but they also have the ability to be nimble and flexible, something the larger companies often have trouble with.

- **Maintain a hopeful outlook.** An optimistic outlook enables you to expect that good things will happen in your life. Try visualizing what you want, rather than worrying about what you fear.

- **Take care of yourself.** Entrepreneurs spend so much time nurturing the company and their employees that they sometimes forget their own needs and feelings. Engage in activities that you enjoy and find relaxing. Exercise regularly. Taking care of you helps to keep your mind and body primed to deal with situations that require resilience.

YOUR ENTREPRENEURIAL CAREER

Now that you have completed this textbook and, presumably, a course in entrepreneurship, you have taken the first step toward an entrepreneurial career. Congratulations. It must be pointed out again, here, at the end of the book as it was at the beginning, that entrepreneurship is a lifelong endeavor. We are under no illusions that this textbook—or any other book on entrepreneurship, for that matter—will somehow transform you into a successful entrepreneur. To the contrary, we have taken great pains to be as realistic as possible throughout this text about the difficulties of entrepreneurship and the need to develop a resilient and flexible mindset.

Naturally, there are some individuals who will become entrepreneurs soon after completing a course in entrepreneurship, but the vast majority will not. You may have an idea in your mind already about a product or service you'd like to perfect and take to the market. Think care-

© Tyler Olson, 2012. Used under license from Shutterstock, Inc.

fully about whether you are ready for such a challenge, and, indeed, whether your market is ready to buy what you are proposing to offer.

Your entrepreneurial career has begun, but you may not decide to launch your own venture until after you have gained some industry experience . Working for someone else for awhile does not mean you are not an entrepreneur—you are simply waiting for the right time and the right place to hatch your plans. Don't be discouraged if this is your path for as many as ten to fifteen years.

Building an entrepreneurial career is not just about building companies, it is about building a lifestyle. Entrepreneurs must shape themselves as much as they shape ventures to be able to handle uncertainty, ambiguity, and occasional failures. This text has provided innumerable ideas, tools, case studies, and suggestions about how to prepare you for a life of entrepreneurship. This preparatory work should have already begun. If not, then you should not hesitate to begin immediately. Some ways for you to begin developing your unique entrepreneurial personality and lifestyle are highlighted in the last Bullet Breakout box.

BULLET BREAKOUT

Suggestions for Launching Your Entrepreneurial Career

- **Don't work for less than you can afford to,** but do offer a discount to customers or clients who sign contracts with you.

- **Find people who will refer jobs to you.** If they send you nightmare jobs, make sure they're balanced out with rewarding (profitable!) ones.

- **Surround yourself with supportive people** and don't be discouraged by anyone. If your idea is good and you're determined to stick with it through the first few difficult years, your chances of success are great.

- **Be flexible in your thinking.** Prepare to change the way you work, the products you use and the services you offer in order to meet the demands of your customers.

- **Admit your mistakes, correct them, and carry on.** For example, if you purchase a piece of equipment that does not meet your expectations, send it back, sell it, or exchange it!

- **Develop a good relationship with your bank manager and creditors.** Show a genuine interest in solving problems. Pay as much as you can afford to, to everyone to whom you owe money.

- **Avoid isolation.** Even if you work closely with your clients, you won't be part of a gang anymore. Develop your own network of entrepreneurs that you see regularly and bounce ideas off. Ideally, they'll allow you to vent your anger and share your successes.

- **Separate your work and personal life.** Set your working hours and stick to a strict timetable. When you're not available to clients, leave a message on your answer machine letting them know when they can expect a reply from you. Let them know how to reach you in an emergency.

- **Plan some "thinking time" into every day.** If you pack your diary with back-to-back activities, your business will never grow.

- **Confirm orders** personally and immediately, especially those you receive on email.

- **When you find someone cleverer than you, employ him or her!**

- **Don't enter a business or a venture that you know nothing about.** You'll be running to catch up for the rest of your business life.

- **Have an existing, loyal customer base** and start locally.

- **Be aware that you will get through any initial investment quickly**, so ensure you are covered financially until at least the end of the second year.

- **Focus on a specific goal** and work at it until it's achieved.[24]

These tips are just a beginning for the aspiring entrepreneur. There is no shortage of resources available to you from here on out. The average bookstore is brimming with stories about entrepreneurs and reference books about how to network, raise money, write a business plan, and myriad other things. You should resolve to continue your education on your own. Your education should include book learning and worldly learning. The latter refers to the many opportunities you will have in nearly every community in the world to interact with entrepreneurs, people who want to be entrepreneurs, investors, teachers, and mentors of all types. It is up to you now. Don't wait a moment longer to begin your entrepreneurial career.

SUMMARY OF LEARNING OBJECTIVES

1. **Recognize and refute** some of the myths of entrepreneurship and set your expectations accordingly. *We looked at the top ten myths of entrepreneurship in this chapter. These myths are used by policymakers, entrepreneurs, and helpers to their disadvantage. Refuting these myths is important to your ability to set your expectations appropriately and avoid the traps that many aspiring entrepreneurs fall into by believing these myths.*

2. **Distinguish** among the various entrepreneurial career types and determine which is right for you. *We examined ten entrepreneur types: acute vs. serial; lead dog vs. perennial partner; pure vs. cause; opportunistic vs. accidental; and project vs. venture. Your knowledge of the entrepreneurial method enables you to choose which type of entrepreneurship is right for you.*

3. **Explore and understand** the various challenges that you'll likely face in your first startup venture and how to handle them. *We discussed several important challenges that entrepreneurs face in setting up their first startup venture. These include setting up the office for productivity and growth, managing liability and other risks, coping with stress and developing resilience. There will be myriad other challenges to be sure, but these are some important and common ones that all first time entrepreneurs face.*

4. **Understand** the issues that are involved in setting up the office for your first venture. *Most of the issues concerning setting up your first office concern either productivity or cost. You need to set up an office that enables workers to do their jobs, which includes appropriate space, work tools, and other considerations. Cost concerns are paramount for all startup ventures, and many find that leasing instead of buying can be a good way to obtain the tools they need to get the job done and preserve precious cash.*

5. **Recognize** the various risks that are associated with entrepreneurial ventures and understand how to manage them. *There are a number of potential risks associated with starting a venture, with liability issues of primary note. Expert entrepreneurs have learned to offset these risks by obtaining appropriate liability insurance. Entrepreneurs should consider purchasing liability insurance appropriate to their industry and that protects key employees and advisors so they can focus on building the venture.*

6. **Develop** resilience and manage stress to maximize your chances for succeeding with your first venture. *Managing stress is always a concern for the startup entrepreneur. Managing stress does not mean eliminating it altogether. That is probably impossible. In fact, there is a positive form of stress, called "eustress" that actually enhances your productivity and performance. Developing resilience is simply a matter of managing stress, reducing the time it takes for you to rebound from setbacks, and improving your chances of succeeding as an entrepreneur.*

STUDY QUESTIONS

1. Identify and discuss the top ten myths of entrepreneurship. How do you think believing these myths could be harmful to the aspiring entrepreneur? Do you think that any of these myths are actually true? Explain.

2. Explain the difference between an acute entrepreneur and a serial entrepreneur. Can you name at least one person who seems to be of each type? Do you have a sense of which type of entrepreneur you might become? Explain your response.

3. What personal qualities do you think a lead dog entrepreneur should possess? Do you think you have these qualities? What is the difference between a lead dog entrepreneur and a perennial partner?

4. How does the pure entrepreneur differ from the cause entrepreneur? Do you think you personally fit one or the other of these? Why do you say that? Can you identify a cause entrepreneur that you admire? Why?

5. Why do you think that many latent entrepreneurs are what we call "accidental entrepreneurs"? What is one danger that many accidental entrepreneurs face?

6. Can you explain how a project entrepreneur would use the entrepreneurial method? Have you ever been involved in a project where knowledge of the entrepreneurial method might have come in handy?

7. Describe some of the common issues that arise for an entrepreneur in setting up the office for the venture. What are some common techniques entrepreneurs use to preserve cash when setting up the office?

8. How can the entrepreneur manage the risks that are associated with starting a venture? Can you think of some other things that can be done besides those discussed in this chapter?

9. What does the term *eustress* mean? What are some strategies that you use to manage stress in your life? Do you think you are ready to manage the stresses that will come from an entrepreneurial career? Explain.

10. What does the term *resilience* mean to you? Do you think you are a resilient person? How do you think you will go about developing your personal resilience as an entrepreneur?

KEY TERMS

Accidental entrepreneurship: The entrepreneur career type where a person was not looking for an economic opportunity but decided to seize such an opportunity due to life circumstances (such as a layoff) or the attractiveness of the opportunity.

Acute entrepreneur: The entrepreneur career type where the entrepreneur launches, operates, and grows only a single venture in his or her career.

Business incubator: A type of organization that exists to help startup entrepreneurs launch their ventures successfully.

Cause entrepreneur: The entrepreneur career type where the entrepreneur is limited by his or her passions and/or interests to pursue ventures in very specific industries.

D&O liability: "Directors and officers" liability; intended to cover the acts or omissions of those in the director or officer position.

Employer liability: Employer liability is also known as "worker's comp"; a mandatory form of liability insurance coverage that all businesses must carry.

Eustress: A positive form of stress that promotes a sense of fulfillment, challenge, and exhilaration.

Executive suites: Office spaces offered to startup ventures that include a number of amenities, such as a receptionist, conference rooms, and office equipment, and that allow for very flexible lease terms.

Latent entrepreneur: A version of accidental entrepreneur, someone who launches a venture late in life due to accidental circumstances.

Lead dog entrepreneur: The entrepreneur career type where the entrepreneur prefers to lead each venture he or she launches.

Opportunistic entrepreneur: The entrepreneur career type where the entrepreneur is actively looking for a venture opportunity and seizes the opportunities that arise.

Perennial partner entrepreneur: The entrepreneurial career type where the entrepreneur prefers not to lead the venture; rather, he or she prefers to be a partner.

Product liability: The responsibility of business firms for negligence in design, manufacture, sale, and operation of their products.

Project entrepreneur: The entrepreneur career type where the entrepreneur applies the entrepreneurial method to a project that has a clear beginning and ending.

Pure entrepreneur: The entrepreneurial career type where the type of venture or industry does not matter to the entrepreneur. The pure entrepreneur is willing and able to pursue economic opportunity in nearly any industry.

Resilience: A term that has been used to refer to the ability to survive and even thrive under conditions of turbulence, change, or trauma. In general, it refers to an ability to absorb defeat and/or bad news without losing one's focus on goals and objectives.

Serial entrepreneur: The entrepreneur career type where the entrepreneur starts numerous ventures throughout his or her career.

Social entrepreneurship: Venture creation that is focused on addressing a social challenge.

Strict product liability: Under strict product liability, the business is responsible for any damages that may result regardless of the care it observes to guard against such damages.

Venture entrepreneurship: The entrepreneur career type where the entrepreneur applies the entrepreneurial method to build a viable venture.

IN-CLASS EXERCISE

In this chapter we identified ten different entrepreneurial career types in terms of five separate dichotomies. For this exercise, students should dig into the popular literature on entrepreneurship and identify several entrepreneurs of each type. Literature that can be consulted for this includes *Entrepreneur* magazine, *Inc.,* magazine and other popular periodicals and websites that provide details on successful entrepreneurs.

In class, write each entrepreneur type on the board and ask students to name the entrepreneur they found in each of the categories. Next, ask students to talk about the entrepreneur they named in a particular category and explain why they believe that entrepreneur belongs in that category.

After you've gone over several examples in each category, have students discuss the different characteristics that seem to be associated with entrepreneurs in each of the categories. The goal of this exercise should be to help students better understand each of these various entrepreneurial career types and better to understand how their own values and personal characteristics might fit each type.

Finally, ask students to articulate what type of entrepreneurial career they think is best suited for them. Ask each volunteer to provide a brief explanation of why he or she thinks that way.

ENDNOTES

[1] Parhankangas, A. and T. Hellstrom, "How Experience and Perceptions Shape Risky Behavior: Evidence from the Venture Capital Industry," *Venture Capital,* 9(3)(2007): 183–205.

[2] Isenberg, D, "Entrepreneurs and the Cult of Failure," *Harvard Business Review,* 89(4)(2011): 36.

[3] Shane, S., *The Illusions of Entrepreneurship: The Costly Myths that Entrepreneurs, Investors, and Policy Makers Live By* (New Haven: Yale University Press, 2008).

[4] Hyytinen, A, and P. Ilmakunnas, "What Distinguishes a Serial Entrepreneur?" *Industrial & Corporate Change,* 16(5)(2007): 793–821.

[5] McIngvale, J., T.N. Duening, and J.M. Ivancevich, *Always Think Big* (Chicago: Dearborn Publishing, 2002).

[6] Eng, D, "Adventures of a Serial Entrepreneur," *Fortune,* 165(6)(2012): 23–26.

[7] Wasserman, N., "The Founder's Dilemma," *Harvard Business Review,* 86(2)(2008): 102–109.

[8] Katzenstein, J., and B.R. Chrispin, "Social Entrepreneurship and a New Model for International Development in the 21st Century," *Journal of Developmental Entrepreneurship,* 16(1)(2011): 87–102.

[9] Doubois, L. 2011. "How to Become a Social Entrepreneur." *Inc.com,* http://www.inc.com/guides/201105/how-to-become-a-social-entrepreneur.html, accessed on May 28, 2012.

[10] Gohmann, S.F., "Institutions, Latent Entrepreneurship, and Self-Employment: An International Comparison," *Entrepreneurship: Theory & Practice,* 36(2)(2012): 295–321.

[11] Romero, D., "Incubators," *Entrepreneur,* 37(5)(2009): 68–77.

[12] Welch, C. 2008. "Victims Plan to Sue over Minnesota Bridge Collapse." *CNN.com,* November 13.

[13] Himelstein, L.,"The Asbestos Case of the 1990s," *Business Week* (January 16, 1995):82–83.

[14] Geyelin, M.,"Product-Liability Groups Take Up Arms," *The Wall Street Journal,* (January 29, 1993):B1, B3.

[15] Kariv, D., "The Relationship Between Stress and Business Performance Among Men and Women Entrepreneurs," *Journal of Small Business & Entrepreneurship,* 21(4)(2008): 449–476.

[16] Ivancevich, J.M., and M.T. Matteson, *Organizational Behavior and Management.* (Chicago: McGraw-Hill/Irwin, 2002), p. 266.

[17] Selye, H., *The Stress of Life.* (New York: McGraw-Hill, 1978).

[18] Williams, S., and L. Cooper, *Managing Workplace Stress: A Best Practice Blueprint* (San Francisco: Jossey-Bass, 2002).

[19] Duening, T.N., "Five Minds for the Entrepreneurial Future," *Journal of Entrepreneurship,* 19(1)(2010): 1–22.

[20] Mangurian, G.E.,"Realizing What You're Made Of," *Harvard Business Review* 85(3)(2007): 125–130.

[21] Timmons, J.A.,"Entrepreneurship and the Creation of High-Potential Ventures,"in D.L. Sexton and R.W. Smilor (Eds.), *The Art and Science of Entrepreneurship* (Cambridge, MA: Ballinger, 1986).

[22] Hayward, M.L.A., W.R. Forster, S.D. Sarasvathy, and B.L. Fredrickson, "Beyond Hubris: How

Highly Confident Entrepreneurs Rebound to Venture Again," *Journal of Business Venturing,* 25(6) (2010): 569–578.

23 Seligman, M., Learned Optimism: *How to Change Your Mind and Your Life* (New York: Vintage Publishing, 2006).

24 Schmae C., "25 Tips by Entrepreneurs for Entrepreneurs." Retrieved from http://www.ivillage. co.uk/workcareer/ownbiz/bizprep/articles/0,,196_156910,00.html.

INDEX

A

CPSIA information can be obtained
at www.ICGtesting.com
Printed in the USA
LVHW03s1509030718
582546LV00006B/14/P

the **ENTREPRENEURIAL** method

Revised Printing

THOMAS N. DUENING

GREGORY N. STOCK

Kendall Hunt
publishing company

Kendall Hunt
publishing company

www.kendallhunt.com
Send all inquiries to:
4050 Westmark Drive
Dubuque, IA 52004-1840

Printed in the United States of America
10 9 8 7 6 5 4 3 2